AA

KEYGUIDE

LONDON

CONTENTS

225

146

179

UNDERSTANDING LONDON

Understanding London is an introduction to the city, its geography, economy, history and its people. Living London gets under the skin of London today, while The Story of London takes you through the city's past.

London is one of the world's most exciting and rewarding cities to visit. Two thousand years have left the capital of the United Kingdom with more than 19,000 buildings officially listed as having special architectural or historic interest. The city has grown largely unplanned, which makes for a piquant unpredictability as the scene and atmosphere change from one corner to the next. It has royal palaces and pageantry, stylish shops, theatres, music and art, and is also a dynamic financial and business hub. London is crowded and noisy and can be hard to get about in — and now and again it rains — but it is vigorously alive.

THE GEOGRAPHY

London lies in the southeast of England, some 64km (40 miles) inland from the North Sea. The rest of Britain has always complained that London and the southeast take up too much attention and too many resources. Greater London is an area of more than 1,550sq km (600sq miles), roughly oval in shape. Inside it is the smaller oval of inner London, covering about 260sq km (100sq miles), and at the heart of that are the two principal areas from the point of view of both Londoners and visitors — the West End and the City. Both lie on the north side of the River Thames, which winds its way through London from west to east before disappearing towards the North Sea.

WEST AND EAST

When Londoners speak of 'the City', they do not mean London as a whole. They mean the City of London itself, the area of just over 2.5sq km (1sq mile) where London's history began. The City is the financial district, crowded with office workers during the week but almost empty at weekends, with a resident population of only about 9,000. Its principal points of interest for visitors are the Tower of London, St. Paul's Cathedral, the Museum of London and the Barbican cultural complex, and there's some extraordinary postmodern architecture.

Lying to either side of the City are the West End, which was always upscale, and the East End, which was not. The East End is the world of the docks and working-class London, of cockneys and rhyming slang (▷ 9), and Jack the Ripper. It took a battering in World War II, and in the last 50 years the area has been substantially rebuilt.

The West End is posh, elegant London, the London of Buckingham Palace, Covent Garden and the National Gallery, Hyde Park, Piccadilly Circus and Trafalgar Square. It is where theatres cluster, along with most of the top shops and restaurants, nightclubs and hotels.

TWO IN ONE

London actually contains two cities, not one, and the West End is set in the second — the City of Westminster. Its nucleus is the area round Westminster Abbey, Big Ben, the Houses of Parliament and Whitehall, from which a quarter of the world's population was ruled in the days of the British Empire. Also in Westminster are Mayfair,

St. James's and Soho, neighbourhoods with distinctive characters of their own.

Mayfair, lying east of Hyde Park, is the most expensive of all London districts to live, shop and eat in. It has the chic Bond Street dress shops, jewellers and art dealers, Park Lane and Berkeley Square, Savile Row, Claridge's, the Royal Academy and the Burlington Arcade. Immediately to the southeast, on the other side of Piccadilly, the St. James's area is known for gentlemen's clubs and gentlemen's tailoring, Fortnum and Mason, the Ritz Hotel and feeding the ducks in St. James's Park.

In contrast, Soho, east of Mayfair, is known for its sex shows, gay venues and a cosmopolitan mix of restaurants, as well as Liberty department store, Carnaby Street and Chinatown.

STYLE, ART AND INTELLECT
Southeast of Hyde Park, Belgravia is an aristocratic district with street after street of gleaming white neoclassical houses and a showcase of exclusive grandeur in Eaton Square. Knightsbridge, Kensington and Chelsea were country villages until London engulfed them. Today Knightsbridge is best known for Harrods and the chic shops in Sloane Avenue and Beauchamp Place, on the way to the museum district of South Kensington. Here you will find the Victoria & Albert Museum, the Natural History Museum and the Science Museum.

Kensington is expensive residential territory, known for the Royal Albert Hall, Kensington Gardens and Kensington Palace, where Diana, Princess of Wales lived. Lying along the river, the pretty streets of Chelsea make another quarter with an artistic and intellectual reputation, spiced with the upscale boutiques around Sloane Square and the King's Road.

To the northeast of Oxford Street, Bloomsbury has a highbrow and arty reputation, partly because of the British Museum, London University and the Slade School of Art, an echo of the Bloomsbury Group of writers and artists, which formed around novelist Virginia Woolf and biographer Lytton Strachey before World War I.

To the east, Holborn (pronounced 'Hoe-b'n') has a quirky mixture of lawyers' offices in Lincoln's Inn and Gray's Inn, diamond dealers in Hatton Garden, and Smithfield's meat market. Out to the northeast, Hoxton, which was, within living memory, one of London's worst slums, has turned into a trendy Brit Art area with galleries and the hippest London music scene.

SOUTH OF THE RIVER
The south bank of the Thames has been the poor relation of the north bank ever since Roman times, when the borough of Southwark (pronounced 'Suthuck') began to evolve at the wrong end of London Bridge. Today, however, it is home to the South Bank cultural complex, Tate Modern, the London Eye, the Globe Theatre and the Saatchi Gallery, not to mention the unspeakable horrors of the London Dungeon.

OUTER SUBURBS
Farther out from the heart of London, more country villages that were swallowed up by the remorselessly expanding city in the 19th century retain a distinctive character. In the west, Richmond has Georgian streets and a highly regarded theatre, Kew has the sumptuous botanical gardens and Wimbledon has the tennis championships.

To the north, on the range of hills called the Northern Heights, Hampstead is known for its village atmosphere and its concentration of high-minded intellectuals, supporting London's largest percentage of psychiatrists per head of population. Highgate, next door, has a Georgian high street and London's most evocative cemetery.

Away to the east, Greenwich is famous for the historic National Maritime Museum, the *Cutty Sark* and Greenwich Mean Time.

MAKING MONEY
A massive share of London's economy is taken up by the financial and business services sector, whose contribution to the city's gross domestic product is nearly 40 per cent—more than double the ratio in the United Kingdom as a whole. The City of London is one of the most successful financial centres in the world. It handles almost a third of the entire global foreign exchange market, nearly twice that of Wall Street. Manufacturing, by contrast, is no longer one of London's strengths. Before World War II, London's factories made beer and sweets, textiles and furniture, and soon moved on to electronics and pharmaceuticals, but there was a dramatic decline in the 1960s and 1970s as businesses found themselves new premises and a cheaper workforce elsewhere.

The same period saw the collapse of the London docks as, after 1960, ships and containers increased in size beyond their capabilities. The East India Dock was closed in 1967 and the others followed over the next 15 years. St. Katharine's Dock, near the Tower of London, was turned into a classy yacht marina and its warehouses were transformed into flats, shops and restaurants. Similar developments occurred farther down the river. From the 1980s the Isle of Dogs was redeveloped as a business and residential district, with the Canary Wharf tower, the London Arena, the Docklands Light Railway and some of the country's most striking postmodern architecture.

While manufacturing and the docks were in decline, London was profiting from an upsurge in the service sector, which brought a noticeable increase in the quantity of office accommodation in the capital. At the same time, the tourist industry boomed with the advent

Camden and Regent's Park In north London, home of the famous Madame Tussauds and the ZSL London Zoo.

Chelsea and Belgravia Upscale, leafy streets just north of the Thames with the King's Road and Sloane Square for shopping.

The City The original settlement, and now the financial heart of the capital, with the major attractions of the Tower of London, Tower Bridge and St. Paul's Cathedral.

Clerkenwell and Islington On the periphery of the City, heading northwards: traditional heartland of radical politics, now very trendy with expensive cafés and craftshops.

Docklands A happy blend of old and modern architecture—shops, offices and apartments—stretching downstream from the City.

Kensington Well-established and well-heeled swathe west of Hyde Park, focused on Kensington Palace and Kensington Gardens.

Knightsbridge High-profile shopping streets lying south of Hyde Park, with Harrods and Harvey Nichols leading the way.

Mayfair Relatively quiet, wealthy residential area east of Hyde Park, sandwiched between Oxford Street and Piccadilly.

Notting Hill and Holland Park Fashionable quarters associated with celebrities, northwest of Hyde Park: home of Portobello Road market and the Notting Hill Carnival.

Piccadilly and St. James's Elegant and expensive: right at the heart of the city, encompassing Green Park and St. James's, two royal parks, and Buckingham Palace.

Soho and Covent Garden Lively, very central areas north of Trafalgar Square, packed with individual shops, restaurants and nightlife.

South Bank Revamped riverside strip from Westminster to London Bridge, now dominated by the London Eye and Tate Modern.

South Kensington and Earl's Court Mansion houses and serious museums southwest of central London.

Westminster and Whitehall Seat of government, with key landmarks Westminster Abbey and the Houses of Parliament.

---

of cheap air travel and the city's 1960s' reputation as 'swinging London'. Visitor numbers swelled from 1 million to 3 million a year between 1960 and 1965, and by 1977 had topped 8 million. The influx of visitors gave shops, restaurants and visitor attractions of all kinds a powerful boost. The number of visitors is now around 14 million a year, or five visitors for each inhabitant of inner London.

GETTING AROUND

London, like every heavily populated city in the world, has its problems. Litter is one of them; getting around is another. The average inner Londoner travels more than 6,500km (4,000 miles) a year inside the city—to get to work and back, on business, for shopping, to take the children to school, to go visiting—by some combination of car, taxi, motorcycle, bus, tube, bicycle or foot. The average inner Londoner walks about 400km (250 miles) a year altogether and cycles only about 50km (30 miles), while spending on transport fares is higher in London than in any other region of the United Kingdom. This is despite the fact that approximately half London's households own a car (10 per cent of London households have two or more cars). The speed of London's motorized traffic is notoriously slow; today's cars and buses move no faster than the horse-drawn traffic of the 1880s. The average daytime speed in central London is currently about 16kph (10mph), but the introduction of congestion charging in the city centre in 2003 is estimated to have cut the number of vehicles clogging the streets by nearly a quarter.

Below *Big Ben and the Houses of Parliament are illuminated at night*

Above *Tower Bridge also looks especially dramatic after dark*

RICH AND POOR

There has always been a gulf between London's rich and poor. The contrast was particularly glaring in Victorian days and the response was slum clearance. A start was made in the 1840s on demolishing the appalling St. Giles 'rookery' (▷ 33) around the eastern end of Oxford Street. Today's theatre-lined Shaftesbury Avenue was carved through an area previously occupied by squalid slums in the 1870s and 1880s.

Although the divide is now less extreme, five of England's ten most deprived municipal areas are in London. Homelessness is a persistent problem and begging, in the street and the Underground, has increased since the start of the 21st century. Still, as big cities go, and provided you behave sensibly, London is not a dangerous place.

POPULATION

The 2001 census produced population figures of 2.8 million for inner London and 4.4 million for outer London. The city has always drawn people from the rest of the country and the rest of the world, and today ethnic minorities account for 30 per cent of the population of inner London (in Greater London as a whole the figure is 25 per cent). The 1980s saw the downward trend in London's population—which had been above 8 million in 1951—beginning to reverse. The city stopped losing more people every year to emigration (mainly to the rest of the country) than it gained from immigration.

London's immigrants have all added to the city's vibrant mix, bringing their languages, traditions and food. As a result, there's a vast choice of ethnic establishments ranging from African crafts emporia to Arab bookshops, Austrian sausage parlours, Caribbean fishmongers, Chinese brocade galleries, Greek jewellers, Israeli crafts outlets, Lebanese butchers and Polish patisseries. Besides the main European, Indian, Chinese and Thai cuisines, you can find restaurants serving food from Brazil, Burma, Cuba, Egypt, Ethiopia, Jamaica, Japan, Mexico, Morocco, Peru, Poland, Russia, Scandinavia, Syria, Vietnam and elsewhere.

The great majority of Londoners speak English, but more than 300 languages from every corner of the globe may be heard on the street.

The majority of incomers to London are aged between 16 and 44. This helps to explain why London's death rate is 6 per cent lower than that of the country as a whole, while the birthrate is higher. The number of people above retirement age, on the other hand, is lower than outside. About 45 per cent of all London dwellings are apartments, compared with 25 per cent nationally.

MAIL ORDER

Greater London is divided up by postal areas, which can be confusing for outsiders. Since World War I, a combination of letters and numbers has been used, the letters indicating which part of the city the street is in: W standing for west, WC for west central, EC for east central, N for north, SW for southwest, and so on (except for NE and S, which are postcodes for other cities— Newcastle and Sheffield).

BETTER ADAM 'N' EVE IT

Cockney rhyming slang's origins are unknown, but some say it was developed to thwart the newly formed police force in the early 19th century. This was when expressions such as 'Would you Adam 'n' Eve [believe] it?' and 'Get up them apples and pears [stairs]' emerged among east Londoners. Some had a particularly sardonic note, as in 'trouble and strife' for wife or 'artful dodger' for lodger. The slang still peppers some Londoners' speech. Anyone lacking cash is 'borassic' (from boracic lint, rhyming with skint); a face is a 'boat' (from boat race) and a hat is a 'titfer' (from tit for tat). Lies are 'porkies' (from pork pies), taking a look is having a 'butcher's' (from butcher's hook) and 'Brahms and Liszt' means intoxicated. Celebrities can also end up as part of the vocabulary. American jockey Tod Sloane provided the expression 'on your Tod (own)', and a Gregory (Peck) is a cheque (check).

SOUTH BANK

The George Inn (▷ 91): Old 17th-century coaching inn with a lovely courtyard and traditional ales and menu.

Imperial War Museum (▷ 74): The country's most impressive military museum.

Ministry of Sound (▷ 87): Huge and famous club where you go to be seen.

Oxo Tower Restaurant (▷ 90): Tasty modern cuisine accompanied by amazing views over the Thames.

Southbank Centre (▷ 77): Top-flight concert halls and theatres in a sprawling complex on the river.

Tate Modern (▷ 80–81): A world-class gallery of modern art set in innovative surroundings.

CITY AND THE EAST END

The Bleeding Heart Tavern (▷ 124): Rustic tavern dating from the mid-18th century, serving good restaurant food.

The Eagle (▷ 124): One of London's first gastropubs, on the edge of Clerkenwell.

Moro (▷ 123): Busy Spanish-North African restaurant, with meals from a wood-fired oven.

Museum of London (▷ 103): Come here to discover the history of London.

The Peasant (▷ 124): Pub with Victorian interior, serving rustic-style food.

St. John (▷ 123): Traditional British food (for carnivores only) in Clerkenwell.

St. Paul's Cathedral (▷ 104–109): Sir Christopher Wren's masterpiece of baroque architecture, its great dome a city landmark.

Smiths of Smithfield (▷ 123): Organic food in a former warehouse near the City.

Tower of London (▷ 112–117): Nearly 1,000 years of Britain's royal history, and the Crown Jewels.

COVENT GARDEN TO BLOOMSBURY

Aldwych Theatre (▷ 156): The Royal Shakespeare Company's former base, with a full programme of drama and dance.

British Museum (▷ 134–139): A vast array of antiquities from around the world.

Cittie of York (▷ 165): Sandwiches and simple dishes in one of London's oldest pubs.

Courtauld Gallery (▷ 150–151): A superb collection in the grand rooms of Somerset House.

Hamleys (▷ 155): Britain's biggest toy shop.

Liberty (▷ 155): Classic clothing and expensive luxuries in a beautiful building.

Orrery (▷ 164): A Marylebone stalwart, serving fine French food.

Ronnie Scott's (▷ 158): Renowned jazz venue.

The Savoy (▷ 167): Back in the swing after its £220 million refit, this is surely the coolest place to stay.

Sir John Soane's Museum (▷ 148–149): One man's taste: an unusual house packed with curiosities.

Theatre Royal Drury Lane (▷ 160): Venue of countless hit musicals in Covent Garden.

WESTMINSTER, ST. JAMES'S AND MAYFAIR

Brown's Hotel (▷ 202): Luxurious, traditional hotel.

The Cinnamon Club (▷ 200): Traditional Indian cookery in the unlikely setting of a former library.

Fortnum and Mason (▷ 198): Famous food emporium.

The Halkin Hotel (▷ 202–203): Elegant, contemporary hotel with an excellent Thai restaurant.

National Gallery (▷ 182–187): European masterpieces from the 13th to the 19th centuries.

National Portrait Gallery (▷ 188–189): Pictures of royalty, the rich and the famous.

Nobu (▷ 201): Upscale restaurant serving exquisite but expensive modern Japanese cuisine.

Pigalle (▷ 199): Sophisticated 1940s'-style club with an amazing atmosphere.

Westminster Abbey (▷ 194–195): London's largest surviving medieval church, packed with famous tombs.

AROUND HYDE PARK

Bibendum (▷ 237): Restaurant known for its wine, and housed in the fabulous art deco Michelin building.

Camden Lock Market (▷ 232): Sprawling market with trendy wares from all over the world.

Claridge's (▷ 243): Quintessentially British hotel, famous for its afternoon teas.

Harrods (▷ 233): Legendary department store selling practically everything you can think of.

Harvey Nichols (▷ 233): Ultra-chic department store with gorgeous window displays.

The Landmark London (▷ 244): One of the city's top hotels, providing every luxury.

Natural History Museum (▷ 220–221): Dinosaurs to lichens: millions of specimens from the natural world.

Portobello Road (▷ 234): Fascinating street market selling everything from antiques to vegetables.

Restaurant Gordon Ramsay (▷ 240): The mothership of the notorious chef's culinary empire offers classic dishes and impeccable service.

Royal Albert Hall (▷ 235): Venue for major classical and contemporary concerts, dance and the summer Promenade Concerts.

Science Museum (▷ 222–223): Innovative hands-on museum that brings science to life.

Victoria & Albert Museum (▷ 224–228): A dazzling collection of decorative art.

Wallace Collection (▷ 229): Exceptional art collection housed in a palatial mansion.

Opposite *The Great Court of the British Museum*
Below *The Landmark London hotel*

TOP EXPERIENCES

Cross the river Stroll across the Millennium Bridge (▷ 77) or Westminster Bridge, preferably at sunset, for classic London river views.

Browse the markets Hunt for bargains and enjoy the atmosphere at a street market, such as Portobello Road (▷ 234) or Petticoat Lane (▷ 120).

Hop on a bus View the city from the top deck of a bus to get your bearings.

Go to Harrods Even if you don't want to buy anything, it's worth visiting this huge, luxurious store (▷ 233).

Shop at Covent Garden Find unusual items in the specialist shops in the area (▷ 142–143).

Ride on the London Eye The huge millennium wheel gives unrivalled views of London (▷ 75).

Take tea Skip lunch and go to Fortnum and Mason (▷ 198), or The Ritz (▷ 203), for a full afternoon tea.

Enjoy the parks and squares Take a picnic to one of the city's many green spaces.

See a live performance Whatever your taste, you'll find it in London. The choice of entertainment is huge.

Watch the Changing of the Guard Witness British tradition in action: daily ceremony outside Buckingham Palace (▷ 176–177).

Go on the river Take a boat trip on the Thames for a different perspective of the city (▷ 266–267).

Drink in a local Have a pint in a traditional London pub—many have changed little since Dickens's day.

Get out of town Leave the city centre for a day and visit at least one of the following: Greenwich, Hampstead Heath, Hampton Court, Kew Gardens (▷ 256–257, 258, 260–261, 268–269).

Wander off the beaten track Take a street map and explore areas such as Bloomsbury or the City on foot.

Lunch in style Try at least a couple of the city's superb restaurants: At lunchtime, prices are usually very reasonable.

Catch a traditional festival or event Look for the events, large and small, that take place year round (▷ 294–295).

Below left *Notting Hill Carnival is a riot of colour and exuberance*
Below right *A trip on the London Eye on a clear day affords fantastic views over the city*

LIVING LONDON

LIVING LONDON

UNDERSTANDING

OPEN 1·00AM MON·THURS 3·00AM FRI·SAT

There's no simple way of defining a Londoner. The city has a population of about 7.5 million, swollen every day by a million commuters coming in to work by train, mainly from southeast England. More than 270 nationalities make up the fabric of the city itself, and ethnic minorities add up to roughly a quarter of all Londoners. Many have family roots in African countries and India, formerly parts of the British Empire. In the 1950s, a huge number of West Indians arrived. Within the city, the Thames provides another means of identification, dividing north London from south; some people never cross the river. Cockneys are east Londoners born 'within the sound of Bow Bells'—the bells of the church of St.-Mary-le-Bow, east of the City. This is a city with a fascinating mix of tradition and change. You'll find the same types—the wealthy City worker, the lawyer in 18th-century wig and gown, the talkative London cabbie—but today they are men and women from a wide range of ethnic and social groups. The typical Londoner doesn't exist, and probably never did.

LONDONERS ALONE

One-third of Londoners live alone. Many are single young people, with good jobs and money. They're at the forefront of a changing society with a 50 per cent divorce rate, serial marriages and freelance or part-time jobs. Many of them will not marry, or cohabit, until they are 30. Their income is more than 15 per cent higher than that of the rest of the country and this pushes up prices, especially for London property, where increases of around 25 per cent a year have been known (though this has slowed considerably in the recession). These young people shop on the internet, eat out and network with their friends, who provide them with the stability once offered by the family group.

Clockwise from above Soho by night is a bustling mix of locals and tourists looking for an entertaining evening out or simply enjoying the atmosphere; the familiar red London buses; Mayor of London Boris Johnson, making a speech at City Hall

BOLLYWOOD IS HERE

The Asian community in London is more than 200 years old and enjoys a thriving cultural and commercial life. There are well over 200 Indian millionaires living in London; Meena Pathak of Pathak Spices, for example, has created a hugely successful food brand. You can enjoy some of the best Indian food in the world at Veeraswamy in Regent Street, the oldest of hundreds of Indian restaurants in the capital, or take your pick from the dozens of inexpensive Bangladeshi eateries along Brick Lane. Or why not see a film in Hindi, released direct from Bombay, in Upton Park. You can check out the saris and jewellery in major centres of the Asian community such as Southall or Tooting, which also offer a huge range of authentic restaurants and spice-filled groceries, catering to the locals.

SPEAKERS CORNER

Speakers Corner is at the northeast tip of Hyde Park, overlooking Marble Arch. Once the site of the Tyburn gallows (▷ 33), where public executions drew massive crowds, it's now a place devoted to free speech. Anyone can stand up, usually on a stepladder, and say anything they like—except, that is, about the Queen, as this is a royal park. Russian revolutionary Lenin (1870–1924) spoke here, as did novelist George Orwell (1903–50) and the Pankhurst family of suffragettes. Most speakers give vent to extreme views on religion, politics and diet at great and tedious length. Meanwhile the heckler plays an equally time-honoured part, shouting jokes or insults, which the best speakers answer back. In this modern age of emails and TV, Speakers Corner still provides that oldest form of communication, the shouting match.

LONDON CABBIES

There are some 21,000 black cabs in London, and an average of 31,000 people looking for a ride each night, so cabbies have to move fast. Since 1851 budding cab drivers have had to take an exam, set up by the Public Carriage Office, to test them on the best routes round 25,000 streets. It's called 'the Knowledge', and it takes three years to prepare for. Scientists have found that parts of the brain used for navigation are actually larger in a cabbie—but this brainpower is now under threat. The PCO wants to computerize the exam, and some companies are actually introducing computerized navigation systems in their cabs. Unsurprisingly, cabbies don't like it. Computers can't tell if a route is traffic-jammed, they say—and how do they know where the best restaurants are?

MAN OF THE PEOPLE

Alexander Boris de Pfeffel Johnson (Boris Johnson, born 1964) is one of London's most recognizable figures, thanks in part to his chaotic blond hair and bumbling style. As Mayor, the former Conservative MP and journalist has surprised his electorate by speaking out on such issues as policing in the city and the culture clash with Islam. Public transport has featured largely in his campaigns; he re-introduced classic red double-decker buses and banned drinking alcohol on the Underground. A pay-as-you-go shared cycle scheme reflects the Mayor's own love of bikes—he often cycles to work. While the press wait eagerly to pounce on Boris's next gaffe, the voters seem, in general, to approve of the job he has done, and he will contend the next election in 2012.

London is the focal point of the three main English sports: football (soccer), rugby and cricket. Wembley Stadium traditionally hosts the Football Association (FA) Cup Final in May, the climax of the football year. The main ground for rugby, invented in 1823 by an English schoolboy tired of kicking the ball, is in the southwest suburb of Twickenham (▷ 263), and cricket has had its headquarters in St. John's Wood since the 1830s, when the Marylebone Cricket Club moved there (▷ 216). London will also host the Summer Olympic Games in 2012 (▷ 40). Many Londoners take part in some form of physical activity, mainly walking, swimming or going to the gym. Some of this energy is expended on good causes. It is estimated that over £500 million has been raised by runners in the London Marathon since it began in 1980. It's the single biggest fund-raising event in the UK. A favourite leisure pastime of Londoners is drinking. There are 4,500 pubs and bars in the city, but they are no longer solely the domain of men and beer. Now you can buy wine, tea or coffee and often excellent food.

ARSENAL VERSUS TOTTENHAM
The long-standing feud between these two great football teams began in 1913. Arsenal moved from southeast London to Highbury, near the north London home of Tottenham Hotspur (Spurs), White Hart Lane. Arsenal needed more fans, and soon the community was split. The teams are very different. Arsenal, under Arsène Wenger, are free-flowing and exciting, while Tottenham are also showing signs of a resurgence since Harry Redknapp took over as manager. One of their famous clashes was the 1991 Football Association Cup Semi-Final. The streets of north London were deserted. After a great match, Spurs won 3–1 and went on to win the Cup Final. Such passionate rivalries ensure the game's popularity in the UK.

Clockwise from above England cricketers display the Ashes urn on a frieze outside Lord's cricket ground in St. John's Wood; Marathon runners coming up to the finish line in the Mall; the new Wembley Stadium and its landmark arch

PUB CRAWL PROTOCOL

One of the best ways to get to know London and see a cross-section of the capital's population is to go on a pub crawl—an afternoon and/or evening spent visiting one pub after another. There's a pub on almost every corner, so areas such as Mayfair or Fleet Street can be studied at close quarters in an enjoyable way. It's not a bad idea to have only a half in each pub, to fit more in and still get home. Until 2003, Britain's licensing laws were a source of amazement and annoyance to visitors as they meant that pubs had to close at 11pm, but local authorities can now decide what time individual pubs and clubs shut their doors. Night owls and visitors certainly welcome the change, and most residents seem happy enough.

THE FIVE-DAY MARATHON

The British love to do mad or strange things to raise money for charity. More than 30,000 people take part in the London Marathon in April and most finish in a few hours, but in 2002 Lloyd Scott took more than five days. He was wearing an antique diving suit weighing 55kg (120lb). In 1987 he had been diagnosed with leukaemia. He beat the disease, and decided to raise money for research. He could walk only 400m (1,300ft) in his suit before stopping to recover his strength. It was all worth it: Scott raised more than £100,000. In 2006 he completed the marathon dressed in armour and in 2007 as Indiana Jones, bringing the total raised to more than £4 million.

A NEW STADIUM

Londoners have a special affection for Wembley Stadium. Its famous two white towers were part of the skyline since 1923. The great athletic, football and rugby events are played at Wembley, and the biggest rock stars in the world have played there. In 1996 a replacement stadium to hold 90,000 people—the world's most expensive, at £715 million—was announced. Then the problems started. The government gave £120 million, but banks refused to lend the rest, demanding to know who was in charge of the project—the government or the Football Association? When demolition of the old towers finally began they proved more stubborn than expected, and work was slow. The new stadium, opened in 2006, has since hosted massive sell-out concerts by Take That, Oasis and Coldplay, as well as international sporting fixtures and events.

SALES MANIA

The traditional post-Christmas sales in London promise to deliver some great bargains after the Christmas spending spree, and Harrods (▷ 233) does it bigger and better than the rest. On the first day of the sale a high-profile film star draws up to the store in a horse-drawn carriage, to the accompaniment of bagpipes, to open the doors which announces the start of the sale. Then, if they have any sense, they run, as it's not unknown for people to be trampled in the consumer frenzy. The daily average of 30,000 visitors swells to a scary 300,000, and staff sometimes have to shut the doors on a packed store. To be first in line shoppers arrive the previous day and sleep on the pavement. Seasoned bargain-hunters know the exact route to their chosen goods and make for them at top speed. With discounts of 50 or 60 per cent, who can blame them?

ROYALTY AND FAME

London's royal pageantry is unique. Members of the royal family, who have been through good times and bad, still star in a regular series of splendid parades and processions. Trooping the Colour in June and the State Opening of Parliament in November, for instance, feature hundreds of soldiers, golden carriages, music and the Queen dressed in diamonds. There are less showy traditions, too: At the New Year's Honours and the Birthday Honours in June, the Queen hands medals and awards to hundreds of people from all walks of life. Her official role as Head of State is reflected in meetings with the Prime Minister every Tuesday to discuss government business. As the head of a very public and expensive monarchy, she attracts both criticism and huge affection. This heady combination of privilege and wealth—seen at the wedding of Prince William of Wales to Catherine Middleton in 2011—has always intrigued and attracted people from overseas: The city was flooded with a million extra visitors for the wedding. Film stars and billionaires still like to be seen mingling with the royals, and the spectacle does its bit to pull in the 14 million tourists from overseas who spend about £8.5 billion every year.

PAGEANTRY TRIUMPHS
The wedding of Prince William to Catherine Middleton in Westminster Abbey on 29 April 2011 was watched live by 34 million viewers in the UK, and billions worldwide, showcasing the capital, which was decked in Union Jack flags. British fashion was under the spotlight, with an elegant wedding gown designed by Sarah Burton of the Alexander McQueen label (with lace hand-made by London's Royal School of Needlework), and fantastic hats by Philip Treacy. The wedding of the year served as a 'warm-up' for the combined Olympics and Queen's Diamond Jubilee in 2012. The signs are that London can still put on a jolly good show.

Clockwise from above *Prince William, Duke of Cambridge, and Catherine, Duchess of Cambridge, depart Westminster Abbey after their marriage; London is peppered with Blue Plaques marking the residences of famous people; in 2015 the Queen, now in her 80s, would become the longest-reigning British monarch*

HOMES OF THE FAMOUS

Would Jimi Hendrix (1942–70) and George Frederick Handel (1685–1759) have got along, swapping notes on chords, tough crowds and the setting alight of instruments? Perhaps; they were neighbours, after all—albeit separated by 270 years, as well as a brick wall. Jimi stayed at No. 23 Brook Street in Mayfair from 1968 to 1969, entertaining, among others, the Beatles. George Frederick lived next door at No. 25 (▷ 178) for much of his life, making his name as a composer. Today this cosmic twist of fate is commemorated by a Blue Plaque, one of some 850 in London marking the homes of notable residents. Look hard enough and you'll spot one on virtually every corner, particularly in the Royal Borough of Kensington and Chelsea. The scheme, now looked after by English Heritage, has been extended across the country.

ROYAL WARRANTS

Keep your eyes open and you'll spot royal warrants everywhere in London. Companies and individuals appointed to provide goods and services to the royal family can display a royal coat of arms for five years. Royal warrants can be granted by the Queen, the Prince of Wales and the Duke of Edinburgh. To qualify, the business must have had the royal patron's custom for at least three years. The practice, which started in the 15th century, gives an interesting insight into the royal lifestyle. There is a royal mole controller and a chimney sweep. No fewer than seven champagne houses have royal warrants, and several chocolatiers—Cadbury's for the staff, Prestat/Bendicks for the royals. This sporty family has providers of riding breeches and fishing tackle, four official gunmakers and a busy royal taxidermist.

THE SEASON HAMPER

Once upon a time Britain's social élite laid out rugs and picnics at the summer race meets and open-air operas that make up The Season. Today you're more likely to find corporate hospitality tents, but it's still worth making the effort to impress with the perfect picnic hamper. Smoked salmon for example, should be wild, not farmed; strawberries should be English rather than Spanish. Scots may prefer to include some specialities from north of the border, such as cullen skink soup or oatcakes. A small tub of Gentleman's Relish, an anchovy paste, adds a touch of class. There are simple rules for drinks: Cans must be avoided. Pimms, a sweet, deceptively alcoholic drink first created in the 1840s, is traditional, and chilled champagne is a must.

THE GREAT AND THE GOOD

In 2002 a portrait of the Queen by Lucian Freud—celebrated as Britain's greatest contemporary painter—was revealed. Although monarchists considered it unflattering, it testifies to the importance of the portrait in British history as a record of who's who. It's difficult to go around a stately home or an established art gallery without being watched by likenesses of the great and the good. The art of portraiture was given a boost by two factors: the fashion for genealogy among the aristocracy, and the Protestant Reformation, when artists sought an alternative market to religious imagery. The best place to see portraits is the National Portrait Gallery (▷ 188–189).

SIR WINSTON CHURCHILL Lived in a house on this site 1921-1924

ARTS AND MEDIA

London has some of the best theatre in the world. There are two government-subsidized companies — the Royal National Theatre and the Royal Shakespeare Company — and Shaftesbury Avenue forms the heart of commercial theatre in the West End. Movie stars such as Nicole Kidman and Kevin Spacey have come to soak up some of its prestige, Spacey taking up the role of artistic director of the Old Vic (▷ 87). BAFTA (British Academy of Film and Television Arts) has moved its film awards ceremony to February, to avoid being overshadowed by the Oscars, and attracts many Hollywood stars. While they're here they have to face the toughest paparazzi in the world, as well as a voracious tabloid press. Art and style are part of the London experience. The Tate Modern gallery (▷ 80–81), one of London's most exciting spaces, is so popular that it stays open until 10pm on Fridays and Saturdays. And the artists of the catwalk, London's fashion designers, are at the peak of their creativity, developing the city's quirky street fashion and producing radicals such as John Galliano, who used to head Christian Dior, to revolutionize haute couture.

THE LOTTERY IN LONDON
Since it started in 1994 the National Lottery has raised hundreds of millions of pounds for big London institutions such as the Royal Opera House. But smaller amounts, which don't attract the headlines, are also distributed across the city to places such as Kentish Town's City Farm, a popular scheme for youngsters who might never have seen animals or the countryside. When the Lottery awarded the farm £47,000 for its drama and arts programme, it set up workshops for young asylum-seekers in the area to create their own stories and attend art classes. Debate about the Lottery continues to rage, but there's no denying that some of its contributions make a real difference.

Clockwise from above *Artists arrive at the Royal Academy of Arts to hand in works completed for the annual Summer Exhibition; modern sculpture outside the British Museum; fashion designer Stella McCartney is the daughter of former Beatle Paul McCartney*

ARCHITECTURAL SUPREMO

How far do you have to go to escape Sir Norman Foster's work? Not Bilbao, where the top British architect has redesigned much of the metro system. Not Berlin, where his renovation of the Reichstag won the Pritzker architecture prize. Nor Hong Kong, if you pass through Chek Lap Kok international airport, built on a man-made island. And certainly not London: Canary Wharf's transcendental tube station, the Great Court in the British Museum (▷ 134–139) and the Greater London Authority's new home, City Hall, are some of the most distinctive buildings in Britain, all designed by Foster and Partners. One of the most striking additions to London's skyline, 30 St. Mary Axe (aka the Gherkin), embodies environmentally friendly architecture with layers of 'light wells' inside its distinctive shape, and largely self-ventilating.

RAGS TO RICHES

From London's East End to the fashion houses of Paris via Savile Row, the Alexander McQueen story crosses the capital and then the English Channel. McQueen was born in 1969, the son of an East End taxi driver, and left school at 16. More interested in couture than cab driving, he served his apprenticeship on Savile Row, before taking an MA at St. Martin's School of Art—other alumni include Stella McCartney and Matthew Williamson. After a celebrated final collection, fashion's *enfant terrible* left London for Paris, working for Givenchy and then Gucci. By 2001 the three-times British Designer of the Year had made his fortune and by the end of 2006 he had 21 boutiques across the globe; an online store was launched in 2008. His personal story has a tragic end: In 2010 McQueen committed suicide, but his fashion label still thrives.

THE PEOPLE'S ART

The Royal Academy Summer Exhibition is held between June and mid-August at the Royal Academy (▷ 181) in Piccadilly. First held in 1769, it is open to every artist in the country from the humblest amateur to the greatest professional. Anything can be submitted: drawings, prints, sculpture, traditional or abstract, and everything is viewed. The exhibition often has a theme which the artists use for inspiration—2010's was 'Raw'; 2011 had no theme. Around a thousand works are chosen for display, every one for sale. There was a time when artists queued all day with their submissions until an Academician shouted a very public acceptance or rejection. The selection process is more civilized these days, and for those whose work is accepted, there's always a chance of seeing their local landscape hanging next to a David Hockney.

THEATRE FOR ALL

Chickenshed is one of the largest theatre companies in the UK, and has a substantial theatre with a recording and dance studio in Southgate, north London. Jo Collins and Mary Ward founded it in 1974 with the simple aim of involving anyone with a love of theatre, including children. One of their most famous performances was *Anansi*, based on African tales, in which 1,000 London children took part. After seeing it, Diana, Princess of Wales became the company's patron, and when she died in 1997 Chickenshed recorded a tribute single, *I Am in Love With the World*, that reached No. 14 in the charts. Chickenshed projects have spread across the country, proving again that the simplest ideas are often the best. In 2007 Chickenshed went one stage further, extending projects into Russia.
www.chickenshed.org.uk

MONEY AND POWER

There are several layers of government in London. The British Parliament, made up of the House of Commons and the House of Lords, sits in the Houses of Parliament (▷ 179–180). Just up the road is Whitehall and the major offices of government, including the Prime Minister's official residence at No. 10 Downing Street. At the top of Whitehall, the Mall leads to Buckingham Palace, official home of the Queen, the constitutional Head of State. Then comes the government of London itself—and this gets even more confusing. The City of London, known as 'the square mile', is its historic heart and financial centre, and still guards its medieval privileges. Since 1189 the Lord Mayor has been head of the fiercely independent Corporation of London, the first local authority in England. The modern city, encompassing its sprawl of suburbs, is known as Greater London and, in 2000, elected its first mayor, Ken Livingstone. He was ousted after two terms in 2008 by Boris Johnson. The Mayor and the Greater London Authority co-ordinate services such as transport across 32 London boroughs and have a budget of £3.2 billion.

POLITICIAN-AUTHORS

As if being part of the world's oldest parliamentary democracy didn't keep them busy enough, dozens of members of parliament (MPs) supplement their £65,000-plus salaries with second jobs. Many are directors of companies or highly paid consultants, some pulling in huge annual salaries. But the most intriguing moonlighters are the novelists. In the 1990s Tory MP Edwina Currie began writing racy novels in her spare time (e.g. *A Parliamentary Affair*). Fellow Tory Ann Widdecombe, known for her uncompromising views, was advanced £100,000 for two rather more restrained novels. Interestingly, one Labour MP's analysis in 2002 of MPs' voting records revealed that those who have second jobs turn up to 30 per cent fewer votes than those who don't.

Clockwise from above *The Houses of Parliament's Central Lobby; a row of highly desirable pastel-coloured houses off the King's Road, Chelsea; the House of Lords Chamber is much more richly decorated than the Commons Chamber*

HOUSE OF LORDS

Historically, the most reliable way of gaining a seat on the red leather benches of Parliament's upper chamber was to inherit it. In 1999 the Labour government reforms threw out all but 92 of the aristocrats. So how do you get a life peerage today? You should be British: former owner of the *Daily Telegraph* Lord Black had to renounce his Canadian citizenship. Senior figures in the military and the judiciary have an advantage, and Britain's 25 bishops are guaranteed a spot. Ex-politicians and business people aren't uncommon — and you needn't be old: Baroness Warsi, the first Muslim woman in the Cabinet, was born in 1971. You can be nominated as a People's Peer — but with brain specialist Professor Susan Greenfield among them, they are hardly average, either.

WHO OWNS LONDON?

After the Queen and the Church, Gerald Grosvenor, 6th Duke of Westminster, is the greatest landowner in London. His ancestor, Mary Davies, married Sir Thomas Grosvenor in 1677. Mary owned 100ha (247 acres) of damp farmland. Today this is Mayfair and Belgravia, some of the most expensive land in the world. The Duke's rents and freeholds have created a fortune worth at least £5 billion. He owns more land elsewhere in the UK and in Canada, Australia and the USA. The present Duke lives simply, but his forebears spent on an imperial scale, splashing out on Old Masters and jewellery by Fabergé. The 4th Duke was a suitor of Paris fashion designer Coco Chanel, and, on finding that the mail was too slow for his liking, set up a private postal system just for her.

VOLATILE HOUSE PRICES

Sixty per cent of Londoners own their homes, but houses don't come cheap. London has among the highest property prices in the world. A small three-bedroom house in Chelsea will cost more than £1 million; a one-bedroom flat in an average area can easily top £200,000. Until 2007 prices were doubling every five years, but the recession had the inevitable effect of sending them back down — by 10 to 15 per cent — and the recovery is only just under way. For those who can afford it, even a small London property is still a great investment, but anyone earning less than £30,000 a year is in trouble. Teachers, nurses, fire and police officers, all vital to the capital, are unable to afford their own homes, and mortgages have become even tougher to secure.

THE UK'S HIGHEST EARNERS

The incomes of the UK's richest 1 per cent are soaring ahead, despite the recent economic crisis, and most of the people earning more than £100,000 a year live in London or its hinterland. The exclusive west London district of Kensington and Chelsea has the highest concentration of high-earners in the country. The City of London, the financial district, is not far behind, and here many employees work for an incentive system that can lead to huge rewards. These districts are also where full-time gross weekly pay is highest — in Kensington and Chelsea it is in the vicinity of a cool £1,250. Seven of the ten best-paid workforces in the UK are in Greater London districts, as are the majority of the UK's millionaires and billionaires.

URBAN WILDLIFE

Along with millions of people, London is home to a surprising amount of wildlife. Within 30km (20 miles) of St. Paul's, 2,000 species of flora and fauna thrive in parks, squares, churchyards, ponds and gardens. Flora includes the London plane tree and the pink-flowered saxifrage called London Pride. Fauna ranges from deer, foxes, badgers and rabbits to grey squirrels, the ubiquitous pigeons, house sparrows (the traditional 'Cockney Sparrows'), and stealthy armies of rats and mice. Voles do so well that the London Wildlife Trust has its own vole officer. The endangered stag beetle finds sanctuary in private gardens, and fish have returned to the once-polluted Thames.

PIGEONS UNDER FIRE

The British have an odd relationship with the pigeon, and the Royal Pigeon Racing Association has around 30,000 members. Meanwhile, the famous pigeons of Trafalgar Square (▷ 190–191), are on the wanted list. These 'rats with wings' carry disease and leave a mess behind them, in many people's opinion, so pigeons are on a diet — in the hope that they will go away. The general public is not allowed to feed them, and hawks go flapping overhead every so often to scare them off. These measures follow the phased eradication programme introduced by former mayor Ken Livingstone, which reduced pigeon numbers considerably from around 4,000 to just 200.

PLANES VERSUS POLLUTION

As well as being beautiful, trees play a vital anti-pollution role. The Trees for Cities charity, started in London, now plants 12,000 of them a year in the city. A characteristic feature of the capital's streets and gardens, the London plane tree *(Platanus x hispanica)*, which periodically sheds its dirt-absorbing bark, is a hybrid of the oriental plane, introduced in 1562, and the western plane, which was imported from Virginia in 1636. The oldest surviving examples in garden squares are the huge ones in Berkeley Square, planted in 1789. William Wordsworth wrote a poem about the ancient plane tree at the corner of Cheapside and Wood Street in the City, which is still there.

FOXES ON THE RUN

Foxes like big cities because it is easy to find food. There are about 20,000 in London. Some people like foxes and encourage them into their gardens, but others are scared, especially since an attack by a fox on twin babies inside their house in 2010. The government officially recommends trapping the foxes and releasing them into the wild, which usually means they just come back, but one area of London has taken the drastic step of employing a hunter to kill the foxes. He traps the foxes and then shoots them. Animal rights activists oppose this and the man has to work anonymously. However, the major cause of fox death is less dramatic: Sixty per cent of them die each year, squashed beneath the wheels of a car. Keep an eye out for them in leafier areas, especially at night.

Clockwise from above An early-morning cycle ride in Kensington Gardens; Trafalgar Square's once ubiquitous pigeons flock around the National Gallery

UNDERSTANDING LIVING LONDON

THE STORY OF LONDON

THE BEGINNINGS OF LONDON

London is where it is because of a decision made by the Roman army commanders after their invasion of England in AD43. A site for a base was chosen on the north bank of the Thames at the highest point of the tide accessible to ships from the European Continent. A bridge was built across the river and quays along the bank, and the military base developed into a town, a busy commercial and administrative district that became the hub of the Roman road network and succeeded Colchester as the capital of Roman Britain. The civic heart was where Leadenhall Market (▷ 120) is now. Besides barracks, houses and shops, there were temples, public baths and an amphitheatre, and from around AD200 the whole town was surrounded by a wall. After the Roman army withdrew from Britain, the Anglo-Saxons established their own town outside the wall on the west, in today's Aldwych area, but attacks by Vikings drove the inhabitants back inside the Roman wall in the ninth century. In the 11th century, King Edward the Confessor founded Westminster Abbey (▷ 194–195) a mile (1.6km) to the west, built a palace and created a second London, the centre of the royal government, alongside the first.

THE PEOPLING OF ROMAN LONDON

All through its history London has grown by attracting settlers from elsewhere. The early population included many Celts from various parts of Britain, but London also imported people from all over the Roman Empire, from across the English Channel in Gaul (France)—such as Julius Classicianus, the first Londoner whose name is known—to Greece and the eastern Mediterranean. Soldiers, officials, doctors, shopkeepers, entertainers, craftsmen, clerks, cooks, slaves—some with their families—brought their gods and goddesses, languages, costumes, traditions and habits with them to create a cosmopolitan mix. Roman London probably resembled a frontier town in the Wild West—crowded, noisy, smelly and often dangerous.

Clockwise from above *Statue of warrior-queen Boadicea (Boudicca) on the Victoria Embankment; King Alfred the Great recaptured London from the Vikings in AD886; Roman head of the god Mithras (second to third century) from the Temple of Mithras, now in the Museum of London*

BOADICEA'S REVOLT
Queen Boadicea (or Boudicca; the name means 'victory'), ruler of the Celtic Iceni people of East Anglia in AD60, was an ally of the Romans until enraged by their arrogance and mistreatment. After Roman soldiers had flogged her and raped her daughters, Boadicea led her tribespeople to sack Colchester and then descended on London in her war chariot, seeking vengeance. She plundered the fledgling town, burned it to the ground and slaughtered those inhabitants who had not fled the city. The Roman army quickly regrouped and defeated the Iceni in battle somewhere to the north, and Boadicea killed herself rather than be captured. London was quickly rebuilt, but archaeologists have found clear traces of extensive fire damage deep below the current ground level.

IN THE ARENA
One of the pleasures of life in Roman London was going to the amphitheatre, near the area now occupied by the Guildhall (▷ 102). Oval in shape, with high earth banks supporting wooden benches for some 5,000 spectators, it was used for entertainment (including executions) and could be hired for private functions. Wild animals were butchered in the arena for the audience's delight, but gladiatorial combats were the star attraction. These might involve a heavily armed fighter against one more lightly armed and more agile, or a contest between a *retiarius* (gladiator equipped with a net and trident) against an opponent with sword and shield. All the gladiators paraded round the arena together before fighting—often to the death, though a defeated gladiator could appeal to the crowd for mercy.

DEATH AND BAY LEAVES
A lavish sarcophagus discovered in the Spitalfields area of the City in 1999 was expected to be that of a powerful citizen of Roman London. When the lead casket inside was opened, however, it was found to contain the skeleton of a young woman. Buried around AD350 and in her 20s when she died, she clearly came from an extremely rich family. The sarcophagus was decorated with scallop shells, symbols of life after death. She had been wrapped in expensive garments of silk and wool, some shot through with gold thread. Also interred with her were glass and jet objects and, touchingly, her head had been put gently to rest on a pillow of fresh, sweet-smelling bay leaves.

THE ROYAL SAINT
Edward the Confessor (*c*.1003–66) was the only English king ever canonized. A deeply religious man, he gave his patronage to a Benedictine monastery on Thorney Island in the Thames marshes west of London, paying for its church to be rebuilt in the Romanesque style, which was fashionable in Normandy, and establishing a royal palace near the site. The monastery relics included fragments of the True Cross, blood from Christ's wounded side, some of the Virgin Mary's milk and one of St. Paul's fingers. When Edward died in 1066, leaving his kingdom without an heir and his throne in dispute, he was laid to rest there—behind the high altar of Westminster Abbey (▷ 194–195).

London's importance was underlined when William I, 'the Conqueror' (1027–87), built the Tower of London to keep the city under control after the Norman conquest. Over the following centuries streets were paved for the first time, hospitals and prisons were built, and church spires studded the skyline. Rich merchant guilds took over the government of the city, which had its own mayor and aldermen. Merchants and financiers came to London from Germany, Denmark, France and Italy; until its expulsion in 1290 there was a flourishing Jewish community. Westminster, meanwhile, became a regular meeting place of Parliament, and magnates built houses along the river between the city and Westminster. In 1500 London had a population of perhaps 50,000, quadrupled by immigration in the Tudor period. City merchants monopolized England's foreign trade, with ships leaving the Port of London for the Mediterranean and the East, America and Africa. Bricks were used in more buildings and the most expensive houses had pumped water. Constables and marshals were employed to deal with crime and vagrancy. Disease was rife, but life was longer on average in London than elsewhere.

OLD LONDON BRIDGE
London's only bridge in the Middle Ages was a remarkable sight. People lived on it in houses along each side, from three to seven floors high. These were not finally removed until 1762. There were shops on the ground floors—more than a hundred of them—and at the core a two-storey chapel dedicated to St. Thomas à Becket. Below, the bridge's 19 arches created dangerous rapids. In 1390 the bridge was turfed over for a great tournament between English and Scottish champions. It had more gruesome uses too. The heads of executed traitors were parboiled in the gatehouse, dipped in tar and stuck on the gateway. One visitor in 1598 counted more than 30 on display.

Clockwise from above *The killing of Wat Tyler in front of King Richard II, from the Chronicles of medieval historian Jean Froissart; The Globe Theatre depicted on Visscher's map of London, 1616; London's first zoo, in the Tower of London*

THE ZOO IN THE TOWER

Until the 1830s the Tower of London (▷ 112–117) housed a royal collection of wild animals, kept for the entertainment of the court, in the Royal Menagerie. Henry III (1207–72) had a polar bear which liked to fish in the Thames, three leopards sent by the Holy Roman Emperor, and an elephant, a gift from France, which caused great excitement when it arrived but survived for only two years. An official Keeper of the King's Lions and Leopards was appointed, and lions still lived in the Tower in the time of James I (1566–1625), who liked to set mastiffs on them. Around 1750 the zoo had lions, tigers, leopards, bears, monkeys, eagles, vultures, kangaroos and an ostrich. In 1832, after several animals had escaped and attacked people, the menagerie was moved to London Zoo.

THE KILLING OF WAT TYLER

In 1381 thousands of rebels objecting to a poll tax journeyed from Kent and Essex to London. The followers of the Peasants' Revolt—whose demands included the redistribution of church wealth—killed several government officials before the 13-year-old king, Richard II (1367–1400), agreed to meet them at Smithfield. After some initial dialogue there was a scuffle, as the Mayor of London, William Walworth, tried to arrest Wat Tyler, the rebel leader. Tyler struck at him with a dagger but Walworth, saved by the mail shirt under his clothes, ran Tyler through with his sword. Richard rode towards the rebels, proclaiming himself their true leader and the crowd fled. Poll taxes were not imposed again—until 1990 by Margaret Thatcher.

QUEEN ELIZABETH AT TILBURY

When the Spanish Armada sailed to invade England in 1588, Elizabeth I (1533–1603) insisted on visiting her troops at Tilbury. Accompanied by her courtiers, she arrived riding a white horse and wearing a steel corselet over her white velvet dress. Having dismounted, she walked through the ranks before delivering a stirring address. The Queen was a superb orator and her defiant speech is famous in English history. 'I know I have but the body of a weak and feeble woman,' she announced, 'but I have the heart and stomach of a king, and of a king of England too.' Elizabeth was still at Tilbury when news arrived of the Armada's defeat. It was the key turning point of the Anglo-Spanish War (1585–1604).

SHAKESPEARE AND THE GLOBE

Bankside in the time of William Shakespeare (1564–1616) was London's most notorious entertainment area, known for its drinking dens and 'stews' (brothels), its bull- and bear-baiting pits and its theatres. A new theatre called the Globe (▷ 78)—polygonal, thatched and built of wood—opened there in 1599 and staged many of Shakespeare's plays, including *Macbeth*, *Othello* and probably *Henry V* (with its veiled reference to the theatre as 'this wooden O'). Bottled ale sold well to the audiences, and buckets served as emergency toilets. When the theatre was destroyed by fire in 1613 the only person hurt was a man whose breeches were set alight, but he resourcefully quenched the flames with a bottle of beer.

When James VI of Scotland (1566–1625) arrived in London to be crowned James I of England in 1603, the city was 10 times the size of any other in the kingdom. The first horse-drawn cabs appeared on the streets in the 1620s, annoying the Thames watermen, who ran London's earliest taxi service, and the development of the West End as a fashionable quarter started in Covent Garden (▷ 142–143). The city guarded its privileges jealously. When Charles I (1600–49) interfered with them he met with fierce opposition, which was to be a major factor of his defeat in the Civil War. The 11-year Commonwealth government brought further encroachments, and London rejoiced when Charles II (1630–85) rode through the streets to reclaim the throne in 1660. Smart neighbourhoods developed, such as St. James's and Bloomsbury, but most of the medieval city was devoured by the Great Fire. Sir Christopher Wren (1632–1723) rebuilt St. Paul's Cathedral (▷ 104–109) and the city churches, but his plan for new streets was rejected. The old layout was restored, though the new buildings were in brick. The city soon recovered its dominance and in 1694 the Bank of England (▷ 101) was founded.

GUNPOWDER, TREASON AND PLOT

A group of conspirators intent on restoring Roman Catholicism in England found a Yorkshire soldier of fortune named Guy Fawkes, who was ready to blow up Parliament, with the aim of killing James I and his ministers gathered for the State opening ceremony in 1605.

After renting a cellar that ran beneath the House of Lords, they filled it with 36 barrels of gunpowder and a quantity of iron bars, concealed under masses of rubbish. Word of the plot leaked out, however; the building was searched and Fawkes was found lurking there with a length of slow-match, tinder and a watch. After interrogation under torture in the Tower of London, he was hanged, drawn and quartered, as were his fellow plotters.

Clockwise from above *The Great Fire of 1666 destroyed most of London; Charles I facing the executioner's block in 1649; the great dome of St. Paul's Cathedral, Christopher Wren's most famous achievement*

THE GREAT FIRE

A catastrophic fire started in a bakery in Pudding Lane, near London Bridge, in the early hours of a September morning in 1666. Fanned by a strong wind and fuelled by wooden houses, it destroyed 80 per cent of the city's buildings and made more than 100,000 people homeless. The death toll remains a mystery — only five were recorded but there were probably more that went unregistered. Charles II sent diarist Samuel Pepys (1633–1703) to the scene to order the construction of fire breaks, and the next day the King and his brother, the future James II, took charge of operations. Flames raged up to 90m (300ft) high and threw out a rain of sparks. The navy was called in and houses were demolished. Finally the wind dropped and after four days the fire burned itself out.

BLOOD AND THE CROWN JEWELS

Colonel Thomas Blood was an adventurous Irishman who had his estates confiscated for supporting Parliament against Charles I. In 1671 he made an audacious attempt to steal the Crown Jewels, which were put on display in the Martin Tower of the Tower of London by the Keeper of Regalia, Talbot Edwards. Disguised as a clergyman, Blood befriended the Keeper and won his trust, returning later with three accomplices to steal the crown, orb and sceptre. They overpowered the Keeper and were making off with their booty when he recovered and raised the alarm. All four were caught, Blood with the crown under his parson's cloak. Charles II, apparently amused by the escapade, pardoned Blood and restored his Irish estate.

THE EXECUTION OF CHARLES I

The Civil War was at an end, and Charles I had been convicted of waging war against his own people. On a cold January afternoon in 1649 he donned an extra shirt — in case his shivers were mistaken for fear — and stepped through a window of the Banqueting House (▷ 175) in Whitehall on to a specially built scaffold, watched by a large crowd. The King pushed his hair up under his cap and knelt awkwardly at the block, which was only 26cm (10in) high. In complete silence he stretched out his arms as a signal to the executioner, who brought the axe down and severed the King's head with one stroke. A groan went up from the crowd, and one or two spectators passed out.

THE GREAT PLAGUE

An epidemic of bubonic plague in 1664–65, though less lethal than the Black Death, still killed around 100,000 people in London, a third of the population. People who could get out of town did so, though many doctors and clergy stayed to fulfil their duties. The disease was transmitted by fleas and spread by flea-ridden rats, but this was not understood at the time, and misguided remedies included a cull of dogs and cats. Plague-stricken houses had a cross daubed on the door, and the inhabitants were locked inside for 40 days' quarantine. To the cry of 'Bring out your dead', carts clattered through the streets collecting corpses, which were thrown into 'plague pits' and covered with a layer of quicklime.

GEORGIAN LONDON

London's population grew towards the million mark as people from all parts of the country flocked in to seek their fortunes in the heart of England's political, commercial and artistic life. London covered more than twice as much ground in 1800 as in 1700. The villages of Knightsbridge, Kensington and Chelsea became extensions of the West End. Elegant squares and streets went up in Mayfair to house wealthy families with their servants. There were fashionable shops in Bond Street, Oxford Street and the Strand, smart coffee-houses and the Vauxhall and Ranelagh pleasure gardens to enjoy. The British Museum (▷ 134–139) and the Royal Academy of Arts (▷ 181) opened their doors, Handel's oratorios were premiered at Covent Garden (▷ 142–143) and exotic plants from around the world were grown at Kew Gardens (▷ 268–269). It was also a London of smoke and stench, open sewers, high infant mortality rates and appalling slum 'rookeries'. Disease, drunkenness, prostitution and thieving were rife. Highwaymen, notably Dick Turpin, preyed on travellers into and out of London. There was no organized police force or fire brigade. Areas such as Seven Dials were avoided altogether by respectable citizens, who hired linkmen with torches to light them through the dark.

AT YE OLDE CHESHIRE CHEESE

The Cheshire Cheese pub in Fleet Street has a list of famous past patrons. Lexicographer Dr. Samuel Johnson (1709–84) lived round the corner and came here or to the Turk's Head in Gerrard Street to gossip with his friends. Other leading lights of the literary and artistic community who drank here were writer James Boswell, painter Sir Joshua Reynolds, author Oliver Goldsmith and actor David Garrick. Johnson's memory has been saluted at the Cheshire Cheese by many later literary figures. Writer G. K. Chesterton once took his part at a Johnsonian dinner, and Irish poet W. B. Yeats and his contemporaries conducted a regular literary circle there in the 1890s.

Clockwise from above *Houses in Bedford Square showing the symmetry and classical lines of Georgian architecture; the Egyptian Room of the British Museum; stone tablet marking the site of Tyburn tree*

THE ST. GILES ROOKERY

A rookery, sometimes also known as a stew, was an old colloquial term for a slum or ghetto. In about the middle of the 18th century the area round the church of St. Giles-in-the-Fields was one of London's worst slums. Its narrow streets, alleys and yards were synonymous with squalor, beggars, prostitution, crime and drink, with up to 50 people crammed into each ramshackle little house. Notorious taverns and gin-shops in the area included the Maidenhead Inn, in Dyott Street, and the Rat's Castle. When the nearby brewery's giant vat burst in 1814 and beer flooded the streets, the slum's inhabitants rushed out with jugs and cups. Even the children brought spoons, and some unfortunate people trying to lap beer from the gutters fell in and were drowned.

COLLECTORS ALL IN A ROW

Sir Hans Sloane (▷ 139) left his cornucopia of antiquities, artworks, manuscripts, natural history specimens and weird curiosities to the nation. The British Museum (▷ 134–139) was founded to house them and other treasures such as the Harleian Collection of manuscripts, assembled by the Earls of Oxford, and the Cotton family's books and antiquities. Money was raised by public lottery to pay for the building in Great Russell Street and the museum opened in 1759. In due course many more collections were purchased or donated, including Sir William Hamilton's antique vases, Egyptian antiquities, classical sculptures, the marble friezes removed from the Parthenon in Athens by Lord Elgin, and King George III's library.

TYBURN TREE

Marble Arch (▷ 216) stands on the site once occupied by the Tyburn gallows. Convicts were brought here to be hanged, travelling from Newgate prison three to a cart, sitting on their own coffins. On the way they were allowed to stop at taverns for free drinks and many, mercifully, arrived drunk. The hangman was sometimes in a similar condition. Huge crowds gathered to watch as the noose was fastened round the prisoner's neck, the horse was whipped up to make the cart move on, leaving the rope to drop. Friends would rush to tug on the dangling victim's legs and shorten the ordeal. From 1783 executions were conducted in Newgate, ending some 600 years of Tyburn hangings, which had claimed more than 50,000 souls.

THE LONDON MOB

In 1780 Member of Parliament Lord George Gordon (1751–93) led a huge demonstration to the Houses of Parliament (▷ 179–180) to protest against the relaxation of penalties on Roman Catholics. Some members of the crowd went on the rampage; Irish people and Roman Catholics were assaulted and their houses destroyed, and Roman Catholic chapels were looted to screams of 'No Popery'. Hoodlums poured out of the slums to drink, rape, kill and steal. Prisons were stormed, the prisoners released, and a mob armed with muskets attacked the Bank of England. After a week of mayhem the government called out the troops. In the ensuing suppression 285 people were killed. Gordon himself was acquitted of high treason, but 25 of the rioters were hanged.

THE GREAT WEN

In the first half of the 19th century 'the great wen' (growth), as journalist William Cobbett called London, continued to expand. It was now the financial capital of the world and improved roads turned villages such as Hampstead and Highgate, Camberwell and Dulwich into suburbs for city commuters. Meanwhile, as the docks expanded down the Thames, cheap housing spread through Whitechapel, Stepney and Bethnal Green in the East End. Architect John Nash (1752–1835) designed Regent's Park, Belgravia was laid out in style, Lord's cricket ground opened and London University was founded. London Zoo (▷ 219) opened and the National Gallery (▷ 182–187) and Nelson's Column were new landmarks in Trafalgar Square (▷ 190–191). Gas lighting made streets seem safer and in the 1820s and 1830s London acquired a police force and a fire brigade. The first horse-drawn omnibuses ran in 1829, and the railways arrived soon afterwards. In stark contrast were the pressing problems of overcrowding and poverty, which spurred on the advocates of sweeping political and social reform.

LORD NELSON'S FUNERAL

Admiral Lord Horatio Nelson (1758–1805) died in action against the Napoleonic fleet at the Battle of Trafalgar. He was brought home in his flagship, HMS *Victory*, and his coffin taken by boat to Greenwich (▷ 256–257) and up the river. At the Admiralty in Whitehall it was placed on a funeral car made to resemble the *Victory*, with a winged figure of Fame at the prow. The Royal Scots Greys led the procession to St. Paul's. Bells tolled, guns boomed and fifes and drums played as the cortège moved through streets lined with people. A dozen sailors from the *Victory* bore the coffin. Darkness was gathering before the service was over and Nelson was lowered into a place of honour directly below the cathedral dome (▷ 107, 109).

Clockwise from above *Glass painting from the National Maritime Museum, Greenwich, showing Nelson's funeral barge; Madame Tussauds exhibition catalogue from 1883; to become a 'peeler'—police officer—men had to be 1.8m (6ft) tall and have a clean record*

THE PEELERS

As Home Secretary in 1829, Sir Robert Peel (1788–1850) introduced London's first effective police force. Called 'peelers' or 'bobbies' after their creator, the officers — many of them ex-soldiers — stepped on to the streets in blue uniforms and top hats, and made their Whitehall headquarters off Scotland Yard. At first the constables were regarded with suspicion and hostility by Londoners, who prized their freedom. 'Blue devils' was another popular nickname. Policemen were often attacked and when one was killed by rioters in 1831 the coroner's jury brought in a verdict of justifiable homicide. Gradually, under their Irish chief, Richard 'King' Mayne, who ran the force until his death in 1868, they acquired a reputation for discipline and restraint.

MADAME TUSSAUD AND THE WAXWORKS

Marie Tussaud (1761–1850), born Anna Maria Grosholtz in Strasbourg, arrived in England from her native France in 1802 with her two sons — having abandoned their father — and toured her waxworks show around the country until settling in London in 1835. In Paris, during the Terror that followed the French Revolution, she had been forced to make wax models of the severed heads of prominent victims of the guillotine, some of whom she had known personally. After fleeing the country she attracted wide attention for her display of lifesized likenesses of famous figures. Madame Tussaud's sons continued the business after her death and moved it to the present site near Baker Street in 1884 (▷ 217).

NEWGATE'S DREADFUL WALLS

Newgate prison was the most famous and dreaded in the country, originally established in the city's west gatehouse in the 12th century. Charles Dickens wrote of 'Those dreadful walls of Newgate, which have hidden so much misery and such unspeakable anguish'. New arrivals were liable to be robbed of everything they had, including clothes, and were bullied by both seasoned inmates and prison officials. Occasionally rich prisoners could buy special treatment and live quite comfortably in an airy room, playing skittles or tennis and drinking in one of the taverns inside the walls. Most prisoners, however, endured grim cells, dirt, lice and vermin, an appalling stench and dreadful food. The prison was demolished in 1902.

THE MUDLARKS

Mudlarks were scavengers who lived by scouring the Thames shore after the tide had gone down to pick up any articles they could sell. They sometimes waded up to their waists in thick, greasy mud, mixed with a nauseating combination of raw sewage and the occasional dead animal. They ranged from small children to bent old women in clothes so tattered and filthy they were scarcely even rags. Most lived near the river and would come out soon after low tide and wait for the chance to scrabble about among barges and boats on the shore. They gathered pieces of coal, wood, rope or iron, bones, tools and copper nails, which were particularly valuable. Coal would be sold to their neighbours and other finds to the local rag-and-bone shops.

THE WORLD'S LARGEST CITY

As the Great Exhibition of 1851 in Hyde Park displayed Britain to the world in the world's largest city, vigorous reform was under way. From the 1860s the Peabody Trust built new housing for the poor; in the 1870s slums were cleared to make way for Shaftesbury Avenue and Charing Cross Road, philanthropist Thomas Barnardo (1845–1905) opened his first homes for destitute children and the London School Board set out to give every London child an elementary education. The population rose steeply, hitting 4 million by the end of the century. In the City and central districts, however, numbers fell as cheap transport allowed people to live farther from their places of work. With the introduction of underground trains and trams, London spread over yet more of the surrounding country, swallowing Hammersmith, Putney, Clapham, Stratford, Tottenham and Hornsey. London County Council was founded in 1888 to run an area of well over 260sq km (100sq miles). By the end of the century electricity lit the streets and new department stores were attracting custom, including Harrods (▷ 233) and Liberty (▷ 155).

THE GREAT STINK

The Thames in 1858 was an open sewer for all the filth of London. That year's hot summer created a stench so horrific that it was dubbed the Great Stink. Noxious fumes penetrated the Houses of Parliament—and consequently something was done. Sir Joseph Bazalgette (1819–91), chief engineer of the new Metropolitan Board of Works, built 800km (500 miles) of main sewers and 21,000km (13,000 miles) of lesser drains, superbly constructed in brick and still working today. The Victoria Embankment (▷ 147) was built along the north bank of the river with a massive sewer inside as well as a tunnel for the new underground trains. On top were gardens and a new road to relieve London's traffic congestion. It was an engineering feat of genius and earned Bazalgette a knighthood.

Clockwise from above The Great Exhibition of 1851 showcased industrial enterprise worldwide; Big Ben takes its nickname from the huge bell that chimes the hour; an 1880s' photograph of Ludgate Hill looking down to St. Paul's Cathedral

JACK THE RIPPER

To this day no one knows the identity of the killer who stalked the cobbled, gas-lit alleys of Whitechapel in 1888, killing prostitutes. The body of Mary Anne Nicholls, the first undoubted victim of the Whitechapel Murderer —as he was known at first—was discovered in Durward Street, with her throat cut, and horribly mutilated. Four more victims were found over the following weeks. The murders caused a sensation in the press, especially when mocking letters signed 'Jack the Ripper' were sent to the police. The police's failure to catch the Ripper led to the resignation of the London Police Commissioner. Suspects have ranged from a deranged policeman to a Russian spy.

THE DIAMOND JUBILEE

Queen Victoria's 60 years on the throne were honoured in 1897 in a spectacular celebration of the British Empire. The little figure in black widow's dress was cheered by huge crowds lining the streets to see her driven in her state landau to a brief thanksgiving service on the steps of St. Paul's Cathedral. The sun blazed down on soldiers in glittering array from every corner of the globe—cavalry from India and Australia, Gurkhas and Sikhs, Africans, Chinese, and Dyaks from Borneo. Governors General of the colonies had a prominent place and were joined by foreign royalty and statesmen, but the main plaudits were for 'the Widow at Windsor', who could not restrain her tears.

BIG BEN

Edmund Beckett Denison, later Lord Grimthorpe (1816–1905), was one of the top barristers of his day. Savagely aggressive and sarcastic, he also knew more about clockmaking than anyone in the country. It was Denison who designed the 5-tonne timepiece in the new clock tower of the Houses of Parliament (▷ 179–180), equipped with its own revolutionary gravity escapement and a giant bell weighing more than 13 tonnes. The clock, nicknamed Big Ben, began operation in 1859. Denison was a difficult character and engaged in prolonged controversy with the architect of the Houses of Parliament, Sir Charles Barry (1795–1860), but his clock keeps excellent time to this day, and its chime is one of London's most familiar and evocative sounds.

ON THE FIRST TUBE

The world's first underground trains began running in 1863 on a line nicknamed 'the Drain', 6km (4 miles) long, between Paddington, Euston, King's Cross and Farringdon Street stations. The steam-powered trains caught on at once. Despite the smoke, grime and smell, Victorian gentlemen in stove-pipe hats rode them with perfect equanimity. The dark green carriages were well lit, trains ran every 10 minutes at peak times and tickets cost from three pence to six pence, depending on class of travel. Almost 10 million journeys were made in the railway's first year. More lines soon opened and in 1890 electric trains appeared in the City, on the first line to be called 'the Tube'. Nearly 150 years after the first Tube, the first air-conditioned carriages have now entered service.

20TH-CENTURY LONDON

The London of 1900 was the capital of the largest empire the world had ever known. Suburban sprawl continued and by 1939 the population was 9 million. The Greater London Council was responsible for an area of 1,550sq km (600sq miles) from 1965 until its abolition in 1986, which left no central London authority. Motor cars and buses replaced horses and hansom cabs, though the average speed of travel in London in 1999 was no faster than in 1899. Damage in World War I was slight, but in World War II the winter Blitz of 1940–41 killed 20,000 people. Later, many more deaths were caused by flying bombs and rockets. Some underground stations served as air-raid shelters, where Londoners bedded down on the platforms. The war was followed by exhaustion, austerity and the collapse of the London docks. Immigration was encouraged to fill the shortage of workers, and new arrivals from the West Indies, Pakistan and Bangladesh added to London's cultural mix. With recovering affluence in the 1960s came the youth culture of coffee bars, boutiques and 'swinging London'. Skyscrapers changed the skyline, while planners and architects replaced houses with concrete tower blocks.

THE UNKNOWN SOLDIER

Garlanded with red poppies and set in the floor near Westminster Abbey's (▷ 194–195) west door is the Tomb of the Unknown Soldier. It contains the remains of a soldier selected at random from among those killed but never identified on the Western Front in World War I. He was reburied in the abbey on Armistice Day in 1920 as a memorial to a lost generation, lying in a coffin of British oak and interred in earth brought from France under a slab of marble from Belgium. The ceremony took place in the presence of King George V and many heads of state and military leaders, with a guard of honour formed by 100 holders of the Victoria Cross. Nearby is the Congressional Medal of Honor, conferred by the United States.

Clockwise from above *The 1951 Festival of Britain; before the Clean Air Act people regularly resorted to masks to protect themselves from pollution in London's dense fogs; poppies are left round the Tomb of the Unknown Soldier in Westminster Abbey on Remembrance Day*

THE CAFÉ DE PARIS BOMB

The Café de Paris in Coventry Street was a well-known nightclub in the heart of the West End. One March night in 1941 customers were dining and dancing in the basement, advertised as 'the safest place to dance in town', when there was a blinding flash as two high-explosive bombs fell on the cinema above. The band leader Ken 'Snakehips' Johnson and some of his musicians were killed, as were entire parties seated at some tables. Survivors staggered up into the night, in shock, bleeding and covered with dust. Some of the first on the scene were looters, stealing wallets and wrenching rings off dead and dying fingers. In all, 34 bodies were eventually brought out.

THE FESTIVAL OF BRITAIN

A century after the Great Exhibition of 1851, the Festival of Britain was held to boost national morale after the war. In London it centred on a site on the South Bank, where 11ha (27 acres) of bomb-blasted Victorian buildings were cleared. The story of Britain's past was told, but the emphasis was on science, technology and the future. In the five months it lasted, 8.5 million people went to admire the futuristic Skylon sculpture and investigate the Dome of Discovery, the Design Review Pavilion, the 3-D polaroid cinema, the crazy Emmet railway and the new Royal Festival Hall (▷ 88), as well as Battersea Park (▷ 211). The festival's permanent legacy was the Southbank Centre (▷ 77).

A CLEANER CITY

The 1956 Clean Air Act, which prohibited coal fires in central London, finally put an end to the city's famous fogs, which would cloak the whole town in thick, impenetrable, clammy mist. On the streets in a fearsome four-day 'pea-souper' smog in December 1952 it was hardly possible to see beyond the end of your outstretched arm. Traffic was brought to a virtual standstill and several people died of aggravated chest and lung complaints. In 1957 there were no fish in the Thames between Richmond and Tilbury. A campaign began to clean up the river, and was so effective that to general astonishment a salmon was caught in the Thames in 1974. Litter, however, remains a problem, and many visitors are quite shocked by the volume of discarded fast food wrappers and plastic bottles on the streets, as well as the free newspapers left on public transport.

MILLENNIUM PROJECTS

London reached the end of the 20th century in a blaze of activity, much of it focused around the Thames. Some projects were huge successes, while others struggled to achieve popularity. Firmly in the latter category was the Millennium Dome (now the O2; ▷ 87), a tent-like arena that hosted a short-lived exhibition, only to fall into disuse for several years. The Millennium Bridge (▷ 77), which provides a new means for pedestrians to get from St. Paul's to the South Bank, wobbled when it first opened, but was eventually fixed. At the southern end of the bridge, the disused Bankside power station was converted into the magnificent Tate Modern (▷ 80–81), which immediately pulled in huge crowds of awestruck art-lovers. Topping even Tate Modern in popularity was the London Eye (▷ 75), a giant sightseeing wheel offering fabulous views over the city.

London hardly had time to draw breath after the excitement of the city's Millennium festivities before preparations for celebrating the Queen's Golden Jubilee in 2002 got under way. The city was host to another display of royal pageantry in the same year, when the Queen Mother died at the age of 101. Her ceremonial funeral was held in Westminster Abbey, which was also the majestic setting of the wedding of her great-grandson, Prince William, in 2011. In the summer of 2012, London will host the Olympic Games.

Clockwise from above *No. 30 St. Mary Axe, popularly known as 'the Gherkin', was opened in 2004 on the site of the old Baltic Exchange and is one of London's most distinctive skyscrapers; Wembley Stadium, one of the venues for the 2012 Olympic Games*

IMPACT OF 2012

In Stratford, in east London, one of the most deprived areas in the UK, news of London's successful Olympic bid was greeted with jubilation. Plans focused on transforming a 200ha (500-acre) swathe of land in the area into a futuristic Olympic Park, 10km (6 miles) from Trafalgar Square. It included an 80,000-seat athletics stadium (later acquired by West Ham United football club), an aquatics centre, a velodrome, a BMX track and a hockey centre, as well as an athletes' village (designed to become 3,500 homes after the Games).

Construction of the Olympic Park also involved huge investment in public transport. New track for the Channel Tunnel Rail Link opened in November 2007, and Heathrow airport's Terminal Five opened in 2008 at a cost of £4 billion.

THE SKY'S THE LIMIT

The most prominent new landmark in London is designed to overtake the Gherkin as the oddest kid on the block: Nicknamed the Shard, it began as a concrete structure resembling a giant nail, hammered into the ground beside London Bridge station, in Southwark. Through 2011 this central service core gradually wrapped itself in a glass cocoon, pointing sharply to the heavens. At 310m tall (1,016ft), it is the tallest skyscraper in Europe (though Moscow's Mercury City Tower promises to eclipse it within months). Visitors will be able to take a high-speed lift to the open-air panoramic observation deck on the 72nd floor, above restaurants, apartments, a hotel, shops and offices. This modern Tower of Babel is to the design of Italian Renzo Piano (best known for Paris's iconic Centre Pompidou and Aurora Place in Sydney), and largely funded by investment from Qatar. Southwark's next big regeneration project is the construction of twin-towered student accommodation—but at a mere 31 floors, the Quill will be no threat to the iceberg glory of its spiky neighbour.

ON THE MOVE

On the Move gives you detailed advice and information about the various options for travelling to London, before explaining the best ways to get you around the city once you are there. Handy tips help you with everything from buying tickets to renting a car.

ARRIVING

ARRIVING BY AIR

This is how most visitors enter the UK. London has air connections to all major world cities. If you are coming from another continent you will almost certainly arrive at either Heathrow, London's biggest airport and one of the busiest in the world, or at Gatwick, which is considerably farther away but the next in size. London's three other airports, Stansted, Luton and London City, serve mainly short-haul destinations. For security reasons there are no luggage lockers at any of the airports.

London Heathrow (LHR), is 19km (12 miles) to the west of central London.

There are five terminals: Terminals 1, 2 and 3 are located in the main central terminal complex; Terminal 4 is on the south side of the airport; Terminal 5 is to the west. Check which terminal you need at www.heathrowairport.com.

» Terminal 1 serves bmi, Air New Zealand, South African Airways, Aer Lingus, Icelandair, LOT, Lufthansa, US Airways and United Airlines.

» Terminal 2 is being redeveloped. The first phase of of rebuilding is scheduled for completion in 2013.

» Terminal 3 serves American Airlines, Cathay Pacific, Iberia, SAS, Virgin Atlantic and other long-haul flights from outside Europe.

» Terminal 4 serves Qantas, Alitalia, Continental, Air France, KLM and a handful of other airlines and a few British Airways flights.

» Terminal 5 is used exclusively by British Airways and serves more than 90 per cent of their flights.

All five terminals are linked to the London Underground, reached by well-signposted moving walkways and elevators. One station serves Terminals 1, 2 and 3, while Terminals

GETTING TO CENTRAL LONDON FROM THE AIRPORT

AIRPORT (CODE)	HEATHROW (LHR)	GATWICK (LGW)
TAXI	£50–£65. 40 min–1 hour	£105. 1 hour 10 min
OVERLAND TRAIN	Heathrow Express to Paddington. Every 15 min 5.10am–11.25pm 365 days a year. £18 single, £32 return. Journey time: 15–20 min. Heathrow Connect to Paddington. Every 30 min 4.42am–11.08pm. Stops at 6 stations. £4.90–£8.50. Journey time: 25–30 min.	Gatwick Express to Victoria. Every 15 min 5am–12.35am, last train 1.35am, first train 4.30am. £17.70 one way, £30.47 return. Journey time: 30 min. Southern trains to Victoria take slightly longer from £11.25 one way. First Capital Connect to London Bridge (from £7.90), every 15 min, journey time 30 min, or to St. Pancras International.
TUBE (UNDERGROUND)	Piccadilly Line from Terminals 1, 2 and 3, Terminal 4 or Terminal 5 stations. Trains run about every 10 min. Runs 5.15am–11.45pm daily. £5 adult/£3 child. Journey time: 50 min.	N/A
BUS	National Express to Victoria Coach Station. Every 15–30 min. £10 one way. Journey time: 40 min–1 hour. Night bus N9 from central bus station and Terminal 5 runs through the night, every 20 min.	National Express from North and South Terminals to Victoria Coach Station. £6.80 one way. Every hour. EasyBus to Earl's Court station. From £2 one way online, £6 cash. Journey time: 1 hour 20 min.
CAR	Terminals 1, 2 and 3: M4 junction 4. Terminal 4: M4 junction 3. Travel eastbound along M4. Terminal 5: M25 junction 14.	M23 Junction 9. Travel northbound along M23.

It serves mainly low-cost charter flights, but some scheduled services operate from here.

London City Airport (LCA) is the capital's smallest airport, 10km (6 miles) from central London. Much used by business travellers, the airport has facilities such as meeting rooms and full secretarial services. The airport now has improved eating and shopping opportunities. Flights operate to over 30 European destinations and several British airports, handling more than 3 million passengers per year. Check-in time is only 15 minutes before departure on some flights.

On arrival, you have several choices of transport to central London. The table below compares the methods of transport from each of the airports, with costs, journey times and frequency.

TIPS
» When departing from Heathrow or Gatwick, check which terminal you will need, as it is cumbersome to move between them—particularly at Heathrow.
» Note that there are no black taxi cabs at Gatwick, Stansted or Luton.

4 and 5 each have their own station. American Airlines, BA, United Airlines and several other major airlines now have check-in facilities at Paddington station. Passengers with connecting flights should follow the signs.

London Gatwick (LGW) is 48km (30 miles) to the south of central London. It has two terminals, North and South, linked by the Gatwick Transit, an efficient and free monorail. Trains run every three to four minutes from each terminal, with a journey time of just under two minutes. The South Terminal handles the bulk of Gatwick's traffic, serving domestic, international and charter flights. BA and American Airlines passengers can check luggage in at Victoria station, central London, which saves time at the airport.

London Stansted (STN), third in size, is 56km (35 miles) northeast of London, in Essex. The passenger terminal occupies a modern glass and steel building (1991) designed by British architect Sir Norman Foster. Driverless rapid transit trains shuttle between this and the airport's other two buildings. Stansted is London's fastest-growing airport.

London Luton (LTN) is 52km (32 miles) north of central London. A new passenger terminal opened in 1999, along with Luton Parkway railway station, from which there are frequent trains to King's Cross.

STANSTED (STN)	LUTON (LTN)	CITY (LCA)
£99. 1–2 hours	£80. 1 hour 45 min	£25–£40. 40 min
Stansted Express to Liverpool Street (Central line). Change at Tottenham Hale for the Victoria line. Runs 5.30am–midnight. Every 15 min. £21 one way (child £10), £27.70 return (child £13.65). Journey time: 45 min.	Shuttle bus from terminal to Luton Airport Parkway station (8 min). £1.50 one way. First Capital Connect or East Midlands services to St. Pancras International. Every 15 min 7am–10pm. £12.50 one way. Journey time: 35 min.	London City Airport DLR station (known as the King George V extension). Trains run every few min 5am–12.30am (www.tfl.gov.uk for timetable and prices). Journey time: 22 min from Bank Station.
N/A	N/A	N/A
National Express A6 to Victoria. Every 15 min. £10.50 one way (child £7.50). EasyBus to Baker Street. From £2 online, £6 cash. Every 20 min. Journey time: 1 hour 30 min. Terravision to Victoria or Liverpool Street. Every 30 min. £9 one way.	Greenline Bus No. 757 to Victoria Coach Station. Every 30 min peak, every hour off-peak. £16 one way (child £12). EasyBus to Victoria (from £2 online). Journey time: 1 hour 30 min.	N/A
M11 Junction 8. Travel southbound along M11.	2 miles (3km) from M1 junction 10. Travel southbound along M1.	N/A

ARRIVING BY TRAIN

Eurostar, the company that operates the Channel Tunnel rail service, links France (Paris and Lille) and Belgium (Brussels) directly to London in less than three hours. Since 2007, Eurostar's high-speed trains arrive in the state-of-the-art transport and retail complex at St. Pancras International station, which boasts Europe's longest champagne bar, a fresh daily farmers' market and world-class brasserie. Look for the 9m (30ft) high evocative statue *The Meeting Place* by artist Paul Day. The station is connected to King's Cross St. Pancras Underground station, which is served by the Northern, Victoria, Circle, Metropolitan and Hammersmith & City lines.

Passports are required for travel and you must check in at least 30 minutes before the train is due to depart. Only one item of hand luggage and two suitcases are allowed per person. Bear in mind that Eurostar trains are long, and it can be quite a walk down the platform to find your carriage.

On arrival you must clear passport control and customs.

The Underground and buses are clearly marked or you can take a taxi from the rank immediately outside the station.

National trains arrive from other parts of Britain into one of London's 11 main railway stations (▷ 62). All stations have Underground links.

ARRIVING BY CAR

Eurotunnel operates the train service for cars, caravans and motorcycles through the Channel Tunnel. The journey between Calais and Folkestone takes 20 minutes, during which time drivers and passengers remain in their vehicles.

Upon arrival at Folkestone in the UK leave the terminal on the M20 motorway northbound, joining at junction 11a. Traffic permitting, the drive to London takes just over one hour.

ARRIVING BY FERRY

Eurostar and Eurotunnel have taken a lot of traffic away but taking a ferry can still be a cheaper way of crossing the Channel. Various ferry companies operate services between British ports and ports on the European continent. Trains run from ports on the south coast— Dover, Folkestone, Ramsgate, Newhaven, Portsmouth and Poole— to various London stations and from Harwich on the east coast to London Liverpool Street.

ARRIVING BY COACH

If you travel to London by long-distance coach you will probably arrive at Victoria Coach Station (VCS) on Buckingham Palace Road, near Victoria main railway station. The coach station is a few minutes' walk from the Underground station, which is on the Victoria, District and Circle lines. Alternatively, there is a taxi rank immediately outside the coach station.

USEFUL TELEPHONE NUMBERS AND WEBSITES

AIRPORTS

Heathrow: tel 0844 335 1801; www.heathrowairport.com

Lost Property: tel 0844 824 3115 (8am–4pm)

Train: Heathrow Express tel 0845 600 1515; www.heathrowexpress.com

Bus: tel 0871 781 8181; www.nationalexpress.com

Taxi: Heathrow Taxis tel 020 8745 7487

Gatwick: tel 0844 335 1802; www.gatwickairport.com

Lost Property: tel 01293 503162

Left Luggage: South Terminal tel 01293 502014, 24 hours.
North Terminal tel 01293 502013.

Trains: The Gatwick Express tel 0845 850 1530; www.gatwickexpress.com
First Capital Connect tel 0845 026 4700; www.firstcapitalconnect.co.uk
Southern Railway tel 0845 127 2920; www.southernrailway.com

Bus: tel 0871 781 8181; www.nationalexpress.com, www.easybus.co.uk

Taxi: Checker Cars tel 01293 567700; www.checkercars.com

Stansted: tel 0844 335 1803; www.stanstedairport.com

Lost Property: Items lost in the airport tel 01279 663293

Left Luggage: tel 01279 663213

Trains: The Stansted Express tel 0845 850 0150; www.stanstedexpress.com

Bus: 0871 781 8181; www.nationalexpress.com

Taxi: Checker Cars tel 01279 661111 or 0800 747 737; www.checkercars.com

Luton: tel 01582 405100; www.london-luton.co.uk

Lost Property: tel 01582 405100

Left Luggage: tel 01582 405100

Trains: First Capital Connect tel 0845 026 4700;
www.firstcapitalconnect.co.uk

Bus: Greenline tel 0844 801 7261; www.greenline.co.uk

Taxi: Cabco tel 01582 737777. Alpha Taxis tel 01582 599499.
Luton Taxi Association tel 01582 735555

London City: tel 020 7646 0088; www.londoncityairport.com

Lost Property: tel 020 7646 0088

Left Luggage: tel 020 7646 0088

Trains: tel 0845 748 950; www.nationalrail.co.uk

Taxi: Taxi rank outside terminal building

General Airport information:
www.world-airport-guide.co.uk

COACH AND TRAIN

Coach Tourism Council: www.coachtourismcouncil.co.uk

Eurolines: tel 0871 781 8181; www.eurolines.co.uk

Eurostar: UK tel 08432 186186; www.eurostar.com

Eurotunnel: tel 0844 353 535; www.eurotunnel.com

National Express: tel 0871 781 8181; www.nationalexpress.com

National Rail enquiries: tel 0845 748 4950

Victoria Coach Station: www.tfl.gov.uk

GETTING AROUND

LONDON TRANSPORT

London is a large city and at some stage you are bound to need to use its extensive public transport system, run by Transport for London (TFL). The Underground (Tube), buses and overground trains principally make up the network, with the Docklands Light Railway (DLR), riverboats and Tramlink as additional options.

Of the two main choices, bus or Underground, the Underground is certainly the quickest way to get around, but it is not always satisfactory and you will have to be patient at least once during your visit as a train is delayed or grinds to a halt for no apparent reason. It can also be very uncomfortable, hot and claustrophobic, involving long walks, escalators and staircases. Buses, on the other hand, offer views and a chance to get to grips with the geography of London.

Taxis are useful for short distances, but longer journeys are expensive.

For train travel and coach (long-distance bus) information, ▷ 61–63.

TRAVEL INFORMATION
» The main London Transport Information Centre, at Piccadilly Circus Underground station, is open Mon–Sat 7.15–9.15, Sun 8.15–8 and supplies free route maps and schedules as well as information brochures in several languages.

You can also phone for around-the-clock information (tel 0843 222 1234).
» Other travel information offices can be found at Heathrow Airport (Terminals 1, 2 and 3), Euston, King's Cross and Liverpool Street Underground stations and Victoria train and coach stations.

CHILDREN AND PUBLIC TRANSPORT
» Accompanied children under the age of 10 travel free on the Underground, DLR, buses and trams.
» Children aged 11–14 can travel at discount rates on the Underground,

DLR and most national rail services, but need an Oyster photocard or child-rate Day Travelcard.
» If a child is younger than 11 but looks older, they may need a child photocard to buy and use any child fare ticket or travel card. These are available from all Underground stations or London Travel Information Centres.
» Reduced rates for unaccompanied older children on the Underground and DLR apply with the Oyster Card (▷ 48).

DISCOUNTS
» Various reductions are available on weekly and monthly travelcards.
» Free travel for people over the age of 60 is available to London residents only with a Freedom Pass.

TICKETS
» You can buy tickets for all forms of public transport at most Underground stations, London Travel Information Centres and national rail stations, and at around 2,500 local ticket outlets, including many newsagents.
» If you know where you want to travel, use the ticket machines. Change is given. Touch-screen ticket machines at Underground stations also accept Electron and Solo cards.
» Ticket offices at Underground stations do close occasionally.
» One-day tickets can be bought four days in advance; try to order and collect tickets outside morning or evening rush hour.
» International visitors can buy Oyster Cards in advance online from www.tfl.gov.uk, or www.visitlondon.com at a slightly reduced rate.

» For further information on London fares, see the individual transport entries following or pick up a copy of the 'Fares and Tickets' leaflet from Underground stations and London Travel Information Centres.

TIPS
» If possible avoid travelling during the rush hour (weekdays 7.30 to 9.30am and 4.30 to 7pm). The Underground in particular gets extremely crowded and many buses are so full that waiting passengers are unable to board.
» Buy a Travelcard, which is valid for the entire transport network, or an Oyster Card if you don't require overground rail.
» Use common sense when travelling alone at night, but there is no need to be unduly concerned about the risk of mugging.

Special fares apply

Bakerloo
Central
Circle
District
Hammersmith & City
Jubilee
Metropolitan
Northern
Piccadilly
Victoria
Waterloo & City
DLR
London Overground

Blackfriars — Station closed
Moor Park — Station in both fare zones
○ Interchange stations
🚶 Step-free access from the platform to the street
≷ National Rail
🚢 Riverboat services
🚊 Tramlink
✈ Airport

MAYOR OF LONDON

Website
tfl.gov.uk

24 hour travel information
0843 222 1234*

© Transport for London   Reg. user Nos. 10/M/1877/P and 11/1894/P

Improvement works may affect your

Transport for London **UNDERGROUND**

pay no more than 5p per minute if calling
a BT landline. There may be a connection charge.
es from mobiles or other landline providers may vary.

TRAVELCARDS AND ZONES

» Travelcards are valid for the entire transport network in selected zones, including buses, Underground (Tube), Docklands Light Railway (DLR), Croydon Tramlink and suburban national rail services within the London area (excluding Heathrow Express).

» Travelcards give you unlimited travel within the zone area paid for, as well as one-third off most riverboat services. They are available from Underground stations, London Travel Information Centres, national rail stations (in the London area) and many newsagents across the capital. You can buy a Travelcard up to four days before you intend to use it.

» For the purposes of transport pricing the London area is divided into zones, central London occupying Zone 1 with Zones 2–6 following in a series of concentric rings (▷ 46–47).

» The concept is simple. The more zones you want to travel in, the more you have to pay. Ensure that your ticket is valid for the zones that you travel in or through, or you may find yourself paying a fine.

» The reusable plastic Oyster Card is a 'smart card' that can store credit for pay-as-you-go services. It automatically works out the cheapest rates for your travel and caps it at the same price as a Day Travelcard. It also charges off-peak fares in Zone 1 (Mon–Fri 4pm–7pm), which can save money.

TRAVELCARDS	VALID	ZONES AND PRICES	NOTES
1 Day Travelcard (Peak)	1am–4.30am the following day, Mon–Fri (except public holidays)	Zones 1 and 2: £8 adult, £4 child Zones 1–4: £10 adult, £5 child Zones 1–6: £15 adult, £7.50 child	If you are using only Underground, bus, Tramlink and DLR services, it is cheaper to use an Oyster Card
1 Day Travelcard (Off-Peak)	From 9.30am Mon–Fri and all day on Sat, Sun and public holidays until 4.30am the following day	Zones 1 and 2: £6.60 adult, £3 child (children must buy a Zone 1–6 ticket). Zones 1–4: £7.70 adult, £3 child. Zones 1–6: £8 adult, £3 child	If you are using only Underground, bus, Tramlink and DLR services, it is cheaper to use an Oyster Card
Oyster Card (a 'smartcard' that can store up to £90 pay-as-you-go)	At all times. Underground trains run from approx 5.30am until 12.30am (time varies on the individual lines). Also for use on DLR, buses, trams and Thames Clippers	All zones and some national rail. A £5 refundable deposit is required on new cards. The £4 single journey in Zone 1 is £1.90 with an Oyster card	Oyster Cards can be obtained online at www.tfl.gov.uk/oyster or at Underground stations and Oyster ticket shops. When making multiple journeys, the card caps payment at 50p less than the cost of a Travelcard
Weekly Travelcard	Valid, with a photocard only, for seven consecutive days and can be used at any time For travel on Underground, buses, Tramlink, DLR and most national rail services in the London area	Zones 1 and 2: £27.60 adult, £13.80 child. Zones 1–4: £39.40 adult, £19.70 child. Zones 1–6: £47.60 adult, £25.20 child	

LONDON UNDERGROUND

London's Underground system is also known as the Tube. The earliest lines, dating from the mid-19th century, were constructed close to the surface using a technique known as 'cut and cover'; builders dug a trench, laid the tracks, then roofed over the trench and replaced the earth. The later, deeper lines were constructed using tunnel boring machines. These lines were called 'tubes', and the name stuck.

The London Underground system is the oldest and most extensive network of its kind in the world, with more than 500 trains and over 260 stations, and maintenance is an on-going challenge. Much of the track is old and subject to repairs, leading to breakdowns and delays. That said, the extended Jubilee line was opened in 1999, providing a state-of-the-art metro system between central and eastern London. It was Europe's biggest engineering project and the new stations built along the line are an attraction in their own right. Prominent architects were chosen to design the stations. Canary Wharf, for example, hailed as an 'underground cathedral', was designed by Sir Norman Foster.

Twelve lines make up the Greater London Underground system and each has its own name and is colour-coded on the Underground map (▷ 46–47). Stations with interchanges with other lines and with suburban rail are marked with a white circle on the map.

Trains run from approximately 5.30am Monday to Saturday (7am Sunday) to approximately midnight Monday to Saturday (11pm Sunday) every day except Christmas Day.

UNDERSTANDING THE UNDERGROUND MAP

TUBE STATION
A simple dash indicates a station with no interchanges

MAINLINE STATION
This symbol indicates a connection with a mainline station.

COLOUR-CODED LINES
Each line is colour-coded to make navigation easy.

STATION WITH INTERCHANGE
Interchanges with other lines and with suburban rail are marked with a white circle. Two white circles show more than one line interchange.

ON THE MOVE | GETTING AROUND

» Stand on the right on escalators so that people in a hurry can walk on the left.

» Be aware that if you cannot produce a valid ticket you will be given an on-the-spot fine of £10.

» Watch out for keys, security passes and some handbag clasps; they may cause magnetic interference and damage your ticket.

» If you are travelling with bulky items, pushchairs (strollers) or folding bicycles, use the special wide gates provided. Ask a member of staff to let you through.

» Stand clear of the train's closing doors. Obstructing them slows trains down and causes delays.

» Mind the gap between the platform and the train.

» Let passengers off the train first before embarking.

» Stand behind the yellow line on the platform when waiting for a train.

» Avoid taking too much luggage on the Underground. Storage space is limited, and there are no porters.

» Keep your bag with you at all times and report any unattended bags.

» Be prepared for heat in summer. There is no air-conditioning, and delays are not uncommon.

» Mobile phones are permitted, but don't expect to get a signal underground.

» Report threats and violent behaviour to members of staff.

» Watch out for pickpockets. Keep your bags securely fastened and don't carry valuables in back pockets or rucksacks. Keep an eye on your bags at all times.

TIPS

» Check the service update section of www.tfl.gov.uk to see if trains are running smoothly. A journey planner on the site helps you plan how to get from A to B in the easiest way.

» Also see www.tfl.gov.uk or tel 020 7222 1234 for up-to-date news and information. There are details on fares and tickets in 14 different languages.

» To avoid ending up at the wrong destination, be sure to check the indicator display on the platform and the front of the train displaying the final destination station.

» Pick up a pocket-size London Underground map, free at all Underground stations.

» Travel after 9.30am and at weekends for cheaper tickets.

» Buy tickets at the machines, or at a sales booth.

» Note that there are two types of machine. One has a few buttons for the most common fares (one destination, single or return ticket and travel cards); the other has lots of buttons, one for every station and ticket type.

» You will need your ticket to get out of the station, so don't throw it away.

Below *Central Underground stations are individually decorated, often with local themes, and frequently have street musicians playing*

From South Ealing to Oxford Circus

Journey time: 42 min
Zones used: 1, 2, 3
Single fare: adult £4, child £2

Find a map and identify the colours of the lines you will need.

Buy a ticket for all the zones you will be travelling through.

Insert your ticket face upwards in the front of the machine at the gates. When it emerges from the top slot, take it out and the gates will open.

Follow signs for the **PICCADILLY LINE**, going down stairs or escalators where necessary.

Check the board between the two platforms and choose the platform for the train heading towards Green Park.

Wait for the **PICCADILLY LINE** train on the platform. The electronic display on the platform tells you when the train is due to arrive and where it terminates.

Get on the train heading for **COCKFOSTERS**, **ARNOS GROVE**, **OAKWOOD** or **KING'S CROSS ST. PANCRAS**.
This information will be displayed on the electronic platform displays as the train arrives and on the front of the train.

Board the train quickly and carefully.

Track the number of stops until you need to change on the route map above the window in the train. On arrival at stations, announcements inform you of the connections available at each one. Stations are easily identified by the large Underground signs mounted on platforms and visible from inside the train. (34 min)

Leave the train at **GREEN PARK**.
Change on to the **VICTORIA LINE**. Follow signs. (2 min)

Wait for the **VICTORIA LINE** train on the platform. (3 min)

Get on the train heading for **WALTHAMSTOW CENTRAL**, **SEVEN SISTERS** or **KING'S CROSS ST. PANCRAS**. (3 min)

Leave the train at **OXFORD CIRCUS**. When you complete your journey, your ticket will be retained in the machine at the exit.

Follow signs to the relevant exit for the street you want.

Fares for the Underground depend on the zones you wish to travel in. If you are travelling through many zones several times a day, consider purchasing a Travelcard or taking advantage of discounted fares (▷ 48). You will make substantial savings by purchasing an Oyster Card, which will also give savings for children. Child fares without any special discount tickets apply to children aged 11 to 15; children aged 11–15 require a photocard. Below are the full price fares without discounted special deals.

ZONES	ADULT (£)	CHILD (£)
Zone 1	4.00	2.00
Zones 2–6	5.00	2.50

ON THE MOVE | GETTING AROUND

BUSES

London's bright red double-decker buses, along with the black cabs (▷ 57), have become an icon. You cannot fail to notice them as you walk around the capital. Increasingly you will see other types of buses travelling around London as well. London bus routes run along most main roads in central London. For short journeys and if you are not in a hurry the buses can be a pleasant way of getting around. On longer journeys they are slower than trains or the Underground but they are always less expensive and quite comfortable.

» Daytime buses in London run Monday to Saturday from around 6am to midnight and Sunday from 7.30am to 11.30pm. In theory, buses run at least once every 10 to 15 minutes in each direction along the route, and much more frequently on heavily used routes. In practice, because of the traffic conditions, you can wait 30 minutes for a bus to arrive, and then three are likely to come along at once.
» Buses come in two styles, so-called Routemaster buses, with a conductor, and driver-only buses.
» Routemaster buses have been phased out and only the No. 9 and No. 15 remain on popular tourist routes. A conductor will sell you a ticket, and Travelcards are also valid on these buses.

» Driver-only buses have two doors: one at the front, where you board, and one midway, where you get off. Buses are lowered to street level when the doors open. Pay the driver when you board. You need to have change ready. Longer, 'bendy' buses operate on some routes.
» Drivers and conductors prefer the exact money, but they will give you change.
» On both types of bus you have to let the driver know you want to get off at a particular stop. Press the red button on a driver-only bus, or pull the cord at the side of the cabin on a Routemaster.
» Hold on to your ticket until the end of the journey, because inspectors regularly board the buses to check tickets and catch fare-dodgers.

TICKET OPTIONS
» The single adult cash bus fare in the whole of the London bus network is £2.20, or £1.30 with an Oyster Card.
» Children 5–10 go free on all buses. Children 11–15, and students up to 18, go free with an Oyster photocard.
» On certain marked routes (including all 'bendy' buses) cash single fares are not available on the buses. If you do not hold a bus pass, an Oyster Card or a Travelcard, you must buy a cash single ticket or a one-day bus pass before boarding. Roadside ticket machines are located at all bus stops on routes where this system applies. Likewise, within Zone 1 you cannot pay cash on the bus.
» You can purchase 7-day passes for £17.80 for adults.

» If you intend to use the Underground as well, you are better off buying an Underground travelcard or Oyster Card, as these are also valid on buses.

NIGHT BUSES

» Night buses (the number is preceded by 'N') run between 11pm and 6am on the main routes through London; the majority pass through Trafalgar Square.
» Night buses stop only at bus stops if requested.
» Fares are the same as daytime fares.

TIPS

» For advice on how to get around the city by bus, call London Transport or look online (tel 020 7222 1234, www.tfl.gov.uk).
» Maps showing all the bus routes are available from London Travel Information Centres.

UNDERSTANDING BUS STOPS

BUS NUMBERS

Each route is marked by a number on the front and the back of the bus corresponding to the numbers on the bus stops. The final destination of the bus is often displayed on the bus along with a brief list of the areas of London on the route.

TIMETABLES

Timetables can be found at bus stops either posted inside bus shelters or attached to individual bus stops. They show the first and last buses on the route you want and allow you to work out the frequency of the service, the times the bus will arrive at your stop and when it will reach the destination you require. The stop that you are standing at will be marked in bold on the timetable.

BUS STOP TYPES

Bus stops are marked by a London Transport circular BUS STOP sign which has a line through the middle with either a white or red background. At main bus stops (signs show a red circle on a white background) you will find information on bus routes, route numbers and times. The bus will stop here automatically.

At request stops (white circle on a red background) you must hail the bus.

At night treat all stops as request stops.

Buy tickets before boarding

MAIN VISITOR BUS ROUTES

Certain routes link key attractions or provide interesting views. Below are seven routes of particular interest.

BUS NO. 8

Buckingham Palace, Westminster Abbey · Wellington Arch · Mayfair · British Museum · St. Paul's Cathedral · The City · Petticoat Lane Market

Victoria Station – Hyde Park Corner – Green Park Station – Berkeley Square – Tottenham Court Road Station – Oxford Circus – Holborn Station – Chancery Lane Station – Holborn Circus – Holborn Viaduct – St. Paul's Station – Bank – Liverpool Street Station – Shoreditch – Bethnal Green – Roman Road – Old Ford – Bow Church

BUS NO. 11

Houses of Parliament, Westminster Abbey, Churchill War Rooms, Whitehall · Buckingham Palace · National Gallery, National Portrait Gallery · Covent Garden · The City

Fulham Broadway – King's Road – Chelsea – Sloane Square – Victoria Station – Victoria Coach Station – Westminster – Trafalgar Square – Strand – Aldwych – Royal Courts of Justice – Ludgate Circus – St. Paul's Cathedral – Mansion House Station – Bank – Liverpool Street Station

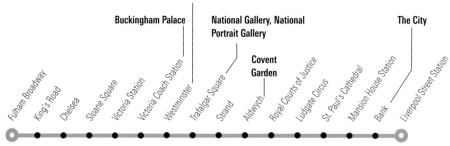

BUS NO. 14

Natural History, Science, V&A museums · Harrods · Buckingham Palace, Wellington Arch · Royal Academy, Shaftesbury Avenue theatres · British Museum

Putney Heath – Putney Station – Putney Bridge – Fulham Road – Fulham Road – Fulham Broadway – Fulham Road – South Kensington Station – Knightsbridge Station – Hyde Park Corner – Green Park Station – Piccadilly Circus – Tottenham Court Road Station

BUS NO. 15

Tower of London · Petticoat Lane Market · Monument · Mansion House · Covent Garden · National Gallery, National Portrait Gallery · Selfridges

Blackwall Station (day) or East Ham (eve) – Poplar – Limehouse – Limehouse Station – Commercial Road – Aldgate Station – Tower Hill – Monument Station – Cannon Street – Mansion House Station – St. Paul's Cathedral – Ludgate Circus – Aldwych – Strand – Trafalgar Square – Piccadilly Circus – Oxford Circus – Bond Street Station – Oxford Street – Marble Arch – Edgware Road Station – Paddington

BUS NO. 74

Madame Tussauds
Buckingham Palace
Natural History, Science, V&A museums
Selfridges
Harrods, Hyde Park

Baker Street Station · Oxford Street · Marble Arch · Hyde Park Corner · Knightsbridge Station · South Kensington Station · Gloucester Road Station · Cromwell Road · Earl's Court Station · Old Brompton Road · West Brompton Station · Lillie Road · Fulham Palace Road · Putney Bridge · Putney High Street · Upper Richmond Road · Dover House Road · Roehampton

N74 NIGHT ONLY

BUS NO. 188

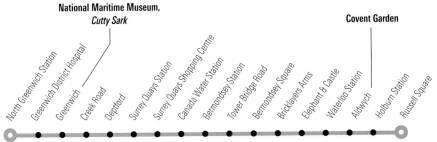

National Maritime Museum, *Cutty Sark*
Covent Garden

North Greenwich Station · Greenwich District Hospital · Greenwich · Creek Road · Deptford · Surrey Quays Station · Surrey Quays Shopping Centre · Canada Water Station · Bermondsey Station · Tower Bridge Road · Bermondsey Square · Bricklayers Arms · Elephant & Castle · Waterloo Station · Aldwych · Holburn Station · Russell Square

RV1 ROUTE

A bus service of particular interest to visitors is Riverside 1, which links the South Bank to the West End and the City. The route, aimed at boosting tourism, employment and accessibility for local communities, brings together more than 30 arts and visitor attractions, five Underground stations, three national rail stations and five river piers. The service runs from Tower Gateway past London Bridge station, Bankside and Waterloo station up to Covent Garden.

The buses, sporting the traditional red livery of London buses, carry a Riverside bus logo and a series of icons identifying the key destinations along the route. In addition, special information screens on board the bus alert passengers to approaching destinations and their attractions.

RV1 buses run daily every 10 minutes between 6am and midnight. On board, you can pick up a guide to local attractions.

For details visit www.southbank london.com/riverside.

BUS RV1

London Bridge City Pier
OXO Tower
London Eye, Waterloo, Millennium Pier
Festival Pier

Tower Gateway Station · Tower Bridge · Tooley Street · London Bridge Station · Southwark Street · Tate Modern · Stamford Street · Broadwall · Royal Festival Hall · Chicheley Street · Waterloo Station · Waterloo Bridge · Aldwych · Covent Garden

The Docklands Light Railway (DLR) and London's river transport network complement London's Underground and buses to provide an integrated public transport system.

DOCKLANDS LIGHT RAILWAY

» The computerized and driverless trains of the Docklands Light Railway (DLR) serve the Docklands area to the east of the City. For the most part they run on an elevated track, allowing panoramic views.

» The DLR is part of the Underground system, so Oyster Cards and Travelcards (▷ 48) may be used.

» From Bank or Tower Gateway station (near Tower Hill Underground station), the system runs south through the Isle of Dogs and Greenwich to Lewisham, north to Stratford, or east to Beckton and the King George V Docks (the station for London City airport).

» The DLR runs Monday to Friday 5.30am to 12.30am with a more limited service operating at the weekend.

» There is a 10 per cent discount for group single, return, One-Day Shuttle and Flyer tickets. They must be booked at least seven days in advance by calling DLR Customer Services (tel 020 7363 9700).

» For more information on the DLR contact DLR Customer Services or visit www.tfl.gov.uk.

LONDON RAIL AND RIVER ROVER TICKETS

» These allow you one full day unlimited hop-on hop-off travel on City Cruises River Boats and the Docklands Light Railway. It is possible to go by boat from Westminster to Greenwich, for example, and return on the DLR to Tower Hill.

» Tickets can be bought at all DLR stations except Bank and Canning Town: £13.50 for adults, £6.80 for children and £33 for a family. Group and family tickets can be bought at a discount seven days in advance.

» For more information visit www.tfl.gov.uk or tel 020 7363 9700.

RIVERBOATS

» Oyster Card holders (▷ 48) receive a third-off discount on most riverboat services and 10 per cent off Thames Clipper single tickets. Most services start and end at Westminster Pier, which is the midway point along the Thames.

» Boats operate from 6.30am to around 9pm but vary according to the route. The network extends from Hampton Court Palace (▷ 260–261) in the west to the Thames Barrier (▷ 263) in the east.

» You can travel on the river with a single, return or DLR River Rover ticket, valid for one day (adult £14.50, child £7.25).

» There are ticket offices on the piers or on the boats themselves in some cases.

» Upriver, you can travel from Westminster Millennium Pier to Hampton Court Pier via Kew and Richmond piers. This service operates, subject to tides, at 10.30am, 11am, noon and 2pm from April to October. A round trip to Hampton Court can take between seven and eight hours. The last boat from Hampton Court is at 5pm. Children travel for half the adult price. For more information about river trips

contact Thames River Boats (tel 020 7930 2062).

» Downriver, you can go from Westminster Pier to Greenwich Pier via Waterloo Millennium Pier, Bankside Pier and Tower Pier. These services depart from Westminster every 30–40 minutes from 10am until 4.20pm. The last boat returns from Greenwich at 4.30pm. Single fares are adult £3–£9.50, child £1.50–£4. For more information contact Crown River Cruises, Thames River Services or Thames Clipper (▷ 267).

TRAMLINK

» Tramlink (www.tfl.gov.uk), the south London tram network, comprises three routes that run between the Wimbledon, Croydon, New Addington and Beckenham areas.

» Tickets must be bought before boarding at the automatic ticket machines at all Tramlink stops. Failure to do so could result in a £50 fine.

» See Travelcards and Zones (▷ 48) for more ticket information.

Below *A boat cruise passes the Thames Barrier*

BY TRAIN

London has 11 mainline rail stations, each serving a different region of the country as well as providing cross-city services (▷ 62). Most parts of the UK can be reached in a day from London: Intercity trains on major routes travel at 225kph (140mph), so journey times from one end of the country to the other can take just a few hours. Conversely, some trains stop at every station so travelling a relatively short distance can seem interminable.

Several different companies now operate the railway network, which can lead to some curious price anomalies as each company determines its own fare structure. It is worth checking whether another company serving the same region can offer an alternative route or price.

There are two classes of train travel: first and second. First is more expensive but does guarantee you a seat on crowded trains as well as complementary drinks and newspapers. Otherwise second class (standard) is perfectly acceptable and you can reserve a seat if you book in advance.

Sleeping compartments can be booked with Scotrail on some overnight services to and from Scotland (tel 0845 755 0033).

Tickets

» You can get a ticket for any company or any destination from any rail station, either from the ticket office or from automated machines. Most Underground stations sell rail tickets, too, as do travel agents. Tickets can also be booked and paid for over the phone or internet.

» Many different ticket options are available, so it pays to do some homework in advance, particularly as the cheapest options generally require that you buy tickets a week or more in advance.

» For a day trip, 'cheap-day' return tickets are the least expensive option, but check the restrictions on when you may travel.

» If you intend to leave London by train on several occasions, it may pay to buy a Network Railcard, valid for a year. It costs £26, for which you get a third off on fares to stations in southeast England for up to four people (www.railcard.co.uk).

» A young person's railcard (for those aged 16 to 25 and mature students in full-time education) costs £26 and gives a third off rail travel across the country (www.railcard.co.uk).

» Senior citizens' railcards cost £26 and give a third off fares.

» To buy railcards, you need a passport-size photo.

» Children under five travel free and 5- to 15-year-olds pay half price for most tickets—but check, as there are exceptions.

SUBURBAN TRAINS

The national rail network offers another way of getting across London and to the edges of the city. This service is particularly important in south and southeast London,

---

LONDON'S MAINLINE RAILWAY STATIONS

Map shows distribution of mainline stations and the interconnecting Underground lines.

© Transport for London   Reg. user No. 02/3702

On Board

» Because many different train operators run services on the national network, the services and conditions on board trains vary depending on the service you use.

» All trains have toilets, and longer routes tend to have some form of catering service on board, usually a refreshments trolley.

» Ask the train operator about any lost property.

» No smoking. In July 2007 a complete smoking ban in enclosed spaces came into force.

» In some carriages, the use of mobile phones is prohibited.

Stations

» All but very small local stations have toilet and refreshment facilities.

» Few stations have left-luggage facilities for security reasons, but King's Cross and Paddington stations provide a good if expensive facility.

» Larger stations have information desks where you can report lost property.

» If you are changing trains, check information screens when you arrive to find the right platform for your connection. The destination of a train should be marked on screens on the platform or on the train.

MAINLINE STATIONS AND MAJOR DESTINATIONS

STATION	REGIONS	MAJOR TRAIN OPERATORS	UNDERGROUND CONNECTIONS	MAJOR DESTINATIONS
Euston	Midlands, Northwest, Scotland	Virgin Trains, Scotrail, London Midland, London Overground	Northern, Victoria	Glasgow, Liverpool, Manchester
St. Pancras	Midlands, North	East Midlands Trains, First Capital Connect, Eurostar	Northern, Victoria, Piccadilly, Hammersmith & City, Circle, Metropolitan	Edinburgh, Manchester
King's Cross	East Midlands, Yorkshire, Northeast, Scotland	Grand Central, Hull Trains, East Coast, First Capital Connect	Northern, Victoria, Piccadilly, Hammersmith & City, Circle, Metropolitan	Cambridge, Edinburgh, York
Liverpool Street	East Anglia, Essex	Stansted Express, National Express East Anglia	Hammersmith & City, Circle, Metropolitan, Central	Cambridge, Norwich
Fenchurch Street	Thames Estuary, Essex	c2c	Circle, District	Southend
London Bridge	Southeast	First Capital Connect, Southeastern	Jubilee, Northern	
Charing Cross	Southeast	Southeastern	Northern, Bakerloo	Brighton, Canterbury, Dover
Waterloo	Southwest, Wales	South West Trains	Northern, Bakerloo, Jubilee, Waterloo & City	Bournemouth, Exeter, Portsmouth, Salisbury, Winchester, Windsor
Victoria	Southern England	Gatwick Express, Southern, Southeastern	Victoria, District, Circle	Brighton, Canterbury
Paddington	South and West Midlands, West Country, Wales	First Great Western, Heathrow Express, Heathrow Connect	District, Circle, Hammersmith & City, Bakerloo	Bath, Bristol, Oxford, Stratford-upon-Avon, Cardiff
Marylebone	Midlands	Chiltern Railways, Wrexham & Shropshire	Bakerloo	Birmingham

where the Underground system is less extensive, although there are many other routes providing efficient travel across the Greater London area. Travelcards (▷ 48) are valid on trains for journeys within the zone system (▷ 46–47).

TIPS

» If you want to be sure of a seat, avoid rush hour (weekdays 7.30 to 9.30am and 4.30 to 7pm). Thousands of London commuters use the services daily at that time.
» Telephone 0845 748 4950 for prices and timetables for all UK trains and destinations, or visit www.nationalrail. co.uk for timetables.
» Discount long-distance train fares can also be found through Megabus (▷ 63).

Left *Oyster Cards are convenient and offer considerable cost savings*

First Capital Connect

» First Capital Connect runs a service from Bedford, north of London, through London. Trains stop at five main London stations (St. Pancras International, Farringdon, City Thameslink, Blackfriars and London Bridge) and continues down to Brighton.

» The Thameslink service, run by First Capital Connect, also connects London with Luton Airport and Gatwick Airport (▷ 43).

Transport for London

» TFL is now running the former Silverlink Metro, a surburban route covering west, north and east London.

London Midland Train Services

» London Midland rail service connects London and Birmingham, stopping at Milton Keynes, Northampton, Hemel Hempstead and Watford.

BY COACH

» Coaches (long-distance buses) run from London to all parts of the country, leaving from Victoria Coach Station (VCS), 164 Buckingham Palace Road SW1W 9TP (tel 020 7027 2520; www.tfl.gov.uk). They provide a much cheaper but slower alternative to rail travel (see the panel below).

» VCS has a travel counter, open 8 to 7 Monday to Friday, 8 to 4.30 Saturday and 8 to 3 Sunday. At this counter you can buy or book airport transfer coach tickets, tours and excursions, London Travelcards, theatre and concert tickets, rail tickets, ferry and hovercraft tickets and travel insurance. It is also possible to arrange a Western Union money transfer.

National Express

» The largest bus company is National Express (tel 0871 781 8181), which operates to all regions of the UK and to Heathrow, Luton and Stansted airports.

» It is best to book your seat in advance. You can do so online at www.nationalexpress.com, or in person at the ticket hall at Victoria Coach Station, which is open 6am to 11.30pm daily. All major credit and debit cards are accepted.

» You can get advance purchase coach tickets until two hours before departure. It is cheaper to book in advance and to travel mid-week.

Other Coach Services

» Oxford Express coaches run to and from Oxford (tel 01865 785400, www.oxfordbus.co.uk).

» Green Line coaches connect local cities and airports to the capital (tel 0844 801 7261, www.greenline.co.uk).

» Megabus offers extremely low fares to major destinations throughout the UK (tel 0900 160 0900, www.megabus.com).

COACH VERSUS TRAIN

Prices vary considerably depending on how tickets are booked and how far in advance. It is best to check online at the various websites. Significant savings can be made on train and bus tickets if they are purchased in advance. To ensure availability, bookings should be made at least 24 hours in advance.

For the relevant mainline stations, ▷ 62.

All coaches leave from Victoria.

BATH
Train 1 hour 25 min
Coach 3 hours 15 min

BRIGHTON
Train 50 min
Coach 2 hours

CAMBRIDGE
Train 45 min
Coach 2 hours

CANTERBURY
Train 1 hour 25 min
Coach 1 hour 50 min

NORWICH
Train 1 hour 50 min
Coach 3 hours

OXFORD
Train 1 hour 30 min
Coach 1 hour 40 min

STRATFORD-UPON-AVON
Train 2 hours 10 min
Coach 3 hours 30 min

WINDSOR
Train (from Waterloo) 56 min
(from Paddington change at Slough) 35min
Coach 1 hour 10 min

YORK
Train 2 hours
Coach 5 hours

Below *Statue of poet Sir John Betjeman at St. Pancras station*

Transport staff in London are aware of the needs of passengers with disabilities and generally go out of their way to help. It is best to phone in advance if you need special help or services. For a good general source of information visit www.tourismforall.org.uk.

AIR

Most airlines have a department for making arrangements for passengers with special requirements; budget airlines may charge.

Designated disabled parking spaces are available in all BAA-run airports (tel 0870 000 1000).

Heathrow

Help Bus free, wheelchair-accessible transport between the bus station and terminals, tel 020 8745 6261, or from Help Bus phone points. Heathrow Express (tel 0845 600 1515) trains are wheelchair-accessible.

Gatwick

Airport helpline for travellers with reduced mobility, tel 0844 335 1802. Only certain train services are wheelchair-accessible.

Stansted

For special needs assistance, tel 0844 335 1803. The Stansted Express train is wheelchair-accessible. Buses from Stansted to other airports and central London are not (tel 0845 600 7245).

Luton

The shuttle bus to Luton Airport Parkway is wheelchair-accessible and there are elevators at the station. First Capital Connect helpline, tel 0800 058 2844.

London City

Wheelchair-accessible shuttle buses run from the airport to Liverpool Street. Information (tel 020 7646 0088).

BUS

» The Stationlink bus service that operates between major rail stations has low entrance ramps, low floors and spaces for wheelchairs.

» All buses are now low-floor for accessibility. Information (tel 020 7222 1234).

COACH

» Coaches tend to have high steep steps that may be difficult to negotiate. People who are sufficiently mobile may use coach services, but staff are not permitted to help passengers with boarding.

» Manual wheelchairs can be carried, but only if folded and if there is room. Powered vehicles or wheelchairs are not permitted on coach services.

» The National Express Disabled Persons travel helpline (tel 08717 818179).

DRIVING
Parking

The City of London Access Team (tel 020 7332 1995 or download from the website: www.cityoflondon.gov. uk) produces a leaflet for people with disabilities.

Breakdown

The Automobile Association (AA) has a disability helpline for members with disabilities (tel 0800 262 0500).

EUROTUNNEL

The Shuttle has been designed with passengers with disabilities in mind. There is no need to get out of your car during the journey, but Eurotunnel does require prior notice of visitors with disabilities. Amenities in the passenger terminal buildings are wheelchair-accessible.

DOCKLANDS LIGHT RAILWAY

» The DLR was constructed much more recently than the main Underground system, so is generally easier to use.

» Most stations are accessible by elevator or ramp. Call the DLR Customer Services (tel 020 7363 9700) during office hours to check more details.

» There are elevators, escalators and/or ramps on every station platform. All platforms are level with the trains for easy access. There is a designated wheelchair bay on every train.

» Platforms have tactile edges for visually impaired passengers and passenger information displays show train information.

FERRY

Improvements have been made to UK ports to cater for passengers with disabilities, but it is still advisable to contact the port in advance.

RAIL

» Portable ramps are available at most stations and some trains carry lightweight versions for use at unmanned stations.

» Increasingly, accessible toilets are available on long-distance trains and many regional services.

» Eurostar trains are wheelchair-accessible (as is the arrival point at St. Pancras International) with space for a maximum of two chairs per train. Reservations and information (tel 08432 186186).

TAXI

» All taxis are wheelchair-accessible.

UNDERGROUND

» For all enquiries (tel 020 7222 1234 24-hour Information Centre or tel 0845 330 9880 Customer Service Centre). An 'accessibility Tube map' is available from www.tfl.gov.uk.

» Guide dogs are permitted on all forms of public transport in London.

REGIONS

This book is divided into five regions of London. Region names are for the purposes of this book only and places of interest are listed alphabetically in each region.

CITY

Tate Modern

Shakespeare's Globe

HMS Belfast

London Eye

THE BOROUGH

LAMBETH

Imperial War Museum

NEWINGTON

VAUXHALL

SOUTH BANK

Occupying the inner curve of the majestic bend that the River Thames traces through the centre of London, the South Bank wears several of the city's most iconic landmarks on its riverfront like jewels on a necklace, while concealing some of central London's most authentic working neighbourhoods in the warren of busy streets beyond. Spanning the northern ends of the boroughs of Lambeth to the west and Southwark to the east, the pedestrianized riverside itself constitutes ideal walking territory, especially from the hi-tech Ferris wheel of the London Eye, which stands proudly in front of imposing County Hall, to the southern end of picturesque Tower Bridge. En route you pass the South Bank cultural complex, the huge brick and glass edifice of Tate Modern with its tall chimney, and the faithful reconstruction of Shakespeare's Globe Theatre, just as it was in the time of the bard himself.

Away from the river, sandwiched between the two busy railway terminals of Waterloo and London Bridge, the sights thin out, although the grand Imperial War Museum lies on the road from Westminster Bridge to the Elephant and Castle, the hub of south London's road system. What most fascinates the visitor here is the sudden transition to the gritty, urban feel of neighbourhoods such as Lambeth, Newington and Walworth, which have remained largely ungentrified despite their proximity to the centre. These are fine spots to wander aimlessly and take in a simple café meal or sip a pint in an unspoiled pub.

One area that has been transformed into something of a gourmet's paradise is Borough Market, which now boasts a fine range of quality food shops as well as trendy restaurants and bars.

CITY

Clockmaker Museum
Guildhall
St Lawrence Jewry Church
St Margaret's Lothbury
No 1 Poultry Shopping Centre
Bank of England & Museum
Royal Exchange
Mansion House
Temple of Mithras
St Stephen Walbrook Church
St Mary Abchurch
CANNON STREET STATION
Monument
Tower 42
The Pinnacle Bishopsgate Tower
30 St Mary Axe (The Gherkin)
Lloyd's
Leadenhall Market
FENCHURCH STREET STATION
London Met University
Synagogue
ALDGATE BUS STATION
Whitechapel Gallery
University

Trinity House
All Hallows-by-the-Tower
Custom House
Tower Hill
Tower of London
Tower Stairs
Tower Millennium Pier
RNLI Lifeboat Station
London Commodity Exchange
Royal Mint Court
ST GEORGE IN THE EAST
East Dock
West Dock
St Katharine Docks

Financial Times
Vinopolis
Clink Prison Museum
Golden Hinde
Southwark Cathedral
Borough Market
London Bridge Hospital
London and City Pier
HMS Belfast
London Dungeon
Hay's Galleria
Southwark Crown Court
The Scoop
Winston Churchill's Britain at War Experience
LONDON BRIDGE STATION
The Shard
Greater London Authority Headquarters (City Hall)
Butler's Wharf Pier
St Katharine Pier
Tower Bridge
Design Museum

Guy's Hospital
Kings College London
London City Mission
Fashion & Textile Museum
St Saviour's Dock
West Providence Square

THE BOROUGH
Henrywood Hall
Empire Square
Tabard Garden

South Bank University
County

KENT ROAD

South London Gallery

SOUTH BANK • SIGHTS MAP

REGIONS

69

BANKSIDE GALLERY

www.banksidegallery.com

Two historic art societies have their homes in this south bank gallery near Tate Modern (▷ 80–81): the Royal Watercolour Society, the world's first institution to specialize in watercolours, and the Royal Society of Painter-Printmakers, founded in 1880 to seek recognition for artists working in etching, engraving and mezzotint. Housed in the converted ground floor of a 1970s' block of flats, the gallery showcases the activities of both societies with shows and themed exhibitions of watercolours and prints.

✚ 68 L5 ✉ 48 Hopton Street SE1 9JH ☎ 020 7928 7521 🕐 Daily 11–6 ✋ Free 🚇 Blackfriars, Mansion House, Southwark 🚌 45, 63, 100 ⛴ Bankside Pier ♿

CLINK PRISON MUSEUM

www.clink.co.uk

A skeleton hanging in a cage marks the entrance to the gloomy basement housing the museum—a taste of what's to come. From the 12th century until 1780, when the building was burned down during the Gordon Riots (▷ 33), this was the site of the notorious Clink Prison, where clerics, heretics, debtors, prostitutes and an assortment of Bankside lowlife were imprisoned in appalling conditions. Its name is said to derive from the 'clinch' irons that were used to pin prisoners down, and 'the clink' has become a slang term for any prison. The museum covers the history of the prison using archive material, tableaux of torture scenes and displays of gruesome instruments.

✚ 69 M5 ✉ 1 Clink Street SE1 9DG ☎ 020 7403 0900 🕐 Jul–Sep daily 10–9; Oct–Jun Mon–Fri 10–6, Sat–Sun 10–5.30 ✋ Adult £6, child (under 16) £5.50, family £15 🚇 London Bridge 🚌 35, 43, 149, RV1 ♿

DESIGN MUSEUM

www.designmuseum.org

In 1989 a 1950s' warehouse on Butler's Wharf was converted into the modernist Design Museum, the first in the world to be dedicated to 20th- and 21st-century design. One of London's most inspiring cultural attractions, it promises to be more than a conventional museum, with a mission 'to excite everyone about design'. An evolving permanent collection presents mass-produced design classics including cars, cameras, furniture, domestic appliances and office equipment, while temporary exhibitions range from retrospectives about great designers to thematic shows.

The first-floor Review Gallery showcases the most innovative contemporary designs and technologies from around the world.

✚ 69 P6 ✉ 28 Shad Thames SE1 2YD ☎ 020 7403 6933 🕐 Daily 10–5.45 ✋ Adult £11, child (under 12) free 🚇 London Bridge, Tower Hill (or Tower Gateway for DLR) 🚌 42, 47, 78, 188, 381 ⛴ Tower of London, St. Katharine's Pier 🍴 ♿

FASHION AND TEXTILE MUSEUM

www.ftmlondon.org

A zingy orange and hot-pink concrete block in the middle of venerable Bermondsey, the Fashion and Textile Museum announces its presence with all the boldness you might expect of a creation founded by flamboyant British designer Zandra Rhodes. It houses around two major exhibitions each year, concentrating on design since the 1950s, in a gallery set on two levels. As part of Newham College, it also runs a variety of related talks and workshops by leading fashion and textile designers—they're very popular, so book ahead.

✚ 69 N6 ✉ 83 Bermondsey Street SE1 3XF ☎ 020 7407 8664 🕐 Tue–Sat 11–6 ✋ Adult £7, child (under 12) free 🚇 London Bridge 🚌 RV1, 43 to London Bridge 🍴 ♿

FLORENCE NIGHTINGALE MUSEUM

www.florence-nightingale.co.uk

Set in a modern annexe of St. Thomas's Hospital, where Florence Nightingale (1820–1910) established the first-ever nurses' training school in 1860, the museum covers her career and contribution to public health. Her work nursing soldiers during the Crimean War, which earned her the title 'the Lady with the Lamp', and her contribution to public health, are evoked with personal mementoes, clothing, furniture, books, letters, portraits and nursing equipment, plus audiovisuals and realistic reconstructions.

✚ 68 K6 ✉ 2 Lambeth Palace Road SE1 7EW ☎ 020 7620 0374 🕐 Daily 10–5 ✋ Adult £5.80, child (5–18) £4.80, under 5s free, family £16 🚇 Westminster, Waterloo 🚌 12, 148, 159, 211, 507, RV1 ⛴ Westminster Pier 🍴 ♿

GARDEN MUSEUM

www.museumgardenhistory.org

The redundant parish church of St. Mary-at-Lambeth provides the setting for this collection of gardening tools and machinery, including everything from spades to cloches and mowers, and temporary exhibition space. Outside, in the church courtyard, a knot garden uses plants popular in the 17th century, including fragrant old roses. Two major figures in the development of English gardening, John Tradescant the elder (1570–1638) and his son, John, gardeners to Charles I and II, are laid to rest here. A window in the church commemorates them.

✚ 68 J7 ✉ Lambeth Palace Road SE1 7LB ☎ 020 7401 8865 🕐 Sun–Fri 10.30–5, Sat 10.30–4. Closed first Mon of month ✋ Adult £6, child (under 16) free 🚇 Lambeth North, Westminster 🚌 3, 344, 77, 507, C10 🍴 ♿

Above *Florence Nightingale statue*
Opposite *Fashion and Textile Museum*

INFORMATION

www.hmsbelfast.iwm.org.uk

⊞ 69 N5 ✉ Morgan's Lane, Tooley
Street SE1 2JH ☎ 020 7940 6300
🕐 Mar–Oct daily 10–6; Nov–Feb
10–5 💷 Adult £13.50, child (under
16—must be accompanied by adult) free
🚇 London Bridge, Monument 🚌 36,
705, RV1 ⛴ London Bridge City Pier,
Tower Pier ☞ Visits take form of self-
guided tours 📖 £3.95, in English, French,
German. Audioguides in English, French,
German and Spanish free with admission
🍴 Walrus Café in zone 3 🎁 Gifts,
models and books with general war/
armed forces theme

TIP

» If you are claustrophobic, you may
not like the deeper regions, and the tour
involves climbing down steep ladders
without much headroom.

Above *Bristling with guns, the Belfast
gives a comprehensive insight into the
lives and work of her crew*

HMS BELFAST

Launched in March 1938, this huge warship had an active career during World
War II and played a leading part both in the destruction of the German battle
cruiser *Scharnhorst* at the Battle of North Cape and in the Normandy landings.
She now floats off the south bank of the Thames near Tower Bridge, the only
surviving example of an armoured warship from this era, and an awesome sight
with her heavy armour and massive gun turrets.

TOURING THE DECKS

A self-guided tour starts on the quarterdeck, where officers and guests of honour
were piped aboard and guards and bands paraded, and leads to the top of the
bridge, with its four Bofors gun mountings, three of which can be aimed by hand
(anyone can have a go). The tour then takes you down through nine decks to see
the triple 6-inch gun turrets, the shell rooms and magazines and the cramped
mess decks, officers' cabins, galley and sick-bay. Life-size models represent
members of the crew going about their business—a surprisingly realistic and
disconcerting touch. The operations room is manned by models, re-enacting
the ship's part in the Battle of North Cape on 26 December 1943. It's a simple
gimmick but an effective one, enhanced by photographs and memorabilia that
emphasize the human cost of the conflict.

The ship's company galley dates from the period after HMS *Belfast*'s
modernization in the 1950s, when meals were prepared by properly trained and
qualified staff and served from the counter; more figures are shown dishing up
and following the precise rules posted up around the galley. In the sick-bay, a
well-equipped operating room reflects the need for every kind of health care on a
cruiser designed to spend long periods at sea.

The tour ends with a visit to the boiler and engine rooms, where massive
boilers produced superheated steam at high pressure to be piped to the turbine
engines, which in turn drove the propeller shafts. It took about four hours to raise
enough steam for the ship to get moving.

VIDEOS AND EXHIBITION

Videos trace the history of each zone on the tour, and officers are on hand to
answer questions and keep crowds flowing. In the exhibition room you can see
the signatures of 36 survivors from a crew of 1,963 on the *Scharnhorst*, sunk on
Boxing Day 1943 off the coast of Norway.

GOLDEN HINDE
www.goldenhinde.com
Nestling in a small dock on Bankside is an exact full-scale replica of the galleon in which Sir Francis Drake (c.1543–96) circumnavigated the globe between 1577 and 1580. In fact the replica has travelled further than the original, twice around the globe. The ship's cramped interior would have been home to more than 80 sailors. Its five decks include a gun deck that holds 22 cannons. During the holiday periods there are occasional tours led by well-versed guides dressed in Elizabethan costume, adding authenticity to your visit.

For those wanting to find out just what it was like to sleep aboard ship, it is possible to stay overnight as part of an educational visit from April to September.

69 M5 St. Mary Overie Dock, Cathedral Street SE1 9DE 020 7403 0123 Daily 10–5.30 Adult £7, child (4–18) £4.50, under 4s free, family £18 London Bridge 17, 35, 43, 47, 48, 133, 501 London Bridge City Pier, Bankside Pier

HMS *BELFAST*
▷ 72.

HOPTON'S ALMSHOUSES
Stroll along behind the modern buildings that line the South Bank and you'll stumble across this appealing little relic of a bygone age, now dwarfed by its surroundings. The brown brick cottages with their cream-painted cornerstones are private, as are the charming gardens in front (adorned with modern art sculptures from the neighbouring Purdy Hicks Gallery), but you may stare through the railings on the open side of the square and wonder at this sturdy, homely survivor. Hopton's Almshouses have stood here since 1749, providing relief for poor single men of Southwark (in recent times, wives have been permitted, too). They were erected at a cost of £2,700, including the land purchase, and were originally homes for 26 men. Room was made for two more in 1825, and the unbroken record of

occupation since 1752 is remarkable. The room at the middle of the east side, with the grand moulding above the doorway, is a panelled committee room for the charity's trustees.

68 L5 Hopton Street SE1 9JJ No public access Southwark, Blackfriars

IMPERIAL WAR MUSEUM
▷ 74.

LONDON DUNGEON
www.the-dungeons.co.uk
Hidden away in the vaults beneath London Bridge railway station is a grisly parade of life-size tableaux, complete with disturbing sound and special effects. Along with scenes of death from disease, early surgery, murder and various methods of torture, the museum presents re-enactments of some of the most horrific events in British history.

The Great Fire of London is a £1 million re-creation of the fire-ravaged streets of London in 1666; Traitor! Boat Ride to Hell and Extremis: Drop Ride are fearsome plummets into murky water and abyss respectively. Jack the Ripper takes you back to

1888 for a terrifying tour through the district of Whitechapel, following the bloody footsteps of the most infamous serial killer of his time.

One of the most spectacular and ambitious exhibitions is the one about the Great Plague; it will certainly challenge the squeamish as it vividly and realistically re-creates the horrors of the plague that claimed more than 100,000 lives in 1665. Expect to see black rats (they carried the disease) running around, and to walk through a tunnel piled up with the ravaged corpses of the plague victims.

Equally as frightening is Labyrinth of the Lost, where visitors find (or rather lose) themselves in a baffling mirror maze of eerie catacombs, with live characters and spooky special effects.

Throughout the museum, actors in period costume help keep you constantly on edge.

69 N5 28–34 Tooley Street SE1 2SZ 020 7403 7221, 0871 423 2240 Daily 10–5.30 (longer hours in school holidays) Adult £23.10, child (4–15) £17.10, under 4s free, family £80.50 London Bridge 35, 43, 47, 133, 149, 343

Below *The replica of Sir Francis Drake's Golden Hinde at St. Mary Overie Dock*

www.iwm.org.uk

✛ 68 K7 ✉ Lambeth Road SE1 6HZ
☎ 020 7416 5000 🕐 Daily 10–6
✋ Free (except for some special
exhibitions) Ⓜ Lambeth North, Elephant
& Castle, Southwark, Waterloo 🚌 3, 12,
344, C10 🎧 Audio tours available, £3.50
📖 £4.95, in English only 💻 On ground
floor, 10–5.30 🎁 Gifts with relevant
themes

TIP

» Note that curators don't recommend
the Holocaust Exhibition for children
under 14, and children under 11 are not
admitted.

IMPERIAL WAR MUSEUM

An imposing pair of naval guns guards the entrance to the country's most
impressive military museum—just a taster of the diverse collection inside, which
covers wars involving Britain or the Commonwealth since 1914. This includes not
only World Wars I and II, but many other international conflicts, from Korea and
Vietnam to Suez and the Arabian Gulf.

GROUND FLOORS

You're first confronted by a confusing array of military equipment in the airy
Large Exhibits Gallery: Tanks, artillery, fighter planes, trucks and submarines are
haphazardly parked—or suspended—in the domed space. Take time to wander
among the vehicles, many of which have stories of bravery attached. There's
the wooden dinghy *Tamzine*, for instance, the smallest surviving boat to have
taken part in the evacuation of 200,000 troops from Dunkirk in 1940. Sometimes
it's simply the sense of scale that impresses, in exhibits such as the colossal V2
rocket or the cramped World War II fighter cockpit.

On the lower ground floor are well-conceived re-creations of the 1940–41
Blitz and World War I trench warfare, complete with sound effects and smells.
The section about the British Home Front is fascinating, and includes evocative
touches such as posters exhorting the women of Britain to 'come into the
factories', or 'dig for victory'.

Elsewhere on the labyrinthine lower floor, collections can easily be overlooked.
World War II receives the fullest coverage, with detailed sections on the eastern
front and war in northwest Europe and the Far East. Extraordinary Heroes, in
the new Lord Ashcroft Gallery, presents the stories behind the world's largest
collection of Victoria Crosses (VCs – the highest award for gallantry in battle) and
George Crosses (the highest civilian award for extreme bravery).

UPPER FLOORS

Move up to the first floor for the absorbing Secret War exhibition. Items on
show include bottles of invisible ink used by German spies and one of the few
remaining German Enigma machines used to encode messages.

The art galleries on the second floor are a popular section of the museum,
with work by Paul Nash, Henry Moore and Stanley Spencer.

On the third floor is the distressing counterpoint to the martial display below.
The Holocaust Exhibition examines the Nazi persecution of Europe's Jewish
communities and other groups, such as gypsies and homosexuals, between
1933 and 1945. Exhibits include shoes collected from prisoners at Majdanek
concentration camp in Poland.

Below *World War I biplane on display in
the Large Exhibits Gallery*

LONDON EYE

The world's largest observation wheel and London's most visible icon is four times wider than the dome of St. Paul's and more than 200 times larger than the wheel of an average racing bicycle. It offers a ride that's enthralling even for those who hate heights, offering spectacular views across the city in every direction.

RIDING HIGH

Passengers ride in one of 32 pod-like capsules that rotate smoothly in a slow-moving, 30-minute flight. Each capsule is fully enclosed and comfortably holds 25 people. Because the capsules are secured on the outside of the wheel (rather than hung from it, as they would be on a Ferris wheel), views through the large glass windows are totally unobstructed. And because the capsules are kept level by a motorized motion stability system, you can walk around inside them quite safely—although seating is provided. For additional safety, each capsule is in touch with the ground via camera and radio links. Note, however, that flights may be cancelled at the last minute owing to weather conditions. You can ask for a flight attendant to accompany you, to point out major landmarks. The wheel is in constant motion, revolving continuously at a quarter of the average walking speed and enabling you to walk straight on and off the moving capsules.

After dark, the trees lining the approach to the London Eye are bathed in green lights, and the boarding platform appears to float on a cloud of blue light. Sunset and after-dark flights are also available.

BACKGROUND

The EDF Energy London Eye was conceived by David Marks and Julia Barfield to celebrate the millennium, using a design that represents the turning of the century. It took seven years and the expertise of hundreds of people from five European countries to realize their vision, and over a week to lift the Eye upright from a horizontal position across the Thames—a procedure previously attempted only in oil-rigging operations. Although originally intended as a temporary structure, the Eye is so popular that it is unlikely that it will disappear from the skyline.

INFORMATION

www.londoneye.com

✚ 68 J6 ✉ EDF Energy London Eye, Riverside Building, County Hall Westminster Bridge Road SE1 7PB ☎ Bookings: 0871 781 3000 🕐 Jul–Aug daily 10–9.30; Sep–Jul 10–8.30 ✋ Adult £19.98, child (4–15) £11.83, under 4s free, family £63.61 🚇 Waterloo, Westminster, Embankment, Charing Cross 🚌 77, 211, 381 ⛴ Waterloo Millennium Pier 📖 *Essential Eye Souvenir Book* and in-flight mini guide available from the ticket hall or shop £5, in English, French, German, Spanish, braille ☕ Zen Café in County Hall and outside in Jubilee Gardens 🏛 In Jubilee Gardens, selling souvenirs and gifts, including Eye-inspired jewellery

TIPS

» Book ahead. Although not essential, it is recommended.
» Arrive 30 minutes before your flight, to allow time for boarding.
» You can always buy tickets on the day but may wait for over an hour.

Above *Survey London from the comfort of a stable pod on the Eye*

LONDON FIRE BRIGADE MUSEUM

www.london-fire.gov.uk

The Great Fire of 1666 marks the starting point for this fascinating journey through the history of firefighting in London. Exhibits housed in two buildings of the London Fire Brigade's Training Centre include original fire engines, pumps, uniforms and uncomfortable-looking breathing apparatus.

Among the museum's prized possessions are the personal belongings of Captain Eyre Massey Shaw. He was in charge of the brigade from 1861 and is credited as the father of the modern fire service. His silver helmet and KCB decoration are on display.

A collection of paintings by World War II firefighters shows telling scenes of the Blitz as they experienced it.

✚ 68 L6 ✉ Winchester House, 94A Southwark Bridge Road SE1 0EG ☎ 020 8555 1200 ext 39894 🕐 Visit by guided tour only (Mon–Fri 10.30 and 2) by prior arrangement ✋ Adult £3, child (7–14) £2, under 7s £1 🚇 Borough, Southwark, Elephant & Castle 🚌 344 🏧

MILLENNIUM BRIDGE

www.arup.com/millenniumbridge

Two of London's famous landmarks—St. Paul's Cathedral (▷ 104–109) in the City and the Tate Modern gallery (▷ 80–81) at Bankside—are connected by this bridge built in 2000, the first pedestrian crossing to be built over the Thames in more than a century.

Architect Sir Norman Foster and engineer Ove Arup designed it to give the impression of a single sweeping 'blade of light', illuminated from deck level with an innovative light pipe system. The steel structure is 325m (1,066ft) high and carries 3,000 tonnes of horizontal force. After some celebrated teething troubles, during which it wobbled when people attempted to use it, it was adjusted and eventually reopened in 2002.

✚ 68 L5 🕐 Open access ✋ Free 🚇 St. Paul's, Southwark 🚌 11, 15, 17, 45, 63, 344, RV1 ⛴ Mansion House, Blackfriars Pier, Bankside Pier

SEA LIFE LONDON AQUARIUM

www.visitsealife.com

More than 3,000 forms of marine life can be found swimming around under the former offices of the Greater London Council in County Hall, one of Europe's largest aquariums. Laid out across three floors, the aquarium displays its residents in tanks representing a variety of environments, from ponds to rivers to oceans.

The aquarium is divided into 14 different zones, in which you will find sharks and stingrays gliding between giant, submerged Easter Island-style heads. There are countless gaudy fish to enjoy in the Reef and Corals and Indian Ocean exhibitions, and children get a thrill from watching the sharks being fed. It takes 2 million litres (440,000 gallons) of Thames water and tons of imported salt to fill the tanks.

The aquarium is committed to conservation and as a way of raising money for research you're invited to adopt from a choice of over 20 different types of fish. Not surprisingly, the sharks, piranhas and rays are the most popular.

✚ 68 J6 ✉ County Hall, Westminster Bridge Road SE1 7PB ☎ 0871 663 1679 🕐 Mon–Thu 10–6, Fri–Sun 10–5 ✋ Adult £17.14, child (3–14) £12.66, family £54 🚇 Waterloo, Westminster, Embankment 🚌 12, 53, 159, 211, 341, RV1 🚻 🏧

SOUTHBANK CENTRE

www.southbankcentre.co.uk

London's premier centre for the performing arts sits on the south side of the river between the Hungerford and Waterloo bridges. It includes the Royal Festival Hall (▷ 87–88), a major concert venue, reopened in June 2007 after a major refurbishment to restore its 1950s ambience; the National Film Theatre (▷ 87), with cinemas, a café and shop; the Queen Elizabeth Hall (▷ 88) and adjoining Purcell

Above *Sharks at Sea Life London Aquarium*
Left *The Millennium Bridge is a handy way to reach St. Paul's from the South Bank*

Room, staging smaller concerts and chamber music respectively; and a clutch of high-profile theatre spaces.

This was the site of the 1951 South Bank Exhibition, part of the Festival of Britain, held as a morale-booster during the post-war years. The only building to survive from that time is the Royal Festival Hall, where exhibitions and events are held in the huge open-plan foyer, and concerts and ballet productions take place in the auditorium above.

To the east is the Hayward Gallery (daily 10–6, charges for some exhibitions), a grim concrete bunker built in 1968, which hosts major contemporary art exhibitions, with the emphasis on British artists. Note that the Southbank Centre hosts many free foyer events so it's always worth asking what's on.

✚ 68 K5 ✉ Belvedere Road SE1 8XX ☎ General information 020 7960 4200. Ticket office 0844 875 0073 (9am–8pm) 🕐 Foyer daily 10am–10.30pm ✋ Performances only 🚇 Waterloo, Embankment 🚌 77, RV1 ⛴ Festival Pier 🚻 🍴 🏧

INFORMATION

www.shakespeares-globe.org
⊞ 68 M5 ✉ 21 New Globe Walk
SE1 9DT ☎ 020 7902 1400. Box office:
020 7401 9919; tours: 020 7902 1500
🕐 Daily 10–5. During theatre season
Mon–Sat 10–6, Sun 10–5. Performances
most afternoons and evenings daily,
Apr–Sep 👁 Exhibition and theatre tour:
adult £11.50, child (5–15) £7, under 5s
free, family £32. Performance: £15–£33,
plus £5 (standing); advance booking
essential 🚇 London Bridge, Mansion
House 🚌 15, 45, 63, RV1 ⛴ Bankside
Pier 📖 *Discovering Shakespeare's
Globe: The Guidebook*, £5.99 🍴 Swan
at the Globe has a bar (11am–late) on
the ground floor for all-day eating and
drinking. The Brasserie with its river view
is for more substantial meals and for
gourmet take-out.

TIP

» The benches are hard—consider hiring
or bring a cushion.

Below *Inside the reconstructed
Elizabethan theatre*

SHAKESPEARE'S GLOBE

Bankside's original Globe was one of England's first true playhouses, built in
1599 by a company that included William Shakespeare. Before this, acting
companies would tour the country, often performing in the courtyards of inns.
Unfortunately, the Globe didn't last long—it was destroyed by fire during a
production of *Hamlet* in 1613. A replacement was built, with a tiled roof, a
year later but was demolished by the Puritans in 1642, and for the next three
centuries the site remained empty.

After visiting Bankside in 1949, American film actor and director Sam
Wanamaker (1919–93) was determined to create an accurate, functioning
reconstruction of the Globe, built as near as possible to the original site
and using materials, tools and craft techniques closely matching those of
Elizabethan times. Although the project began in 1969, reconstruction wasn't
started until 1987, with completion in 1997.

Small by modern standards, the Globe is an O-shaped, white-plastered
building constructed with unseasoned oak and held together with 6,000 oak
pegs. It's crowned with the first thatched roof to be built in the city since the
Great Fire in 1666; the modern version plays it safe with a sprinkler system. In
the middle, an elevated stage and a yard are surrounded on three sides by tiers
of benches.

In the interests of authenticity, productions are held during the afternoon,
much as in Shakespeare's day, without artificial lighting. As with the original,
there is standing room in front of the stage, where groundlings (the term used
in Shakespearean times for standing members of the audience) can heckle the
actors in Elizabethan fashion. Performances continue, whatever the weather—
but no umbrellas.

UNDERGLOBE

Beneath the theatre, the huge space called the UnderGlobe houses the
Shakespeare's Globe Exhibition. Here the roles of actor, musician and audience
are brought to life through text, film, music and multimedia. You can learn about
the techniques used to design and make the costumes in the Theatre Workroom,
and in Special Effects you discover what was used for blood and how the sound
of thunder in *Macbeth* was created.

Above *Come to Vinopolis to relive London's wine-trading history*

SOUTH LONDON GALLERY

www.southlondongallery.org

This renowned contemporary art gallery shows work by local, national and international artists. Acclaimed artists who have exhibited here include Tracy Emin, Barbara Kruger, Christian Boltanski and Keith Tyson. A permanent collection of nearly 2,000 works can be viewed by appointment.

✚ Off map 69 M8 ✉ 65 Peckham Road SE5 8UH ☎ 020 7703 6120 🕐 Tue, Thu–Sun 11–6, Wed 11–9 💷 Free; admission charge to individual events 🚇 Elephant & Castle, then bus 12, 171, 343; Oval then bus 36, 436 🚌 12, 36, 171, 343, 345, 436 🛍 🏛

SOUTHWARK CATHEDRAL

www.cathedral.southwark.anglican.org

This stone building, originally built between 1220 and 1420 as part of a medieval priory, is tucked away near London Bridge on the south bank of the Thames. Prior to 1905, when it was given cathedral status, it was the parish church of St. Saviour. Inside the nave retains some original stonework and fascinating 15th-century ceiling bosses — look for the one which depicts the devil swallowing Judas Iscariot. It's also worth seeking out many of the tombs and memorials, including that of Shakespeare's brother, Edmund, who died in 1607. A monument to the playwright himself (who lived in Southwark from 1599 to 1611) depicts various characters from his plays.

✚ 69 M5 ✉ London Bridge SE1 9DA ☎ 020 7367 6700 🕐 Mon–Fri 8–6, Sat–Sun 8.30–6 💷 Free; donations welcomed 🚇 London Bridge 🚌 15, 35, 40, 133, 149, 344, 381, RV1 🍴 🏛

TATE MODERN

▷ 80–81.

VINOPOLIS

www.vinopolis.co.uk

London has a rich history of wine trading and this is the starting point for this unusual exhibition. Set in historic vaults that were once at the centre of Europe's wine trade, this multi-award-winning visitor attraction takes you on an encyclopaedic trawl from Alsace wines to Zinfandel grapes, visiting every major wine-producing region in the world. The basic tour (self-guided) includes sampling six different wines plus a cocktail — this must be the only museum in the world where you are actually encouraged to saunter around with a glass of wine in your hand. Touch-screen technology, audioguides and assisted tastings aim to educate your taste buds.

✚ 69 M5 ✉ 1 Bank End, Bankside SE1 9BU ☎ 020 7940 8300 🕐 Thu–Sat 12–7.30, Sun 12–3.30 💷 Basic tours, tasting six wines plus a cocktail £21. More tours available 🚇 London Bridge 🚌 17, 21, 35, 40, 43, 48, 133, 149, 343, 501, 521, RV1 🍴 Cantina Vinopolis ▷ 89–90

WINSTON CHURCHILL'S BRITAIN AT WAR EXPERIENCE

www.britainatwar.co.uk

Here you can learn something of what it was like to be on Britain's Home Front during World War II, the most turbulent period in the nation's 20th-century history. Winston Churchill's Britain at War Experience is not a war museum devoted to the instruments of destruction but a tribute to ordinary people who lived their lives against the backdrop of air raids, the blackout, rationing and evacuation.

Begin your journey by taking an elevator down into the converted railway arches beneath London Bridge train station, where a mock-up of an underground air-raid shelter serves as a prelude to a huge collection of evocative photographs and assorted items ranging from rolls of toilet paper, ration books, gas masks and bombs to a complete Anderson shelter.

You can also see re-creations of a 1940s' shopping arcade, a BBC radio studio, a theatre dressing room and a club for GIs.

Special effects re-create the sights, sounds, even smells of a London street during the Blitz, and you can walk through the reconstructed shattered remains of a bombed department store, a cinema, a pub and homes.

✚ 69 N5 ✉ Churchill House, 64–66 Tooley Street SE1 2TF ☎ 020 7403 3171 🕐 Apr–Oct daily 10–5; Nov–Mar 10–4.30. 💷 Adult £12.95, child (5–15) £5.50, under 5s free, family £29 🚇 London Bridge 🚌 47, 381, RV1 🏛

INFORMATION

www.tate.org.uk

✚ 68 L5 ✉ Bankside SE1 9TG ☎ 020 7887 8888 🕐 Sun–Thu 10–6, Fri–Sat 10–10 💷 Free, donations welcome. Charge for special exhibitions 🚇 Southwark, Mansion House, St. Paul's 🚌 45, 63, 100, 344, 381, RV1 ⛴ Bankside Pier; Tate Boat (▷ 192) 🎧 Choice of audiotours covering permanent collection, architecture, children's trail, tour for the visually impaired. Available from near the Turbine Hall information point and Level 3, £2, in English, French, German, Italian, Spanish 📖 Official guide £3, in English, French, German, Italian, Spanish, Japanese; audioguides in English, French, German, Italian, Spanish £3.50 🍴 Restaurant on Level 7 with exceptional views ☕ Cafe on Level 2; espresso bar on Level 4 🛍 Large shop on Level 1 with comprehensive range of art books, posters, prints, stationery and postcards; shops also on levels 2 and 4

Above *States of Flux Room 2*

INTRODUCTION

Towering over the Millennium Bridge on the south bank of the Thames, Tate Modern opened in 2000 as one of the world's leading museums of modern art, and it's been pulling in huge crowds ever since.

By the early 1990s the Tate Gallery, now called Tate Britain (▷ 192–193), needed more space. Its international modern art collection had nearly doubled in 40 years, and the decision was made to divide the collection between British and other works of art. A major new gallery was planned to house the international work, and the venue chosen was a decommissioned power station, a huge 1950s' brick and steel-frame building designed by Sir Giles Gilbert Scott (1880–1960). A competition was mounted for the best plan to transform the site, and the winners, out of 148 entrants, were Swiss architects Herzog & de Meron. Renovation began in 1995 and the gallery opened five years later. In March 2009 revised plans were announced for the museum to add the uniquely shaped Tate Modern 2 directly behind the current gallery. Using the old power house's oil tanks as its foundation, the design, also by Herzog & de Meron, will add 5,000sq m (54,000sq ft) of exhibition space. It is expected to open during 2012.

You can use entrances on the western or the northern side of the former power station. On the west side there are two; the main entrance takes you down an access ramp into the enormous, airy Turbine Hall, which acts as a dramatic interior plaza for temporary installations. Another entrance on this side of the building gives level access to the second floor. The main shop and information point are on Level One (the basement) and escalators take you up to the galleries on the upper levels.

The collection is divided into four broad themes: Material Gestures, Poetry and Dream, Energy and Process, and States of Flux. Each has combinations of film media, installations, painting, photography and sculpture, linking historic works with contemporary. Every year there are additional special loan exhibitions and several shows focusing on a single artist, theme or period.

WHAT TO SEE

Tate Modern continues the story of art where the National Gallery (▷ 182–187) leaves off. Its displays are changed regularly, but they always include works by the most influential artists of the 20th century, such as Picasso, Matisse, Dalí, Moore, Bacon, Gabo, Giacometti and Warhol.

LEVEL 3
Material Gestures (Room 2)
Venice Woman IX by Alberto Giacometti
Giacometti (1901–66) began to sculpt his series of emaciated human figures in the 1940s, providing a sober answer to the 'superman' philosophy of the pre-war Futurists. The fragility and dignity of this bronze piece, with all its resonance of human suffering, underlines Giacometti's own view that his thin sculptures were truer to humanity than larger works.

Poetry and Dream (Beyond Surrealism: Room 2)
Naked Man with Knife by Jackson Pollock
Before developing his famous 'drip' technique, American artist Jackson Pollock (1912–56) painted this powerful work as he was beginning to assert his own style. The image of the interlocking figures conveys a brooding violence and was based on Mexican painter Orozco's lost work depicting Abel and Cain.

LEVEL 5
States of Flux (After Impressionism: Room 3)
Reading Woman with Parasol by Henri Matisse
Matisse (1869–1954) painted this work in 1921, while staying in a house near Nice. It is typical of the artist's work in the 1920s and an excellent example of his mastery of everyday subjects. The colours are more subdued than in his early Fauvist works.

States of Flux (After Impressionism: Room 3)
Girl in a Chemise by Pablo Picasso
During his Blue Period, Picasso (1881–1973) produced a series of portraits of people from society's margins. This study of a melancholy, thin young girl is included in the Naked and Nude collection in contrast to the idealized nude. It's a poignant work, which goes beyond the depiction of a model and into the realms of social commentary.

States of Flux (Umberto Boccioni and Roy Lichtenstein: Room 1)
Unique Forms of Continuity in Space by Umberto Boccioni
The Futurist movement was founded by writers and artists such as Umberto Boccioni (1882–1916) in the early 20th century, when industrialization was engulfing Italy and innovations such as cars and electricity seemed to promise a dynamic and thrusting age ahead. This 1913 sculpture shows the air in the wake of the moving figure, giving a vivid sense of speed and progress.

States of Flux (Cubism, Futurism and Vorticism: Room 3)
Mandora by Georges Braque
Braque (1882–1963) was a leading light among the Cubists, whose experiments in form and perception revolutionized the art world. Braque collected early musical instruments and in this image of a mandora, a small lute, he uses his fragmented style to suggest rhythm and sound—an unusually active kind of still-life painting.

GALLERY GUIDE
LEVEL ONE
Turbine Hall: temporary exhibitions
LEVEL TWO
Starr Auditorium, Seminar Rooms
LEVEL THREE
Material Gestures (New Painting and Sculpture 1945–60)
Poetry and Dream (Surrealism & Beyond)
LEVEL FOUR
Changing exhibitions
LEVEL FIVE
Energy and Process (art inspired by transformation and natural forces)
States of Flux (Cubism, Futurism and Vorticism)

TIP
» Tate Boat links Tate Britain, the London Eye and Tate Modern (every 40 min).

Below *The entrance lobby is in what used to be the turbine hall in the old power station*

ALONG THE SOUTH BANK

A walk past Westminster, Britain's seat of government, and London's premier centre for the performing arts, the South Bank, with spectacular views along the Thames.

THE WALK

Distance: 5km (3 miles)
Time: 2 hours minimum
Start at: Westminster Underground station
End at: St. Paul's Underground station

HOW TO GET THERE

🚇 Jubilee, Circle or District line to Westminster
🚌 11, 12, 24, 453

★ This well-trodden route exudes a sense of space in an otherwise highly populated city.

Leave Westminster Underground station by exit 1 (Pier) to reach the bank of the Thames near Big Ben. You can take boat trips from here up and down the river (▷ 266–267).
Cross the road, skirt around the base of Big Ben and turn left along the Parliament Green side of the Houses of Parliament (▷ 179–180).

At the end of the complex of buildings you can see St. Stephen's Tower—make for this now. On your right you'll pass Westminster Abbey (▷ 194–195). When you come to the gardens on your left, enter and follow them to Lambeth Bridge. Turn left across the bridge, then left along the Thames path. Across the road to your right are Lambeth Palace and the Garden Museum (▷ 71).

❶ Since 1197 Lambeth Palace, a largely medieval complex of domestic buildings, has been the official residence of the archbishops of Canterbury. The medieval crypt and Great Hall, rebuilt in the 17th century, house the palace library (the first public library in England) and grand 19th-century reception rooms. The palace is open for pre-arranged tours only—you will need to apply in writing in advance.

Continue to the edge of Westminster Bridge by St. Thomas's Hospital, where you'll find the Florence Nightingale Museum (▷ 71). Cross the road and go down the steps to the former County Hall, now housing the London Aquarium (▷ 77). Unless you want to visit the aquarium, continue along the river path to the London Eye (▷ 75).

❷ Behind the wheel are the Jubilee Gardens, laid out in 1977 to commemorate Queen Elizabeth's silver jubilee. The former Shell Centre, behind them, has the largest clock facade in the world. *Jubilee Oracle*, the statue on the pavement by Alexander, was completed in 1980. Street performers are often here, entertaining passers-by.

With the river on your left, continue under Hungerford Bridge (officially

Left *The London Eye and County Hall seen from Westminster Bridge*

landmark of inner-city regeneration. The tower and the building opened to the public in 1996 as a mix of social housing, retail design studios, restaurants, cafés, bars, a gallery and an exhibition.

Back outside, pass the Sea Containers House and Doggets pub and go under Blackfriars Bridge, where subway murals tell the story of various historical designs for the bridge that were considered before the current version was accepted.

You'll see the Founders' Arms pub in front and then Tate Modern (▷ 80–81) to the right. Opposite Tate Modern, turn left over the Millennium Bridge (▷ 77) and continue straight ahead up Peter's Hill and up the steps to St. Paul's Cathedral (▷ 104–109). The Underground station is behind the cathedral, to your right.

WHEN TO GO
» Try to go early or late to see the sun rising or setting on the river.

WHERE TO EAT
There are places to go for a drink all along the river. Consider EAT, behind the Oxo Tower, the National Film Theatre café or the Gourmet Pizza Company at Gabriel's Wharf.

shows outside in Theatre Square. Notice the statue *London Pride*, by Frank Dobson (1886–1963), on the right. Street painters can sometimes be seen at work here, and on the left there is a guide to sights along the river on the North Bank.

Continue on the riverside path to Gabriel's Wharf on your right, where houses have been painted onto the former warehouse walls.

❹ Gabriel's Wharf is a lively collection of design workshops, restaurants and bars—a great place for unusual textiles, fashion, jewellery, ceramics and furnishings.

Continue past Bernie Spain Gardens and on to Oxo Tower Wharf.

❺ The Oxo Tower, former headquarters of the famous British stock-cube makers, is a witty 20th-century building with windows that spell out the word 'OXO'. It is a

the Golden Jubilee Bridge) and past the Royal Festival Hall and Festival Pier, where you could catch a boat along the river or to Westminster.

Continue under Waterloo Bridge, where there is often an open-air book market near the entrance to the National Film Theatre. Continue to the Royal National Theatre.

❸ In summer there are often live performances and stand-up comedy

AROUND SOUTHWARK

This section of the borough of Southwark covers a fascinating area just south of the Thames. It combines some interesting attractions and two lively markets with an authentic neighbourhood feel.

THE WALK

Distance: 5km (3 miles)
Time: 2 hours
Start at: Borough Underground station
End at: London Bridge Station

HOW TO GET THERE

🚇 Northern line to Borough
🚌 35, 40, 153, 343, C10

★ The attraction of this walk is that it takes you from the bustle of Borough to Southwark's scenic eastern riverfront. The route also affords a glimpse into the evolving neighbourhood of Bermondsey, which was actually quite a rural haven during the Middle Ages, dominated by an abbey; the advent of the railways and spillover from the docklands saw social conditions deteriorate during the 19th century. While some of the area away from the Thames remains staunchly working class, as you approach the river you will come across trendy flats and loft conversions.

From Borough Underground station turn left to cross Marshalsea Road and continue along Borough High Street. Turn left on to Southwark Street. The Menier Chocolate Factory is on the corner at 53 Southwark Street (▷ 87).

❶ The Menier Chocolate Factory, now housing a theatre and art gallery, was just one industrial building in this fascinating corner of the city. There are many old warehouses between here and Bermondsey Street, many now converted to chic living, but names such as Tanner Street and Leathermarket Street are clues to a working past.

Retrace your steps along Southwark Street and turn left on to Redcross Way and immediately right on to Park Street, which brings you to the Borough Market on the opposite side of Stoney Street.

❷ Borough Market (▷ 86) is the last remaining early morning wholesale fruit and vegetable market in central London, where traders are joined on Thursdays, Fridays and Saturdays by a variety of specialist food retailers. Expect to see stalls selling anything from French cheeses and Cumbrian wild boar meat to barbecued burgers and organic vegetables. The enclave has now been enhanced by a few gourmet restaurants and the odd trendy bar.

From Borough High Street turn right on to St. Thomas Street, then take the second right on to Weston Street, until Leathermarket Street, where you turn left. (At the far end of Leathermarket Street, the Fashion and Textile Museum is on the opposite side of Bermondsey Street at No. 83.)

❸ The Fashion and Textile Museum (▷ 71) was founded by renowned British designer Zandra Rhodes and occupies a building designed by Mexican architect Ricardo Legoretta. Situated in gentrified Bermondsey Village, the museum showcases constantly revolving exhibitions of cutting-edge fashion, textiles and jewellery.

Turn right from Leathermarket Street on to Bermondsey Street (or head south from the Fashion and Textile Museum if you have stopped for a visit) until it meets Long Lane, where you turn left. Bermondsey Antiques Market is on the right.

Left *The fish on sale at Borough Market is temptingly fresh*

❹ Bermondsey Antiques Market is a stalwart affair that operates on Friday only from 4am to 1pm. The serious traders have all done their business in the early hours before it opens, leaving tons of bric-a-brac for the average shopper to pore over later on. Confusingly, the place is sometimes still also referred to as the New Caledonian Market, as it has its roots in a pre-war flea market near the Caledonian Road in Islington.

Turn left on to Tower Bridge Road and then head north until Queen Elizabeth Street. Turn right on to that and left at the end on to Shad Thames. The Design Museum is at No. 28.

❺ The Design Museum (▷ 71) is located in a converted 1950s' warehouse and contains a growing permanent collection tracing developments in the design of items as diverse as cars, cameras and cabinets. There are also temporary exhibits on a range of themes related to all aspects of innovation in design.

From the river side of the Design Museum at the end of Shad Thames, turn left along the Thames Path, continuing underneath Tower Bridge. Turn left up Battle Bridge Lane and then right on to Tooley Street. London Bridge station is on the left.

❻ This section of the South Bank not only gives you a close-up view of the city's most iconic bridge, whose castle-like turrets rise above you as you admire them from below, but you will also pass in front of the lopsided beehive that is London's new City Hall, where the Mayor's offices are, and beside veteran battleship the HMS *Belfast* (▷ 72). As you approach London Bridge station on Tooley Street there are two more highly popular attractions; the absorbing Winston Churchill's Britain At War Experience (▷ 79) at Nos. 64–66 and the gruesomely entertaining and ever-popular London Dungeon (▷ 73) at Nos. 28–34.

PLACE TO VISIT
BERMONDSEY ANTIQUES MARKET
✉ 63 Bermondsey Street ☎ 020 7407 1096 🕑 Fri 4am–1pm

WHEN TO GO
The earlier you can set off on this walk the more of the genuine action you will catch at the two markets. For food buying and sampling, Borough Market is livelier at weekends, while Bermondsey Antiques Market only operates on Friday.

WHERE TO EAT AND DRINK
You're spoiled for choice at Borough Market. If you fancy a splurge, Roast in the Floral Hall at the market is a good choice, better if you've done the walk in reverse. Pubs along the way include quaint George Inn on Borough High Street and the Rose on Snowsfields.

SOUTH BANK • WALK

REGIONS

85

SHOPPING
BOROUGH MARKET
www.boroughmarket.org.uk
A wholesale fruit and vegetable market has operated here for many years, but there is now a very successful weekend international food market, with up to 70 stalls. It sells top-quality fish, meat, vegetables, cider, cheese, bread, coffee, cakes and patisseries to London's foodies and top chefs so you will be in good company.
✚ 95 M5 ✉ Borough High Street/Bedale Street/Stoney Street/Winchester Walk SE1 1TL ☎ 020 7407 1002 🕐 Thu 11–5, Fri 12–6, Sat 8–5 🚇 Borough, London Bridge 🚌 344, 381, RV1

FUNKI FRESH
www.funkifresh.co.uk
It's been a long road to this chic riverfront location for Funki Fresh from its 1997 beginnings at Portobello and Spitalfields markets. On offer are a range of fine ladies'

garments, all individually hand-made, from casual tops through evening attire to coats and hats.
✚ 94 K5 ✉ 13 Gabriel's Wharf, 56 Upper Ground SE1 9PP ☎ 020 7928 1100 🕐 Tue–Sat 11.30–6, Sun 12–6 🚇 Waterloo, Southwark 🚌 4, 26, 59, 68, 76, 168, 171, 188, 243, 341, 521

GANESHA
www.ganesha.co.uk
This delightful shop is at once fun and fair trade, importing high-quality home furnishings and accessories from co-operatives in India, Nepal and other locations. Items include baskets, bedding, cushions, leather bags, silk scarves, shawls and woolly hats. There is also a range of scented candles, incense and even Bollywood CDs.
✚ 94 K5 ✉ 3 Gabriel's Wharf, 56 Upper Ground SE1 9PP ☎ 020 7928 3444 🕐 Mon–Fri 11.30–6, Sat–Sun 12–6 🚇 Waterloo, Southwark 🚌 4, 26, 59, 68, 76, 168, 171, 188, 243, 341, 521

KONDITOR & COOK
www.konditorandcook.com
This little gem of a bakery, in a side street within wafting distance of Waterloo station, is simply cake heaven. The purple-liveried shop sells imaginative and wacky cakes and biscuits (using organic, free-range eggs), and you can glimpse them being made in the bakery behind. Its tiny size belies its reputation. There is also a branch at Borough Market.
✚ 94 K5 ✉ 22 Cornwell Road SE1 8TW ☎ 020 7261 0456 🕐 Mon–Fri 7.30–6.30, Sat 8.30–3 🚇 Waterloo, Southwark 🚇 Waterloo

ENTERTAINMENT AND NIGHTLIFE
AMERSHAM ARMS
www.amersham-arms.co.uk
The performance space at this popular New Cross pub is small enough for intimacy but big enough to generate a decent atmosphere. The wide range of entertainment here

includes Monday comedy nights, alternative gigs, ukelele evenings, discos and student events. The beer and snacks are not bad either.

✚ Off map 95 P8 ✉ 388 New Cross Road SE14 6TY ☎ 020 8469 1499 ⏰ Sun–Wed 12–12, Thu 12–late, Fri–Sat 10–late 🎫 Fri £3, free before 11pm; Sat £1, free before 11pm 🚌 21, 36, 136, 171, 177, 436, 453 🚇 New Cross Gate

BFI IMAX
www.bfi.org.uk
A 500-seat cinema in a space-age balloon, with the biggest film screen in Britain, showing exhilarating 2-D and 3-D movies.

✚ 94 K5 ✉ 1 Charlie Chaplin Walk, South Bank SE1 8XR ☎ 020 7199 6000 🚇 Embankment, Waterloo 🚌 68, 77, 171, 176, RV1 🎫

GLOBE, SHAKESPEARE'S
▷ 78.

INDIGO2
www.theo2.co.uk/indigo2
Although the Indigo2 is dwarfed by the neighbouring Arena, it is well designed and can hold up to 2,400 people. The club has hosted a diverse range of acts from rock legends like The Who to more eclectic performers such as Daniel Johnson.

✚ Off map 95 P6 ✉ The O2, Peninsula Square SE10 0DX ☎ 020 8463 2000, tickets 0844 856 0202 🚇 North Greenwich 🚌 108, 129, 132, 161, 188, 422, 472 ⛴ O2 Express link from Waterloo Pier

MASS NIGHTCLUB
www.mass-club.com
This popular club in buzzing Brixton consists of three rooms over two levels. Mass Club hosts events such as Ibiza Underground and the Torture Garden fetish night, while Babalou is the stage for emerging bands and has more ambient trance nights.

✚ Off map 94 L8 ✉ St. Matthew's Church, Brixton Hill SW2 1JF ☎ 020 7738 7875 ⏰ Fri 7.30–11, Sat 10–5 🎫 £5–£15 🚇 Brixton 🚌 45, 59, 109, 118, 133, 159, 250, 333

MENIER CHOCOLATE FACTORY
www.menierchocolatefactory.com
One of London's most exciting small theatres opened in 2004, in a factory building dating from 1870. There are just 150 seats, but the theatre punches way above its weight in talent—and they'll let you finish your dessert in the restaurant before they start the show.

✚ 96 M5 ✉ 53 Southwark Street SE1 1RU ☎ 020 7378 1712, tickets: 020 7907 7060 🎫 Around £33 🚇 London Bridge 🚌 381, RV1 🎫 🍴

MINISTRY OF SOUND
www.ministryofsound.com
Perhaps the most famous club in London, the Ministry is a huge place playing house music. Never mind the unfriendly bouncers, long queues and high admission price: just party.

✚ 94 L6 ✉ 103 Gaunt Street SE1 6DP ☎ 0870 060 0100 ⏰ Fri 10.30pm–6.30am, Sat 11pm–7am 🎫 £15–£25 🚇 Elephant & Castle 🚌 12, 188, 453, C10

NATIONAL FILM THEATRE (NFT)
www.bfi.org.uk
Part of the Southbank Centre (▷ 77), with two cinemas showing both British and international films. Focus of the London Film Festival (▷ 295).

✚ 94 K5 ✉ Southbank Centre, Belvedere Road SE1 8XT ☎ 020 7928 3232 ⏰ Daily 11–11 🎫 £5–£9 🚇 Embankment, Waterloo 🚌 1, 26, 68, 76, 77, 168, 171, 176, 188, RV1 🎫 📷

THE O2
www.theo2.co.uk
London's biggest arena, seating 20,000, shows the biggest pop concerts, from the likes of Elton John, Take That and Kylie Minogue. The former Millennium Dome also hosts major sporting events.

✚ Off map 95 P6 ✉ The O2, Peninsula Square SE10 0DX ☎ 020 8463 2000, tickets 0844 856 0202 🚇 North Greenwich 🚌 108, 129, 132, 161, 188, 422, 472 ⛴ O2 Express link from Waterloo Pier

OLD VIC
www.oldvictheatre.com
Historic building (1818) where Britain's National Theatre began before transferring to the South Bank in the 1970s, achieving great success under artistic director Kevin Spacey.

✚ 94 K6 ✉ The Cut, Waterloo Road SE1 8NB ☎ 0844 871628 🎫 £10–£50 🚇 Waterloo, Southwark 🚌 68, 168, 171, 176, RV1

Below Food stalls at Borough Market

PURCELL ROOM
www.southbankcentre.co.uk
Smallest of the three concert halls at the Southbank Centre (▷ 77). An intimate space for chamber music, accompanied singers, solo singers, musicians and more.
✚ 94 K5 ✉ Southbank Centre SE1 8XX ☎ 0844 875 0073 ✋ £10–£50 🚇 Embankment, Waterloo 🚌 68, 77, 171, RV1 ⛴ Festival Pier

QUEEN ELIZABETH HALL
www.southbankcentre.co.uk
The middle-sized of the three auditoriums at the Southbank Centre hosts small orchestral concerts, bands, small-scale opera and dance productions, and chamber music.
✚ 94 K5 ✉ Southbank Centre SE1 8XX ☎ 0844 875 0073 ✋ £10–£50 🚇 Embankment, Waterloo 🚌 68, 77, 171, RV1 ⛴ Festival Pier

ROYAL FESTIVAL HALL
www.southbankcentre.co.uk
Part of the Southbank Centre (▷ 77), the RFH has major classical music performances, with regular appearances by the Philharmonia and the London Philharmonic. There's also jazz, ballet and other genres.
✚ 94 K5 ✉ Southbank Centre SE1 8XX ☎ 0844 875 0037 ✋ £15–£40 🚇 Embankment, Waterloo 🚌 68, 77, 171, RV1 ⛴ Festival Pier

ROYAL NATIONAL THEATRE
www.nationaltheatre.org.uk
There are three auditoriums here: the Cottesloe, accommodating 300, with no fixed seats or staging; the 890-seat proscenium Lyttleton; and the Olivier (1,080), which is named after Sir Laurence Olivier, the National Theatre's first director.
✚ 94 K5 ✉ South Bank SE1 9PX ☎ 020 7452 3000 ✋ £10–£50 🚇 Waterloo 🚌 68, 77, 171, 176, RV1 🎭 🍴

THE VENUE
www.thevenuelondon.com
Once this was a stage for the then-unknown band Radiohead; now the live acts are almost exclusively tribute bands. The Venue actually comprises six separate spaces.

✚ Off map 95 P7 ✉ 2a Clifton Rise, New Cross SE14 6JP ☎ 020 8692 4077 🕐 Fri 9pm–4am, Sat 9pm–5am ✋ Fri £7, £1–£3 before midnight with flyer; Sat £12, £5 before 10pm with flyer 🚌 21, 36, 136, 171, 177, 436, 453 🚉 New Cross Gate

SPORTS AND ACTIVITIES
CRYSTAL PALACE NATIONAL SPORTS CENTRE
www.gll.org
A venue for major athletics events, where world-class competitors do battle in the summer. There is also a fitness centre, including a pool and climbing wall.
✚ Off map 94 J8 ✉ Ledrington Road, Crystal Palace SE19 2BB ☎ 020 8778 0131 🕐 Fitness centre Mon–Thu 7am–9.30pm, Fri 7am–9pm, Sat–Sun 9–5 🚌 63, 322 🚉 Crystal Palace

MILLWALL FOOTBALL CLUB
www.millwallfc.co.uk
Since moving to the 20,000 all-seater New Den in 1993, the club has cultivated a more family-oriented atmosphere and are currently going well in the Championship.
✚ Off map 95 P6 ✉ The New Den, Zampa Road, Bermondsey SE16 3LN ☎ 020 7232 1222 🚇 Surrey Quays 🚌 1, 21, 47, 53, 172, 188, 381, P12 🚉 New Cross, South Bermondsey

HEALTH AND BEAUTY
THE CLUB AND SPA AT COUNTY HALL
www.theclubandspaatcountyhall.com
Located on the south bank of the Thames between Westminster and the London Eye, this private club within the Marriott Hotel offers a 25m (82ft) pool, steam room, sauna, Jacuzzi, gym and beauty treatments.
✚ 94 K6 ✉ County Hall SE1 7PB ☎ 020 7928 4900 🕐 Mon–Wed 9–8, Thu–Fri 8am–9pm, Sat–Sun 10–6. Booking essential ✋ Day membership from £25 (as guest of member, or by separate negotiation) 🚇 Westminster, Waterloo 🚌 12, 53, 159, 211

SOUTH BANK CLUB
www.southbankclub.co.uk
This huge health and fitness club has a great gym, equipped with state-

of-the-art apparatus, where you can work out alone or in a class. There are also squash courts, sauna and steam facilities and a spa pool.
✚ Off map 94 J8 ✉ 124–130 Wandsworth Road SW8 2DL ☎ 020 7622 6866 🕐 Mon–Thu 6.30am–11pm, Fri 6.30am–9pm, Sat–Sun 8–8 ✋ Treatments from £30 🚇 Vauxhall 🚌 77, 87

FOR CHILDREN
ALL FIRED UP
www.allfiredupceramics.co.uk
This is a fun place to be creative and solve any gift or souvenir headaches at the same time. You can hand-paint a range of durable ceramics from plates to piggy banks at very reasonable prices and collect them a few days later. There's a nice café too.
✚ Off map 95 N8 ✉ 34 East Dulwich Road SE22 9AX ☎ 020 7732 6688 🕐 Mon–Wed, Fri, Sat 9.30–6, Thu 9.30am–10pm, Sun 11–5 ✋ Adult £4.50 paint/fire ceramic pieces, child (3–16) £3, under 3s free. Price for ceramics varies 🚌 12, 40, 63, 78, 176, 185, 484 🚉 East Dulwich 🚉

NAMCO STATION
www.namcostation.co.uk
There is action-packed interactive entertainment on three levels here. You'll find everything from tenpin bowling to dodgems and every kind of video game and simulator imaginable, including downhill skiing, skateboarding, Grand Prix racing, martial arts, jet-skiing, football and horse-racing.
✚ 94 K6 ✉ County Hall, Riverside Buildings, Westminster Bridge Road SE1 7PB ☎ 020 7967 1067 🕐 Daily 10am–12am ✋ Free entry 🚇 Waterloo, Westminster 🚌 77, RV1

TATE MODERN
www.tate.org.uk/families
Engaging Saturday workshops are organized for the over-fives, which regularly feature storytelling and poets. 'Start' runs on Saturdays and Sundays from 11am until 4pm (tel 020 7887 8888 for more information), with Tate-related games and puzzles (▷ 80–81).

ANCHOR BANKSIDE
TERRACE
FOR PATRONS USE ONLY
Users of Terrace do so at their own risk
No children allowed unless accompanied
by an adult.

PRICES AND SYMBOLS

The prices given are the average for a two-course set lunch (L) and a three-course à la carte dinner (D) for one person, without drinks. The wine price is for the least expensive bottle.

For a key to the symbols, ▷ 2.

BALTIC

www.balticrestaurant.co.uk
The Polish vodka bar is trendy, the restaurant even trendier. White walls, steel chairs and abstract paintings provide the setting for predominantly traditional Eastern European cuisine. You might start with *kopytka* (potato dumplings) with tomato sauce, and follow with a leek and wild mushroom risotto made from *kasza*, a type of barley with a nutty taste. Jazz every Sunday at 7pm.
✚ 94 L6 ✉ 74 Blackfriars Road SE1 8HA ☎ 020 7928 1111 ◷ Daily 12–3, 6–11. Closed 25–26 Dec, 1 Jan, public hols ✋ L from £14.50, D from £30, Wine £16.50 (carafe £13.50) ⊕ Southwark

BLUEPRINT CAFÉ

www.danddlondon.com
A bustling, stylish restaurant in the Design Museum (▷ 71) with unrivalled views over the River Thames to Tower Bridge and the City. The decor is sophisticated and simple, as is the menu, which changes daily. Modern European dishes are presented in a straightforward manner—for example, baked pork with mustard and parsley crust. A splendid place for summer dining.
✚ 95 P6 ✉ The Design Museum, 28 Shad Thames SE1 2YD ☎ 020 7378 7031 ◷ Mon–Sat 12–3, 6–11, Sun 12–4. Closed 25–28 Dec, 1 Jan ✋ L £15, D from £32, Wine £19 ⊕ Tower Hill, London Bridge

CANTINA DEL PONTE

www.danddlondon.com
Lots of lusty Italian flavours are to be savoured at this modern riverside location. Apart from the tasty pizzas and pastas, there are traditional delights such as veal

Milanese and excellent seafood. The outdoor seating has a huge canopy and patio heaters.
✚ 95 P5 ✉ The Butler's Wharf Building, 36c Shad Thames SE1 2YE ☎ 020 7403 5403 ◷ Mon–Sat 12–3, 6–11, Sun 6–10 ✋ L £10.95, D £32, Wine £15 ⊕ Tower Hill, London Bridge 🚌 47, 188, 381, C10

CANTINA VINOPOLIS

www.cantinavinopolis.com
This vivacious, wine-themed restaurant with understated furnishings, bare brick walls, terracotta floor tiles and high ceilings is just a few minutes' walk from the Thames and has a relaxed, brasserie style. Simple dishes with a strong Mediterranean influence are prepared in the open-view kitchen, and might include spiced grilled squid with tomatoes, chorizo and olive salsa, or succulent lamb rump with

Above Enjoy good views of the river and St. Paul's from the Anchor (▷ 91)

89

dauphinoise potatoes. There's an extensive and inspiring international wine list and a huge choice available by the glass.

✛ 95 M5 ✉ 1 Bank End SE1 9BU
☎ 020 7940 8333 🕓 Mon–Sat 12–3, 6–10.30, Sun 12–4. Closed 25–26 Dec, 1 Jan
✋ L £25.95, D £33.50, Wine £20
🚇 London Bridge

CHAMPOR-CHAMPOR
www.champor-champor.com
This is a small, wonderfully bohemian, southeast Asian restaurant in the Borough district. The name, which can be roughly translated from Malay as 'mix and match', is the key to the menu, which reflects Asian cuisines with roots in Malaysia plus a taste of the exotic. A two-course, fixed-price meal might include poached king prawns in Chinese rice wine followed by boneless quail, botok-botok, coconut rice and lemon grass gravy.

✛ 95 N6 ✉ 62–64 Weston Street SE1 3QJ ☎ 020 7403 4600 🕓 Mon–Sat 6.15–10.15. Closed Sun, Easter, 24 Dec–2 Jan, public hols ✋ D £33, Wine £15
🚇 London Bridge

Below *The Oxo Tower Restaurant offers great food in an enviable location*

MAGDALEN
www.magdalenrestaurant.co.uk
The food here is basically British with European, especially French, influences, served in a warmly decorated, two-storey restaurant. Starters such as potted Devon crab can be followed by treats like roast pheasant with braised red cabbage, bacon and chestnuts. Round it all off with a sticky rum baba.

✛ 95 N5 ✉ 152 Tooley Street SE1 2TU ☎ 020 7403 1342 🕓 Mon–Fri 12–2.30, 6.30–10.30, Sat 6.30–10.30 ✋ L £15.50, D £34, Wine £20 🚇 London Bridge 🚌 47, 48, 149, 381, 512, RV1

THE OXO TOWER RESTAURANT
www.harveynichols.co.uk
With its amazing views through floor-to-ceiling windows overlooking the River Thames and the City, this cubed tower tends to impress all those who visit. Cuisine is modern European with elements of fusion; typical dishes on offer could be salt cod pasties with fiery harissa emulsion and a fennel salad, or rabbit pie with Earl Grey prunes and pickled carrots. Desserts might include wild strawberry soufflé with milk ice cream.

✛ 94 L5 ✉ 8th Floor, Oxo Tower Wharf, Barge House Street SE1 9PH ☎ 020 7803 3888 🕓 Mon–Sat 12–2.30, 6–11, Sun 12–3,

6.30–10. Closed 25–26 Dec ✋ L £26, D £45, Wine £22.50 🚇 Blackfriars

LE PONT DE LA TOUR
www.lepontdelatour.co.uk
This modern riverside establishment, set in a revitalized wharf, offers splendid views of Tower Bridge. The elegant and upmarket French menu includes delights such as oysters grilled with spinach, bacon and a parmesan crust, and Label Anglais chicken with braised cabbage and morel sauce. There's an impressive wine list too.

✛ 95 P5 ✉ The Butler's Wharf Building, 36d Shad Thames SE1 2YE ☎ 020 7403 8403 🕓 Mon–Sat 12–3, 6–11, Sun 6–10
✋ L £27.50, D £44.50 (set 3 courses), Wine £30 🚇 Tower Hill, London Bridge 🚌 47, 188, 381, C10

RSJ
www.rsj.uk.com
RSJ is set a block back from the river but is very handily placed for the South Bank theatre scene and convenient to Waterloo station. The modern British food is top quality and excellent value (particularly the fixed-price dinner menu) and the charming, simple, modern and informal surroundings are very relaxing. Expect the likes of roast rump of lamb with French beans,

spinach, dauphinoise potatoes and red wine sauce.

🏛 94 K5 ✉ 33 Coin Street SE1 9NR ☎ 020 7928 4554 🕐 Mon–Fri 12–2.30, 5.30–11, Sat 5.30–11. Closed Christmas, 1 Jan 🍴 L £16.95, D £33, Wine £16.95 🚇 Waterloo

TAS

www.tasrestaurant.com

This busy Turkish restaurant offers good hearty food in a wood-framed environment. Meats are barbecued and stewed with spices, and vegetarians are well catered for, with dishes such as *bamya* (okra with potatoes, onions, tomatoes and herbs, served with couscous and yogurt). Save room for desserts such as baklava. There is also a branch on Borough High Street.

🏛 94 L6 ✉ 33 The Cut, Waterloo SE1 8LF ☎ 020 7928 1444 🕐 Mon–Sat 12–11.30, Sun 12–10.30 🍴 L (set menu) £6.95, D £20, Wine £13.40 🚇 Southwark

ZUCCA

www.zuccalondon.com

This popular new restaurant has caused quite a stir. The food is imaginative modern Italian, with big flavours in starters such as sardines and gremolata, and mains including braised ox cheek and polenta, or sea bass served with porcini mushrooms and salsa verde. Watch the food being prepared in the open-plan kitchen, from the cool comfort of the shiny white furnishings out front.

🏛 95 N6 ✉ 184 Bermondsey Street SE1 3TQ ☎ 020 7378 6809 🕐 Tue–Sat 12.30–3, 6.30–10, Sun 12.30–3 🍴 L £19, D £24, Wine £18 🚇 London Bridge

PUBS

THE ANCHOR

This historic pub lies in the shadow of Shakespeare's Globe (▷ 78). Diarist Samuel Pepys supposedly watched the Great Fire of London from here in 1666, and regulars over the years have included writer Oliver Goldsmith and painter Sir Joshua Reynolds. There are excellent river views, black beams, faded plasterwork and a maze of tiny rooms. A varied menu includes scallops and

smoked haddock linguine, and chocolate pudding. Garden and patio overlooking the River Thames.

🏛 95 M5 ✉ Bankside, 34 Park Street SE1 9EF ☎ 020 7407 1577 🕐 Mon–Sat 11–11, Sun 12–10.30. Restaurant: Mon–Sat 12–2.30, 5.30–10, Sun 12–9.30 🍴 Bar meals from £6, D from £19 🚇 London Bridge, Mansion House

THE ANCHOR & HOPE

With two rosettes for its excellent food, good Eagle IPA beer and a family-friendly policy, this award-winning gastropub manages to appeal to most tastes without diluting its strengths. For sunny days there's a garden and street-seating. It is convenient for Waterloo station and the South Bank. Groups will also appreciate its innovative policy of pricing selected main courses for up to six diners (such as rib of beef, chips and Béarnaise sauce).

🏛 94 L6 ✉ 36 The Cut SE1 8LP ☎ 020 7928 9898 🕐 Tue–Sun 12–11, Mon 5–11. Restaurant Tue–Sat 12–2.30, 6–10.30, Sun 12.30–5, Mon 6–10.30 🍴 Bar meals from £16, D from £18.50 🚇 Waterloo, Southwark

THE FIRE STATION

www.thefirestationwaterloo.com

An early Edwardian fire station is the unusual setting for this popular gastropub, handy for Waterloo station, the Old Vic theatre and the Imperial War Museum. The menu includes the likes of ham and pea risotto, or perhaps a vegetable curry with rice. Also open for tasty breakfasts.

🏛 94 K6 ✉ 150 Waterloo Road SE1 8SB ☎ 020 7620 2226 🕐 Mon 11–11, Tue–Thu 9am–12am, Fri–Sat 9am–1am, Sun 11–10.30 🍴 Bar meals from £8.50 🚇 Waterloo 🚆 Waterloo

FOUNDERS ARMS

www.foundersarms.co.uk

This modern Youngs pub has a trendily designed interior and offers tasty bar food such as beer-battered fish and chips, steak and ale pie and pastas, salads and sandwiches. However, the real attraction is the riverside patio, where you can watch

a Waterloo sunset (blankets and hot water bottles are offered to intrepid customers in winter).

🏛 94 L5 ✉ 52 Hopton Street, Bankside SE1 9JH ☎ 020 7928 1899 🕐 Mon–Thu 10am–11pm, Fri 10am–12am, Sat 9am–12am, Sun 9am–11pm; food served until 10pm 🍴 Bar meals from £7.50 🚇 Southwark 🚌 45, 63, RV1

THE GEORGE INN

This 17th-century coaching inn is now owned by the National Trust. It has a lovely courtyard and fading plasterwork, black beams and a warren of tiny rooms inside. Food is along the tried and trusty lines of steak, ale and Guinness pie and traditional fish and chips, and they also serve some decent real ales (beers made in the barrel by the traditional method).

🏛 95 M5 ✉ 77 Borough High Street SE1 1NH ☎ 020 7407 2056 🕐 Mon–Sat 11–11, Sun 12–10.30. Meals: Mon–Sat 12–9, Sun 12–5. Closed 25 Dec 🍴 Bar meals from £5.50, D from £20 🚇 London Bridge

KINGS ARMS

A hidden gem of a pub, tucked away in a lovely residential street only a few minutes' walk from Waterloo. There is a pleasant, down-to-earth atmosphere and a good range of real ales and lagers, as well as quality Thai food.

🏛 94 K5 ✉ 25 Roupell Street, Waterloo SE1 8TP ☎ 020 7207 0784 🕐 Mon–Sat 11–11, Sun 12–10.30; food served Mon–Fri 12–3, 6–10.30, Sun 12–4 🍴 Meals from £8 🚇 Southwark, Waterloo 🚌 4, 26, 68, 139, 171, 176, 243, 381

THE ROYAL OAK

This lovely Victorian pub stands in the heart of Borough and attracts many locals as well as City workers. The fine pub grub includes the likes of rabbit casserole, quality meat pies and proper Sunday roasts, which can all be accompanied by real ales or a range of fine wines.

🏛 95 M6 ✉ 44 Tabard Street SE1 4JU ☎ 020 7357 7173 🕐 Mon–Sat 11am–11.30pm, Sun 12–6 🍴 Bar meals from £6 🚇 Borough 🚌 21, 35, 40, 133, 343, 344, 381

PRICES AND SYMBOLS

The prices given are the lowest and highest for a double room for one night, unless otherwise stated. Breakfast is not usually included. All the hotels listed accept credit cards unless otherwise stated. Note that rates can vary widely throughout the year.

For a key to the symbols, ▷ 2.

ALL SEASONS LONDON SOUTHWARK ROSE

www.all-seasons-hotels.com
Very conveniently located for all the South Bank attractions, this modern hotel offers comfortable rooms at reasonable rates, as well as six spacious family rooms. All rooms have 32in flat-screen TVs and complementary WiFi. The stylish restaurant offers hearty British fare.
✚ 95 M5 ✉ 43–47 Southwark Bridge Road SE1 9HH ☎ 020 7015 1480 ⑭ £95–£300 ① 84 🛇 🚾 🚹 🚊 London Bridge 🚌 344, 381, RV1

CANNIZARO HOUSE

www.cannizarohouse.com
Once frequented only by London's elite, this extremely elegant 18th-century mansion stands amid beautifully landscaped grounds in

peaceful Wimbledon. Fine paintings, murals and fireplaces feature throughout the building and each room is furnished separately with the utmost attention to detail. The restaurant serves quality, largely organic produce.
✚ Off map 94 J8 ✉ West Side, Wimbledon Common SW19 4UE ☎ 020 8879 1464 ⑭ £145–£585 ① 46 🚊 Wimbledon 🚌 93, 200

DAYS HOTEL WATERLOO

www.hotelwaterloo.com
Conveniently located opposite the Imperial War Museum and within a short walk of Waterloo station, this modern budget hotel offers great value for money. Bedrooms are stylish and spacious. It has a bar, and the restaurant is open for breakfast and dinner.
✚ 94 K7 ✉ 54 Kennington Road SE1 7BJ ☎ 020 7922 1331 ⑭ £69–£169 ① 162 (15 family) 🚊 Lambeth North 🚌 59, 159, 148 🚇 Waterloo

DEVONPORT HOUSE

www.devere.co.uk
Set in the leafy grounds of the Maritime Museum, there are few more imposing buildings to stay in

than this World Heritage Site. The rooms have all been modernized tastefully to ensure comfort while maintaining character, and there are 22 meeting and training rooms. The restaurant is highly recommended.
✚ Off map 95 P8 ✉ King William Walk, Greenwich SE10 9JW ☎ 0844 980 2304 ⑭ £60–£200 ① 94 🚊 Cutty Sark 🚌 129, 177, 180, 188, 199, 266, 386 ⛴ Greenwich Pier

EXPRESS BY HOLIDAY INN

www.exhisouthwark.co.uk
In this good-value modern hotel, suitable for both families and business travellers, the rooms are simple but spacious, with Sky TV and power showers. Only the complimentary breakfast is served but there are several pubs and restaurants nearby.
✚ 94 L5 ✉ 103–109 Southwark Street SE1 0JQ ☎ 020 7401 2525 ⑭ £79–£225 ① 88 🚊 Southwark, London Bridge 🚌 344, 381, RV1

H10 LONDON WATERLOO HOTEL

www.hotelh10londonwaterloo.com
This hotel conveniently close to Waterloo station and the South Bank

Left The stylish entrance lobby at the London Bridge Hotel

is modern and stylish, with its own restaurant. The gym and spa on the eighth floor offer great views over the city.

➕ 95 L6 ✉ 284–302 Waterloo Road SE1 8RQ ☎ 020 7928 4062 👜 £135–£255 ⓘ 176 📺 🚇 Lambeth North, Waterloo 🚉 Waterloo

IBIS HOTEL GREENWICH
www.ibishotel.com

This modern hotel offers comfortable accommodation in bright and practical rooms. There's a self-service breakfast buffet and dinner is also available. It's only minutes from the Royal Observatory, the vast park and the heart of trendy Greenwich.

➕ Off map 95 P8 ✉ 30 Stockwell Street, Greenwich SE10 9JN ☎ 020 8305 1177 👜 £75–£150 ⓘ 82 🚇 Cutty Sark 🚌 129, 177, 180, 188, 199, 266, 386 🚢 Greenwich Pier

LONDON BRIDGE HOTEL
www.londonbridgehotel.com

The elegant, independently owned hotel enjoys a prime location on the edge of the City, next to London Bridge railway station. Bedrooms include a number of spacious deluxe rooms and suites. The public areas are small yet sophisticated. The popular Londinium restaurant offers modern British food in a colonial setting and the stylish contemporary Borough bar is a good place for drinks and casual dining. There's a well-equipped gym on site.

➕ 95 M5 ✉ 8–18 London Bridge Street SE1 9SG ☎ 020 7855 2200 👜 £105–£320 ⓘ 138 🚇 📺 🚉 London Bridge 🚌 47, 343, RV1

LONDON MARRIOTT HOTEL COUNTY HALL
www.marriott.co.uk

A luxury hotel in an enviable position, this occupies the riverside building that formerly housed the Greater London Council, the city's governing body. Bedrooms have excellent facilities and enjoy superb London views. Public areas include

the library lounge and a crescent-shaped restaurant overlooking Westminster, which serves a range of contemporary cuisine. Residents here have access to the extensive spa and health complex (▷ 88).

➕ 94 K6 ✉ Westminster Bridge Road, County Hall SE1 7PB ☎ 020 7928 5200 👜 £205–£1,150 ⓘ 200 🚇 ♨ Indoor 📺 🚇 Westminster, Waterloo 🚌 12, 77, 148, RV1

MAD HATTER HOTEL
www.fullershotels.com

An attractive hotel, the Mad Hatter has maintained the 19th-century facade of a former millinery factory. The stylish theme of the exterior is continued inside, with all the rooms decked out in lavish period furnishings. Unsurprisingly, as it is owned by the renowned west London brewery Fullers, there is an attached pub serving excellent beer and bar food.

➕ 94 L5 ✉ 3–7 Stamford Street SE1 9NY ☎ 020 7401 9222 👜 £125–£180 ⓘ 30 🚇 Waterloo, Southwark 🚌 45, 63, RV1

NOVOTEL LONDON CITY SOUTH
www.novotel.com

One of the Novotel chain's new generation, this location has a contemporary design, with smart, modern bedrooms and spacious public areas. Guests can relax in the sauna and steam room or work up a sweat in the gym.

➕ 95 M5 ✉ 53–61 Southwark Bridge Road SE1 9HH ☎ 020 7089 0400 👜 £119–£295 ⓘ 182 📺 🚇 Southwark, London Bridge 🚌 344, 381, RV1

PARK PLAZA RIVERBANK
www.parkplaza.com

The uber-cool Plaza Riverbank is located just south of Lambeth Bridge, and makes for a stylish and extremely comfortable place to stay, with views across the Thames to London's best-loved landmarks. WiFi and flat-screen TVs are standard, and there are power sockets to take EU and US plugs. The Chino-Latino brasserie serves Pan-Asian food.

➕ 94 J7 ✉ 18 Albert Embankment SE1 7TJ ☎ 020 7958 8000 👜 £159–£224 ⓘ 394 🚇 📺 🚇 Westminster, Vauxhall

PREMIER INN LONDON COUNTY HALL
www.premierinn.com

The rooms here are simple but functional, neatly designed and quite comfortable. All have their own bathrooms and will accommodate up to two adults and two children (under 15) So, if all you really want is a bed for the night in the heart of central London (right next to the London Eye and opposite the Houses of Parliament, though sadly with no views in this direction) then you can't beat the value/location equation that this chain hotel offers. It occupies the modern part of the old County Hall, which was formerly the headquarters of the Greater London Council.

➕ 94 K6 ✉ County Hall, Belvedere Road SE1 7PB ☎ 0871 527 8648 👜 £90–£180 ⓘ 313 🚇 Waterloo, Westminster 🚌 12, 77, 148, RV1

YHA LONDON THAMESIDE
www.yha.org.uk

This modern, purpose-built youth hostel offers good basic accommodation at very affordable prices, especially for families sharing. It is convenient for the Thames Path. All rooms have private bathrooms, and the hostel has its own café and restaurant. Continental breakfast is included in the rate. For YHA membership ▷ 298.

➕ Off map 95 P6 ✉ 20 Salter Road SE16 5PR ☎ 0845 371 9756 👜 From £18.65 per person ⓘ 70 🚇 Rotherhithe, Canada Water 🚌 381, C10

Below A room at the London Bridge Hotel

Map: South Bank — Eating and Staying

Thames

Grid markers: 4, 5, 6, 7 (left margin); J, K, L (bottom)

Streets, landmarks and places:

- New Oxford St, Whetstone, Lincoln's Inn Fields, Sir John Soane's Museum, Royal College of Surgeons, Lincoln's Inn
- London Silver Vaults, Norwich St, Cursitor St, Bream's Buildings, New Fetter Lane, Holborn Viaduct, St Bartholomew's Hospital
- Newgate Street, King Edward St, Stock Exchange, St Paul's
- HIGH HOLBORN, KINGSWAY, Oasis Sports Centre, Drury Lane, Covent Garden, Royal Opera House, St Paul's Church, The Piazza, London Transport Museum
- Old Curiosity Shop, London School of Economics & Political Science, Royal Courts of Justice (Law Courts), Maughan Library, Dr Johnson's House, Bridewell Church, Ludgate Circus, Old Bailey Central Criminal Court, St Paul's Churchyard, College of Arms
- STRAND, Aldwych, Bush House, Australia House (BBC), India House, St Mary-le-Strand, Roman Bath, King's College, Courtauld Institute of Art, Hermitage Rooms, Somerset House
- FLEET STREET, Temple Church, Inns of Court, Middle Temple, Inner Temple, Temple
- Royal Society of Arts, Proud Galleries, Savoy, Cleopatra's Needle, Embankment
- Blackfriars Station, Blackfriars Bridge, Queen Victoria Street, City of London School
- VICTORIA EMBANKMENT, HQS Wellington (Master Mariners), HMS President, Blackfriars Millennium Pier, Blackfriars Pier, Millennium Bridge, Panorama Pier
- Charing Cross Station, Golden Jubilee Bridges, Festival Pier, Queen Elizabeth Hall, Southbank Centre, Royal Festival Hall, Hayward Gallery, National Film Theatre, National Theatre, The London Television Centre, Gabriel's Wharf
- **The Oxo Tower Restaurant**, **Founders Arms**, Bankside Gallery, Purdy Hicks Gallery, **Tate Modern**, Shakespeare's
- DEFRA, Old War Office, Hispaniola, BFI London IMAX Cinema, King's College London, Schiller University, London Nautical School
- **Mad Hatter Hotel**, **Express by Holiday Inn**, SOUTHWARK, **RSJ**, **Kings Arms**, STAMFORD, Burrell Street
- Waterloo East Station, **The Anchor & Hope**, **Baltic**, **The Tas**, Southwark College, Union Street, Copperfield Street, London Fire Brigade Museum
- London Eye, Millennium Pier, Jubilee Gardens, Shell Centre, County Hall, **Premier Inn London County Hall**, **London Marriott County Hall**, SEA LIFE London Aquarium, **The Fire Station**
- Westminster Bridge, Big Ben, Palace of Westminster, Houses of Parliament, Cenotaph, Government Offices, Derby Gate, Portcullis House, Banqueting House, Ministry of Defence, Richmond Terrace, Horse Guards Avenue
- WATERLOO STATION, Waterloo Road, Westminster Bridge Road, Florence Nightingale Museum, St Thomas' Hospital, Lambeth North
- **H10 London Waterloo Hotel**, St George's Circus, ST GEORGE'S CIRCUS, St George's Cathedral, BOROUGH, South Bank University
- LAMBETH, Archbishop's Park, Lambeth Palace, Garden Museum, **Park Plaza Riverbank**, **Days Hotel Waterloo**, Imperial War Museum, Geraldine Mary Harmsworth Park
- NEWINGTON, London College of Communication, Elephant & Castle Shopping Centre, ELEPHANT & CASTLE STATION, Metropolitan Tabernacle, Newington Court Business Centre
- Jewel Tower, Victoria Tower Gardens, St John's Concert Hall, Thames House, Millbank Tower, Tate Britain, Millbank Millennium Pier, Lambeth Bridge
- VAUXHALL, Albert Embankment

Cannizaro House ↓

Clockmaker Museum
Guildhall
St Margaret's Lothbury
St Lawrence Jewry Church
Coleman Street
Moorgate
Great Winchester Street
WORMWOOD STREET
CAMOMILE STREET
A1211
Devonshire Square
HOUNDSDITCH
BEVIS MARKS
Cutler Street
University
Whitechapel Gallery
Goulston Street
Aldgate East
WHITECHAPEL HIGH STREET
WHITE CHURCH
Adler Street
A11
B134

Tower 42
St Helen's Place
St Helen's
ALDGATE BUS STATION
Aldgate High
ST BOTOLPH STREET
Aldgate High
A13
Graham Street

CITY
Temple of Mithras
Bank of England & Museum
Royal Exchange
Mansion House
30 St Mary Axe (The Gherkin)
London Met University
MINORIES
A1211
A1210
MANSELL STREET
LEMAN STREET
ALIE STREET
West Tenter Street
East Tenter Street
Scarborough Street
South Tenter Street
PRESCOT STREET

St Stephen Walbrook Church
St Mary Abchurch
Cornhill
Lombard Street
Leadenhall
Lloyd's
Leadenhall Market
Fenchurch Avenue
Carlisle Avenue
Vine Street
Crosswall
GOODMAN'S YARD
Chamber Street

CANNON STREET STATION
Monument
FENCHURCH STREET STATION
Mark Lane
Seething Lane
Crutched Friars
Pepys Street
Cooper's Row
Tower Gateway
TOWER HILL A100
A1211 SHORTER STREET
A1202 ROYAL MINT STREET
Cartwright Street
Ensign Street
DOCK STREET
B126

LOWER THAMES STREET
All Hallows-by-the-Tower
Custom House
Tower Hill
Trinity House
Tower Hill
Royal Mint Court
ST GEORGE IN THE EAST
SMITHFIELD
Thomas More Street

SOUTHWARK BRIDGE
London Bridge Sports Centre
Fishmonger's Hall
Swan Lane Pier
LONDON BRIDGE
Tower Stairs
Tower of London
Tower Millennium Pier
RNLI Lifeboat Station
Thames
BYWARD STREET
London Commodity Exchange
West Dock
St Katharine Docks
East Dock
Nesham St
Mews Path

Financial Times
The Anchor
Clink Prison Museum
Golden Hinde
London Bridge Hospital
London and City Pier
Thames Path
HMS Belfast
Hay's Galleria
St Katharine's Way
Tower Bridge
St Katharine Pier

Cantina Vinopolis
All Seasons London Southwark Rose
Southwark Cathedral
Borough Market
London Bridge Hotel
London Dungeon
Southwark Crown Court
The Scoop
Butler's Wharf Pier

Novotel London City South
DUKE STREET HILL
Battle Bridge Lane
Greater London Authority Headquarters (City Hall)
Cantina del Ponte, Le Pont de la Tour
Shad Thames

The George Inn
Guy's Hospital
Magdalen
Shad Thames
Gainsford
Blueprint Café
Design Museum

Kings College London
Champor-Champor
Snowsfields
CRUCIFIX LANE
DRUID
London City Mission
St Saviour's Dock
Bermondsey Wall
West Providence Square
Jacob Street
John Felton Road

THE BOROUGH
The Royal Oak
A2198
Porlock Street
Leathermarket Gardens
Kipling Street
Tyers Gate
Fashion & Textile Museum
Brunswick Court
JAMAICA
Dockhead
Wolseley Street
George Row

Leathermarket Street
Zucca
Lamb Walk
Tanner Street
TANNER STREET
Millstream
JAMAICA ROAD

LONG LANE
Morocco St
YHA London Thameside

Tabard Garden
Clumy Place
Purbrook Street
ABBEY
Maltby Street
GRANGE WALK
B202
Enid
Spa

Henrywood Hall
A2
GREAT DOVER STREET
Tabard Street
TOWER BRIDGE ROAD
A2206
GRANGE ROAD
Grange Yard
SOUTHWARK PARK ROAD
A2206

KENT ROAD
A2
NEW KENT ROAD
A100
TOWER BRIDGE ROAD
OLD KENT ROAD
B203
MANDELA WAY
Willow Walk

M
N
Devonport House, Ibis Hotel Greenwich
P

0   400 m
0   400 yds

95

ENTRY TO THE TRAITORS' GATE

HOXTON

BETHNAL
GREEN

SHOREDITCH

ST LUKE'S

CLERKENWELL

SPITALFIELDS

**Museum of
London**

**St Paul's
Cathedral**

CITY

WHITECHAPEL

**Tower of
London**

**Tower
Bridge**

CITY AND THE EAST END

Nestling on the north bank of the Thames, the densely built-up area between the erstwhile home of the newspaper industry in Fleet Street and the hallowed turrets of the Tower of London encompasses some of the capital's oldest structures. It has at its core the traditional economic heart that is the City of London. Although the bowler hats are a thing of the past, there is still a palpable sense of purpose in the stride of the current generation of wheelers and dealers as they dart to and fro from their lairs in the tightly packed banks and other financial institutions. There might not be the mass of soaring skyscrapers as in Manhattan, but some of London's narrowest alleys run in maze-like fashion between these hives of money-making activity and, of the few high-rise buildings that do exist, the iconic post-millennial edifice at 30 St. Mary Axe has become affectionately known as the Gherkin because of its shape.

It's not all about business, though. The City has a soul too, exemplified in most dramatic fashion by the heaven-piercing dome of St. Paul's Cathedral, one of the world's great places of worship. At the far west end of Fleet Street, Britain's moral code is personified in the gilt statue of Justice that stands atop the Old Bailey criminal court. Justice of a more summary nature used to be meted out to traitors at the Tower of London, of course, usually in the form of an axe and chopping block. Another structure of historical note is the stone column known simply as the Monument, which marks the spot where the Great Fire started in 1666, while just north of the Tower and near the Barbican Centre you can see some of the best remains of the original Roman city walls.

CITY AND THE EAST END • SIGHTS MAP

400 m
400 yds

PENTONVILLE

SHOREDITCH

CLERKENWELL

ST LUKE'S

FINSBURY SQUARE

HOLBORN

CITY

Order of St John

Barts & The London School of Medicine & Dentistry

The Barbican

Museum of London

Guildhall School of Music & Drama

Central London Markets (Smithfield)

St Bartholomew's The Great

St Bartholomew's Hospital

Clockmaker Museum

Guildhall

Bank of England & Museum

Royal Exchange

Old Bailey (Central Criminal Court)

Stock Exchange

St Paul's Cathedral

One New Change Shopping Centre

No 1 Poultry Shopping Centre

Mansion House

Dr Johnson's House

Bridewell Church

Temple Church

College of Arms

Temple of Mithras

St Stephen Walbrook Church

St Mary Abchurch

Royal Courts of Justice (Law Courts)

Royal College of Surgeons

Lincoln's Inn

Maughan Library

Middle Temple

Inner Temple

Monument

HMS President

Blackfriars Millennium Pier

Blackfriars Pier

City of London School

HQS Wellington (Master Mariners)

Victoria Embankment

London Bridge Sports Centre

Swan Lane Pier

Thames

Hayward Gallery

National Film Theatre

Royal National Theatre

BFI London IMAX Cinema

The London Television Centre

National Nautical School

London College London

Purdy Hicks Gallery

Tate Modern

Shakespeare's Globe

Financial Times

Rose Theatre Exhibition

Golden Hinde

Clink Prison Museum

Southwark Cathedral

London Bridge Hospital

Guy's Hospital

Kings College London

Wesley's Chapel, House & Museum

Armoury House

Moorfields Eye Hospital

Old Street Station

Finsbury Leisure Centre

Ironmonger Row Baths

City University

London Weather Centre

London Silver Vaults

BANK OF ENGLAND MUSEUM

www.bankofengland.co.uk/museum
The Old Lady of Threadneedle Street, the nation's central bank, occupies a massive, undistinguished, seven-storey office building designed and erected by English architect Sir Herbert Baker between 1925 and 1939. Sculptures on its facade of Britannia are by sculptor Sir Charles Wheeler (1892–1974), and inside there's a museum (entrance on Bartholomew Lane) tracing the history of the nation's finances from the bank's foundation in 1694 to today's hi-tech environment. On display are a faithful restoration of the 1790s' bank stock office, a late 18th-century banking hall by Sir John Soane (▷ 148–149) and chronological displays of minted coins, bank notes, gold bars from ancient times to the modern market bar, plus unexpected items such as pikes and muskets used to defend the bank. There are also documents relating to such famous customers as Horatio Nelson and George Washington.

Interactive displays reveal the intricacies of bank note design and production. A computerized simulation allows you to play at wheeling and dealing on the stock market. You also get the unusual chance to lift a genuine gold bar. Don't miss the £1-million note, used for accounting purposes only.

➕ 98 M4 ✉ Bank of England, Threadneedle Street EC2R 8AH, entrance on Bartholomew Lane ☎ 020 7601 5545 ⏰ Mon–Fri 10–5 ✋ Free 🚇 Bank 🚌 8, 11, 25, 26, 47 ♿

THE BARBICAN

www.barbican.org.uk
This area of the city was once a maze of small streets and warehouses, before its devastation by bombs in December 1940. Today's Barbican complex, 14ha (35 acres) of concrete buildings, was built over the site between 1971 and 1982. It

incorporates flats, an arts centre and premises for the Guildhall School of Music and Drama. At its heart is the D-shaped arts centre, Europe's largest multi-arts and conference venue and home of the London Symphony Orchestra. A wide range of innovative exhibitions of 20th-century and current art and design is staged in the gallery on Level 3 and in The Curve (ground floor). There's also a lively programme of jazz, classical, contemporary and world music, and two cinemas showing independent, art-house and mainstream films. Stage productions take place in the Barbican Theatre or the smaller Pit.

➕ 98 M3 ✉ Silk Street EC2Y 8DS ☎ 020 7638 4141; 020 7638 8891 (box office) ⏰ Mon–Sat 8am–11pm, Sun 11–11. Box office Mon–Sat 9–8, Sun 11–8 ✋ Free; separate charges for productions and exhibitions in Level 3 gallery, and for walking tours Wed, Sat–Sun 🚇 Barbican 🚌 8, 11, 23, 26, 56, 153 🍴 🚻 ♿

DR. JOHNSON'S HOUSE

www.drjohnsonshouse.org
This large, dark-brick house buried in a maze of courtyards and passages is one of the few residential 18th-century buildings surviving in the City of London. It was the home and workplace of journalist, poet and lexicographer Dr. Samuel Johnson (1709–84) from 1748 to 1759, and it was here that Johnson compiled the first comprehensive English dictionary, published in 1755.

Restored to its original condition, with panelled rooms and a pine staircase, the house contains a collection of period furniture, prints and portraits, as well as first editions of the dictionary. While Johnson worked on his entries for the dictionary in his own corner of the house, six copyists stood in the garret to transcribe them.

➕ 98 K4 ✉ 17 Gough Square EC4A 3DE ☎ 020 7353 3745 ⏰ May–Sep Mon–Sat 11–5.30; Oct–Apr Mon–Sat 11–5 ✋ Adult £4.50, child (10–16) £1.50, under 10s free, family £10 🚇 Temple, Holborn, Chancery Lane (closed Sun) 🚌 4, 11, 15, 23, 26, 76, 172 ♿

GEFFRYE MUSEUM

www.geffrye-museum.org.uk
A series of rooms decorated and furnished in period style takes you through 400 years of domestic life. You start with an oak-panelled, 17th-century room, and pass through Georgian restraint and elaborate Victorian design eventually to reach a 20th-century converted warehouse space.

A 1998 extension brings displays up to the present, and includes modern furniture and interiors, as well as a temporary exhibition gallery and design centre. Changes in horticultural style are reflected in the gardens, arranged as outdoor rooms and including a walled herb garden.

The Geffrye Almshouses—14 houses and a chapel—are open on the first Saturday, and the first and third Wednesday of the month (guided tours). They were originally built for elderly and impoverished ironmongers and their widows in 1715 on land bequeathed by Sir Robert Geffrye, a former Lord Mayor of London.

➕ 99 N1 ✉ 136 Kingsland Road, Shoreditch E2 8EA ☎ 020 7739 9893 ⏰ Tue–Sat 10–5, Sun 12–5. Garden open Apr–Oct during museum opening hours ✋ Free; almshouses £2 adult, children free 🚇 Old Street, Liverpool Street 🚌 67, 149, 242, 243, 394 🚃 Hoxton 🍴 ♿

Left *Dr. Johnson's House*
Right *A 19th-century drawing room in the Geffrye Museum*

GUILDHALL

www.guildhall.cityoflondon.gov.uk

England's third-largest civic hall, begun in 1411, is the City's only secular stone structure to have survived the Great Fire of 1666 (▷ 31). The Corporation of London, which governs the City, still has its home here.

Beyond the unusual entrance, designed in 1788 with Gothic and Indian influences, is a medieval great hall with stained-glass windows and monuments to national heroes such as Lord Nelson, the Duke of Wellington and Sir Winston Churchill. Beneath is the most extensive medieval crypt in London and London's most important recent archaeological find, the remains of the capital's only Roman amphitheatre (▷ 27).

Above *Stained-glass window in the Order of St. John Museum, St. John's Gate*

The Guildhall library contains prints, drawings and books about the history of London, as well as the Clockmakers' Museum, which has some 600 watches, 30 clocks and 15 marine timekeepers dating from the 15th to the 20th century.

Since the 17th century the Corporation has collected works of art, mostly portraits, and paintings of naval battles and views of historic London; a changing selection of these works is displayed in the Guildhall art gallery.

✚ 98 M4 ✉ Gresham Street EC2P 2EJ ☎ 020 7332 1313 🕐 Mon–Sat 9–5. Closed during ceremonies/events. Art gallery Mon–Sat 10–5, Sun 12–4. Clockmakers' Museum Mon–Sat 9.30–4.45 ♿ Free. Charge for special exhibitions. Gallery free tours Fri 12.15, 1.15, 2.15, 3.15 🚇 Bank, St. Paul's, Mansion House, Moorgate 🚌 8, 11, 15

MONUMENT

www.themonument.info

The devastating Great Fire of 1666 (▷ 31) wiped out the medieval heart of London. The Monument commemorates this event and the later rebuilding. Built between 1671 and 1677 to a design by Sir Christopher Wren, chief architect of the new city, it stands on the northern bank of the Thames, east

of London Bridge. The fluted column of Portland stone is 62m (203ft) high, which equals the distance from the start of the fire in Pudding Lane. At the top a flaming gilded urn symbolizes the fire.

The 311 steps of a steep internal spiral stairway lead to the viewing platform, 41m (133ft) up.

✚ 98 N4 ✉ Monument Street EC3R 8AH ☎ 020 7626 2717 🕐 Daily 9.30–5.30 ♿ Adult £3, child (under 16) £1 🚇 Monument 🚌 17, 21, 43, 133, 521 ⛴ London Bridge City Pier

MUSEUM OF LONDON

▷ 103.

OLD BAILEY (CENTRAL CRIMINAL COURT)

www.cityoflondon.gov.uk

Its correct title is the Central Criminal Court, but everyone knows the courthouse as the Old Bailey, a name borrowed from the nearby street. Major criminal trials from all over England and Wales are heard in this baroque building, erected in 1907 on the site of the notorious Newgate prison (▷ 35).

A bronze, gilded figure of Justice carrying her sword and scales (but not blindfolded) crowns the green copper dome, echoing the design of nearby St. Paul's Cathedral.

Public galleries are open for viewing of trials in session.

✚ 98 L4 ✉ Central Criminal Court, Old Bailey EC4M 7EH ☎ 020 7248 3277 🕐 Mon–Fri 10–1, 2–5 (approx); reduced court sitting Aug. No admission for children under 14 ♿ Free 🚇 St. Paul's 🚌 8, 15, 25, 242

ST. JOHN'S GATE

www.sja.org.uk/museum

Clerkenwell's medieval priory of St. John was the base of the Knights Hospitallers, who sent men, money and supplies to hospitals situated on the great pilgrim routes in Europe. Today all that remains of the priory buildings are the crypt of the Norman church and the Tudor gatehouse. They house a museum of the history of the Order of St. John, with exhibits such as Crusader treasures from the Holy Land, and the beautiful 15th-century Weston Triptych.

Victorian pioneers began the St. John Ambulance voluntary first-aid movement here. Its service continues today, and a small gallery relates its history.

✚ 98 L3 ✉ St. John's Lane EC1M 4DA ☎ 020 7324 4005 🕐 Mon–Fri 10–5, Sat 10–4; tours Tue, Fri, Sat 11am, 2.30pm ♿ Free. Donations requested for tours 🚇 Farringdon 🚌 63, 55, 243 ♿

MUSEUM OF LONDON

The history of this vibrant city is brilliantly told in these two very modern and exciting museums—one in the heart of London, near the Barbican, and the other in the docks that once supplied so much of the city's wealth. Visit both sites for a fuller understanding of the people who shaped the capital.

CENTRAL LONDON SITE

Displays here are chronological, starting with the auroch's skull that dates from around 245000BC and ending with a glimpse into the future for the city in an age of global warming and environmental concerns. As you work your way down through the two levels, highlights include the reconstructed Roman shops, including the glassmaker's and the cutler's stall. You can admire a suit of medieval chainmail from Whitechapel and contrast it with a pair of pointed fashionable shoes from the same century. Try on a leather fireman's hat, of the style worn at the time of the Great Fire of London in the 1660s.

On the lower level, don't miss the extraordinary Fanshawe dress of 1752, with its emblematic silken embroidery representing the trades of brewer and merchant. It was worn by Ann Fanshawe when she served as Lady Mayoress. A video wall of costumed actors brings the pleasure gardens so popular at that time in London to life, and you can wander a mini-maze of Victorian streets lined with nostalgic shops. Film and video enable Londoners to tell the story of the Blitz, and there's a great section on fashion which is right up to date. Don't miss the Lord Mayor's ceremonial coach of 1757, displayed in a special room devoted to ceremonies within the city. It is still used in the annual Lord Mayor's Show parade, and requires six horses to pull it.

DOCKLANDS SITE

The museum's second site is located within a 19th-century warehouse, set on the city's first purpose-built cargo handling docks. Dwarfed by the glass tower blocks of the financial district, this modest brown brick structure is one of the few historic buildings to have survived fires, bombings and redevelopment.

Exhibits over two floors (start at the top) tell the story of London as a world port, from its growth in Roman times to the present. On the second floor you can even lose yourself in the atmospheric labyrinth of a reconstructed 'Sailortown', recalling the murky and often sinister alleyways of the port area in the 1840s. London was the fourth biggest slavery port in the world (after Rio, Bahia and Liverpool)—an unpleasant truth which is not shirked in the moving exhibition here. Later exhibits recall wartime destruction of the docks, and the massive redevelopment in the 1980s.

INFORMATION

Central London site

www.museumoflondon.org.uk

✚ 98 M3 ✉ 150 London Wall EC2Y 5HN ☎ 020 7001 9844 🕐 Daily 10–6 ✋ Free 📖 Souvenir guide £5 (English only); map/guide free, in English, French, German, Italian, Spanish 🚇 Moorgate, Barbican, St. Paul's 🚌 4, 8, 25, 56, 100, 521 ☕ Entrance Hall café, and Sackler Hall Café for hot and cold drinks, snacks, salads, light lunches 🎁 Excellent range of London souvenirs

Docklands site

www.museumindocklands.org.uk

✚ Off map 99 Q4 ✉ West India Quay, Canary Wharf E14 4AL ☎ 020 7001 9844 🕐 Daily 10–6 ✋ Free 🚇 Canary Wharf 🚌 D3, D7, D8, 277, D6, 15, 115, 135 🚈 West India Quay 🍴 1802 serves drinks, sandwiches, cakes and meals 🎁 Small bookshop, some London souvenirs

TIPS

» Free guided tours take place daily at 11, 12, 3 and 4pm, each visiting a different gallery – check at the desk.

» Every hour there's a free object in focus session, when museum staff pick one object in the collection to talk about—sign up in the foyer to join.

» Lightweight folding chairs are available free for visitors with tired feet to carry with them.

Below *The Lord Mayor's fabulous coach, displayed on the lower level*

INTRODUCTION

The first St. Paul's was built in AD604, possibly on the site of a Roman temple of Apollo. Rebuilt three centuries later after a Viking attack, the structure was replaced by a huge Gothic cathedral, now known as Old St. Paul's, built by the Normans in 1087. By the 17th century this had a dubious reputation as the home of several obscure cults, such as that of the odd bearded St. Uncumber, who was most likely a figment of somebody's imagination, and the site of horse fairs and secular entertainments. After the Civil War its nave was used as a cavalry barracks, and shops were set up in its portico.

Following its destruction in the Great Fire of 1666, Sir Christopher Wren (1632–1723) was commissioned to build a new version. His first design was rejected for proposing radical European elements and the second was abandoned; the final version was an uneasy compromise between the architect and the clergy. Even then, monetary problems plagued the project, which finally got off the ground in 1675 and was completed in 1710, during the reign of Queen Anne.

Since the first service was held in 1697, the cathedral has shared with Westminster Abbey some of the most momentous ceremonies in Britain's history. These include the funerals of Lord Nelson, the Duke of Wellington and Winston Churchill; Queen Victoria's Jubilee; peace ceremonies to mark the ends of both world wars; the wedding of Charles and Diana; and thanksgiving services for both the Golden Jubilee and the 80th birthday of Queen Elizabeth II. The noble structure survived attempts by Hitler's Luftwaffe to undo Wren's work during the Blitz, and photographs of St. Paul's standing unbent among the surrounding wreckage provided strongly symbolic images of the British people's resilience.

St. Paul's is the cathedral of the Diocese of London, comprising the five episcopal areas of London, Kensington, Willesden, Edmonton and Stepney, which together account for a large part of Greater London. The Bishop of London oversees four area bishops, who are assisted in turn by archdeacons and deacons, who themselves oversee groups of parishes. In 2004 special services were held at the cathedral to celebrate the 1,400th anniversary of the diocese.

A wide flight of steps leads up to the west front entrance, flanked by two clock towers. Wren's original Classical design, using a Greek cross with the dome over the central intersection, was modified to provide an impressive processional space for the clergy, and the first view on entering is of the three-bay-long nave provided for this purpose. To the left are All Souls' Chapel and the bell tower, then St. Dunstan's Chapel. To the right is the Chapel of St. Michael and St. George. Farther down, in one of the nave arches, is the Wellington memorial, and ahead is the massive dome. Nelson's memorial is to the right, in the south transept, and beyond it is the entrance to the crypt and shop. The choir stalls and the organ case are ahead, and behind the high altar is the American Memorial Chapel. Stairs at the southwest corner of the crossing lead up to the dome and its galleries.

WHAT TO SEE

THE DOME AND GALLERIES

Eight pillars support this huge structure, over 111m (364ft) high and weighing about 65,000 tonnes. It's a stiff climb up 259 steps to the Whispering Gallery, which runs around the dome's interior. Here, acoustics are such that someone standing on the opposite side of the gallery can hear your whispers quite clearly after several seconds' delay—though only early visitors have the peace to test

INFORMATION

www.stpauls.co.uk

✚ 98 L4 ✉ St. Paul's Churchyard EC4M 8AD ☎ 020 7246 8357 🕐 Mon–Sat 8.30–4, Sun worship only. Times of daily services vary—call or check online for details 🖐 Adult £14.50, child (6–18) £5.50, under 6s free, family £34.50. Services free 🔲 Mon–Sat free guided tours (90 min) at 10.45, 11.15, 1.30, 2; book on admission. Free introductory talks last 20 min. Touch-screen multimedia guides in 12 languages free with admission 🚇 St. Paul's, Mansion House 🚌 4, 11, 15, 23, 25, 26, 100, 242 🚉 Blackfriars, City Thameslink 📖 £3.99, in English, Chinese, French, German, Italian, Japanese, Spanish 🍴 Restaurant at St Paul's serves seasonal meals. Sat brunch from 11am ☕ Traditional British cakes at Café; fresh salads at the Barrow in the Crypt 💿 CDs of psalms, organ and choral music; books; religious merchandise; Christmas decorations

Opposite The cathedral nave is a dramatic combination of vast space and elaborate decoration

Below A statue on the Classical facade of the cathedral

the theory properly. There are fine views down to the nave below and up to the frescoes of the dome above, where scenes from the life of St. Paul were painted by Sir James Thornhill between 1716 and 1719.

Another 119 steps lead to the Stone Gallery, which encircles the exterior of the dome's base, 53m (173ft) up. Climbing higher still you pass through the timberwork that rests on the inner dome, supporting the wooden skin of the outer, lead-covered dome. Between these two domes is a third: the brick cone supporting the elegant lantern that crowns the whole structure. This can be viewed from the Golden Gallery, the smallest of the galleries, which runs around the highest point of the outer dome, 85m (279ft) and 528 steps from ground level. A hole in the floor gives a dizzying view straight down to the cathedral floor. Above are the ball and cross at the very top, originally added in 1708 and replaced in 1821. For safety reasons visitors are not allowed into the interior of the ball.

THE CHANCEL

This part of the cathedral, near the choir and altar, is a riot of Byzantine-style gilding, with mosaics of birds, fish and animals, dating from the late 19th century. In the north choir aisle is a marble sculpture by Henry Moore (1898–1986), *Mother and Child*. French master metalworker Jean Tijou (*fl.* 1689–*c.* 1711) designed the wrought-iron gates and most of the cathedral's decorative metalwork.

A statue of the Virgin and Child, originally part of the Victorian altar screen, which was damaged by a bomb during World War II, stands in the south choir aisle. Also here is a marble effigy of poet John Donne (1572–1631), who was dean of the cathedral. This is one of few effigies to have survived the Great Fire of London in 1666, and you can still make out the scorch marks on its base.

Below *The dome behind one of the towers of the west front*

The organ is the third-largest in Britain, with 7,189 pipes, 5 keyboards and 138 organ stops. Its case was carved by Grinling Gibbons (1648–1721), as were the choir stalls. The high altar, made of marble and carved and gilded oak with a canopy based on a sketch by Wren, replaced its bomb-damaged predecessor in 1958.

WELLINGTON'S TOMB

The Duke of Wellington (1769–1852), military hero of the Napoleonic Wars and prime minister from 1828 to 1830, lies in a simple Cornish granite casket under the crossing. Designed in 1858 by F. C. Penrose, it has echoes of the style of Napoleon's tomb in Les Invalides in Paris. Banners made for Wellington's funeral procession hang around the tomb, but the Prussian flag that originally hung there was removed during World War I and has never been reinstated.

NELSON'S TOMB

Admiral Nelson (1758–1805), who died in action against Napoleon at the Battle of Trafalgar, lies in the middle of the crypt, one of around 200 tombs contained in this huge space, which was part of the medieval cathedral. Nelson's coffin—carved from the mast of a defeated French ship—went with him into battle and was kept handy behind his desk. After his death, Nelson was preserved in French brandy for the journey home, and at Gibraltar the coffin was placed into a lead-lined casket and steeped in distilled wine. Finally, his remains were encased

TIPS

» The cathedral sometimes closes for special events so it's wise to check before a visit.

» Buy guidebooks at the west end of the cathedral or from the shop in the crypt, or online.

» If you come to one of the free organ recitals at 4.45pm every Sunday, bring some loose change for the collection at the end.

» A good way to get a free glimpse of the cathedral and sample its atmosphere is to attend a service.

» To test the acoustics of the Whispering Gallery, face the wall as you whisper.

Above *Looking up at the dome's painted ceiling*

107

1 West Doorway
2 All Souls' Chapel
3 St. Dunstan's Chapel
4 Wellington Memorial
5 Font
6 Martyr's Chapel
7 Choir
8 High Altar
9 American Memorial Chapel
10 St. Mary's Chapel
11 Pulpit
12 Steps down to crypt
13 Nelson Memorial
14 Steps up to Whispering Gallery and
   Upper Galleries
15 Chapel of St. Michael
   and St. George

in two more coffins before being buried in the crypt under Cardinal Wolsey's 16th-century sarcophagus, which had remained empty since its confiscation by Henry VIII. The monument to Nelson shows two naval cadets being introduced to their hero by Britannia. It was sculpted by John Flaxman (1755–1826), an internationally famous artist in his time.

THE LIGHT OF THE WORLD

Quietly resplendent in the north transept, the cathedral's most famous painting makes for a good place to sit and reflect. The work in question is *The Light of the World* by pre-Raphaelite William Holman Hunt, who in 1900 made this copy of his own original, which adorns the chapel of Keble College, Oxford. The painting is deeply symbolic, showing Christ knocking at the handleless, overgrown door of the human soul and awaiting the answer from within. Note how the lamp of the spirit gently radiates through the dark surroundings.

THE TREASURY

In the southwest section of the crypt, just before the entrance to the shop and restaurant, is the cathedral's collection of gold, silver and precious objects. Much of the cathedral's original gold and silver was stolen during a robbery in 1810, and more than 200 of the ceremonial items in the current display are on loan from other London churches. One of St. Paul's own possessions is the 1977 Jubilee Cope, made for a thanksgiving service in honour of the 25th anniversary of Queen Elizabeth II's accession and worn by Gerald Ellison, Bishop of London. Its ornate decoration depicts 73 embroidered London church spires. Other exhibits are two effigies dating from before the Great Fire. Though they look like wood, these are stone effigies, originally painted in vivid colours. The heat of the fire fused the paint to the surface and turned them the colour of polished oak.

SIR CHRISTOPHER WREN'S MEMORIAL

A plain black slab in the crypt pays tribute to the cathedral's architect, with the exhortation *circumspice si monumentum requiris* ('if you require a memorial, look about you'). It was inserted in the late 18th century by the surveyor of St. Paul's, Robert Mylne, after a heated debate about a suitable monument; a grand statue had also been proposed. It was Wren's son who provided the memorial's telling phrase. Other architects are commemorated nearby, along with scientists, musicians and artists, including William Blake (1757–1827) and J. M. W. Turner (1775–1851).

MUSIC AT ST. PAUL'S

St. Paul's choir first appears in the records in 1127, when the Bishop of London, Richard de Belmeis, founded a choir school. To celebrate the opening of Wren's cathedral the choir sang an anthem composed by its leader, John Blow, accompanied by the new organ, described by diarist John Evelyn as the best in Europe. After 1860, when the screen that originally supported the organ was taken away, a bigger choir was needed as well as a new organ, to fill the now much larger space. The organ was built in 1872 and the choir increased to a total of 58 voices, which enabled it to establish a wider repertoire of works. Today the choir consists of 30 choristers (boy trebles), eight probationers (who will become choristers) and 12 adults—all chosen by audition. It still follows the monastic tradition of singing services: daily evensong and matins, eucharist and evensong on Sundays. It also has a busy schedule of concerts, broadcasts and recordings. The choirboys are given a normal schooling along with their musical training, which involves learning the piano and another instrument and attending two daily choral rehearsals.

Left *Both of the west front towers were originally intended to have a clock-face*
Below *View from the choir of the elaborate canopy above the high altar*

TEMPLE, INNER AND MIDDLE
www.innertemple.org.uk
www.middletemple.org.uk
Two Inns of Court (▷ 140 and 144) make up the Temple, named after the crusading Knights Templar, who acquired the land in 1160. The 12th-century circular Temple Church still stands at the heart of this network of gardens and courtyards.

In addition to the church, you can visit the Inner and Middle Temple gardens and the 16th-century Middle Temple Hall, where the first recorded performance of Shakespeare's *Twelfth Night* took place. It has an impressive hammerbeam roof, some fine Elizabethan tables and several royal portraits.

Black-gowned lawyers stroll between their chambers and the Royal Courts of Justice (▷ 147) on the other side of Fleet Street.

✚ 98 K4 ✉ Inner Temple EC4Y 7HL; Middle Temple EC4Y 9AT ☎ Inner Temple 020 7797 8250; Middle Temple 020 7427 4800 🕓 Inner Temple Gardens Mon–Fri 12.30–3. Middle Temple Hall Mar–Nov Mon–Fri 10–12, 3–4. Middle Temple Gardens May–Jul, Sep Mon–Fri 12–3. Church Mon–Fri 2–4, plus services (tel 020 7353 3470) ✋ Free 🚇 Temple (closed Sun), Blackfriars 🚌 11, 15, 23 🚢 Savoy Pier

TOWER BRIDGE
▷ 111.

TOWER OF LONDON
▷ 112–117.

V & A MUSEUM OF CHILDHOOD
www.vam.ac.uk
With nearly 6,000 exhibits spanning 400 years of childhood, this is one of the biggest and oldest collections of its kind in the world. The museum opened in 1872 as the east London branch of what would eventually become the Victoria & Albert Museum (▷ 224–228) and was redeveloped in 2002. Permanent collections are displayed in three main galleries: Moving Toys, Creativity and Childhood.

Exhibits include swaddling bands (cloth used to wrap babies) from the 16th century, dolls from the 17th (don't miss the Nuremberg Dolls' House, made in 1673 — the only example of its type outside Germany), games from the 18th, toy theatres from the 19th, model trains from the 20th and construction kits from the 21st. Children's events and activities take place at weekends and during school holidays.

✚ 99 Q2 ✉ Cambridge Heath Road E2 9PA ☎ 020 8983 5200 🕓 Daily 10–5.45 ✋ Free, small charge for some activities 🚇 Bethnal Green 🚌 8, 106, 254, 309, 388, D6 🎫 📷

WHITECHAPEL ART GALLERY
www.whitechapelgallery.org
Founded in 1901 to 'bring great art to the people of the East End of London', the gallery shows a changing programme of contemporary and 20th-century art, featuring new and acknowledged artists in solo shows, group exhibitions and commissions. Media range from painting and sculpture to video and photography.

The Arts and Crafts building, designed by Charles Harrison Townsend, was the first purpose-built British gallery to host changing exhibitions. In 2009 it doubled its size at a cost of £13 million.

✚ 99 P4 ✉ 77–82 Whitechapel High Street E1 7QX ☎ 020 7522 7888 🕓 Tue–Wed, Fri–Sun 11–6, Thu 11–9 ✋ Free 🚇 Aldgate East 🚌 15, 25, 67, 253 🎫 📷

Left *Middle Temple Hall garden in the Inns of Court*

TOWER BRIDGE

London's best-known bridge, linking the Tower of London (▷ 112–117) and the South Bank promenade, has been a tourist attraction since 1982, with access to the upper walkways and engine rooms and a Tower Bridge exhibition tracing its history. There are stupendous views across London from the high-level walkway, 43m (140ft) above the Thames, and interactive computer displays help pick out the most famous buildings on the skyline, but the hydraulically operated bascules (from the French for 'see-saw') are the main attraction. Originally designed (in the late 19th century) to allow tall ships to sail through, they are still lifted more than 900 times a year for cruise liners and other large river craft. If you want to time your visit to coincide with the bridge opening, a list of times is posted daily in the entrance kiosk to the exhibition or you can call 020 7940 3984. Vessels have to give at least 24 hours' notice if they want to pass through.

The famous neo-Gothic towers, with their mock-medieval turrets, are an attraction in themselves. DVD shows and graphic display panels in the towers and on the walkways give an idea of the debates and controversies that led to the construction of the bridge, discussed since 1800 but not officially planned until 1876. Some of the designs submitted over the following seven years included a futuristic-looking structure with sliding roadways, a rolling bridge and an under-river arcade. The winning design, submitted by Sir Horace Jones and adapted by engineer John Wolfe Barry, took eight years to build.

From the south tower, follow the blue guideline to the engine rooms, which house the beautifully crafted Victorian machinery used to power the bridge between 1894 and 1976.

PLANNING THE BRIDGE

Between 1750 and 1850 10 new bridges had been built along the Thames to cope with the increasing trade and traffic of a booming city. East of London Bridge, where the population had expanded to over a million by the late 19th century, there was no river crossing. Plans were delayed and disrupted by wharfingers and shipping traders, who feared the decline of river business, and by the need for 43m (140ft) of clearance for tall-masted ships. A competition was finally opened for a new design. The winning architect, Sir Horace Jones, died in 1887 before the foundations were complete, and the task was passed on to his assistant, George Daniel Stevenson, who had an even greater passion for the Victorian Gothic style.

INFORMATION

www.towerbridge.org.uk

✚ 99 P5 ✉ Tower Bridge SE1 2UP
☎ 020 7403 3761 🕓 Apr–Sep daily 10–6.30 (last entry 5.30), Oct–Mar 9.30–6 (last entry 5) 🎟 Adult £8, child (5–15) £3, under 5s free, family £11 🚇 Tower Hill, London Bridge 🚌 15, 42, 78, 100, RV1 ⛴ Tower Pier 🎧 £3, in English, French, German, Dutch, Japanese 🍴 Café Most under north tower; indoor and outdoor seating 🛒 Small kiosk in engine rooms selling limited range of souvenirs

TIP

» The main access is in the northwest tower of the bridge.

Below The bridge was given a royal opening in 1894, with a gun salute from the Tower of London to greet the first raising of the bascules

INTRODUCTION

The White Tower was built in the 11th century on a commanding site on the Thames, which probably had earlier royal significance. It was constructed over one of the defensive structures that William the Conqueror had hastily erected in the aftermath of the Battle of Hastings in 1066, when he had effectively won the succession to the English throne by defeating King Harold II. William saw the necessity of having a strong fortress from which to subdue the feisty people of London, already a huge city by medieval standards, and thus began the Tower's history proper. Between 1190 and 1285 it was encircled by two towered curtain walls and a moat, and in the 14th century the wharf was added. This major expansion, which saw the Tower more or less take the shape it retains to this day, was begun during the reign of Richard the Lionheart (1189–99), under the auspices of his chancellor, William Longchamp, while Richard went off on crusade. Henry III (reigned 1216–72) then strengthened the defences after a group of rebellious barons made him seek refuge in the Tower in 1238.

It was left to his successor, Edward I (reigned 1272–1307), however, to supervise the transformation of the fortress into Britain's largest and sturdiest concentric castle. During his reign the Tower was also used as a prison for the first time, setting in train the lengthy list of captives, many of them royal, who were incarcerated and often executed here. Among the most celebrated inmates were several of Henry VIII's wives, Catholic martyr Sir Thomas More and Guy Fawkes, mastermind behind the failed Gunpowder Plot of 1605 (▷ 30).

Further additions included the Chapel Royal and Queen's House, built in Henry VIII's reign, and the 17th-century New Armouries. Strong bastion though it was, the Tower could not protect Charles I and it was taken and controlled by Cromwell and the Parliamentarians throughout the Civil War (1642–49) and subsequently used mostly as a munitions store. The Tower was last used to assert power over people during the Chartist rebellion of the 1840s. Since then it has played a ceremonial and, finally, a touristic role. In 1988 the Tower of London was designated a World Heritage Site.

The Tower's layout illustrates its development from William the Conqueror's White Tower to the complex of defences completed by Edward I and Henry III and essentially unchanged today.

Entry to the Tower is through the Middle Tower in the southwest corner of the site. Once inside, you can wander at will. At the heart of the complex is the White Tower, 36m (118ft) across and 27m (88ft) high, with weathervanes topping the corner turrets. It is surrounded by 13th-century outer and inner walls, the latter punctuated by 12 towers.

A complex of later buildings within the inner wall includes the New Armouries, Waterloo Barracks and the Fusiliers' Museum.

WHAT TO SEE

WHITE TOWER

At the heart of the Tower is its oldest medieval building, thought to date from 1078 and probably marking a site of political significance for many centuries before that. It earned its name in the 13th century, when Henry III had the exterior whitewashed, but the original stone, brought over from Caen in Normandy, has mainly been replaced over the years with Portland stone from Dorset. The windows and doors are also replacements, added in the 17th and 18th centuries, and the turret roofs are a 16th-century feature.

The White Tower was built to serve as a fortress, armoury and a royal residence, and is split inside into three floors and a basement, where the

INFORMATION

www.hrp.org.uk

✚ 99 N5 ✉ London EC3N 4AB
☎ 0844 482 7777; tickets: 0844 482 7799
🕐 Tue–Sat 9–4.30, Sun–Mon 10–4.30.
All buildings inside the gates close 30 min after last admission; Tower closes 1 hour after last admission. To watch the nightly Ceremony of the Keys apply in advance in writing enclosing an S.A.E. (▷ 294)
✋ Adult £18.70, child (5–16) £10.45, under 5s free, family £51.70 🚇 Tower Hill
🚌 15, 42, 78, 100, RV1 ⛴ Tower Pier
📷 Audioguides with a choice of five tours £4, in English, French, German, Italian, Spanish, Japanese, Russian, Mandarin, Dutch, Portuguese, Korean
📖 £3.95, in English, French, Russian, Japanese, Spanish, Italian, German
🍴 New Armouries restaurant 🍽 Paul French for pastries on wharf 🎁 Tower Shop at main entrance in the Salvin Pumphouse; Jewel House Shop in Lower Martin Tower; White Tower Shop, in basement of White Tower; Medieval Palace Shop; Beefeater Shop in Water Lane

Opposite *The White Tower, which replaced an earlier wooden building*

TIPS

» Crowds can be a problem in the summer. To save queueing, buy tickets in advance by calling 0844 482 7799 or online at www.hrp.org.uk and obtain a small discount as well.

» In the Martin Tower there's a display on the making of the Crown Jewels.

» Check at the main entrance near the Middle Tower for times of entertaining, free daily guided tours by Yeoman Warders, every 30 minutes.

11th-century well still holds fresh water. On the ground floor is an exhibition about small arms, from the Royal Armouries collection; spiral stairs lead to the first floor, with the gloriously simple Chapel of St. John the Evangelist, a double-height room original to the building. Used as chapel throughout the Middle Ages, from the 16th to the 19th centuries it stored state records. The adjacent large room may have been used for banquets and royal ceremonies.

Temporary exhibitions are held on the top floors and stairs lead to the turrets above, where Charles II's astronomer, John Flamsteed, observed the stars until a new observatory was built at Greenwich (▷ 256–257).

JEWEL HOUSE

First stop for many visitors is the Jewel House (in the Waterloo Barracks), north of the White Tower. Here you pass through a series of displays giving a history of the Coronation Regalia (Crown Jewels) before reaching the treasury, where the collection is kept. An excellent visual story of the jewels entertains those waiting to view the exhibits, and it is possible to repeat the circuit round the actual jewels immediately for a second look at no extra cost.

The jewels mainly date from the restoration of the monarchy in 1660; the older regalia were melted down on Oliver Cromwell's orders, and only three swords and a coronation spoon survive. The sovereign's orb and sceptre (topped with a dove), made for Charles II in 1661, have been used in every coronation since, but there are also many later additions, such as the new sets made for

Below *The Jewel House houses the magnificent Crown Jewels*
Opposite *Armour on display in the White Tower*

James II's wife, as queen consort, and for Mary II, crowned with William III but queen in her own right. Among the priceless stones used in the regalia are the world's biggest cut diamond, the 530-carat First Star of Africa, set in the head of the sceptre. The 317-carat Second Star of Africa diamond is part of the Imperial State Crown, made for the coronation of George VI in 1937 and set with no fewer than 2,868 diamonds, as well as 17 sapphires, 11 emeralds, 5 rubies and 273 pearls.

TOWER GREEN

Endlessly fascinating to visitors are the Tower's famous prisoners and their grisly deaths. Tower Green, west of the White Tower, is the main focus for stories of suffering and heroics: some of the tower's best-known prisoners were held in the buildings around this area of garden, including Sir Walter Raleigh, whose stay in the Bloody Tower led to the addition of a new floor to provide room for him and his family. The tower's name derives from the supposed murder of the two princes, Edward V and Richard, Duke of York, sons of Edward IV and allegedly the victims of their ambitious uncle, Richard III. They disappeared in 1483, aged around 13 and 10.

The Queen's House, a black-and-white, half-timbered building next to the Bloody Tower, was the scene of Guy Fawkes' interrogation in 1605 (▷ 30) and of a daring escape when the Earl of Nithsdale, imprisoned after the 1715

BEHEADED

The Scaffold Site in front of the Chapel of St. Peter ad Vincula saw the executions of the only five women to be beheaded for treason—four of them during Henry VIII's reign. First on the block was Anne Boleyn in 1536; she and the next victim, wife No. 5, Catherine Howard, were both accused of adultery. Catherine's lady-in-waiting Jane, Viscountess Rochford, met her fate along with her mistress. In 1541, 70-year-old Margaret Pole, Countess of Salisbury, was executed for her Catholic faith and Yorkist loyalty. Henry's daughter Mary I continued the family tradition by dispatching the fifth woman, Lady Jane Grey, proclaimed queen in 1553 in an attempt to secure a Protestant succession.

TRADITIONS

The Tower has many ancient traditions.
One is the nightly Ceremony of the Keys
(▷ 294), when the Chief Yeoman Warder
locks the main gates of the Tower at
9.53pm, after which a bugler sounds the
Last Post. This ceremony has scarcely
changed in more than 700 years, except
that it now takes place under floodlights
with an audience.

Seven ravens live in the gardens, well
cared for by the official Ravenmaster;
legend has it that the Tower will collapse
if they fly away, but in fact their wings are
clipped so this will never happen.

On 21 May members of Eton College
and King's College, Cambridge put white
roses and lilies in Wakefield Tower in
memory of Henry VI, who founded both
institutions and who was murdered here
in 1471.

Jacobite rebellion, dressed as a woman and made his getaway. Particularly
high-ranking prisoners were kept in the 13th-century Beauchamp Tower. In the
upper chamber you can still see inscriptions carved by the prisoners, some with
amazing skill and intricacy.

TRAITORS' GATE

Just beyond the entrance to the medieval palace, opposite the gateway of
the Bloody Tower, is a great stone archway. Above it is Tudor timber-framing
and below are the wooden watergates that gave direct access from the river.
Its name derives from the number of prisoners accused of treason who were
brought by boat through this entrance. Until the 1860s there was an engine in
the pool behind the gate that used water power or horsepower to raise water to
a tank on the roof of the White Tower.

WAKEFIELD TOWER

Next in size to the White Tower, this was built in the 13th century to house
King Henry III's main private room and included a private river entrance, still
visible in Water Lane. Its impressive upper chamber was the king's bedroom,
and has been decked out according to accounts written in his son Edward I's
reign, when it served as a throne room. The current throne is a copy of the
Coronation Chair in Westminster Abbey, and sits flanked by candelabra under
the magnificent vaulted ceiling. A painted timber screen divides the main room
from the chapel, reputed to be the site of Henry VI's murder while at prayer,
though like many of the Tower's legends this is probably more convenient than
true (see side panel).

Above left *Yeoman Warders carrying out
the Ceremony of the Keys*
Above right *Anne Boleyn was one of those
who passed through Traitors' Gate*

FUSILIERS' MUSEUM

King James II established the Royal Regiment of Fusiliers in 1685 to guard the Tower's arsenal. They took their name from the 'fusil', a then-state-of-the-art musket which they were the first to use. The museum and the regiment headquarters occupy a 19th-century building which was initially the officers' mess. Inside is a display tracing the Fusiliers' service in the American War of Independence, the Crimean War, World War I and World War II, among many other campaigns, up to their more recent peace-keeping missions in Northern Ireland and the Balkans.

Most of the items on display are uniforms, medals and paintings. Some of the quirkier exhibits include a metal boot worn by a soldier who had avoided action for more than three years during the Napoleonic Wars by putting a corrosive lotion on his leg to create an open sore. His leg was cured within days of the boot being fitted.

GUIDE TO THE TOWER

1 Middle Tower
2 Byward Tower
3 Bell Tower
4 Traitors' Gate
5 St. Thomas's Tower
6 Bloody Tower
7 Wakefield Tower
8 White Tower
9 Chapel of St. John the Evangelist
10 Queen's House
11 Gaoler's House
12 Tower Green
13 Scaffold Site
14 Beauchamp Tower
15 Royal Chapel of St. Peter ad Vincula
16 Waterloo Barracks with Crown Jewels
17 Devereux Tower
18 Flint Tower
19 Bowyer Tower
20 Brick Tower
21 Martin Tower
22 Fusiliers' Museum
23 Former Hospital
24 Workshop
25 Constable Tower
26 Broad Arrow Tower
27 Salt Tower
28 Lanthorn Tower
29 Cradle Tower
30 Well Tower
31 Develin Tower
32 Brass Mount
33 Legge's Mount
34 Tower Wharf
35 Queen's Stair

Main Entrance

Tower Green

Ticket Office

Traitors' Gate

Tickets

Moat

Moat

White Tower

Wakefield Tower

Moat

Fusiliers' Museum

AROUND THE CITY

The City is the financial heart of Britain, a compact area of modern buildings, medieval lanes and churches designed by Sir Christopher Wren.

THE WALK
Distance: 2 miles (3km)
Time: 2 hours minimum
Start at: Monument Underground station
End at: Bank Underground station

HOW TO GET THERE
🚇 Circle or District line to Monument 🚌 15, 35

★ The charm of this walk is that it covers one of the oldest parts of London, at the same time home to the city's most modern buildings.

Take the London Bridge/King William Street (south) exit from Monument station. Walk straight ahead past the Monument on your left and on to London Bridge for views along the river. Tower Bridge (▷ 111) is to your left, with HMS *Belfast* (▷ 72) moored nearby. To the west is the Tate Modern tower (▷ 80–81). Return towards the station and turn right on to Monument Street. Follow this to the Monument (▷ 102).

Climb Fish Street Hill to Eastcheap and then turn right. Pudding Lane, where the Great Fire of London started in 1666, is the next road on the right. Cross Eastcheap to turn left into Philpot Lane. The Lloyd's Building is ahead of you.

❶ Sir Richard Rogers (co-architect of the Pompidou Centre in Paris) designed this 'inside-out' building for insurance underwriters Lloyd's of London in 1978. The 14-storey glass, concrete and aluminium office block, with its exterior tangle of ventilation ducts and fire stairs, attracts admiration and derision in equal measure.

At the end of Philpot Lane, cross Fenchurch Street into Lime Street and follow the cobbled street on the left, Lime Street Passage, into Leadenhall Market.

❷ Leadenhall Market (▷ 120), now under a wrought-iron and

glass roof, has been operating as a meat and fish market since the 14th century. Today its alleys are a mix of market stalls, as well as pubs and upmarket fashion shops. Have a drink or lunch at the historic Lamb Tavern (closed weekends).

Take Whittington Avenue from the market and turn right into Leadenhall Street by Lloyd's. Cross the road and an open square. To your right looms the startling 30 St. Mary Axe (aka the Gherkin). St. Helen's Bishopsgate is behind the tower block in the middle of the square.

❸ St. Helen's is a rare survivor of the Great Fire of London and is London's largest medieval church. It contains several fine memorials (open daily 9.30–5).

At the church turn left to follow Great St. Helen's to Bishopsgate. Turn left here and at the traffic lights cross into Threadneedle Street. Continue

From the church turn left along Walbrook and then right at the end towards the Royal Exchange building at the far side of the junction. On the right is the Mansion House (tours Sep–Jul Tue 2pm; adult £6, child free).

❻ This is one of London's grandest surviving Georgian town palaces, with magnificent interiors including elaborate plasterwork and carved timber ornament. Built in the mid-18th century, it is the home of the Lord Mayor of London.

Bank Underground station is at this road junction.

Above *Leadenhall Market*
Left *The porticoed Mansion House*

TIP

» Do this walk on a weekday, when the streets are busy with City workers. At weekends the area is deserted and some places close.

WHERE TO EAT

Stop at one of the cafés or pubs in Leadenhall Market, or at an outdoor café by the George Peabody statue. Café in the Crypt at St. Mary-le-Bow (tel 020 7329 0789) serves good vegetarian food.

past a statue of US philanthropist George Peabody on the left, and turn right down Bartholomew Lane alongside the Bank of England (▷ 101).

At the end of Bartholomew Lane turn left along Lothbury and into Gresham Street. Guildhall (▷ 102) is to your right, behind St. Lawrence Jewry Church. Facing away from Guildhall, cross Gresham Street into King Street and on to Cheapside. Turn right here and head for the steeple of St. Mary-le-Bow.

❹ Sir Christopher Wren designed 51 churches in the City, of which St. Mary-le-Bow is one. Its bells once sounded the curfew for Londoners, and to be born within earshot was the definition of a Cockney.

Go round the back of the church and turn right into Bow Lane. Williamson's Tavern is on the right. Turn left into Watling Street and as you turn look right to see the dome of St. Paul's Cathedral (▷ 104–109). According to tradition, Wren conducted his business in Ye Olde Watling Pub while building St. Paul's.

Follow Watling Street to a major junction and cross the intersection bearing left into Queen Victoria Street. Turn right into Bucklersbury to St. Stephen Walbrook Church.

❺ St. Stephen Walbrook is the Lord Mayor's official church, and considered to be Wren's finest City church. Its dome was probably built as a prototype (1672–79) for that of nearby St. Paul's. Centrally placed beneath it is the altar by English sculptor Henry Moore (1987). This asymmetrical lump of stone is at odds with its classical setting.

SHOPPING

BRICK LANE MARKET
www.visitbricklane.org
Never mind the quality, feel the atmosphere at this vibrant multi-ethnic street market. Come for clothes (especially leather), furniture, fruits, kitchenware and kitsch. Or just follow the streets to see where they lead and sift the jewels from the junk.
127 P2 ⊠ Brick Lane/Cheshire Street/ Sclater Street 🕐 Sun 8–2 🚇 Liverpool Street, Aldgate East 🚌 26, 28, 35, 43

LEADENHALL MARKET
www.leadenhallmarket.co.uk
Probably the most chic of the city's markets, with meat, fish, poultry, cheese, wine and chocolate. Worth visiting for the atmospheric building in the heart of the City (▷ 118), which comes to life early lunchtime.
127 N4 ⊠ Gracechurch Street EC3V 1LR ☎ 020 7929 1073 🕐 Mon–Fri 11–4 🚇 Cannon Street, Bank 🚌 8, 25, 40

MONT BLANC
www.montblanc.com
Superbly crafted pens and other writing implements are the signature items on sale at this plush boutique. However, there is also plenty in the way of watches, leather accessories,

jewellery, eyewear and perfumes, all at prices that reflect the quality.
126 M4 ⊠ 10–11 Royal Exchange EC3V 3LL ☎ 020 7929 4200 🕐 Mon–Fri 9–5.30 🚇 Bank 🚌 8, 11, 15, 23, 25, 26, 43, 76, 344

ONEDEKO
www.onedeko.co.uk
This is a good place for high-end designer furniture. Quirky accessories such as flower-shaped and tube map mirrors, shoe racks and kitchen equipment are also available. Smaller gift items include the morse code tea towel and dog and cat holders to hang it on.
127 P3 ⊠ 103 Commercial Street E1 6BG ☎ 020 7375 3289 🕐 Mon–Fri 10.30–6, Sat–Sun 10.30–5.30 🚇 Liverpool Street, Aldgate East 🚌 15, 25, 67, 78, 254

PETTICOAT LANE
London's most famous market was named after the garments sold by French immigrants in the 1700s. Look for clothing at bargain prices— especially fabrics and leather jackets. Around 1,000 stalls on Sundays.
127 N4 ⊠ Middlesex and Wentworth streets E1 ☎ 020 7377 8963 🕐 Mon–Fri 10–2.30, Sun 9–2 🚇 Liverpool Street, Aldgate, Aldgate East 🚌 8, 42, 344

R TWINING & CO
www.twinings.co.uk
One of London's oldest firms, Twinings has been trading in tea for more than 300 years. This shop— still on its original site opposite the Royal Courts of Justice—sells a wide range of teas, fruit and herb infusions plus teapots, cups, mugs and biscuits. There's a small museum at the back.
126 K4 ⊠ 216 Strand WC2R 1AP ☎ 0844 324 5000 🕐 Mon–Fri 9–5 🚇 Temple 🚌 9, 11, 13, 15, RV1

ENTERTAINMENT AND NIGHTLIFE

333 MOTHER
www.333mother.com
This City club and bar offers a mix of styles that might include soul, funk, reggae, drum 'n' bass and hip-hop. Resident DJs and special events.
127 N2 ⊠ 333 Old Street EC1V 9LE ☎ 020 7739 5949 🕐 Daily 8pm–3am 🎟 Free; events at 333 £5–£7 🚇 Old Street 🚌 43, 55, 243

BARBICAN CENTRE
www.barbican.org.uk
A 2,000-seat concert hall in the confusingly laid-out arts complex (▷ 101). Home of the world-class

London Symphony Orchestra and the English Chamber Orchestra.
126 M3 ✉ Silk Street EC2Y 8DS ☎ 020 7638 4141; box office 020 7638 8891 🖐 Tickets £12.50–£35. Supper Club daily 6–9 £25 🚇 Barbican 🚌 8, 11, 23, 26, 56, 153

THE BOOK CLUB
www.wearetbc.com
Two floors of a Victorian warehouse are the spacious setting for this arts meeting house, where night club rubs shoulder with evening class. Cocktails, poetry, workshops and dancing are on the cultural menu.
127 N2 ✉ 100 Leonard Street EC2A 4RH ☎ 020 7684 8618 🕐 Mon–Wed 8am–12am, Fri–Sat 8am–2am, Sun 10am–2am 🖐 Free 🚇 Old Street 🚌 55, 205, 243

CARGO
www.cargo-london.com
A cool East End bar in a cavernous building has a restaurant with tables for sharing. Not particularly friendly, but has top DJs and bands.
127 N2 ✉ 83 Rivington Street, Shoreditch EC2A 3AY ☎ 020 7739 3440 🕐 Club: Mon–Thu 6pm–1am, Fri–Sat 6pm–3am, Sun 6pm–12am. Restaurant: Mon–Thu 12pm–1am, Fri–Sat 12pm–3am, Sun 12–12 🖐 Free most nights; £10–£12.50 🚇 Old Street, Liverpool Street 🚌 26, 35, 47, 48, 67, 78, 149, 242

CHARLIE WRIGHT'S INTERNATIONAL BAR
www.charliewrights.com
This lively Thai restaurant and bar in Hoxton is frequented by a diverse crowd. Music Friday to Sunday.
126 N2 ✉ 45 Pitfield Street N1 6DA ☎ 020 7490 8345 🕐 Mon–Wed 12pm–1am, Thu–Fri 12pm–4am, Sat 6pm–4am, Sun 6–1 🖐 Free or £5–£10 🚇 Old Street 🚌 55, 203, 243

COMEDY CAFÉ
www.comedycafe.co.uk
Dine in comfort during shows by established stand-up acts—and a no-heckling policy. Dancing afterwards.

127 N2 ✉ 66–68 Rivington Street, Shoreditch EC2A 3AY ☎ 020 7739 5706 🕐 Wed–Sat 7–11.15 🖐 £10–£16, Wed free 🚇 Old Street 🚌 55, 243

FABRIC
www.fabriclondon.com
Fab superclub with mainly techno music, an easygoing 20-something crowd and less well-known DJs.
126 L3 ✉ 77A Charterhouse Street EC1M 3HN ☎ 020 7336 8898 🕐 Fri 10pm–6am, Sat 11pm–8am, Sun 11pm–6am 🖐 £12–£18 🚇 Farringdon 🚌 4, 55, 63, 243

LSO ST. LUKE'S
www.lso.co.uk
A handsome 18th-century church, designed by Nicholas Hawksmoor, is the venue for concert performances and community workshops run by the London Symphony Orchestra. Book ahead for occasional open rehearsals, and enjoy regular Thursday lunchtime concerts at 1pm (also broadcast on BBC Radio 3).
126 M2 ✉ 161 Old Street EC1V 9NG 🖐 From £9 🚇 Old Street 🚌 43, 55, 76, 243 🚗

PLASTIC PEOPLE
www.plasticpeople.co.uk
This small basement club prides itself on the breadth and quality of its eclectic music, rotating the very best in latin, Afro jazz, hip-hop, house, techno, soul, rock 'n' roll, punk, funk, even folk, plus genres you suspect they may have concocted, such as future jazz.
127 N3 ✉ 147–149 Curtain Road, Shoreditch EC2A 3QE ☎ 020 7739 6471 🕐 Thu 10pm–2am, Fri–Sat 10pm–3.30am, Sun 7–11 🖐 £5–£10 🚇 Old Street, Liverpool Street 🚌 8, 11, 23, 26, 35, 42, 43, 47, 48, 55, 67, 76, 78, 100, 133, 141, 149, 214, 242, 243, 271, 344, N8, N11, N26, N35, N149, N243

SADLER'S WELLS THEATRE
www.sadlerswells.com
Europe's finest dance venue offers classical ballet, modern dance and opera. The building, opened in 1998, replaces the theatre founded by Lilian Bayliss in 1931.

126 L2 ✉ Rosebery Avenue EC1R 4TN ☎ 020 7863 8198; box office 0844 412 4300 🖐 £10–£50 🚇 Angel 🚌 19, 38, 341

SHOREDITCH ELECTRICITY SHOWROOMS
www.electricityshowrooms.com
A place with atmosphere where you drink at bashed-up tables and strut your stuff on a light-up dance floor. Full of City boys—macho business types—on weekdays but more mellow on Saturday and Sunday.
127 N2 ✉ 39A Hoxton Square N1 6NN ☎ 020 7739 3939 🕐 Sun–Thu 12–12, Fri–Sat 12pm–1am 🖐 Phone for details 🚇 Old Street 🚌 55, 205, 243

SPORTS AND ACTIVITIES
ARSENAL FOOTBALL CLUB
www.arsenal.com
Famous north London club that usually finishes near the top of the Premiership. The club relocated to the new Emirates Stadium at Ashburton Grove in 2006.
Off map 126 M1 ✉ Emirates Stadium, 75 Drayton Park N5 1BU ☎ 020 7619 5003 🚇 Arsenal 🚌 4, 30 🎫 Tours adult £16, child (under 17) £8, tel 020 7619 5000

TOTTENHAM HOTSPUR FOOTBALL CLUB
www.tottenhamhotspur.com
A match at White Hart Lane is usually guaranteed to provide goals and entertainment, whether Spurs—one of England's most historic clubs, with an exceptionally fine tradition in Cup football—win, lose or draw.
Off map 127 N1 ✉ White Hart Lane, Bill Nicholson Way, 748 High Road, Tottenham N17 0AP ☎ 0844 499 5000 🚇 White Hart Lane, Northumberland Park 🚌 76, 149, 259 🎫 Tours adult £16, child (under 16) £9; book in advance tel 0844 844 0102

WEST HAM UNITED FOOTBALL CLUB
www.whufc.com
The highly respected Hammers—the club of legendary captain Bobby Moore—have a proud history.
Off map 127 R2 ✉ Boleyn Ground, Green Street, Upton Park E13 9AZ ☎ 020 8548 2748 🚇 Upton Park 🚌 15, 115

PRICES AND SYMBOLS

The prices given are the average for a two-course set lunch (L) and a three-course à la carte dinner (D) for one person, without drinks. The wine price is for the least expensive bottle.

For a key to the symbols, ▷ 2.

1 LOMBARD STREET – THE FINE DINING RESTAURANT

www.1lombardstreet.com

A typical City building with large-scale windows, opposite the Bank of England. Behind the busy, informal brasserie is a fine dining area in a quiet back room, with formal service. The cooking is primarily French, with dishes such as seared foie gras with muscatel grapes in Armagnac; roasted turbot on the bone with woodland mushroom and herb ragoût; and a wonderful *feuillantine* of caramelized Granny Smith apples with Guinness ice cream and glazed hazelnuts. The slightly cheaper sister restaurant, The Brasserie, within the same building, is also recommended.

➕ 126 M4 ✉ 1 Lombard Street EC3V 9AA ☎ 020 7929 6611 🕓 Mon–Fri 12–2.30, 6–10. Closed 25–26 Dec, 1 Jan, public hols 🖐 L £43.50, D £52.50, Wine £21 🚇 Bank

ALBA

www.albarestaurant.com

This contemporary restaurant, a short stroll from the Barbican, offers a taste of northern Italy. Like the olive-green walls and brightly hued prints, the menu is modern and has such daily specials as Piedmont ravioli and tagliolini with butter, sage and white truffles. Desserts include twin nougat parfait with chocolate sauce.

➕ 126 M3 ✉ 107 Whitecross Street EC1Y 8JD ☎ 020 7588 1798 🕓 Mon–Fri 12–3, 6–11 🖐 L £16.90, D £30, Wine £16.50 🚇 Barbican

BARBECOA

www.barbecoa.com

The brainchild of the ubiquitous Jamie Oliver and American chef Adam Perry Lang, this is a tribute to barbecued, smoked and charred British meats (superb quality, available to cook for yourself from the butcher's shop below), on the lofty upper floor of One New Change shopping mall, within sight of St. Paul's Cathedral. The ultra-modern interior includes seating on banquettes lightly caged in with iron rods. Reviews have been mixed as the new venture settles down. Sample a house hamburger, with cheese, smoked bacon, onions and pickles, or perhaps lamb skewers with polenta and girolles. Fishy options might include crab cakes.

➕ 126 M4 ✉ 20 New Change Passage EC4M 9AG ☎ 020 3005 8555 🕓 Daily 12–11 🖐 L £26, D £38, Wine £12 🚇 St. Paul's 🚌 4, 8, 25, 56, 100, 172, 242, 521

LE CAFÉ DU MARCHÉ

www.cafedumarche.co.uk

Actually three cosy restaurants under one roof. Le Café offers a three-course fixed-price menu, accompanied by live jazz in the background every evening. The first floor Le Grenier also has fixed-price menus and is strong on grilled meat and fish. Le Rendezvous is a smaller brasserie, open for lunch.

➕ 126 L3 ✉ Charterhouse Mews, Charterhouse Square EC1M 6AH ☎ 020 7608 1609 🕓 Mon–Fri 12–2.30, 6–10, Sat 6–10 🖐 L £28.50, D £34.85 (set 3 courses), Wine £16.95 🚇 Farringdon, Barbican

CANTEEN

www.canteen.co.uk

This unpretentious eatery in Spitalfields Market opened in 2006 to rave reviews and has heaved with an eclectic mix of foodies, locals and City types ever since.

Glass-walled on three sides, it teams retro booth seating with long shared tables and prides itself on offering high-quality cuisine at reasonable prices. The all-day menu includes breakfast items and designated 'fast service' dishes, as well as a daily roast, home-made pies and fish options. Expect British classics conjured from the freshest of ingredients, plus a diet-busting array of comfort desserts, such as steamed syrup pudding and custard, or orange jelly with ice cream and shortbread.
✚ 127 N3 ✉ 2 Crispin Place E1 6DW ☎ 0845 686 1122 🕙 Mon–Fri 8am–11pm, Sat–Sun 9am–11pm. Closed 24–26 Dec ✋ B from £3, L £19, D £24.50, Wine £12.50 🚇 Liverpool Street

EYRE BROTHERS
www.eyrebrothers.co.uk
Tucked amid gentrified Shoreditch lofts, this dining spot has dark wood, cool leather and a long, trendy bar. The cuisine is a mixture of regional Portuguese and classic Spanish, featuring earthy flavours and bright colours. Try the seafood, potato, sweet pepper and saffron stew, or Mozambique tiger prawns piri piri.
✚ 127 N2 ✉ 70 Leonard Street EC2 4QX ☎ 020 7613 5346 🕙 Mon–Fri 12–3, 6.30–11, Sat 6.30–11. Closed Christmas–New Year ✋ L £27.50, D £37.50, Wine £16 🚇 Old Street

HIX OYSTER & CHOP HOUSE
www.hixoysterandchophouse.co.uk
Seasonal produce cooked without fuss is the flavour at this restaurant, with its dark-wood panelling and tiles, which opened in 2008 on the site of a former sausage factory. Oysters are at the top of the menu, but the meat is also star quality—as you might expect from a venue so close to Smithfield meat market. Try a Barnsley chop, or hanger steak with baked bone marrow.
✚ 126 L3 ✉ 36–37 Greenhill Rents, Cowcross Street EC1M 6BN ☎ 020 7017 1930 🕙 Daily 12–3, 5.30–11 ✋ L £24.50, D £39, Wine £19.50 (£13.50 for carafe) 🚇 Barbican, Farringdon

MEHEK
www.mehek.co.uk
Stunningly decorated by a Bollywood designer, there is more room inside this popular Indian restaurant than appears from the hole-in-the-wall exterior. The cuisine is mostly standard north Indian with a modern twist, and some dishes from other parts of the subcontinent, such as guinea fowl in Bengali herbs and Goan fish curry.
✚ 126 M3 ✉ 45 London Wall EC2M 5TE ☎ 020 7588 5043 🕙 Mon–Fri 11.30–3, 5.30–11 ✋ L £22, D £26, Wine £15.95 🚇 Moorgate, Liverpool Street

MORO
www.moro.co.uk
Value for money is the key at this lively and always busy Spanish/ North African restaurant. The menu changes weekly but many of the dishes are inspired by the wood-fired oven, ranging from simple grilled chicory with ham and sherry vinegar to roasted turbot with roast beetroot, lentils and spicy red chilli *churrasco* sauce. Warm goat's cheese with pine nuts, raisins and orange blossom water in filo pastry might provide an interesting and unusual dessert. There's also a great choice of sherries.
✚ 126 K2 ✉ 34–36 Exmouth Market EC1R 4QE ☎ 020 7833 8336 🕙 Mon–Sat 12.30–2.30, 7–10.30. Tapas served all day Mon–Sat. Closed Sun, 25–26 Dec, 1 Jan, public hols ✋ L £26.50, D £32.50, Wine £15.50 🚇 Farringdon, Angel

RHODES TWENTYFOUR
www.rhodes24.co.uk
This top-notch addition to the empire of celebrity chef Gary Rhodes sits on the 24th floor of the NatWest Tower, enjoying panoramic views across the City. Friendly, casually dressed staff serve starters such as crisply breaded duck egg with mushroom toast, and main courses such as monkfish with smoked bacon hash and salsify. Note that security is tight here and reservations are essential.
✚ 127 N4 ✉ Tower 42, 25 Old Broad Street EC2N 1HQ ☎ 020 7877 7703 🕙 Mon–Fri 12–2.30, 6–9. Closed 24 Dec–

2 Jan ✋ L £42, D £51, Wine £24 🚇 Bank, Liverpool Street

ST. JOHN
www.stjohnrestaurant.com
Approached through an archway and big iron gates, with a café/bakery below, this restaurant has a menu that nods to traditional British meat cuisine and has a pig motif with butchery markings. There's plenty of offal—salted kid's liver, rabbit's heart, kidneys and liver—and unusual ingredients such as smoked eel with bacon and mash, sausage and chickpeas, and the freshest of game in season. If the meat-fest gets too much, you could go for oysters, and there's always at least one vegetarian dish on the menu.
✚ 126 L3 ✉ 26 St. John Street EC1M 4AY ☎ 020 7251 0848 🕙 Mon–Fri 12–3, 6–11, Sat 6–11, Sun 1–4. Closed 25–26 Dec, 1 Jan, Easter ✋ L £30, D £37, Wine £20.65 🚇 Farringdon, Barbican, Chancery Lane

SMITHS OF SMITHFIELD
www.smithsofsmithfield.co.uk
This sizeable building started life as a warehouse in around 1886 before the completion of the Smithfield Meat Market that lies next door. The upper two floors have panoramic views that take in the City (▷ 118–119), St. Paul's Cathedral and the Old Bailey (▷ 102). The organic and additive-free modern British cooking, of TV *MasterChef*'s John Torode, includes the likes of crisp belly of pork, mashed potato and green sauce, roast monkfish with baby leeks, game chips and caviar butter sauce. Enjoy the Wine Rooms on the first floor, too, serving lighter dishes.
✚ 126 L3 ✉ Top Floor, 66–67 Charterhouse Street EC1M 6HJ ☎ 020 7251 7950 🕙 Mon–Fri 12–3.30, 6.30–12, Sat 6.30–12, Sun 12.30–3.30. Ground floor café Mon–Fri from 7am, Sat 10am, Sun 9.30am ✋ L £33.50, D £40, Wine £13.95 🚇 Farringdon, Barbican

WASABI
www.wasabi.uk.com
The perfect place to take a break when you've shopped till you drop in the shiny One New Change mall,

with the dome of St. Paul's in view, this is the latest in the popular chain of Japanese sushi and bento restaurants. The food is prepared freshly on site every day—you can watch it happening in the open kitchen—and offers quality and great value. Select from 30 different varieties of sushi from the chill cabinet, or tasty hot food such as noodles or salmon teriyaki, from the counter, to eat in or take away. Order *tappan* (savoury pancakes) from the hot plate. Service is friendly and fast. ✚ 126 M4 ✉ One New Change EC4M 9AF ☎ 020 7236 3619 ⏰ Mon–Fri 11–8, Sat 11–7, Sun 11–6 🍴 Bento boxes from £6.95 🚇 St. Paul's 🚌 4, 8, 25, 56, 100, 172, 242, 521

PUBS

THE BLEEDING HEART TAVERN
www.bleedingheart.co.uk/tavern
The original tavern opened in 1746 and was named after a murder in nearby Hatton Garden 100 years earlier. Ales are from Adnam's Brewery, there's an impressive wine list and a menu of traditional pub food, such as spit-roast, grilled gammon steak and rib-eye steak with Béarnaise sauce. No children. ✚ 126 L3 ✉ 19 Greville Street EC1N 8SQ ☎ 020 7242 8238 ⏰ Mon–Fri 7–11.30 (breakfast), 11.30–10.30. Closed 24 Dec–2 Jan, public hols 🍴 Bar meals from £8.95, D from £20 🚇 Farringdon

THE CROWN
www.geronimo-inns.co.uk
In this carefully restored 1860s' building, everything from the building materials and the second-hand furniture to the organic menu and wine list is green—based on sound environmental practices. The menu changes with the seasons, and is a mix of European dishes, such as leek and parsnip soup. The bitter chocolate mousse is a delicious end to the meal. There's also a garden. ✚ Off map 127 Q2 ✉ 223 Grove Road E3 5SN ☎ 020 8880 7261 ⏰ Mon 5–11, Tue–Fri 12–11, Sat–Sun phone for times. Restaurant: Tue–Sun 12.30–3, Mon–Sun 7–10pm. Closed 25 Dec 🍴 L £18, D £29 🚇 Mile End, Bethnal Green

THE DUKE OF CAMBRIDGE
www.dukeorganic.co.uk
This stylishly modernized building in a residential street in trendy Islington was one of London's first pubs to specialize in organic food, wine and beer. Changing chalkboard menus might include seasonal European dishes such as pumpkin and sage soup or grilled asparagus with anchovy. Try to leave space for desserts such as lavender crème brûlée and the pear and chocolate soufflé cake. Garden and patio. ✚ Off map 126 L1 ✉ 30 St. Peter's Street N1 8JT ☎ 020 7359 3066 ⏰ Mon–Sat 12–11, Sun 12–10.30. Restaurant Mon–Fri 12.30–3, 6.30–10, Sat 12.30–3.30, 6.30–10.30, Sun 12.30–3.30, 6.30–10. Closed 25–26 Dec, 1 Jan 🍴 L £22, D £28 🚇 Angel

THE EAGLE
On the fringe of Clerkenwell, London's focus on cool, The Eagle was one of Britain's first pubs to concentrate on the quality of its food. The pub has even published its own cookbook, *Big Flavours and Rough Edges*. The straightforward, rustic blackboard menu favours a Mediterranean style. The post-work City buzz can be truly intoxicating. ✚ 126 K2 ✉ 159 Farringdon Road EC1R 3AL ☎ 020 7837 1353 ⏰ Mon–Sat 12–11, Sun 12–5. Food served Mon–Fri 12.30–3, 6.30–10.30, Sat 12.30–3.30, 6.30–10.30, Sun 12.30–3.30 🍴 Meals from £10 🚇 Angel, Farringdon

THE JERUSALEM TAVERN
www.stpetersbrewery.co.uk
This dimly lit bar dates from 1720, when it was a merchant's house, and it has often been used as a film set. It derives its name from the Priory of St. John, originally on the site. There are bare floorboards, rustic tables and a selection of magazines and newspapers. Bar food is simple—speciality sandwiches, sausage baguettes and beef casserole. Try one of the pub's own excellent cask ales. ✚ 126 L3 ✉ 55 Britton Street EC1M 5UQ ☎ 020 7490 4281 ⏰ Mon–Fri 11–11. Meals: 12–3. Closed 25 Dec, Good Fri, Easter Mon 🍴 Bar meals from £8 🚇 Farringdon

THE OLD BANK OF ENGLAND
www.fullers.co.uk
London's grandest pub, with tall ornate ceilings, this building, formerly the Law Courts branch of the Bank of England, lies by legend between the site of Sweeney Todd's barber shop and his mistress's pie shop; it was in the tunnels and vaults below the present building that Todd's hapless victims were butchered before being cooked and sold in Mrs Lovett's pies. Don't let that put you off, especially as the pub does great pies. The menu ranges from light snacks to traditional English offerings. No children. ✚ 126 K4 ✉ 194 Fleet Street EC4A 2LT ☎ 020 7430 2255 ⏰ Mon–Fri 11–11. Meals: Mon–Thu 12–8, Fri 12–9. Closed public hols 🍴 Bar meals from £10 🚇 Chancery Lane, Temple

THE PEASANT
www.thepeasant.co.uk
Here, the original Victorian features have been restored, including an inlaid mosaic floor, horseshoe bar and conservatory. The peasant-style food with a Mediterranean leaning includes dressed Dorset crab with bacon croquettes, or pan-fried pollock with saffron mash. Children not allowed in the bar area. Terrace. ✚ 126 L2 ✉ 240 St. John Street EC1V 4PH ☎ 020 7336 7726 ⏰ Mon–Sat 12–11, Sun 12–10.30. Restaurant: Tue–Fri 12.30–3.30, 6.30–11 🍴 Bar meals from £10, D from £28 🚇 Angel, Farringdon

YE OLDE CHESHIRE CHEESE
This rambling institution is full of nooks and crannies and has a long history of entertaining literary greats such as Sir Arthur Conan Doyle and Charles Dickens, and journalists when Fleet Street was the hub of Britain's newspaper world. One of the few remaining chop houses rebuilt after the Great Fire of 1666, it serves Olde English pub food. ✚ 126 L4 ✉ Wine Office Court, 145 Fleet Street EC4A 2BU ☎ 020 7353 6170 ⏰ Mon–Sat 11–11, Sun 12–6. Restaurant: Mon–Fri 12–9.30, Sat 12–8.30, Sun 12–5. Closed 25–26 Dec, public hols 🍴 Bar meals from £10, D from £19 🚇 Blackfriars, Chancery Lane, Temple

COVENT GARDEN TO BLOOMSBURY

From the grand old Strand that runs parallel to the Embankment on the River Thames's north bank, this area fans out to include London's principal entertainment and commercial districts, Covent Garden and Soho. Here you will find the vast majority of the city's renowned theatres, as well as many of its more mainstream nightlife venues and a dazzling selection of shops. Covent Garden itself is blessed with more attractive streets and buildings than its brash neighbour, all centred upon its famous Piazza, a haven for tourists, street performers and the odd pickpocket following in the footsteps of Charles Dickens's Fagin.

Across the other side of Charing Cross Road, famous for its bookshops, the architecture is a tad more functional throughout most of Soho, although its main hubs of Leicester Square and Piccadilly Circus, presided over by the impish Eros, always manage to attract hordes of visitors, if not that many Londoners. Just to the north, the city's modest Chinatown provides a colourful break and the chance of grabbing an inexpensive bite to eat. Continuing north from here, the rest of Soho develops a split personality, partly a seedy series of sex shops, partly an elegant set of streets around Soho Square, interspersed with more upscale restaurants and pubs.

Forming a distinct northern boundary to this part of the city is London's most famous consumer honeypot, Oxford Street, where most of the huge department stores vie for business. To the east and north of here, beyond the West End's lone skyscraper, Centre Point, you will find a completely different atmosphere in the classy area of Bloomsbury. With the magnificent British Museum as its cultural centrepiece and several leafy squares, the surprisingly quiet streets contain some of the capital's most desirable and expensive property.

Regent's Park

SOMERS TOWN
Community Sports Centre

REGENT'S PARK

EUSTON STATION

Open Air Theatre

The Holme

Queen Mary's Garden

St John's Lodge

Cumberland Gate

Clarence Gardens

Netley Street

University of Westminster

Euston Tower

University College Hospital

University College London

Petrie Museum of Egyptian Archaeology

Royal College of Physicians

Sherlock Holmes Museum

Madame Tussauds

University of Westminster

The London Clinic

Royal Academy of Music

Regent's Park

Royal National Orthopaedic Hospital

BT Tower

University of Westminster

UCL

LISSON GROVE

PADDINGTON

MARYLEBONE

Central Synagogue

Wallace Collection

All Saints' Church

Wigmore Hall

Photographers' Gallery

West End Great Synagogue

Selfridges

ST GILES CIRCUS

Tottenham Court Road

SOHO

CHINATOWN

Handel House Museum

St George's Church

US Embassy

Roosevelt Memorial

Leicester Square

London Trocadero

Piccadilly Circus

Eros

MAYFAIR

Royal Institution

Royal Academy of Arts

St James's Church

Hyde Park

Green Park

ALL SAINTS' CHURCH

www.allsaintsmargaretstreet.org.uk

All Saints' soars up from its crowded site north of Oxford Street. Designed by William Butterfield (1814–1900) in 13th-century Gothic style, its lofty architecture and lavish interior of granite, marble and polychrome tiles make it one of the most impressive Victorian churches in London. At 69m (227ft), the cross-banded spire is the second highest in the city. Visit after dark if possible, as the church looks its best in candlelight.

✚ 130 H4 ✉ 7 Margaret Street W1W 8JG ☎ 020 7636 1788 🕐 Daily 7–7 ✋ Free Ⓜ Oxford Circus 🚌 7, 8, 10, 176

BRITISH LIBRARY

www.bl.uk

Britain's national library, formerly housed in the British Museum (▷ 134–139), gained its own purpose-built complex in 1998—the UK's biggest 20th-century public building. This stunning new package consists of a spacious piazza, three public galleries, new public artworks, a restaurant, a café, a shop and plenty of activities and tours. Eight of its fourteen floors are above ground, six below; beneath these are basements extending to a depth of 25m (82ft).

Before entering the galleries, go up the steps by the information desk and walk around the floor-to-ceiling central glass shaft to enjoy some of the beautiful bindings of the King's Library, George III's 60,000 volumes donated by his son George IV in 1823. The outer walls store the British Library's stamp collection—the world's finest—and you can pull out the vertical trays of stamps to examine specimens.

The John Ritblat Galleries display more of the library's treasures, including various editions of the Magna Carta (the 13th-century charter of public liberties), Leonardo da Vinci's notebook and the only surviving manuscript in Shakespeare's own hand. You can listen to recordings of rare bird song or a speech by Sir Winston Churchill. The Paccar Gallery is a major space

Above *The British Library occupies striking modern premises in St. Pancras*
Left *Statues atop the former Flower Market building, Covent Garden*

for temporary exhibitions. These change regularly, but popular recent exhibitions included Magnificent Maps (2010), and in 2011–12 highlights of the royal collection of illuminated manuscripts were shown here.

The reading rooms are accessible only to pass-holders, who can consult any work from the collection, including every book printed since 1911. There are more than 150 million items in more than 400 languages; some 8,000 titles are added each working day.

✚ 131 J2 ✉ 96 Euston Road NW1 2DB ☎ 0843 208 1144 🕐 Public areas, galleries and bookshop: Mon, Wed–Fri 9.30–6, Tue 9.30–8, Sat 9.30–5, Sun 11–5. Reading rooms open to readers only ✋ Free Ⓜ King's Cross, St. Pancras, Euston, Euston Square 🚌 10, 30, 73, 91 🖥 🏛

BRITISH MUSEUM

▷ 134–139.

THE CARTOON MUSEUM

www.cartoonmuseum.org

This is London's first dedicated cartoon museum, which opened in 2006 close to the British Museum. The collection conserves and displays a fascinating range of British cartoons, caricatures and comics. The reference library contains some 4,000 books on cartoons and aspects of the art, as well as more than 2,500 comics. The museum hosts lectures and workshops for adults and children.

✚ 131 J3 ✉ 35 Little Russell Street WC1A 2HH ☎ 020 7580 8155 🕐 Tue–Sat 10.30–5.30, Sun 12–5.30 ✋ Adult £5.50, child (under 18) free Ⓜ Tottenham Court Road, Holborn 🚌 7, 38, 91, 188 🏛

INTRODUCTION

Wealthy physician Sir Hans Sloane (1660–1753) spent his life collecting assorted coins, books and natural history specimens, which by his death amounted to some 80,000 items. The government bought this collection and it was first put on display as the British Museum in 1759, at Montague House, which occupied the museum's present site. However, augmented by donations from benefactors, travellers, historians and archaeologists, the museum soon outgrew its home and Sir Robert Smirke's Classical building (1823–47) was constructed to replace Montague House. As the museum continued to grow, more galleries were added, but space was still a major problem and by the late 20th century it became clear that a more radical solution had to be found. So in 1998 the British Library (▷ 133), which had occupied the famous Reading Room, was moved to St. Pancras and the Great Court was given a complete overhaul.

There are two entrances to the museum: one (the main entrance) on Great Russell Street (south) and the other on Montague Place (north). Both lead into the covered Great Court, which is the hub of the museum, forming the crossroads between all the galleries. It also serves as the main information centre and the location of the shops and eateries.

The museum's collections are arranged by geography, culture and theme, but the layout and sheer size of the place can still be bewildering. Note that collections from the same culture are not necessarily on the same floor (▷ 138). The best way to tackle the museum is to focus on the highlights or on one or two collections.

WHAT TO SEE

GREAT COURT AND READING ROOM

Entering Sir Robert Smirke's imposing, neoclassical building has become a pleasure in itself since the addition in 2000 of Sir Norman Foster's glorious, curved glass canopy over the central Great Court, turning the previously dark and confusing area cluttered with storerooms into a huge, light space—now Europe's largest covered square. It's worth lingering here to enjoy the sculpture displays set around the Great Concourse Gallery (such as the Easter Island statue and a reconstructed chariot) while deciding which galleries to visit.

In the middle of the court is the circular Reading Room, completed in 1857 to the design of Smirke's brother, Sydney. Karl Marx and other intellectuals once worked here. From a viewing area at the front, you can enjoy the domed ceiling, restored to its original colour scheme of blue, cream and gold, the low-lit desks and the floor-to-ceiling bookcases. There's an information desk near the entrance.

MAIN FLOOR

Rosetta Stone (Room 4)

Though not particularly impressive to look at, the Rosetta Stone was instrumental in solving many of the puzzles of the ancient Egyptian world. The slab of black basalt, discovered by Napoleon's army in the Nile Delta in 1799, reproduces the same (not very exciting) text in three languages: Greek, Demotic and Egyptian. This offered the first opportunity for modern scholars to crack the code of Egyptian hieroglyphics by comparing them with known scripts.

Elgin Marbles (Room 18)

The question of where they should be—in Greece or in Britain—still causes passionate debate. In fact, such is the controversy raging around them that

INFORMATION

www.britishmuseum.org
131 J3 ✉ Great Russell Street WC1B 3DG ☎ 020 7323 8000 🕐 Sat–Thu 10–5.30, Fri 10–8.30. Great Court Sat–Wed 9–5.30, Thu–Fri 9–8.30. Check times for temporary exhibitions. Late views: selected galleries only; check ahead 👆 Free; charges for some temporary exhibitions 🚇 Holborn, Tottenham Court Road, Russell Square, Goodge Street 🚌 1, 7, 8, 19, 25, 38, 55, 98, 242 🎧 Various audiotours in 10 languages, £5. Multimedia guide for children £3. 30–40-minute introductory tours: choose from Japan, Gods of Roman Britain, Ancient Greece, Ancient Iraq, Africa, China, Enlightenment Gallery, South Asia, Mexico, Art of the Middle East, The World of Money, Ancient Egypt, Early Medieval Europe, Ancient Rome, Assyrian reliefs; daily starting at 11 until 3.45; free 📖 A good selection for adults and children from £6. Available in English, French, German, Italian, Spanish, Korean, Chinese, Japanese, Russian, Polish, Arabic 🍴 Court Restaurant on upper floor of Great Court serves hot and cold meals, afternoon tea, evening dinner. Open Sat–Wed 12–5.30, Thu–Fri 12–8. Reservations: 020 7323 8990 ☕ Court Café (east and west) serving hot drinks, light meals. Open Sat–Wed 9–5.30, Thu–Fri 9–8. Gallery Café serving hot and cold light meals, morning coffee and afternoon tea. Open daily 10–5 🛍 Bookshop by Room 6, selling titles on art, history, archaeology etc. Family shop on north side of Great Court concourse. Collections shop on west side of Great Court concourse. Culture shop on east side of the main entrance, next to Room 3, selling replica sculpture, jewellery, silk scarves and ties

Opposite *Iron and gilt bronze helmet from the ship burial at Sutton Hoo, dating from the seventh century*

REGIONS COVENT GARDEN TO BLOOMSBURY • SIGHTS

135

the marbles' quality can be overlooked. These frieze reliefs, taken from the Parthenon, the temple to Athena on the Acropolis at Athens, are some of the finest sculptures of antiquity. Displayed in a vast room, they are best viewed as a kind of cartoon strip depicting a festival to commemorate Athena's birthday.

Following a visit to Athens in 1800 Lord Elgin, then British ambassador in Constantinople, obtained a licence from the Turkish Sultan to remove the stones, which had suffered severe damage during a skirmish between the Turks and a Venetian fleet in 1687. Arguing that the marbles would not survive if they remained in Greece, Elgin had them transported to Britain. The eventful journey involved a shipwreck and Elgin's detention in France.

Assyrian Reliefs (Rooms 6–10)
Vivid carved figures carrying pots and weapons, taking part in daily activities or military campaigns, were cut into panels for the Assyrian kings' palaces and temples, and have survived since about 880–612BC. Originally set on the buildings' mud-brick walls—some to a height of 2.6m (8.5ft), they were coloured with paint, traces of which can sometimes still be seen. Like comic strips, they relate their stories from one end of a wall to the other. Some of the most striking friezes come from the great palace—known as the Southwest Palace—of King Sennacherib, who came to the throne of Assyria in 704BC and moved his capital from Dur-Sharrukin (modern Khorsabad) to the ancient city of Nineveh, which he rebuilt in magnificent style. The palace was his great showpiece, many of its rooms covered with alabaster wall reliefs.

UPPER FLOORS
Portland Vase (Room 70)
This ancient cameo-glass vase was probably made in Rome between AD5 and AD25. Nothing is known about it prior to its appearance in the description of Cardinal del Monte's art collection in Italy in 1601. After passing to a series of buyers, it eventually reached the hands of the 3rd Duke of Portland in 1786.

Above *Smirke's Greek-inspired colonnaded facade on Great Russell Street*

He lent it to potter Josiah Wedgwood, who copied its cameo design and made it world-famous. The 4th Duke deposited it in the British Museum, which eventually bought it outright in 1945.

Love and marriage are the themes of its decoration, with a mythological slant, and one theory is that it was made as a wedding gift, at a time when glass-blowing was a relatively new technique.

Sutton Hoo Treasure (Room 41)
This comprises the collection of treasures from an Anglo-Saxon royal burial ship that survived intact in Suffolk and was excavated in 1939. The ship was probably a monument to Raedwald, the last great pagan king of East Anglia, who died in about AD625. Besides fine gold jewels, the boat contained a sceptre, a gold purse, silver bowls and plates, mounted silver drinking horns, bronze cauldrons and silver and gold ship fittings. Among a number of weapons were a shield, a sword with jewelled gold hilt, and an iron helmet with bronze and silver fittings and 'eyebrows' edged in garnets (▷ 134).

Lewis Chessmen (Room 40)
Carved from the tusks of walruses, these squat, sometimes comical-looking little figures were discovered on the island of Lewis in the Outer Hebrides of Scotland in 1831 by a crofter while working his land. Scandinavian in origin, they depict the figures used on a chess-board and are believed to date from the mid-12th century. There are 80 pieces in all.

Mildenhall Treasure (Room 49)
A farmer ploughing his field near Mildenhall in Suffolk in 1942 unearthed an entire set of late-Roman silver tableware. There were no coins, so it was not easy to date, but the collection's design suggests it was used during the fourth century AD, by someone of high standing. The level of decoration on the platters, ladles and spoons, bowls and dishes is superb, and includes handles shaped like dolphins and depictions of Bacchus, god of wine—a fashionable touch in silver dining sets throughout the Roman period.

TIPS
» Get your bearings in the Great Court, where you can pick up plans and information.
» Don't expect to see everything in a day; focus on what interests you and make for one or two galleries.
» Make a trip here in the evening on Thursday to Saturday, when the Great Court's restaurants and shops remain open. On Thursdays and Fridays the major galleries stay open late.

Left *Detail from the Elgin Marbles*
Below *The light and airy Great Court under its vast glass canopy*

GALLERY GUIDE
UPPER FLOOR
Rooms 38–39: Clocks and Watches
Rooms 40–51: Europe
Room 49: Roman Britain
Room 50: Britain and Europe 800BC–AD43
Room 51: Ancient Europe 4000–800BC
Rooms 52–59: Middle East
Rooms 61–66: Egypt
Room 68: Money
Rooms 69–73: Ancient Greece and Rome
Rooms 92–94: Asia—Japan

GROUND FLOOR
Room 1: Enlightenment
Room 2: Changing museum
Room 3: Special exhibitions
Room 4: Ancient Egypt
Room 5: Special exhibitions
Rooms 6–10: Middle East
Rooms 11–23: Ancient Greece and Rome
Room 24: Living and Dying
Rooms 26–27: The Americas
Rooms 33–33a, 67, 95: Asia
Room 34: The Islamic World

RAISED LEVEL
Room 67: Korea
Room 95: Chinese ceramics

LOWER FLOORS
Clore Education Centre
Room 25: Africa
Room 77: Greek and Roman architecture
Room 78: Classical inscriptions

Egyptian Mummies

Portland Vase

Lindow Man

Mildenhall Treasure

Sutton Hoo Treasure

Lewis Chessmen

Percival David Collection

MONTAGUE PLACE ENTRANCE

Elgin Marbles

Rosetta Stone

THE GREAT COURT

Bookshop

Shop

Reading Room

GREAT RUSSELL STREET ENTRANCE

Clore Education Centre

Ford Centre for Young Visitors

Egyptian Mummies (Rooms 62–63)

One of the most popular displays in the British Museum is that of Egyptian mummies and sarcophagi. Row after row of preserved bodies, wrapped in bandages and surrounded by their prized possessions and favourite food, exercise a gruesome fascination, especially for children. Most disturbing of all is the preserved body of 'Ginger', a Predynastic Egyptian from 3400BC in a reconstructed grave pit. Not just people were mummified: there are also elaborately wrapped cat mummies which were buried by pious Egyptians in special cat cemeteries. The craftsmanship and elegance of the items surrounding and celebrating the dead are superb—such as the intricately painted wooden coffin of Passenhor, its body busy with figures and texts, its head painted to represent a serene, young face framed by a headdress. Discovered in Thebes, it was created in about 700BC.

Lindow Man (Room 50)

Nicknamed 'Pete Marsh' by the archaeologists who found him in a waterlogged peat bog in Cheshire, the Lindow Man is an almost perfectly preserved—albeit somewhat leathery—2,000-year-old corpse. One of the current theories is that he was sacrificed during a Druid ceremony. There are signs of a blow to his head and a wound to his throat, and mistletoe grains were found in his gut, suggesting that he was fed a hallucinatory meal before being knocked out, strangled and drowned.

Percival David Collection (Room 95)

This outstanding collection of Chinese ceramics was amassed by scholar and collector Sir Percival David, who acquired pieces sold off by the Chinese imperial household in the 1920s. He presented the collection, along with his extensive library of books relating to Chinese art and culture, to the University of London in 1950, and for many years both were housed in an elegant Georgian town house in Gordon Square. Lack of funding forced the Percival David Foundation to close in 2007, but in 2009 the ceramics were installed on permanent loan in a specially built new gallery in the British Museum.

In all there are about 1,700 Chinese ceramics, reflecting court taste and dating mainly from the 10th to the 18th centuries. Items range from bowls, teapots, cups and vases to incense burners and perfume baskets, spittoons, garden seats, flower-holders, lamp stands and candleholders, animal figurines and figures of Buddhas and deities.

Highlights include a collection of stoneware from the Song (960–1279) and Yuan (1279–1368) dynasties, as well as blue and white, polychrome and monochrome porcelains.

SIR HANS SLOANE

Having developed a keen interest in nature as a child in Ireland, Hans Sloane studied chemistry and botany in London, and medicine in France. A three-month voyage to Jamaica as physician to the new governor, the 2nd Duke of Albemarle, gave him the chance to observe the local fauna and flora, customs and natural phenomena such as earthquakes, and to collect plants, molluscs, insects and fish. He was intrigued by a popular local drink, cocoa, and concocted a variation adding milk to reduce its bitterness. On his return to England Sloane's version was sold as a medicine before passing to Messrs. Cadbury, who turned it into their famous drinking chocolate. Sloane continued his career as a distinguished physician while collecting curiosities and publishing works on his travels and studies. By the time of his death at the age of 93, his precious collection took up a large part of his house, and was looked after by a full-time curator.

Above *Monumental figures in the Egyptian Sculpture Gallery*

CHARLES DICKENS MUSEUM

www.dickensmuseum.com

Charles Dickens (1812–70), the prolific novelist and commentator on Victorian society, lived at no fewer than 15 addresses during his life. This Georgian terraced house in Bloomsbury is where he lived from 1837 to 1839. Now a museum of his life and work, it houses original manuscripts, first editions, personal effects, memorabilia, including the Dickens family tree, and 19th-century paintings, and includes the study where Dickens completed his first full-length novel, *The Pickwick Papers*, and later the famous *Oliver Twist* and *Nicholas Nickleby*.

The cluttered drawing room where the novelist entertained has been restored to its original Regency style. A £2 million revamp means the museum will close at the end of 2011, re-opening in 2012 for the bicentenary of Dickens's birth.

➕ 131 K3 ✉ 48 Doughty Street WC1N 2LX ☎ 020 7405 2127 🕐 Mon–Sat 10–5, Sun 11–5 ✋ Adult £6, child (under 16) £3, family £15 🚇 Russell Square, King's Cross, Chancery Lane (closed Sun) 🚌 19, 38, 45, 55, 243 ♿

CHINATOWN

www.chinatownlondon.org

This vibrant enclave around pedestrianized Gerrard Street is crammed with Asian shops and eateries. Since the 1950s Chinese immigrants have made the area their own and the community congregates here to shop and socialize. Ornate gateways stand at either end of the pedestrian area, and even the phone boxes have pagoda-style roofs. At Chinese New Year (late January/early February, ▷ 294), huge papier-mâché lions dance through the streets against a background of firecrackers and street events.

➕ 130 H4 🕐 Open access ✋ Free 🚇 Leicester Square, Tottenham Court Road 🚌 14, 19, 24, 38, 176

CLEOPATRA'S NEEDLE

www.akhet.co.uk/cleo.htm

This pink granite obelisk—the twin of the one in New York's Central Park—was constructed for the Egyptian Pharaoh Tuthmose III in about 1500BC, and its elaborately carved hieroglyphics and inscriptions were added to mark the victories of Rameses II. Its association with Cleopatra began when it was moved to Alexandria. In the 19th century it was given to the British by the Egyptian viceroy, but its weight made shipment impossible for several decades.

Plaques mounted round the base of the obelisk give a brief history of the needle and commemorate the men who died during its transportation, when the ship carrying it ran into a storm in the Bay of Biscay. It was placed here beside the Thames in 1879, flanked by two Victorian bronze sphinxes. Nearby benches are also decorated with an Egyptian motif of winged sphinxes.

➕ 131 J5 🕐 Open access ✋ Free 🚇 Embankment 🚌 68, 171, 176, 188, RV1 ⛴ Embankment Pier

COVENT GARDEN

▷ 142–143.

THE FOUNDLING MUSEUM

www.foundlingmuseum.org.uk

The Thomas Coram Foundation was set up in 1739 to provide shelter and education for orphaned and abandoned children. The founder was sea captain and philanthropist Thomas Coram, who enlisted the composer Handel and artist William Hogarth as governors and benefactors.

The Foundling Museum was founded in 1998 and after a major refurbishment opened as a state-of-the-art museum in 2004. It tells the story of the Foundling Hospital for abandoned children and displays a fine collection of art and social history. It is next to the Foundation now known as Coram, which continues the work of helping vulnerable children.

➕ 131 J2 ✉ 40 Brunswick Square WC1N 1AZ ☎ 020 7841 3600 🕐 Tue–Sat 10–5, Sun 11–5 ✋ Adult £7.50, under 16s free 🚇 Russell Square, King's Cross 🚌 10, 19, 45, 68, 73, 168, 243

GRAY'S INN

www.graysinn.info

Gray's Inn is one of the four Inns of Court (along with Lincoln's Inn, ▷ 144, and Inner and Middle Temple, ▷ 110) established in the 14th century to provide accommodation for lawyers and their trainees. Together they now serve as the home of London's legal profession.

Although wartime bombing destroyed much of Gray's Inn, the most important buildings have been well restored. These include the 17th-century gateway on High Holborn, which gives access to the gardens, the only part open to the public. Known as the Walks, the gardens were first laid out in 1606 by English philosopher and statesman Sir Francis Bacon (1561–1626) when he was treasurer here.

Paths lead through quadrangles of varying character. Red-brick Georgian buildings line South Square, a quiet precinct with lawns and a statue of Bacon at its centre. Late 17th-century houses and a chapel can be found in Gray's Inn Square. Field Court is distinguished by 18th-century houses bordering a paved and cobbled courtyard.

➕ 131 K3 ✉ 8 South Square WC1R 5ET ☎ 020 7458 7800 🕐 Public access to gardens only Mon–Fri 12–2.30. Chapel Mon–Fri 10–6 ✋ Free 🚇 Chancery Lane (closed Sun), Holborn 🚌 8, 17, 25, 45, 46, 243, 521

Right Ornamental gates mark the entrances to Chinatown

Below Blue plaque at No. 48 Doughty Street, one-time home of Charles Dickens

COVENT GARDEN

INFORMATION

www.coventgardenlife.com

131 J4 Open access Free

Covent Garden 9, 13, 15, 23, 24, 139, 153

INTRODUCTION

Covent Garden Piazza was London's first residential square, laid out in the 1630s by architect Inigo Jones and the model for numerous other squares around the city. Jones had been commissioned by the Earl of Bedford to model its Palladian-style arcades on the central piazza of Livorno in Italy. It was an immediate hit as promenading territory with the upper echelon of England's Renaissance society but it gradually metamorphosed into a thriving fruit and vegetable market, renowned for its flower-sellers and for the costermongers (a term originally meaning 'apple-sellers'), who effortlessly balanced towering stacks of baskets on their heads. This transformation ironically returned the area to its earlier usage, when it served as kitchen garden of the Convent ('covent' in Middle English) of St. Peter during the medieval period. Subsequent centuries saw the area's reputation decline further as brothels supplemented the market stalls, and it remained the province of pimps, whores and lowlifes well into the Victorian era. Indeed, this was the location chosen by playwright George Bernard Shaw for his character Henry Higgins to find the perfect cockney accent as spoken by flower-seller Eliza Doolittle in *Pygmalion*.

WHAT TO SEE

THE PIAZZA

When the traders moved out to Nine Elms near Vauxhall, south London, in the 1970s, the market area was transformed into the Piazza, a mix of specialist shops, stalls and eating places, with street entertainers to amuse the crowds. The central halls, still covered with their 1870s' iron roofs and fronted at the eastern end, the original entrance, by grand stone columns, form the heart of this buzzing area.

Steps lead down to the converted cellar area of the halls, now housing more shops and the Punch and Judy pub. It was here that diarist Samuel Pepys made the first recorded mention of seeing a Punch and Judy puppet show in May

Above *The converted cellar area at the heart of the Piazza is filled with shops and cafés*

1662. Shoppers sitting at the outdoor tables or leaning on the balcony above are entertained by street performers who must prove their worth by audition before being let loose on the public.

Retailers, too, are carefully chosen for their suitability to the Covent Garden spirit, so the Piazza's shops all have a certain character—such as Culpeper the Herbalist, or Benjamin Pollock's Toy Shop, which specializes in toy theatres, Punch and Judy, antique toys, miniatures and games.

There's still a daily market here (10–6), set up in the North Hall and collectively known as the Apple Market. More than 200 stallholders are registered to trade in it, and because most exhibit only once or twice a week, there is always an enormous variety of crafts, jewellery, clothing and accessories (Tue–Sun). On Mondays, the market is turned over exclusively to stalls selling antiques and other collectables.

AROUND AND BEYOND THE PIAZZA

On the northeast corner of the Piazza is the magnificently refurbished Royal Opera House (▷ 158, 160). Its design incorporates the original iron framework of the market's Floral Hall. Across the Piazza is the former Flower Market, now the site of the refurbished London Transport Museum (▷ 145), while the Italianate St. Paul's Church (▷ 147), on the west side of the Piazza, is about the only building not to have changed its purpose. The area in front of it is another space often devoted to street performances. To the east are two of the area's famous theatres, the elegant Theatre Royal Drury Lane (▷ 160) and the Lyceum (▷ 158), on Wellington Street.

The area known as Covent Garden spreads well beyond the Underground station and into the narrow streets leading off the Piazza, themselves full of arty specialist shops. Long Acre is a particularly good hunting ground, as is King Street and the small roads that radiate out from Seven Dials, to the northwest.

TIP
» Petty thieves operate more around Covent Garden than in any other part of London, so you should guard your valuables against sleight of hand.

Left *Old buses and trams on display at the London Transport Museum*
Below *One of the specialist shops in Neal Street, off Long Acre*

REGIONS COVENT GARDEN TO BLOOMSBURY • SIGHTS

LEICESTER SQUARE

www.officiallondontheatre.co.uk/tkts for cut-price tickets

By night, particularly on a Friday or Saturday, this pedestrianized central London square is one of the most crowded places in the city, teeming with people on their way to or from cinemas, nightclubs, restaurants, fast-food outlets and bars. By day its tiny central garden is a popular lunchtime resting place. In the middle of the garden is the marble Shakespeare Memorial Fountain (1874) by Giovanni Fontana, facing a bronze statue of Charlie Chaplin (1981) by John Doubleday. Around the perimeter are busts of some of the square's former local residents—Sir Joshua Reynolds, Sir Isaac Newton, William Hogarth and John Hunter.

The tkts ticket booth in the clock tower building on the south side of the square is the best place to buy discounted theatre tickets.

✚ 130 H5 ✉ Leicester Square WC2H 7NJ 🕐 Open access to the square. Cut-price tkts ticket booth: Mon–Sat 10–7, Sun 11–4 ✋ Free 🚇 Leicester Square 🚌 24, 29, 176 🍴 🖳 🏛

LINCOLN'S INN

www.lincolnsinn.org.uk

The buildings of Lincoln's Inn, one of London's four Inns of Court (▷ 110 and 140), cover 400 years and a number of architectural styles. The 15th-century Old Hall, where the Court of Chancery sat between 1733 and 1873, is the setting for the protracted Jarndyce v Jarndyce case in Charles Dickens's novel *Bleak House*. A 17th-century chapel built above a beautiful open undercroft (crypt) has massive pillars and dramatic vaulting, and gas lamps still light the 17th-century houses in New Square. The mock-Tudor Great Hall, with its red brick and black frame, is a 19th-century addition.

An archway at the northwest corner of New Square leads to Lincoln's Inn Fields, at 5ha (12 acres) the largest square in London and once a popular venue for fighting duels. Today lawyers battle it out instead on the tennis courts here in their lunch hour. On the north side is Sir John Soane's Museum (▷ 148–149).

✚ 131 K4 ✉ Lincoln's Inn WC2A 3TL ☎ 020 7405 1393 🕐 Public access to grounds only, Mon–Fri 8.30–7. Chapel 12–2.30 ✋ Free 🚇 Chancery Lane (closed Sun), Holborn 🚌 8, 25, 242, 521

LONDON CANAL MUSEUM

www.canalmuseum.org.uk

Here on Regent's Canal, within striking distance of one of the city's busiest areas, you can see inside a narrowboat cabin, trace the history of London's canals and learn about the cargoes they carried and the people who lived and worked on the waterways when they formed the nation's commercial arteries. The museum is housed in a former warehouse built for famous ice-cream-maker Carlo Gatti, and also explores the history of the ice trade and ice cream. Don't miss the opportunity to look down into the Victorian ice well.

✚ 131 J1 ✉ 12–13 New Wharf Road, King's Cross N1 9RT ☎ 020 7713 0836 🕐 Tue–Sun 10–4.30 ✋ Adult £3, child (8–15) £1.50, under 8s free 🚇 King's Cross 🚌 10, 46, 73, 205 🚉 King's Cross 🏛

Left *Charlie Chaplin's statue in Leicester Square*

LONDON TRANSPORT MUSEUM

www.ltmuseum.co.uk

Covent Garden's former Flower Market (▷ 142–143) now houses the London Transport Museum, which tells the story of the city's transport since the early 1800s and explores its impact on the growth of the capital and the lives of Londoners.

The museum's permanent displays draw from more than 370,000 items—the most comprehensive collection of historic urban transport in the world. Fulfil your childhood fantasies by clambering into the driving seat of a bus or operating a simulated Tube train, and admire the handsomely designed horse-drawn and electric trams. Discover the story of wartime London when the city's transport workers played a key role.

In addition to the vehicles themselves, there are maps, posters, models, uniforms, signs and other equipment. Touch screens provide more information about the exhibits, and there are many working models and hands-on exhibits.

The museum reopened in November 2007 after a £22 million refurbishment. It still tells the history of transport in the city but there is also an emphasis on future developments, including other major city projects in Delhi, New York, Paris, Shanghai and Tokyo. The museum will take a major role over the coming decades in the debate on the environmental impact of transport in the city and its effect on the inhabitants.

➕ 131 J4 ✉ Covent Garden Piazza, WC2E 7BB ☎ 020 7379 6344 or 020 7565 7299 (24-hour recorded information) 🕐 Sat–Thu 10–6, Fri 11–6 💷 Adult £13.50, under 16s accompanied by an adult free 🚇 Covent Garden, Leicester Square, Holborn, Charing Cross 🚌 9, 11, 15, 13, 23, 139, RV1 ☕ The Upper Deck café 🏪

PETRIE MUSEUM OF EGYPTIAN ARCHAEOLOGY

www.ucl.ac.uk/museums/petrie

This collection, kept in the University of London's Institute of Archaeology building, consists of about 80,000 Egyptian and Sudanese items.

Above *Street artists congregate in Leicester Square and will rustle you up a portrait on the spot; they vary in quality, so choose carefully*

It was started by Victorian enthusiast Amelia Edwards and expanded by Professor William Flinders Petrie (1853–1942), who excavated dozens of major sites. Treasures include finds from the Roman cemeteries at Hawara, famous for its beautiful mummy portraits, El-Amarna, the city of King Akhenaten, and the first true pyramid, at Meydum. Fresh presentation in 2010 has introduced interactive displays, a focus on the Nile Valley and a look at the people and places behind the historic objects.

➕ 130 H3 ✉ University College London, Malet Place WC1E 6BT ☎ 020 7679 2000 🕐 Tue–Sat 1–5 💷 Free. Donations welcome 🚇 Euston, Euston Square, Warren Street, Goodge Street 🚌 18, 24, 29, 73

PHOTOGRAPHERS' GALLERY

www.photonet.org.uk

Britain's first independent photographic gallery, founded in 1971, is now a leading venue for contemporary shows with a full schedule of exhibitions and educational events. Temporary exhibitions cover aspects of the history of photography. (The portrait painter and founder of the Royal Academy, Sir Joshua Reynolds, lived here in the 18th century.) Two buildings off Charing Cross Road accommodate the three galleries, a bookshop and a café.

➕ 131 J4 ✉ Ramillies Street WC2H 7HY ☎ 0845 262 1618 🕐 Scheduled to open autumn 2011. Check for opening times 💷 Free 🚇 Oxford Circus 🚌 12, 24, 29, 176 ☕ 🏪

Opposite *Statue of Eros in Piccadilly Circus*

PICCADILLY CIRCUS

One of the world's busiest traffic circles, formed by the junction of five streets in the West End, the Circus has become a byword for urban clamour and crowds. It was created by John Nash as part of a scheme to link St. James's with Regent's Park. Neon advertisements flash above the constant flow—or crawl—of traffic and the tourists, workers and shoppers who throng the area at all hours.

Its focal point is the aluminium statue known as Eros, above a bronze fountain erected in 1892 as a memorial to the philanthropic 7th Earl of Shaftesbury. Sir Alfred Gilbert, the designer, intended it as an angel of Christian charity rather than the Greek god of love, and was so upset by changes to his design that he refused to attend the unveiling.

Piccadilly is believed to take its name from a 16th-century frilly collar called a pikadil. A dressmaker who made his fortune selling these fashion items built his house nearby.

130 H5 Open access Free Piccadilly Circus 9, 12, 15, 19, 23, 139, 159

ROYAL COURTS OF JUSTICE (LAW COURTS)

www.hmcourts-service.gov.uk
Crowds, news cameras and reporters eager for a verdict often congregate outside the Royal Courts of Justice, at the end of the Strand. The country's most important and high-profile civil cases are tried in this elaborate neo-Gothic building, designed by George Edmund Street in the 1870s. A concoction of spires and pinnacles, it houses more than 50 courtrooms. Public galleries are open to anyone, but security is very tight and to enter you'll have to undergo stringent checks.

On reaching the Main Hall ask for a plan and guide to the complex at the information desk. Cases being heard that day are posted here. An exhibition in the minstrels' gallery traces the history of lawcourt dress.

131 K4 Strand WC2A 2LL 020 7947 6000 Mon–Fri 9–4.30. Cases start around 10am and break for lunch at 1pm Free Chancery Lane, Holborn, Temple 4, 11, 15, 76

ST. CLEMENT DANES

www.raf.mod.uk/stclementdanes
This small and elegant building surrounded by traffic in the middle of the Strand is the latest in a succession of churches on the site. The 11th-century church was first rebuilt by William the Conqueror, then again in the 14th century, demolished and rebuilt by Wren in 1680–82 and virtually destroyed by bombs in 1941, leaving only the steeple (1719) and walls. The interior was rebuilt and dedicated to the Royal Air Force in 1958, and daily prayers and memorial services are held here for its members. Don't miss the black Welsh slate badges of units of the RAF set into the church floor.

131 K4 Strand WC2R 1DH 020 7242 8282 Mon–Sat 8.30–5, Sun 9–1; choral Sun service 11am Free Temple (closed Sun), Embankment 4, 11, 15, 76

ST. PAUL'S CHURCH

actorschurch.org
St. Paul's was conceived as an integral feature of Inigo Jones's 17th-century Italianate piazza, Covent Garden (▷ 142–143), and its Tuscan pillars and columns still dominate the west side of the square. This portico was never used, as the church's main entrance is on Bedford Street.

With the Theatre Royal Drury Lane (▷ 160) and the Royal Opera House (▷ 158, 160) nearby, St. Paul's has always been associated with the theatre and is consequently known as the actors' church. Dozens of plaques commemorate distinguished figures of the thespian world, such as London-born film actor and director Charlie Chaplin (1889–1977).

Other memorials in the church include those for artist J. M. W. Turner, baptized here in 1775, and woodcarver Grinling Gibbons, buried here in 1721.

The space in front of the church is used by all kinds of street performers—clowns, fire-eaters, musicians and acrobats. At the costermongers' harvest festival (▷ 295), cockney market stall-holders converge, dressed for charity in the traditional outfits of pearly kings and queens.

131 J4 Bedford Street WC2E 9ED 020 7836 5221 Mon–Fri 8.30–4.30, Sun service 11am (also evensong 2nd Sun of month, 4pm) Free Covent Garden, Leicester Square 9, 11, 13, 15, 23, RV1

SIR JOHN SOANE'S MUSEUM
▷ 148–149.

SOMERSET HOUSE
▷ 150–151.

VICTORIA EMBANKMENT
The Victoria Embankment, built in the late 1860s to 1870s, was a massive engineering project, reclaiming land from the north bank of the River Thames to create a buffer against flooding. This is where you'll find Cleopatra's Needle (▷ 140), the city's oldest monument, dating from around 1500BC.

131 K5 Open access Free Embankment, Charing Cross 3, 11, 12, 15, 88, 148 Blackfriars, Embankment, Westminster

Below *Italianate St Paul's Church in Covent Garden dates from 1633*

SIR JOHN SOANE'S MUSEUM

INFORMATION

www.soane.org

🕂 131 K4 ✉ 13 Lincoln's Inn Fields WC2A 3BP ☎ 020 7405 2107 ☻ Tue–Sat 10–5; first Tue each month also 6–9pm ♿ Free; donations box provided Ⓠ Chancery Lane (closed Sun), Holborn 🚌 8, 25, 242, 521 🕭 Museum tour Sat 11am, £5 📖 £1, in English and French (includes floor plan) 🏬 Shop selling books on art and architecture, cards and museum-related merchandise

Above *Sir Thomas Lawrence's portrait of Sir John Soane (1827) dominates the library/dining room*

INTRODUCTION

From the moment you arrive it's apparent that this is a museum unlike any other. The entrance is through the front door of No. 13; don't be disconcerted if it's shut—just climb the steps and knock for admission. This is one of three town houses containing the vast collection of sculptures, paintings, carvings and curios amassed by Sir John Soane (1753–1837).

Soane was Professor of Architecture at the Royal Academy (▷ 181) and made his collection of curios, casts and models available to his students and to enthusiastic amateurs. For that purpose he acquired three houses in succession on the north side of Lincoln's Inn Fields between 1792 and 1824. He lived in No. 12 first, then purchased and rebuilt No. 13 and rented out No. 12. He lived in No. 13 from 1813 until his death, when he left it to the nation as a museum. The house at No. 14 was purchased in 1824 and Sir John extended the museum across the back of that property, renting out the house. The museum was open to visitors the day before and the day after each of his lectures, and by 1827 was already known as the Academy of Architecture.

It's possible to wander at will, but a floorplan suggests the route Soane recommended. This starts with the dining room and library and continues to the study and dressing room, crammed with antique marble fragments. You're now overlooking Monument Court, a central light well with relics rescued from demolished buildings. Across the corridor full of marbles and casts is the picture room, on the site of No. 14's old stableyards. A staircase then leads down to the basement, with the Monk's Parlour and yard and the crypt, full of plaster prototypes of classical monuments. Stairs lead back up to the ground floor and the colonnade, which overlooks the basement under a high dome.

The trail leads on through the New Picture Room; the peaceful breakfast parlour; a dining room housing changing exhibitions as the Soane Gallery; another breakfast parlour, and up the curved staircase to the spacious first-floor drawing rooms, where you can see a pencil sketch of Mrs Soane and portraits of Soane and of his sons, John and George.

Opposite Middle Temple Hall looks on to a pretty garden

Barber of Fleet Street. The vaults and tunnels that run below the Old Bank of England public house and the nearby buildings are where barber Sweeney Todd is reputed to have killed and butchered clients, the remains of whom were served as fillings in the nearby pie shop of his mistress, Mrs Lovett.

Turn left to continue along Fleet Street and cross at the pedestrian lights. Continue to the Old Bank of England pub.

❹ The Old Bank of England pub (▷ 124) was a subsidiary branch of the Bank of England until the mid-1970s, when it became the flagship public house for London brewers Fuller, Smith & Turner. It's a grand affair with chandeliers and high ceilings and some cosy corners.

After the Old Bank of England pub turn right into Bell Yard and continue ahead on the path that runs alongside the Royal Courts of Justice (▷ 147). Turn left and then right through the archway into New Square; follow the avenue of trees.

Take the path on the far right past Lincoln's Inn Chapel to reach Stone Buildings and, ahead, go through the gates that lead to Chancery Lane, via a narrow lane. Cross this road and turn left into the street called Southampton Buildings. After just 18m (20yds) this veers sharply left, past the London Silver Vaults. At the end cross High Holborn and pass through a gateway to Gray's Inn (▷ 140) on the right.

❺ The young Charles Dickens spent a year as a solicitor's clerk in Gray's Inn. Later he mastered the art of shorthand and took a job as a reporter on the *Morning Herald* before producing a series of pieces for monthly and weekly publications, writing these under the pseudonym of 'Boz'.

A few paces farther, after Gray's Inn Hall, turn left into Field Court. Continue to the end of Field Court then turn right and go up the steps into Jockey's Fields. Bear left and take the second road on the left, Hand Court. Just past the Bunghole Cellars at the end, turn right along High Holborn to reach Holborn Tube.

WHERE TO EAT AND DRINK
The Old Bank of England pub has London Pride real ale on hand pump. Bar food is served from noon until 9pm. The Bunghole Cellars is a Davy's Wine Bar with sawdust on the floor, where ale is served by the half-gallon. Food is served in the Char Grill all day. Both places are open from 11 to 11.

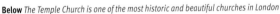

Below The Temple Church is one of the most historic and beautiful churches in London

REGIONS   COVENT GARDEN TO BLOOMSBURY • WALK

153

WHAT TO DO

SHOPPING

ALGERIAN COFFEE STORES
www.algcoffee.co.uk
This splendid Soho shop has been around since 1887 and is one of the oldest in the country. It offers around 80 blends of coffee and 120 types of tea. The shop retains its original wooden floorboards, fixtures and fittings and the wonderfully old-fashioned window display looks as if it has changed little in decades.
✚ 168 H4 ✉ 52 Old Compton Street W1D 4PB ☎ 020 7437 2480 ⏰ Mon–Wed 9–7, Thu–Fri 9–9, Sat 9–8 🚇 Leicester Square, Piccadilly Circus 🚌 10, 14, 19, 25, 38

THE ASTROLOGY SHOP
www.londonastrology.com
Those curious about the cosmic forces will find this shop rather fascinating. Books, games, maps and other astrology-related products are available, and you can have your star chart prepared while you wait.
✚ 169 J4 ✉ 78 Neal Street WC2H 9PA ☎ 020 7813 3051 ⏰ Mon–Sat 11–7, Sun 12–6 🚇 Covent Garden 🚌 1, 9, 11, 13, 15

BENJAMIN POLLOCK'S TOY SHOP
www.pollocks-coventgarden.co.uk
Benjamin Pollock started selling theatrical sheets—a penny plain, twopence coloured—to children in the 19th century, and this extraordinary shop carries on the tradition of selling beautifully made toy theatres, as well as old-fashioned, hand-crafted items such as Punch and Judy puppets, dolls, paper gifts and unusual toys.
✚ 169 J4 ✉ 44 The Market, Covent Garden WC2E 8RF ☎ 020 7379 7866 ⏰ Mon–Sat 10.30–6, Sun 11–4 🚇 Covent Garden 🚌 9, 13, 15, 23, 24, 153

BERWICK STREET
This fruit and vegetable market tucked away in Soho also sells cheese, bread, herbs and spices. Loud stall-holders, media and fashion folk plus a few shady characters set a lively scene. Best at lunchtime.
✚ 168 H4 ✉ Berwick Street W1F 8TW ⏰ Mon–Sat 9–6 🚇 Tottenham Court Road, Oxford Circus 🚌 10, 14, 19, 25, 38

BLACKWELL'S
www.blackwell.co.uk
Set on a corner of the book-lover's paradise, Charing Cross Road, Blackwell's is part of an Oxford-based chain that stocks academic titles as well as fiction and general interest. Look for the Expresso Book Machine, which can print and bind a book of your choice in less than six minutes.
✚ 169 J4 ✉ 100 Charing Cross Road WC2H 0JG ☎ 020 7292 5100 ⏰ Mon–Sat 9.30–8, Sun 12–6 🚇 Leicester Square 🚌 14, 19, 24, 29, 176

CHAPPELL OF BOND STREET
www.chappellofbondstreet.co.uk
Established in 1811 and once frequented by Beethoven, Richard Strauss and Charles Dickens, this store has the largest selection of classical and popular printed music in the UK. Also keyboards and brass/woodwind instruments.
✚ 168 H4 ✉ 152–160 Wardour Street W1F 8YA ☎ 020 7432 4400 ⏰ Mon–Fri 9.30–6, Sat 10–5.30 🚇 Oxford Circus, Tottenham Court Road 🚌 8, 10, 25, 55, 73

Left *Hamleys toyshop celebrated its 250th birthday in 2010*

COVENT GARDEN
www.coventgardenlondonuk.com
It's worth a visit to Covent Garden just to see the street performers and soak up the lively atmosphere. The central area, the Piazza, hosts an antiques and collectables market on Mondays and an arts and crafts market selling jewellery, clothing, silverware and pottery the rest of the week (▷ 142–143).
✚ 169 J4 ✉ Office: 41 The Market WC2E 8RF ☎ 020 7836 9136 🕐 Daily 10–6 🚇 Covent Garden 🚌 9, 13, 15, 23, 24, 153

CULPEPER THE HERBALIST
www.culpeper.co.uk
Culpeper is a reliable brand for herbs, oils, gifts and food. You can make your own cosmetics by adding essential oils to the store's face, hand, body and bath products.
✚ 169 J4 ✉ 8 The Market, Covent Garden WC2 8RB ☎ 020 7379 6698 🕐 Mon–Sat 10–7 (Thu until 8), Sun 10–6 🚇 Covent Garden 🚌 9, 13, 15, 23, 24, 153, RV1

FOYLES
www.foyles.co.uk
This enormous bookshop stocks around 200,000 titles—and a promise that you're more likely to find that elusive title here than in any other bookshop. It has an active schedule of literary luncheons, a big music section, a snazzy jazz café and a gallery, which hosts special exhibitions.
✚ 168 H4 ✉ 113–119 Charing Cross Road WC2H 0EB ☎ 020 7437 5660 🕐 Mon–Sat 9.30–9, Sun 11.30–6 🚇 Tottenham Court Road 🚌 14, 19, 24, 29, 176

GERRY'S WINES & SPIRITS
www.gerrys.uk.com
Whatever your tipple, Gerry's probably stocks it, and if it doesn't you'll find more than enough to catch your eye in the extraordinary collection of wines and spirits. This classic store encapsulates the spirit of Soho (pardon the pun). Friendly expert service.

✚ 168 H4 ✉ 74 Old Compton Street W1D 4UW ☎ 020 7734 4203 🕐 Mon–Thu 9–6.30, Fri 9–7.30, Sat 9–6.30, Sun 12–6 🚇 Leicester Square, Piccadilly Circus 🚌 10, 14, 19, 25, 38

HAMLEYS
www.hamleys.com
The 'World's Finest Toyshop' and great fun for all ages, the store was 250 years old in 2010. Five large floors full of the latest playthings—soft toys, dolls, dressing up, computer games, train sets, kites, LEGO and much more. The knowledgeable and switched-on staff demonstrate the latest gadgets.
✚ 168 H4 ✉ 188–196 Regent Street W1B 5BT ☎ 0871 704 1977 🕐 Mon–Wed 10–8, Thu–Fri 10–9, Sat 10–8, Sun 12–6 🚇 Oxford Circus 🚌 8, 10, 12, 13

HAROLD MOORES RECORDS
www.hmrecords.co.uk
This shop may have England's largest and most comprehensive selection of classical music LPs and CDs, both new and second hand. Perfect for browsing.
✚ 168 H4 ✉ 2 Great Marlborough Street W1F 7HQ ☎ 020 7437 1576 🕐 Mon–Sat 10–6.30 🚇 Oxford Circus 🚌 8, 10, 12, 13, 23

HEAL'S
www.heals.co.uk
Heal's has been a top destination for contemporary interior design and furnishings for the past two centuries, with striking, high-quality furniture, rugs, beds, furnishing fabrics, bed linen and home accessories. The main store, on Tottenham Court Road, is immense.
✚ 168 H3 ✉ The Heal's Building, 196 Tottenham Court Road W1T 7LQ ☎ 020 7636 1666 🕐 Mon–Wed 10–6, Thu 10–8, Fri 10–6.30, Sat 9.30–6.30, Sun 12–6 🚇 Goodge Street 🚌 11, 19, 22, 211, C1 📶

JAMES SMITH & SONS
www.james-smith.co.uk
This very traditional old London shop, established in 1830, manufactures umbrellas by hand—a real craft. You'll also find shooting sticks,

parasols and walking sticks in which you can keep dice—or a dram of whisky.
✚ 169 J4 ✉ 53 New Oxford Street WC1A 1BL ☎ 020 7836 4731 🕐 Mon–Fri 9.30–5, Sat 10–5 🚇 Tottenham Court Road 🚌 8, 14, 98

LIBERTY
www.liberty.co.uk
The mock-Tudor building, complete with creaky timber staircase and sloping ceilings, was actually built in the 1920s. The interior contains an eclectic stock, ranging from ornaments and rugs that seem to have been gathered on some explorer's travels, to designer apparel. The menswear boutique stocks shirts and ties of every colour imaginable, and don't miss the famous fabric collection.
✚ 168 G4 ✉ Great Marlborough Street W1B 5AH ☎ 020 7734 1234 🕐 Mon–Sat 10–9, Sun 12–6 🚇 Oxford Circus, Piccadilly Circus 🚌 3, 6, 12, 13, 15, 23, 53, 88, 94, 139

MRS KIBBLE'S OLDE SWEET SHOPPE
www.mrskibbles.co.uk
Step back in time for a taste of nostalgia at this adorable retro time warp in the middle of Soho. Wall-to-wall jars are filled with sweets from the past that will bring back childhood memories: sugar mice, bon-bons, flying saucers, toffee apples, and lots more.
✚ 168 H4 ✉ 57a Brewer Street W1F 9UL ☎ 0333 123 2345 🕐 Mon–Wed 10–6, Thu–Fri 10–7, Sat 11–7, Sun 12–6 🚇 Piccadilly Circus 🚌 9, 14, 19, 22, 38

NEAL'S YARD DAIRY
www.nealsyarddairy.co.uk
The queen of cheese shops in Covent Garden concentrates on cheese made by small-scale makers in the British Isles. Owner Randolph Hodgson buys direct from farms and sells around 60 to 70 varieties in the dairy, a wonderful place displaying vast round cheeses, where you can sample the wares.
✚ 169 J4 ✉ 17 Shorts Gardens WC2H 9AT ☎ 020 7240 5700 🕐 Mon–Sat 10–7 🚇 Covent Garden 🚌 6, 9, 13, 23, 87

PAPERCHASE

www.paperchase.co.uk

The most design-led stationer in the UK carries a huge range of art papers and materials, including hand-made Japanese papers. This is the vast flagship store.

✚ 168 H3 ✉ 213–215 Tottenham Court Road W1T 7PS ☎ 020 7467 6200 🕙 Mon–Thu 8.30–8, Fri 8.30–7.30, Sat 9–7, Sun 11.30–6 🚇 Goodge Street 🚌 10, 24, 29, 73, 134

PLAYIN' GAMES

Central London's only indoor games specialist is set a stone's throw from the British Museum and among a number of fine bookshops and print galleries. The store offers board games, and classic, family and role-playing games.

✚ 169 J3 ✉ 33 Museum Street WC1A 1LH ☎ 020 7323 3080 🕙 Mon–Wed, Fri–Sat 10–6.30, Thu 10–7 🚇 Tottenham Court Road 🚌 7, 188

ENTERTAINMENT AND NIGHTLIFE

100 CLUB

www.the100club.co.uk

Billed as Europe's most famous live music venue, and opened in 1942, the 100 Club originally focused exclusively on jazz until the 1960s, when the Rolling Stones and The Kinks played here. Music from soul, funk and jazz to R&B, swing, rock and Latin.

✚ 168 H4 ✉ 100 Oxford Street W1D 1LL ☎ 020 7636 0933 👋 £5–£50 🚇 Tottenham Court Road 🚌 7, 8, 10, 25, 55, 98, 176, N8, N25, N176, N207

ADELPHI THEATRE

www.reallyuseful.com

The Adelphi was built in 1806, but its cool black livery dates back to 1930. It stages popular shows and long-running musicals including *Love Never Dies*.

✚ 169 J5 ✉ Strand WC2R 0NS ☎ 0844 412 4651 👋 £25–£67.50 🚇 Charing Cross 🚌 9, 11, 13, 15, 23

ADMIRAL DUNCAN

This cheerful, friendly gay bar in the middle of Soho defies homophobic

oppression—it was rebuilt after a bombing in 1999.

✚ 168 H4 ✉ 54 Old Compton Street W1D 4UD ☎ 020 7437 5300 🕙 Mon–Thu 12–11, Fri–Sat 12–12, Sun 12–10.30 👋 Free 🚇 Leicester Square 🚌 14, 19, 24, 29, 176

ALDWYCH THEATRE

www.aldwych-theatre.co.uk

For 22 years the London home of the Royal Shakespeare Company (1960–82), the Aldwych now stages plays and musicals under Michael Codron's watchful eye.

✚ 169 K4 ✉ 49 Aldwych WC2B 4DF ☎ 020 7379 3367 👋 £33–£72.50 🚇 Covent Garden, Charing Cross 🚌 1, 4, 11, 15, 69, 98

AMBASSADORS THEATRE

www.theambassadorstheatre.co.uk

The West End's smallest theatre mounts an interesting programme of drama by contemporary artists. Seats 400.

✚ 169 J4 ✉ West Street WC2H 9ND ☎ 0844 811 2334 👋 £25–£50 🚇 Leicester Square 🚌 14, 19, 24, 29, 38, 176

BARCODE SOHO

www.bar-code.co.uk

This gay men's bar has a lively, sweaty basement dance floor, plus fruit machines and a pool table. The crowd is flirtatious and easy-going.

✚ 168 H4 ✉ 3–4 Archer Street W1D 7AP ☎ 020 7734 3342 🕙 Mon–Sat 4pm–1am, Sun 4–11 👋 Free; Fri–Sat £4 after 10pm 🚇 Piccadilly Circus 🚌 14, 19, 38

BORDERLINE

www.meanfiddler.com

A famous venue (capacity 275), this place has seen many big names in its time. Music ranges from country to heavy metal and beyond.

✚ 168 H4 ✉ Orange Yard, Manette Street W1D 4JB ☎ 020 7734 5547, tickets 0843 221 0100 👋 £6–£16 🚇 Tottenham Court Road 🚌 8, 10, 14, 24

CAFÉ DE PARIS

www.cafedeparis.com

Elegant and original, this nightspot, established in 1924, has velvet

sash curtains and a long sweeping staircase to the dance floor and bar. There's live jazz and cabaret nightly. Drinks are expensive and there is a strict door policy; no sportswear. There's also a restaurant if you want to eat first, and a burlesque cabaret on Saturdays.

✚ 168 H5 ✉ 3–4 Coventry Street W1D 6BL ☎ 020 7734 7700 🕙 Club nights Fri, Sat 10pm–3am (restaurant 6–9pm) 👋 £12–£99 🚇 Leicester Square, Piccadilly Circus 🚌 9, 12, 13, 15, 23

CAMBRIDGE THEATRE

www.reallyuseful.com

Tucked away on Seven Dials and normally home to short-lived musicals, the Cambridge Theatre was restored in 1987 to its 1930s' gold and silver art deco splendour.

✚ 169 J4 ✉ Earlham Street WC2 9HU ☎ 0844 412 4652 👋 £32–£63 🚇 Tottenham Court Road, Covent Garden 🚌 14, 19, 38

CANDY BAR

www.candybarsoho.com

This leading lesbian bar in central London attracts a large crowd and has DJs every night. Male guests are also welcome if with two women. It's a decidedly relaxed atmosphere, and there is no dress code.

✚ 168 H4 ✉ 4 Carlisle Street, off Dean Street W1D 3BJ ☎ 020 7287 5041 🕙 Mon–Wed 4–1, Thu 4–3, Fri–Sat 3–3, Sun 4–12.30 👋 Free Sun–Thu, £4 Fri–Sat after 9pm 🚇 Tottenham Court Road 🚌 7, 10, 73, 390, N7, N10, N73

CHUCKLE CLUB

www.chuckleclub.com

A student bar with cheap drinks and an established comedy club, the Chuckle pulls in some of the best in the business.

✚ 169 K4 ✉ The Albany, 240 Great Portland Street W1W 5QU ☎ 020 7476 1672 🕙 Sat 7.45pm–3am 👋 £12 🚇 Regent's Park

CINEWORLD SHAFTESBURY AVENUE AT THE TROCADERO

www.cineworld.co.uk

A seven-screen multiplex is provided by this major cinema chain.

Above *The Garrick Theatre, noted for its comedies and comedy dramas, has an auditorium decorated with gold leaf*

🚇 168 H5 ✉ 13 Coventry Street W1D 7DH
☎ 0871 200 2000 🚇 Leicester Square,
Piccadilly Circus 🚌 14, 19, 22, 38

COMEDY STORE

www.thecomedystore.co.uk
The best in stand-up comedy features
improvised sketches from the
Comedy Store Players. Big British TV
and radio names who cut their teeth
here include Ben Elton, Julian Clary,
Josie Lawrence, Paul Merton and
Steve Coogan. Over-18s only.
🚇 168 H5 ✉ 1a Oxendon Street SW1Y
4EE ☎ 0844 871 7699 🕐 Tue–Sun, doors
open 6.30, shows from 8pm ✋ £14–£20
🚇 Piccadilly Circus, Leicester Square
🚌 14, 19, 38

COWARD THEATRE

www.delfontmackintosh.co.uk
Dating from 1903 and formerly called
the Albery, the Coward Theatre has
an impressive roll-call of stars from
Olivier to Izzard.
🚇 169 J4 ✉ 85–88 St. Martin's Lane
WC2N 4AU ☎ 0844 482 5141 ✋ £19–£50
🚇 Leicester Square 🚌 24, 29, 176

DONMAR WAREHOUSE
THEATRE

www.ambassadortickets.com
Housed in a refurbished 19th-century
warehouse in trendy Covent Garden,
the Donmar Warehouse was led for
a decade by Sam Mendes, attracting
the starriest of casts. Since 2002
Michael Grandage has continued
its eclectic programming, including
classic drama and new plays.
🚇 169 J4 ✉ 41 Earlham Street WC2H 9LX
☎ 0844 871 7624 ✋ £15–£29 🚇 Covent
Garden, Leicester Square 🚌 14, 19, 24,
29, 38, 176

EGG

www.egglondon.net
One of London's most exciting
nightspots attracting an up-for-it, up-
to-the-minute crowd who come for
the live bands as well as DJs playing
house, techno and electro. Intimate
Mediterranean atmosphere.
🚇 169 J1 ✉ 200 York Way, King's
Cross N7 9AX ☎ 020 7871 7111 🕐 Fri
10pm–7am, Sat 10pm–noon ✋ £20
🚇 King's Cross 🚌 390

EMPIRE

www.empirecinemas.co.uk
The Empire is a large central cinema
showing new releases.
🚇 168 H4 ✉ 190 J4 ✉ 5–6 Leicester
Square WC2H 7NA ☎ 0871 471 4714
🚇 Leicester Square, Piccadilly Circus
🚌 14, 24, 29

GARRICK THEATRE

www.nimaxtheatres.com
This small theatre was named
after the 18th-century actor
and entrepreneur David Garrick
(1717–79).
🚇 169 J5 ✉ Charing Cross Road WC2H
0HH ☎ 0844 412 4662 ✋ £20–£50
🚇 Leicester Square, Charing Cross
🚌 24, 29, 176

GIELGUD THEATRE

www.delfontmackintosh.co.uk
Opened in 1906, the Gielgud was
known as the Globe until the mid-
1990s, when, with Shakespeare's
Globe about to open on the South
Bank, it changed its name to honour
Sir John Gielgud (1904–2000), who

frequently performed here. The theatre stages high-profile works and was refurbished in 2007.

✚ 168 H4 ✉ 33–37 Shaftesbury Avenue W1D 6AR ☎ 0844 482 5130 ✋ £20–£49.50 🚇 Piccadilly Circus 🚌 14, 19, 38

GUANABARA
www.guanabara.co.uk
Decadent Latino cocktails and exotic Brazilian dance music—you could well be in Rio. There's also a restaurant.

✚ 169 J4 ✉ Parker Street WC2B 5PW ☎ 020 7242 8600 🕐 Mon–Sat 5pm–2.30am, Sun 5–12 ✋ £5–£10; free Mon and before 9pm 🚇 Covent Garden, Holborn 🚌 6, 9, 13, 23, 87

LONDON COLISEUM
www.eno.org
The Coliseum is home to the English National Opera (who always sing in English) with regular visits from Welsh National Opera, Opera North and the English National Ballet. ENO aims to offer opera to the widest possible audience and is known for some innovative productions.

✚ 169 J5 ✉ St. Martin's Lane WC2N 4ES ☎ 020 7836 0111, tickets 0871 911 0200 ✋ £5–£70 🚇 Charing Cross, Leicester Square 🚌 24, 29, 176

LONDON PALLADIUM
www.reallyuseful.com
A colossal theatre built in 1910, the Palladium has been home to the biggest musicals (including a flying car in *Chitty Chitty Bang Bang*) and a series of television specials and Christmas pantomimes.

✚ 168 H4 ✉ Argyll Street W1F 7TF ☎ 0844 412 2704 ✋ £32–£62.50 🚇 Oxford Circus 🚌 8, 10, 73, 453

LYCEUM THEATRE
lyceum-theatre.co.uk
Once a concert hall, and then a waxworks, the Lyceum Theatre's famous colonnaded entrance reopened in 1996, and has been home to Disney's *The Lion King* for more than 10 years.

✚ 169 J4 ✉ 21 Wellington Street WC2 7RQ ☎ 020 7420 8113 ✋ £27–£57 🚇 Charing Cross 🚌 9, 13, 23

LYRIC THEATRE
www.nimaxtheatres.com
The oldest of the four fine, if faded, Victorian theatres on Shaftesbury Avenue, the Lyric opened in 1888 and now stages entertaining dramas and musicals.

✚ 168 H4 ✉ 29 Shaftesbury Avenue W1D 7ES ☎ 0844 412 4661 ✋ £20–£50 🚇 Piccadilly Circus 🚌 14, 19, 38

MARKET PLACE
www.marketplace-london.com
Market Place, set on two floors, is a classic London DJ bar, popular with Londoners after work, with panelled walls and very good food. Downstairs is larger, with room to dance and alcove tables.

✚ 168 H4 ✉ 11 Market Place W1H 8AH ☎ 020 7079 2020 🕐 Mon–Wed 11am–12am, Thu–Fri 11am–2am, Sat 12pm–2am, Sun 1–11 ✋ Free 🚇 Oxford Circus 🚌 7, 8, 10, 73, 176

NOVELLO THEATRE
www.delfontmackintosh.co.uk
The Novello was built as a pair with the Aldwych Theatre in 1905. The auditorium seats 1,143.

✚ 169 K4 ✉ Aldwych WC2B 4LD ☎ 0844 482 5170 ✋ £12–£51 🚇 Covent Garden 🚌 9, 13, 19, 77A

ODEON LEICESTER SQUARE
www.odeon.co.uk
This famous central mega-cinema and West End showpiece is used for many film premieres. Six screens show new-release blockbusters in luxurious comfort.

✚ 169 J5 ✉ 24–26 Leicester Square WC2H 7JY ☎ 0871 224 4007 🚇 Leicester Square, Piccadilly Circus 🚌 24, 29, 176

PICCADILLY THEATRE
www.ambassadortickets.com
Tucked away behind Piccadilly Circus, and principally the home of comedies and musicals, this theatre has seen the likes of Al Jolson, Evelyn Laye and Henry Fonda tread the boards over the years.

✚ 168 H4 ✉ 16 Denman Street W1D 7DY ☎ 0844 871 7627 ✋ £20–£55 🚇 Piccadilly Circus 🚌 24, 29, 176

Right *Bronze ballerina outside the Royal Opera House*

PIZZA EXPRESS JAZZ CLUB
www.pizzaexpresslive.com
All kinds of modern and contemporary jazz are played in a basement under the main branch of Pizza Express in Soho. A popular combination, so book ahead.

✚ 168 H4 ✉ 10 Dean Street W1D 3RW ☎ Jazz club 0845 602 7017; restaurant 020 7437 9595 🕐 Jazz shows Mon–Thu 8.30, Fri–Sat 9, Sun 8 ✋ £20 🚇 Tottenham Court Road 🚌 8, 10, 14, 24, 73

PRINCE CHARLES
www.princecharlescinema.com
A central independent cinema offers seats at lower than usual West End prices. Foreign-language films shown with English subtitles.

✚ 168 H4 ✉ 7 Leicester Place WC2H 7BH ☎ Box office 020 7494 3654 🚇 Leicester Square, Piccadilly Circus 🚌 24, 29, 176

RENOIR
www.curzoncinemas.com
The two-screen cinema shows art-house and foreign-language films (English subtitles) and classics from the repertory.

✚ 169 J2 ✉ Brunswick Centre, Brunswick Square WC1N 1AW ☎ 020 7837 8402 🚇 Russell Square 🚌 7, 59, 68, 91, 168, 188

RONNIE SCOTT'S
www.ronniescotts.co.uk
Britain's top jazz venue and one of the most famous jazz clubs in the world. The best players line up to perform here.

✚ 168 H4 ✉ 47 Frith Street W1D 4HT ☎ 020 7439 0747 🕐 Nightly, with two shows Fri–Sat, plus Sun lunchtime ✋ £20–£38.50; more for special gigs 🚇 Tottenham Court Road 🚌 8, 10, 14, 24, 73

ROYAL OPERA HOUSE
www.roh.org.uk
The principal venue for world-class opera and ballet was reopened in 1999 after extensive redevelopment. The building, in Covent Garden, hosts major operatic productions and is home to the Royal Ballet. The Opera

House also stages regular exhibitions of costumes and memorabilia of former stars.

✚ 169 J4 ✉ Bow Street WC2E 9DD ☎ 020 7304 4000 ✋ £3–£180 🚇 Covent Garden 🚌 4, 9, 13, 15, 176, RV1

SAVOY THEATRE
www.ambassadortickets.com

Built in 1881 by Richard D'Oyly Carte to stage operettas by Gilbert and Sullivan, the Savoy was redesigned in the 1920s. Seats 1,100.

✚ 169 J5 ✉ Savoy Court, Strand WC2R 0ET ☎ 0844 871 7627 ✋ £40–£55 🚇 Charing Cross 🚌 9, 11, 13, 15, 23, 176

SCALA
www.scala-london.co.uk

This former cinema turned clubbing venue with four floors and several bars hosts hip-hop and breakbeat nights plus big names from the pop world. Phone or check website for live music nights in the week.

✚ 169 J1 ✉ 275 Pentonville Road N1 9NL ☎ 020 7833 2022 🕐 Mon–Thu 7–11, Fri–Sat 10pm–6am ✋ £8–£15 🚇 King's Cross 🚌 30, 73, 214

SHADOW LOUNGE
www.theshadowlounge.co.uk

This pretentious gay club in the heart of Soho, more like an overcrowded bar, is one of the few gay venues with a straight bar-style dress code—that is, smart and fashionable. Over-21s only.

✚ 168 H4 ✉ 5 Brewer Street W1F 0RF ☎ 020 7317 9270 🕐 Mon–Sat 10pm–3am ✋ £5–£10 🚇 Piccadilly Circus 🚌 12, 13, 15, 23, 139

SHAFTESBURY THEATRE
www.shaftesbury-theatre.co.uk

Independent theatre built in 1902 on the corner of Shaftesbury Avenue, staging mainly musicals and comedies. Seats 1,400.

✚ 169 J4 ✉ 210 Shaftesbury Avenue WC2H 8DP ☎ 0870 906 3798 ✋ £22–£62 🚇 Covent Garden 🚌 14, 19, 38

SHAW THEATRE
www.shaw-theatre.com

Named after Irish playwright George Bernard Shaw, once a local

councillor here. Now refurbished and associated with the next-door hotel, the Novotel London St. Pancras. Stages family shows and international dance productions.

✚ 169 J2 ✉ 100–110 Euston Road NW1 2AJ ☎ 020 7666 9000, tickets 0844 248 5075 ✋ £12–£20 🚇 King's Cross, Euston 🚌 10, 30, 73, 168

THEATRE ROYAL DRURY LANE
www.reallyuseful.com

The present theatre, built in 1812, is the fourth on this site and stages mostly musicals. And there are ghosts—the Man in Grey walks around the Upper Circle during successful productions. Seats 2,196.

✚ 169 J4 ✉ Catherine Street WC2B 5JF ☎ 0844 412 4648 ✋ £15–£45 🚇 Covent Garden 🚌 6, 9, 13, 23, RV1

VAUDEVILLE THEATRE
www.nimaxtheatres.com

This small venue, which opened in 1870, was the third theatre to occupy this site. It stages musicals and comedy. Seats 714.

✚ 169 J5 ✉ 404 Strand WC2R 0NH ☎ 0844 412 4663 ✋ £27–£66 🚇 Charing Cross 🚌 9, 11, 13, 176

VILLAGE SOHO
www.village-soho.co.uk

A young, relaxed crowd enjoys this stylish, late, gay café-bar, which fills three floors. There is karaoke on Tuesday and Wednesday, Discolicious Thursday and Friday, and gogo dancing Thursday to Saturday.

✚ 168 H4 ✉ 81 Wardour Street W1D 6QD ☎ 020 7478 0530 🕐 Mon–Sat 4pm–1am, Sun 4pm–11.30pm ✋ Free 🚇 Piccadilly Circus 🚌 12, 14, 19, 38

VUE WEST END
www.myvue.com

Nine-screen multiplex (including 3-D) in the heart of London's 'movieland'.

✚ 168 H4 ✉ 3 Cranbourn Street WC2H 7AL ☎ Bookings 0871 224 0240 🚇 Leicester Square 🚌 24, 29, 176

WALKABOUT
www.walkabout.eu.com

This is the Covent Garden venue for the popular country-wide chain of

relaxed Australian sports-themed bars. Giant screens show football, rugby and motorsport from around the world. Live music.

✚ 168 4J ✉ 11 Henrietta Street and 33 Maiden Lane WC2E 8PY ☎ 020 7379 5555 🕐 Mon–Thu 12–11, Fri–Sat 12–12, Sun 12–10.30 🚇 Covent Garden

THE YARD BAR
www.yardbar.co.uk

This friendly gay haven in the middle of frenetic Soho is a good place for a pre-club drink. The central courtyard makes a welcome change from crammed bars and there's an upstairs loft bar. Reasonable prices, good food and friendly staff.

✚ 168 H4 ✉ 57 Rupert Street W1D 7LP ☎ 020 7437 2652 🕐 Mon–Thu 1–11.30, Fri 4–12, Sat 2–12, Sun 2–10.15 ✋ Free 🚇 Piccadilly Circus, Leicester Square 🚌 12, 14, 19, 38

SPORTS AND ACTIVITIES
CENTRAL YMCA CLUB
www.ymca.co.uk

The original site of the first YMCA (established 1844) houses a huge sports centre, offering almost any kind of physical activity you want—gym, pool, sports hall, playing fields, dance studio, climbing wall and more.

✚ 168 H4 ✉ 112 Great Russell Street WC1B 3NQ ☎ 020 7343 1700 🕐 Mon–Fri 6.30–10.30, Sat 10–8.30, Sun 10–7 ✋ Day membership £15, weekly £52.95 (use of all facilities) 🚇 Tottenham Court Road 🚌 7, 19, 24, 29, 38, 134

THE GYM COVENT GARDEN
www.jubileehalltrust.org

Central, well-equipped gym which also offers classes. Gym and sports centre are open access. Also offers a range of beauty therapies and treatments. Book ahead.

✚ 169 J4 ✉ 30 The Piazza, Covent Garden WC2 8BE ☎ 020 7836 4007 🕐 Mon–Fri 6.45am–10pm, Sat 9–9, Sun 10–5 ✋ £6.50–£12 🚇 Covent Garden 🚌 6, 9, 13, 23, RV1 🎫

OASIS SPORTS CENTRE

There are indoor and outdoor swimming pools, a sauna, gym,

massage, squash, badminton, martial arts and fitness training on offer at the Oasis.
🏛 169 J4 ✉ 32 Endell Street WC2H 9AG ☎ 020 7831 1804 🕐 Mon–Fri 6.30am–9pm, Sat, Sun 9.30am–6pm ✋ Call for details 🚇 Covent Garden 🚌 14, 19, 38, RV1

SOMERSET HOUSE
In winter, the central courtyard of this magnificent building becomes an ice rink (▷ 150–151).

HEALTH AND BEAUTY
CHARLES WORTHINGTON
www.charlesworthington.com
Award-winning but never intimidating, this chic salon in a Georgian town-house wants to make you feel at ease and offers a drink and snacks as you sit down. There are two other London salons. Booking is essential.
🏛 168 H3 ✉ 7 Percy Street W1T 1DH, ☎ 020 7631 1370 🕐 Mon–Thu 8–7.45, Fri 10.15–6.45, Sat 9.15–5.45, Sun 10–4.45

🚻 Cut and blow dry from £50 🚇 Goodge Street, Tottenham Court Road 🚌 10, 24, 29, 73, 134

THE SANCTUARY
www.thesanctuary.co.uk
This famous women-only Covent Garden spa has an atrium pool complete with swing, and a relaxation area with a koi carp pool.
🏛 169 J4 ✉ 12 Floral Street WC2E 9DH ☎ 0844 875 8443 🕐 Mon–Fri 9.30–6, Sat–Sun 9.30–8. Booking essential ✋ Treatments from £43 🚇 Covent Garden 🚌 6, 9, 11, 13, 15, 24, 29, 87, 91, 176 🍴

FOR CHILDREN
CORAM'S FIELDS
www.coramsfields.org
Outdoor fun for young and older children is the name of the game here, with lawns for running and picnics, plus a sand pit, Astro Turf football pitch, basketball court, climbing equipment and pets' corner. Adults without children not permitted to enter.

🏛 169 J2 ✉ 93 Guilford Street WC1N 1DN ☎ 020 7837 6138 🕐 Daily 9–7. Closes at dusk in winter ✋ Free 🚇 Russell Square 🚌 17, 46, 59, 91 🚻

COVENT GARDEN
Punch and Judy shows using hand-operated puppets have been staged here since the 17th century (▷ 142–143). There's also an excellent range of children's shops, such as Benjamin Pollock's Toy Shop (▷ 154).

TROCADERO
www.troc.co.uk, www.funland.co.uk
Seven storeys of ten-pin bowling, Ripleys Believe It or Not, computer games and simulator rides.
🏛 168 H5 ✉ 7–14 Coventry Street W1D 7DH ☎ 020 7292 3642 🕐 Sun–Thu 10am–midnight, Fri–Sat 10am–1am ✋ Bowling from £6.95 per person 🚇 Piccadilly Circus 🚌 9, 14, 19, 22, 38

Below *The Sanctuary atrium pool*

PRICES AND SYMBOLS

The prices given are the average for a two-course set lunch (L) and a three-course à la carte dinner (D) for one person, without drinks. The wine price is for the least expensive bottle.

For a key to the symbols, ▷ 2.

ACORN HOUSE

www.acornhouserestaurant.com
Acorn House is widely regarded as the first truly eco-friendly restaurant in London, using organic and recycled material, and offering local people training in hospitality. Only the best seasonal ingredients are used. Lunchtime take-aways include hot soup and wholesome sandwiches. The dining room is stark but the food is utterly appetizing—try main courses such as creamed spinach and mushroom farinata (chickpea pancake) with beetroot salad and parmesan, and try to leave sufficient room for the scrumptious desserts.
✚ 169 K2 ✉ 69 Swinton Street WC1X 9NT ☎ 020 7812 1842 🕔 Mon–Fri 12–3, 6–10, Sat 6–10, Sun 12–4. Closed 23 Dec–2 Jan, public hols 🍴 L £18.50, D £24.50, Wine £14.50 🚇 King's Cross, Russell Square

ARBUTUS

www.arbutusrestaurant.co.uk
This Soho-based restaurant opened to great acclaim in 2006 and it continues to delight at the highest level. The brainchild of Will Smith and Anthony Demetre, both highly respected chefs, it features classic seasonal dishes with a definite modern twist. This includes smoked eel, squid and mackerel burger, saddle of rabbit and the most delectable English plum sorbet you could wish to try.
✚ 168 H4 ✉ 63–64 Frith Street W1D 3JW ☎ 020 7734 4545 🕔 Mon–Sat 12–2.30, 5–11, Sun 12–3, 5.30–10.30 (pre-theatre 7–11). Closed 24–26 Dec, 1 Jan 🍴 L £16.95, D £32, Wine £14.50 🚇 Tottenham Court Road, Leicester Square

ARCHIPELAGO

www.archipelago-restaurant.co.uk
Archipelago dares to be different. The international dishes on the menu are inspiring and adventurous, transporting diners to the four corners of the globe. It's not the best place for the timid, with exotic concoctions like spiced Australian kangaroo fillet with spinach and pak choi, peanut-crusted wildebeest or African crocodile bites.
✚ 168 H3 ✉ 110 Whitfield Street W1T 5ED ☎ 020 7383 3346 🕔 Mon–Fri 12–2.15, 6–10.15, Sat 6–10.15. Closed 2 weeks at Christmas, public hols 🍴 L £18.50, D £33, Wine £18 🚇 Warren Street

CARLUCCIO'S

www.carluccios.com
The flagship restaurant of this popular Italian chain announces its presence on the street with its distinctive blue blinds. Inside, the service from Italian staff is friendly, the food is freshly prepared and full of flavour, and the atmosphere is congenial and buzzing. Enjoy a salad of soft goat's cheese, roasted red pepper and pine nuts on mixed leaves, or a plateful of *fritto misto* (deep-fried calamari, prawns and whitebait), or perhaps hand-made tortellini stuffed with wine-braised venison. The standard menu is augmented by daily specials. A gluten-free menu is also available.
✚ 169 J4 ✉ Garrick Street, Covent Garden WC2E 9BH ☎ 020 7836 0990 🕔 Mon–Fri 8am–11.30pm, Sat 9am–11.30pm, Sun 9am–10.30pm 🍴 L £16, D £24, Wine £13.95 🚇 Covent Garden, Leicester Square

Left *The sophisticated dining space at L'Escargot*

CHRISTOPHER'S
www.christophersgrill.com
Christopher's is based on the grand steak and lobster restaurants of the US and is set in an elegant Victorian town house with curving staircase and high ceilings. The simpler dishes on the modern American menu are particularly successful, with plenty of flavour in the Maryland crab cake and a really succulent Aberdeen Angus steak. Desserts include fresh fruity sorbets and classic US cheesecakes. The modern wine list includes a good selection by the glass, and cocktails are served at the Martini Bar.
✚ 169 J4 ✉ 18 Wellington Street WC2E 7DD ☎ 020 7240 4222 🕓 Mon–Fri 12–3, 5–11.30, Sat 11.30–3.30, 5–11.30, Sun 11.30–3.30, 5–10.30. Closed Easter, 25–26 Dec 🖐 L £28.95, D £40, Wine £19.75 🚇 Embankment

CIGALA
www.cigala.co.uk
Tucked away in the back streets of Holborn, this popular Spanish restaurant is regularly crowded with local customers in both the light, understated upstairs restaurant and the basement tapas bar. The open-plan kitchen keeps things slightly steamy and turns out dishes such as *venado asado*—fillet of venison wrapped in ham, potato bake and wild mushrooms. A good range of Spanish wines.
✚ 169 K3 ✉ 54 Lamb's Conduit Street WC1N 3LW ☎ 020 7405 1717 🕓 Mon–Fri 12–10.45, Sat 12pm–12.30am, Sun 12–9.45. Closed 25–26 Dec, 1 Jan, Easter, public hols 🖐 L £15, D £31.75, Wine £13.50 🚇 Holborn

L'ESCARGOT—THE GROUND FLOOR RESTAURANT
www.whitestarline.org.uk
A Soho landmark, L'Escargot has been serving classy French cuisine since 1927. This was the first restaurant to offer fresh snails in Britain and they're still a speciality. Alongside starters such as carpaccio of beef with rocket salad, you might find snail ravioli accompanied by parsley purée. Fine art decorates the walls—the collection includes original works by Joan Miró, Henri Matisse, David Hockney and Andy Warhol.
✚ 168 H4 ✉ 48 Greek Street W1D 4EF ☎ 020 7439 7474 🕓 Mon–Sat 12–2.15, 5.30–11.30. Closed 25–26 Dec, 1 Jan 🖐 L £15, D £33.50, Wine £19 🚇 Tottenham Court Road, Leicester Square

THE IVY
www.the-ivy.co.uk
There's still a buzz at the Ivy; people clearly want to be heard as well as seen here. In the heart of theatreland, the V-shaped building opens into a small bar, which leads on to the main room with leaded windows and coloured glass. The menu offers simple dishes, ranging from snacks to a main meal, with international influences. Vegetarians and vegans are well catered for.
✚ 169 J4 ✉ 1–5 West Street, Covent Garden WC2H 9NQ ☎ 020 7836 4751 🕓 Mon–Sat 12–3, 5.30–12, Sun 12–3.30, 5.30–11.30. Closed L 27 Dec, D 24 Dec, 25–26 Dec, 1 Jan, Aug public hol 🖐 L £32, D £39.50, Wine £25 🚇 Leicester Square, Covent Garden

J. SHEEKEY
www.j-sheekey.co.uk
This much-loved establishment, off the beaten track in theatreland, is in a class of its own when it comes to fish. The freshness of the catch is second to none. Look for Cornish fish stew, roast whole gilthead bream with herbs and olive oil and grilled sardines *piri piri*. Oak panelling, portraits of theatre stars and bench seating set the scene. The Olympia Bar is also popular.
✚ 169 J4 ✉ 32–34 St. Martin's Court WC2N 4AL ☎ 020 7240 2565 🕓 Mon–Sat 12–3, 5.30–12, Sun 12–3, 6–11. Closed D 24 Dec, 25–26 Dec, 1 Jan, public hols 🖐 L £26.50, D £35, Wine £21.75 🚇 Leicester Square

KAYA
www.kayarestaurant.co.uk
Korean food of the highest calibre is served in the elegant minimalist surroundings of this well-established restaurant, a short hop from the Burlington Arcade. It's a cuisine noted for its healthy balance, and culture of sharing. If the variety of the menu is bewildering, set menus offer a great way in, starting with *naengchae* (jelly-fish and seafood in a mustard sauce), followed by beef and noodle dishes, side dishes and rice. Advance booking is strongly recommended.
✚ 168 G5 ✉ 42 Albemarle Street W1S 4JH ☎ 020 7499 0622 🕓 Mon–Sat 12–3, 6–11 🖐 L (set menu) £10, D £38 (traditional full-course menu), £45 (royal platter) 🚇 Green Park

KOYA
www.koya.co.uk
Great value and excellent noodles ensure the success of this no-frills Japanese eatery, so be prepared to queue for a space at a shared table. Thick udon noodles, made with imported Japanese wheat flour, are the speciality of the house, served in three classic ways: *atsu-atsu* (in a hot broth), *hiyashi* (cold with a dipping or pouring sauce), or *hiya-atsu* (cold with a hot broth accompaniment). Broths and sauces might be flavoured with mushrooms and walnut, or smoked mackerel and green leaves. Other options include rice dishes, and tempura prawns and vegetables.
✚ 168 H4 ✉ 49 Frith Street W1D 4SG ☎ 020 7434 4463 🕓 Mon–Sat 12–3, 5.30–10.30 🖐 L £14.50 D £20, Wine £21.50 🚇 Tottenham Court Road

MELA
www.melarestaurant.co.uk
An unusual Indian restaurant that uses traditional Indian cooking methods and spices and combines them with Western ingredients, for example, the *batakh sula shashlik*—chargrilled chunks of duck supreme marinated in yoghurt and spices, served on a skewer with onions, courgettes (zucchini), tomatoes and peppers. All dishes are freshly prepared and service is friendly and prompt. The simple, minimalist decor makes a pleasant backdrop.

✚ 169 J4 ✉ 152–156 Shaftesbury Avenue WC2H 8HL ☎ 020 7836 8635 🕐 Mon–Fri 12–11.30, Sat 1–11.30, Sun 12–10.30. Closed L 25–26 Dec ✋ L £9.95, D £26, Wine £13.95 🚇 Leicester Square

MON PLAISIR

www.monplaisir.co.uk

This is the oldest French restaurant in London, run by the same family for 50 years. An unassuming entrance leads to a maze of comfortable rooms, including a mezzanine-style loft, brightly decked with modern abstract paintings. The menu mixes classics such as *cassoulet d'escargots* and *coquilles St.-Jacques* with more contemporary fare such as steamed sea bass with broccoli and shellfish sauce. All desserts are hand-made by the chef patissier. Bustling, friendly French service with closely packed tables creating a Gallic atmosphere.

✚ 169 J4 ✉ 19–21 Monmouth Street WC2H 9DD ☎ 020 7836 7243 🕐 Mon–Sat 12–2.30, 5.45–11.15. Brasserie menu Mon–Fri 2.30–5.45, Sat 2.30–3. Closed 25–26 Dec, 1 Jan, public hols ✋ L £16.95, D £40, Wine £18 🚇 Covent Garden, Leicester Square, Tottenham Court Road

Below *The French House, a watering hole where writers and artists drank in the 1950s*

ORRERY

www.danddlondon.com

Orrery is in the heart of Marylebone and one of the smartest restaurants in London, with huge, round windows and long rows of tables attended by professional French staff. The menu is Modern European with dishes such as terrine of *foie gras* with Sauternes *gelée*, fillet of bream with roast artichokes and truffles or saddle of venison with black pudding.

✚ 168 F3 ✉ 55–57 Marylebone High Street W1U 5RB ☎ 020 7616 8000 🕐 Mon–Sat 12–2.30, 6.30–10.30, Sun 12–2.30, 6.30–10. Closed 25–26 Dec, 1 Jan, Good Fri ✋ L £26.50 (3 courses), D £48 (set 3 courses), Wine £21 🚇 Baker Street, Regent's Park

OZER

www.ozerrestaurant.com

Huseyin Ozer's restaurant is stylish and contemporary, with a rich bold interior tempered with neutral linens, cool tiles and intricate lighting. Dishes are Mediterranean, but with strong North African and Middle Eastern accents. A wide choice of menus and dishes makes selecting tricky as they cover grills, seafood, casseroles, vegetarian, set menus and hot or cold mezes as either starters or main courses. There's a great breakfast menu, too.

✚ 168 G3 ✉ 5 Langham Place W1B 3DG ☎ 020 7323 0505 🕐 Daily 12–12 ✋ L £18, D £22.60, Wine £13.95 🚇 Oxford Circus

RASA SAMUDRA

www.rasarestaurants.com

The name means 'a taste of the ocean', and this authentic Indian restaurant specializes in the home cooking of the coastal state of Kerala in southwest India, particularly fish and seafood. The exterior is hard to miss, with its bold pink, and the interior is decorated with bright silks and vibrant oil paintings. Try a crab *varuthathu* cooked dry with ginger, curry leaves, chilli and mustard seeds accompanied by rice tossed in lemon juice, curry leaves and mustard seeds.

✚ 168 H3 ✉ 5 Charlotte Street W1T 1RE ☎ 020 7637 0222 🕐 Mon–Sat 12–3, 6–11, Sun 6–11. Closed 2 weeks Dec ✋ L £13.75, D £22, Wine £15 🚇 Tottenham Court Road, Goodge Street

SITAARAY

www.sitaaray.com

The exuberantly glamorous Bollywood theme sets this popular restaurant apart. Theatrical red curtains lead through to an interior decorated with gilt and movie posters, and cocktails are named after favourite Indian films (try the '3 Idiots' if you dare…). The fixed-price Great Indian Grill menu offers an unlimited choice of superb kebabs and curries, plus delicate dishes such as Amritsari fish—fish fried with cardamom. It's perfect for sharing, and there's a full vegetarian version, too. Puddings include mango kulfi (a type of Indian ice cream). Authentic Indian street food sets the tone for a lighter lunch.

✉ 167 Drury Lane, New London Theatre Building WC2B 5PG ☎ 020 8269 6422 🕐 Mon–Sat 12–3, 5.30–11.30 ✋ L £14.50, D £26.95, Wine £19.95 🚇 Covent Garden, Holborn

TOM'S KITCHEN

www.tomskitchen.co.uk

Young chef Tom Aikens has made a great success of this new restaurant since it opened towards the end of 2010, winning awards for its breakfasts (try waffles, or perhaps porridge with raisins and banana). The brasserie spreads over three rooms, with a menu that combines the best of classic British cooking with European flavours. Try the fish and chips, or perhaps the signature dish of slow-braised lamb.

✚ 169 K4 ✉ Somerset House, The Strand WC2R 1LA ☎ 020 7845 4646 🕐 Mon–Fri 8–11, 12–3, 6–10, Sat 10–4, 6–10, Sun 10–4 ✋ L £33.50, D £45.50, Wine £20.50 🚇 Charing Cross

PUBS

THE ARGYLL ARMS

There has been a tavern here since 1740, but the present building is mid-Victorian and notable for its stunning floral displays. There's a range of sandwiches and the hot food menu might offer vegetarian moussaka, beef and Guinness pie, traditional haddock and chips or the popular lasagne. Children are not allowed in the bar area.

✠ 168 G4 ✉ 18 Argyll Street W1F 7TP ☎ 020 7734 6117 🕐 Mon–Sat 10am–11pm, Sun 10am–10.30pm. Meals: daily 10–10. Closed 25 Dec ✋ Bar meals from £13 Ⓜ Oxford Circus

THE BOUNTIFUL COW

www.thebountifulcow.co.uk
This funky bistro pub, under the flamboyant leadership of proprietor Roxy Beaujolais, is devoted to beef. Steaks are the order of the day, cut six ways, or try the excellent 14oz 'Bountyburger'. The 'Almost Free Lunch' deal, Monday to Saturday, offers a great value main course such as corned beef hash, or eggs Benedict, when you buy an accompanying drink.

✠ 169 K3 ✉ 51 Eagle Street WC1R 4AP ☎ 020 7404 0200 🕐 Mon–Sat 11–11 ✋ L (set menu) £6, D £25, Wine £15.40 Ⓜ Holborn

CITTIE OF YORKE

A pub has stood on this site since 1430. In 1695 it was rebuilt as the Gray's Inn Coffee House and the large cellar bar dates from this time. The panelled front bar has an original chandelier and portraits of illustrious locals, including Charles Dickens and Sir Thomas More. Bar food includes sandwiches, salads and soups, plus a handful of hearty hot dishes.

✠ 169 K3 ✉ 22 High Holborn WC1V 6BN ☎ 020 7242 7670 🕐 Mon–Fri 11.30–11, Sat 12–11. Meals: 12–3, 6–9.30. Closed 25–26 Dec ✋ Bar meals from £8 Ⓜ Holborn

THE FRENCH HOUSE

www.frenchhousesoho.com
Notable for its custom of serving only half pints of beer, this small Soho bar holds an annual Pint Day dedicated to the long-established British charity, the National Society for the Prevention of Cruelty to Children (NSPCC). The bar remains

much as it was in the 1950s, when it was popular with writers and artists such as Brendan Behan, Dylan Thomas and Francis Bacon. Weekly changing menus might feature navarin of lamb or roasted monkfish with ham.

✠ 168 H4 ✉ 49 Dean Street W1D 5BG ☎ 020 7437 2799 🕐 Mon–Sat 12–11, Sun 12–10.30. Restaurant: Mon–Sat 12–3, 5.30–7. Closed 25 Dec ✋ Bar meals from £8.50, D from £32 Ⓜ Tottenham Court Road

THE LAMB

www.youngs.co.uk
This traditional watering hole, with a distinctive green-tiled facade, was built around 1729 and sends you back in time the minute you walk in the door, with its dark polished wood, original sepia photographs of music hall stars, rare glass 'snob screens', and an old phonograph in the bar that can be wound up to play discs by request. Home-cooked bar food covers all bases, including vegetarian choices, a fish dish, light bites and traditional meals such as sausage and mash. No children allowed in the bar area. Meals are served on the patio.

✠ 169 J3 ✉ 94 Lamb's Conduit Street WC1N 3LZ ☎ 020 7405 0713 🕐 Mon–Wed 12–11, Thu–Sat 12–12, Sun 12–10.30. Meals: 12–9 ✋ Bar meals from £7, D from £18 Ⓜ Holborn, Russell Square

THE LAMB AND FLAG

www.pubs.com
The oldest pub in Covent Garden, its cosy atmosphere attracts City workers and visitors to partake of a beer or some traditional pub grub.

✠ 169 J4 ✉ 33 Rose Street WC2E 9EB ☎ 020 7497 9504 🕐 Mon–Sat 11–11, Sun 12–10.30. Meals: Mon–Sat 12–3, Sun 12–4 ✋ Bar meals from £7 Ⓜ Covent Garden, Leicester Square

THE SEVEN STARS

The clientele of this pub, built in 1602, is drawn from the adjacent Law Courts. This highly individual free house serves fresh, home-made dishes. A changing selection of options might include oysters, steak, herrings and Caesar salad. Adnam's ales. No children.

✠ 169 K4 ✉ 53 Carey Street WC2A 2JB ☎ 020 7242 8521 🕐 Mon–Fri 11–11, Sat 12–11, Sun 12–10.30. Meals: Mon–Fri 12–3, 5–9. Closed 25–26 Dec, 1 Jan, Easter Mon ✋ Bar meals from £10, D from £19 Ⓜ Chancery Lane

Above *The Argyll Arms, bedecked with flowers, is close to Oxford Circus*

PRICES AND SYMBOLS

The prices given are the lowest and highest for a double room for one night, unless otherwise stated. Breakfast is not usually included. All the hotels listed accept credit cards unless otherwise stated. Note that rates vary widely throughout the year.

For a key to the symbols, ▷ 2.

BLOOMS TOWNHOUSE

www.grangehotels.com

The Grange Blooms is part of an 18th-century row of town houses in Bloomsbury, just round the corner from the British Museum (▷ 134–139). The elegant bedrooms are furnished in Regency style (including some with four-poster beds), and there are several day rooms: a lobby lounge, a garden terrace, a breakfast room, restaurant and the Malt Library bar with around 30 specially selected malt whiskies to choose from.

✚ 169 J3 ✉ 7 Montague Street WC1B 5BP ☎ 020 7323 1717 🖐 £250–£280 ⓘ 26 🚇 Holborn, Russell Square 🚌 7, 68, 188

CLINK 261

www.clinkhotels.com

Stylish and rather funky, this hostel is just two minutes' walk from King's Cross station. Safe and clean accommodation and the friendly staff make it a popular choice for backpackers. It is close to London's nightlife action and well positioned for access to most of the city's major sights. Single, twin and multi-bedded rooms are available. There's a lounge for chilling out, WiFi internet access and a laundry room. Continental breakfast is included in the price.

✚ 169 J2 ✉ Ashlee House, 261–265 Gray's Inn Road W1X 8QT ☎ 020 7833 9400 🖐 £50–£65, beds from £10 ⓘ 25 🚇 King's Cross 🚌 17, 45, 46

DOUBLETREE BY HILTON

www.doubletree.hilton.co.uk

A smart, newly renovated hotel central to the city, the British Museum (▷ 134–139) and Covent Garden (▷ 142–143). The public areas, all with plenty of space, include the restaurant and a comfortable lobby lounge with bar.

Bedrooms include a number of superb executive rooms and suites.

✚ 169 J3 ✉ 92 Southampton Row WC1B 4BH ☎ 020 7242 2828 🖐 £117–£215 ⓘ 247 🚇 Russell Square, Holborn 🚌 7

EURO HOTEL

www.eurohotel.co.uk

This friendly bed-and-breakfast is in a leafy Georgian crescent. Russell Square Underground station, which links direct to Heathrow Airport, is only a few minutes' walk away. Most bedrooms have private bathrooms. Breakfast (included) is served in the attractive dining room, but note that there are no meals in the evening. There are good family rooms and tennis courts.

✚ 169 J2 ✉ 51–53 Cartwright Gardens, Russell Square WC1H 9EL ☎ 020 7387 4321 🖐 £105–£110 ⓘ 34 🚇 Russell Square 🚌 7, 59, 68, 91, 168, 188

GUILFORD HOTEL

www.guilfordhotel.co.uk

Within walking distance of the British Museum (▷ 134–139), the Guilford

has single, double, triple and family rooms, all with private shower. Continental breakfast.
✚ 169 K3 ✉ 6 Guilford Street WC1N 1DR ☎ 020 7430 2504 🖐 £80–£100 ⓘ 12 🚇 Russell Square, King's Cross 🚌 17, 45, 46

KINGSWAY HALL

www.kingswayhall.co.uk
Close to Covent Garden, this is a modern, stylish and comfortable hotel. Air-conditioned bedrooms have such extra facilities as a safe deposit box and an iron. The compact lounge bar serves drinks and light snacks and the Harlequin Restaurant provides more formal dining on the premises. There's a fitness centre and steam rooms in the basement.
✚ 169 J4 ✉ 66 Great Queen Street WC2B 5BX ☎ 020 7309 0909 🖐 £155–£350 ⓘ 170 🚭 🛗 🚇 Holborn 🚌 1, 59, 68, 91, 168, 171, 188

MENTONE HOTEL

www.mentonehotel.com
This impressive bed-and-breakfast in a row of Victorian houses overlooking pleasant gardens in Bloomsbury is close to many central London attractions and a few minutes' walk from Russell Square Underground station. All bedrooms have private bathrooms; five provide facilities for visitors with disabilities. Breakfast (included) is taken in the downstairs dining room and free internet access is available. Tennis courts are just opposite. No evening meals are served.
✚ 169 J2 ✉ 54–55 Cartwright Gardens WC1H 9EL ☎ 020 7387 3927 🖐 £96–£101 ⓘ 42 🚇 King's Cross, Russell Square, Euston 🚌 10, 30, 73, 91, 205

ONE ALDWYCH

www.onealdwych.co.uk
One Aldwych is well known for its chic and contemporary style set in an Edwardian building. There's a host of interesting features: a swimming pool with underwater music in the health club, the dramatic amber city

mural in the lofty Axis Restaurant— acclaimed for its modern British cooking—and the contemporary lobby bar where American martini cocktails are the thing to drink. There is a coffee bar and Indigo for lighter dining. Bedrooms are no less stylish, with giant pillows, down duvets and granite bathroom surfaces.
✚ 169 J4 ✉ 1 Aldwych WC2B 4RH ☎ 020 7300 1000 🖐 £219–£615 ⓘ 105 (18 family) 🏊 Indoor 🛗 🚇 Charing Cross, Covent Garden 🚌 521

RADISSON EDWARDIAN HAMPSHIRE HOTEL

www.radissonedwardian.com
This popular hotel is in central Leicester Square. The public areas are all elegantly furnished, with wood-panelled lounges and sitting rooms. Bedrooms and suites are air-conditioned. There is an excellent restaurant and you can have drinks in the plush chairs of the Hampshire Bar.
✚ 169 J5 ✉ 31 Leicester Square WC2H 7LH ☎ 020 7839 9399 🖐 £250–£310 ⓘ 127 🛗 🚇 Leicester Square 🚌 24, 29, 176

REGENCY

www.regencyhotelwestend.co.uk
The Regency Hotel is close to Madame Tussauds (▷ 217) and the West End. The bedrooms are well furnished and include some suitable for families. Breakfast (included) is served in a light and cheerful basement breakfast room.
✚ 168 F3 ✉ 19 Nottingham Place W1U 5LQ ☎ 020 7486 5347 🖐 £85–£120 ⓘ 20

🚇 Euston, King's Cross, Baker Street 🚌 2, 13, 27, 30, 74, 82, 113, 139, 189

THE SAVOY

www.fairmont.com
After a £220 million gutting and total restoration, completed in 2010, this iconic hotel has once again taken its place in the top echelons of glamorous Edwardian-style luxury, where staff strive to obey your every whim. Some bedrooms look directly on to the river, and suites come with their own butler. Sip cocktails in the art deco American Bar, or champagne in the new Beaufort Bar, or simply indulge in the fresh pastries of the new tea room. Chef Gordon Ramsay now has charge of the famous Savoy Grill restaurant.
✚ 169 J5 ✉ Strand WC2R 0EU ☎ 020 7836 4343 🖐 £354–£750 ⓘ 268 🏊 🛗 🚇 Charing Cross, Covent Garden

STRAND PALACE

www.strandpalacehotel.co.uk
At the heart of theatreland, the Strand Palace is a vast hotel, with rooms that vary in style, including Club rooms with enhanced facilities. The extensive public areas include four restaurants and bars in which to eat and a popular cocktail bar. Prices include breakfast.
✚ 169 J4 ✉ 372 The Strand WC2R 0JJ ☎ 020 7379 4737 🖐 £175–£250 ⓘ 786 🚇 Charing Cross

Below *The grand entrance to The Savoy*

Map labels:
- STRAND
- MAYFAIR
- National Portrait Gallery
- National Gallery
- ST JAMES'S
- Buckingham Palace
- Houses of Parliament
- Westminster Abbey
- LAMBETH
- BELGRAVIA
- WESTMINSTER
- Tate Britain
- VAUXHALL
- PIMLICO
- KENNINGTON

WESTMINSTER, ST. JAMES'S AND MAYFAIR

At once the architectural jewel in London's crown, the seat of Britain's parliament, and the home of the nation's constitutional monarchy and Mayfair, London's most exclusive district, this part of the borough of Westminster is the city at its most alluring and beautiful. With Big Ben standing sentry over the River Thames at one end of the Houses of Parliament, and Admiral Nelson gazing imperiously in that direction down Whitehall from the lofty perch of his column in Trafalgar Square, you could barely ask for a more imposing introduction to the area. And yet these are only two of the magnificent structures that catch the eye wherever you turn. On the far side of Parliament Square from the famous clock stands the medieval masterpiece of Westminster Abbey, while behind Nelson at the top of Trafalgar Square, the stylish facade of the National Gallery heralds the wealth of artistic treasures within. Some way southwest down the river, Tate Britain holds another world-class collection of art.

Passing from Trafalgar Square through Edward VII's colossal Admiralty Arch, you can stroll down Pall Mall, as the green expanse of St. James's Park unfolds to your left and the outline of Buckingham Palace comes gradually into focus in front of you. As you near the official residence of Queen Elizabeth II and the royal family, another fine patch of nature, Green Park, stretches out to the right, lined by a row of splendid mansions. It's a shame, however, not to detour at least for a little while, so that you can stand on the small footbridge that spans the elongated lake in St. James's Park and be rewarded by the breathtaking view as the grandeur of the city manifests itself all around.

BANQUETING HOUSE

www.hrp.org.uk

The Banqueting House is all that remains of Whitehall Palace, the sovereign's main residence from 1530 until its destruction by fire in 1698. English architect Inigo Jones (1573–1652) amazed the public with his Palladian design of three central bays and Ionic columns, giving London (and Britain) its first glimpse of neoclassical architecture. State occasions, plays and masques were held in the magnificent main hall in which the painted canvas ceiling by Peter Paul Rubens allegorically glorifies the reign of James I. A less propitious period for the monarchy was marked when Charles I stepped out of the first-floor balcony to face his execution in 1649.

The spacious undercroft (crypt), designed as a drinking den for James I, is still hired out for private parties.
⊞ 173 J5 ✉ Whitehall SW1A 2ER ☎ 020 3166 6154 🕓 Mon–Sat 10–5. May close at short notice for state functions 🖐 Adult £4.80, child (under 16) free 🚇 Westminster, Embankment 🚌 3, 11, 12, 24, 53, 77A, 88, 159 ❓ Lunchtime concerts

BENJAMIN FRANKLIN HOUSE

www.benjaminfranklinhouse.org

Opened to the public on Franklin's 300th birthday (he was born on 16 January 1706) after extensive restoration, this house, built around 1730, holds a Grade I architectural listing for its many original features, including 14 fireplaces, ceilings, shutters, floors and a marvellous central staircase.

Franklin lived here from 1757 to 1775, and it is the only home of his remaining in the world. The museum highlights the many accomplishments and inventions of this brilliant man, some of which were discovered here. The Historical Experience combines the latest technology with lively performances to show Franklin's integral role in politics, science and philosophy. The interests of this highly social and gregarious man ranged from bifocal spectacles and an energy-saving oven to health issues such as inoculation and cures for the common cold.

The museum holds key artefacts such as bones studied at the anatomy school run by Dr. William Hewson, who lived here during Franklin's stay. The house is also home to the Student Science Centre, which through hands-on experiments demonstrates Franklin's significant discoveries such as electricity, and medical processes studied by Dr. Hewson.
⊞ 173 J5 ✉ 36 Craven Street WC2N 5NF ☎ 020 7839 2006 🕓 Wed–Sun 12–5. Shows at 12, 1, 2, 3.15, 4.15 (arrive 10 min before start 🖐 Adult £7, child (under 16) free 🚇 Charing Cross, Embankment 🚌 6, 9, 11, 13, 15, 23, 91, 77A, 176 (to Strand) 🚶 Guided tours Mon 📅

BUCKINGHAM PALACE

▷ 176–177.

BURLINGTON ARCADE

www.burlington-arcade.co.uk

Leather goods, bespoke shoes, antique and contemporary jewellery, cashmere garments, perfumery and unusual gifts can all be found behind the Regency-style mahogany shopfronts of this Piccadilly arcade. Built in 1819 with a central, timberframe glass canopy, its original purpose was to prevent passers-by tossing rubbish into the garden of Burlington House (see Royal Academy of Arts, ▷ 181). Former soldiers of the regiment of the 10th Hussars were recruited to keep order. 'Beadles' in Edwardian frock coats and top hats still enforce Regency laws of courtesy and decorum, which forbid whistling, singing, hurrying and carrying large packages.
⊞ 130 H5 ✉ Piccadilly W1 🕓 Mon–Wed, Fri 8–6.30, Thu 8–7, Sat 9–6.30, Sun 11–5 🖐 Free 🚇 Green Park, Piccadilly Circus 🚌 8, 9, 14, 19, 22, 38

CHURCHILL WAR ROOMS

cwr.iwm.org.uk

Nowhere is the personal experience of war and the sense of crisis more keenly felt than in these cramped underground rooms in Whitehall, where the most senior figures of Britain's government and armed forces worked and slept during World War II. Most interesting of those rooms open to the public are the Map Room, its walls covered in pinhole-riddled maps as the progress of the war was tracked; the Cabinet Room, where the work of government carried on during bombing raids; the Transatlantic Telephone Room, which had direct communication with Washington's White House; and the Prime Minister's Room, where Sir Winston Churchill broadcast to the nation. More rooms make up this evocative museum dedicated to the life of Winston Churchill, with an interactive 'Lifeline'.

A free audioguide navigates you through corridors that reverberate to the sound of sirens and the voices of guards as bombs explode and fires rage outside.
⊞ 173 J6 ✉ Clive Steps, King Charles Street SW1A 2AQ ☎ 020 7930 6961 🕓 Daily 9.30–6 🖐 Adult £16.95, child (under 16) free 🚇 Westminster, St. James's Park 🚌 3, 11, 12, 24, 53, 88 🛍 📅

Opposite *The main hall of the Banqueting House, with its superb Rubens ceiling*
Below *The Map Room in the Churchill War Rooms has been left as it was in August 1945*

INFORMATION

www.royal.gov.uk

➕ 172 G6 ✉ Buckingham Gate SW1A
1AA ☎ 020 7766 7300 🕐 Aug–Sep
(precise dates vary) 9.45–6.30 (last entry
3.45); timed ticket system with admission
every 15 min 💷 Adult £17.50, child
(5–17) £10, under 5s free, family £46
🚇 Victoria, Green Park, Hyde Park Corner
🚌 11, 211, C1, C10 🎫 Entry includes
free audioguide. Exclusive tours available
Dec–Jan, Apr–May, Aug–Sep, £65.
Advance booking essential 📖 £5.25,
in English, French, German, Italian,
Japanese, Spanish, Chinese, Russian
🛍 🏛 Royal Collection souvenirs

Above *The splendid Victoria Memorial sits
opposite the entrance to the palace*

INTRODUCTION

The palace so familiar to millions from newsreels and postcards took shape
comparatively recently, after centuries of piecemeal architectural changes.
Originally plain Buckingham House, it was built as the Duke of Buckingham's
country mansion at the western end of St. James's Park and Green Park.
George III snapped it up as a private residence in 1761 and work began on
embellishments and additions to the shell of the Duke's old home. When Queen
Victoria and Prince Albert moved into the palace in 1837 a whole new wing was
added to accommodate their fast-growing family. There are 775 rooms in total,
including offices for the extensive administration of the monarchy.

The palace is owned by the British state, as is Windsor Castle, and is not the
private property of the monarch like Sandringham House or Balmoral Castle.
Consequently there was not much the Queen could do about the decision—
controversial to some—made in 1993 to generate funds for the restoration
of Windsor Castle after fire damage, by opening the 19 State Rooms to the
public. They are open in August and September, when the royal family is not
in residence.

Without even entering the grounds at all, you can enjoy the Changing of the
Guard through the surrounding railings. This splendid bit of pomp takes place at
11.30am daily from May to July and on alternate days the rest of the year, when
the new guard arrives from Wellington Barracks, accompanied by a brass band.

WHAT TO SEE
THE STATE ROOMS

You enter the palace through the Ambassadors' Court, in the south wing, and go through John Nash's dramatic Grand Hall to climb the curving Carrara marble stairs of the Grand Staircase to the first-floor State Rooms. Beyond the small Guard Room, hung with Gobelin tapestries, is the Green Drawing Room, an antechamber to the Throne Room, where official visitors gather before being presented to the Queen. Ahead is the Throne Room, a theatrical space leading up to the Chairs of State under a baroque proscenium arch.

From here you go into the Picture Gallery, 47m long (155ft), hung with works by Rubens, Rembrandt, Canaletto and Van Dyck. The Silk Tapestry Room, with its monumental French pedestal clock, links the Picture Gallery with the East Gallery, part of Queen Victoria's new block, leading into the Ball Supper Room and the vast Ballroom, now used for investiture ceremonies (when knighthoods and other honours are awarded) and state banquets.

More Gobelin tapestries are displayed in the smaller West Gallery, which leads to the State Dining Room, vividly decorated in white and gold with deep-red walls and carpet. Next comes the sumptuous Blue Drawing Room, with a dazzling ceiling by John Nash and huge Corinthian columns. The opulent decoration continues in the Music Room, with its vaulted, domed ceiling and columns of lapis lazuli scagliola (imitation stone, made of glue and plaster).

A blaze of white and gold greets you in the White Drawing Room, where there are more pieces of wonderful French furniture. The intricately designed Minister's Staircase leads back to the ground floor and the Marble Hall, displaying statues of nymphs and portraits of Victoria's relations. From the Bow Room tours exit into the garden.

Other visitor attractions are the Queen's Gallery (▷ 181) and the nearby Royal Mews (▷ 181). Combined tickets are available.

TIPS
» To avoid the queues, book a timed ticket in advance.
» For same-day tickets on the day go to the Visitor Entrance, Buckingham Palace Road.
» The Royal Standard flies above the palace when the Queen is in residence.

Left *The Royal Guards do not just guard the Queen but are also serving soldiers*
Below *The Grand Staircase takes you up to the State Rooms*

REGIONS WESTMINSTER, ST. JAMES'S AND MAYFAIR • SIGHTS

GREEN PARK

www.royalparks.gov.uk

Henry VIII bought this swathe of land for hunting, along with Hyde Park (▷ 212) to the west and St. James's Park (▷ 190) on the other side of the Mall. Famous for its mature trees and avenues, Green Park's 19ha (42 acres) are less formal than London's other royal parks. In the southwest corner is the Wellington Arch (▷ 191).

✚ 172 G6 ☎ 020 7930 1793 🕐 Open access ✋ Free 🚇 Green Park, Hyde Park Corner 🚌 8, 14, 19, 82 🔲

GUARDS MUSEUM

www.theguardsmuseum.com

The Guards are the monarch's personal bodyguard, made up of soldiers from the Grenadier, Coldstream, Scots, Irish and Welsh Guards. Their 350-year regimental history is explored using more than 30 displays of uniforms, weapons and tableaux depicting famous battles from the 17th-century English Civil War to the present day.

All this is found under the parade ground at the east end of Wellington Barracks, whose classical facade overlooks St. James's Park (▷ 190).

✚ 173 H6 ✉ Wellington Barracks, Birdcage Walk SW1E 6HQ ☎ 020 7414 3271 🕐 Daily 10–4. Closed on ceremonial days ✋ Adult £4, under 16s free 🚇 St. James's Park 🚌 11, 24, 148, 211 🏛

HANDEL HOUSE MUSEUM

www.handelhouse.org

No. 25 Brook Street was the home of German-English composer George Frederick Handel (1685–1759) from 1723 until his death. It was here that he composed some of his best-loved works, including the *Messiah*, *Zadok the Priest* and the *Music for the Royal Fireworks*. Portraits of Handel and his contemporaries, scores, prints and sculpture are on display. Part of No. 23, next door (▷ 19), is being developed to reflect Jimi Hendrix's life there.

✚ 209 G4 ✉ 25 Brook Street W1K 4HB ☎ 020 7495 1685 🕐 Tue, Wed, Fri, Sat 10–6, Thu 10–8, Sun 12–6. During busy periods, tickets may be timed ✋ Adult £5, child (5–16) £2, under 5s free 🚇 Bond Street, Oxford Circus 🚌 3, 8, 25, 55, 176 🏛

HOUSES OF PARLIAMENT

▷ 179–180.

INSTITUTE OF CONTEMPORARY ARTS (ICA)

www.ica.org.uk

English art critic and historian Sir Herbert Read (1893–1968) established the ICA soon after World War II. Originally housed in Dover Street, it was moved in 1968 to Carlton House Terrace, a long and elegant white-stone building fronted by neoclassical columns and designed by John Nash (1752–1835). Behind its formal facade the Institute presents contemporary films, exhibitions of avant-garde art, talks and dance productions.

✚ 173 H5 ✉ The Mall SW1Y 5AH ☎ 020 7930 3647 🕐 Wed 12–11, Thu–Sat 12pm–1am, Sun 12–9. Gallery daily 12–7; until 9pm on Thu (during exhibitions) ✋ Exhibitions free; check ahead for individual events 🚇 Charing Cross, Piccadilly Circus 🚌 3, 9, 11, 12, 13, 19, 23, 88 🔲 🏛

JEWEL TOWER

www.english-heritage.org.uk

The three-storey brick-built Jewel Tower was built in about 1365 as part of the original Palace of Westminster and used to store Edward III's treasures. A moat surrounded it at that time. On the first floor an exhibition records the history of Parliament from 1066 to the present day, and on the second floor a 50-minute video explains the workings of government, and a virtual tour takes you round the Houses of Parliament.

✚ 173 J6 ✉ Abingdon Street SW1P 3JX ☎ 020 7222 2219 🕐 Apr–Oct daily 10–5; Nov–Mar daily 10–4 ✋ Adult £3, child (5–16) £1.50, under 5s free 🚇 Westminster 🚌 3, 12 🏛

Below The Canada Memorial fountain in Green Park, dedicated to Canadian soldiers

INTRODUCTION

Despite their Gothic appearance, the present Houses of Parliament, the headquarters of state power, are quite recent. The medieval Palace of Westminster was virtually destroyed by fire in 1834, and a competition was held to design a replacement in the Elizabethan style. It was won by architect Charles Barry (1795–1860) and his assistant, Augustus Pugin (1812–52).

WHAT TO SEE

PARLIAMENT

At the State Opening of Parliament (usually November) (▷ 295) the Queen processes through the building. Her route can be followed on a public tour during the summer recess, when Members of Parliament take their annual break. After passing through the Norman porch, tours enter the Queen's Robing Room, a dazzle of gold and crimson. This is where the Queen puts on the Imperial State Crown (▷ 114) and her crimson parliamentary robe. The Royal Gallery comes next, hung with portraits of monarchs. Huge Victorian portraits of the Tudors decorate the Prince's Chamber. From here you enter the Lords' Chamber, where the Queen addresses Parliament from the royal throne, and the Lord Chancellor takes up position on the Woolsack, a wool-stuffed cushion representing British prosperity.

This is the end of the Queen's journey, but visitors continue through the Peers' Lobby to the Central Lobby, between the two Chambers. This is where members of the public can come face to face with their political representatives to plead their particular cause—that is, to lobby. From here a corridor leads into the Commons Lobby, with a red line marking the boundary between

INFORMATION

www.parliament.uk

✚ 173 J6 ✉ Parliament Square SW1A 0AA ☎ House of Commons 020 7219 4272, House of Lords 020 7219 3107, tickets for Saturdays and summer tours 0844 847 1672 🕙 Sat all year 9.15–4.30, Aug–Sep dates and times may vary. Tour during summer recess. Clock Tower by request only 👆 Strangers' Gallery and Clock Tower free 🚇 Westminster 🚌 3, 11, 12, 24 🚢 Westminster Millennium Pier ☛ Tour during summer recess: adult £14, child (5–15) £6, under 5s free, family £35. Foreign-language tours in French, Spanish, German or Italian at set times 📖 Free 'Brief Guides' in several languages. Various souvenir guidebooks ☕ Jubilee Café in Westminster Hall 🎁 Gift shop in Westminster Hall

Above *The Houses of Parliament at dusk*

TIP
» Tours last around 75 minutes and involve lots of walking—not recommended for younger children.

Government and Opposition members—traditionally seated at just over two swords' lengths apart, for safety's sake. Although there is not much chance of a violent confrontation between opposing MPs these days, it is common for some pretty barbed comments to be cast back and forth during the more heated debates, leading to the frequent demands for 'Order! Order!' from the Speaker of the House. Next comes St. Stephen's Hall, on the site of the original chapel, and finally the 11th-century Westminster Hall, now used only occasionally for ceremonial occasions.

Free tours are available throughout the year for UK residents, while foreign visitors can only book tickets on Saturdays and during summer recess. You can attend debates in the House of Commons or the House of Lords. You can also watch committees and judicial hearings. Wait outside St. Stephen's Entrance, but note that queues can be long for the most interesting debates or for Prime Minister's Questions. UK residents can arrange free tickets for entry in advance by contacting their local MP's office or a Lord. Advice on how to go about this can be found on the website. To arrange a tour of the Big Ben clock tower, UK residents can contact their MP; overseas visitors are not permitted at the time of writing.

BIG BEN

If it's the Astronomer Royal at the Meridian a few miles east in Greenwich that sets the time, then it is the clock tower of the Houses of Parliament that keeps it in most people's minds. Better known as Big Ben, the most famous clock in the world is renowned for keeping remarkably accurate time and, as its chimes are broadcast by the BBC, people all over Britain and beyond set their watches by it. Completed in 1859, its four ornate faces, made of gilt and cast iron and 7m (23ft) in diameter, are positioned about four-fifths of the way up the 96m (315ft) Gothic Revival tower. It remains a matter of debate whether it is named after the former Commissioner of Works, Benjamin Hall, or a popular boxer of the period, Benjamin Caunt.

To be exact, the name Big Ben only refers to the huge 13-tonne bell inside, not the rest of the clock or tower. The hammer weighs 200kg (440lb) and when struck the great bell emits the musical note E in an unhurried, ponderous manner. This is the sound by which thousands of revellers, waiting half a mile away in Trafalgar Square, see in the New Year every 31 December. Indeed, it is worth making a point of seeing Big Ben at least once when it is lit up at night, whatever the date is.

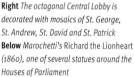

Right *The octagonal Central Lobby is decorated with mosaics of St. George, St. Andrew, St. David and St. Patrick*
Below *Marochetti's Richard the Lionheart (1860), one of several statues around the Houses of Parliament*

THE NORTH WING
Rembrandt van Rijn (1606–69), *Belshazzar's Feast*
One of the Dutch master's more dramatic creations, this painting was commissioned by a wealthy Jewish patron. It depicts the biblical scene from Daniel Chapter 5, where Belshazzar, king of Babylon, throws a lavish feast for his nobles, during which he blasphemously uses the sacred goblets his father Nebuchadnezzar had looted from Jerusalem Temple. Using his trademark technique of drawing attention to the important features of the canvas by illuminating them in stark contrast to the dark background, Rembrandt shows the moment when the hand of God appears and prophesies the king's imminent death with the inscription on the wall. This, incidentally, is the origin of the phrase 'the writing is on the wall'.

Pieter de Hooch (1629–84), *The Courtyard of a House in Delft*
This domestic scene dating from 1658 is a masterpiece of composition and light, showing a woman and child in a brick courtyard, a passage along the side of a burgher's house and another woman looking out towards the canal and the neighbour's house. The contrasts of light and colour in the red and yellow brick,

TIPS
» Visit on a Friday if your schedule is tight. There's an extra tour at 6.30pm and late opening to 9pm.
» Paintings are moved around so check at the desk or call first to find your favourite.

Below *Vincent van Gogh's* Sunflowers *(1888) was one of many pictures of the same subject painted to decorate his yellow house in Provence*

INFORMATION

www.npg.org.uk

✚ 173 J5 ✉ St. Martin's Place WC2H
OHE ☎ 020 7312 2463 🕔 Sat–Wed
10–6, Thu–Fri 10–9 ✋ Free. Charge for
some special exhibitions 🚇 Leicester
Square, Charing Cross 🚌 24, 29, 176
🎧 Audio-visual guide with choice of five
tours, plus options for children (7–11),
£3. Also available in French, German,
Italian, Japanese, Spanish 📖 Visitor's
Guide £5 🍴 The Portrait Restaurant on
the top floor (▷ 201); tea from 2.30pm
☕ The Portrait Café in the basement
🛍 Art-themed books, posters, cards,
jewellery, frames, stationery, bookshop
(basement), selling titles on British history,
art, portraiture, photography, costume,
literature and biography. Exhibition shop
outside Wolfson Gallery

INTRODUCTION

The National Portrait Gallery was founded in 1856 by the 5th Earl Stanhope,
historian, politician and trustee of the British Museum, to collect the likenesses
of famous British men and women. After 40 years of being moved around
London to a succession of unsuitable homes it was finally given a permanent
new gallery on St. Martin's Place. After several appeals for permission to
increase the gallery space it was agreed in 1928 that a new wing could be
built along Orange Street, and in the 1990s there was further expansion into
the old Royal Dental School (now home to the Heinz Archive and the
reference library).

In 2000 the Queen opened the Ondaatje Wing, named after benefactor
Christopher Ondaatje.

The gallery entrance is a surprisingly modest doorway tucked away at the
back of the National Gallery (▷ 182–187). Exhibits are arranged chronologically,
but a little confusingly, over three floors, with the selection beginning on the
second floor and ending on the ground floor.

To reach the start of the collection, take the escalator up from the main hall
to the Tudor Galleries, the 17th century and work from the 18th century, which
follows themes such as the Kit-Cat Club, the arts, and science and industry. The
Victorians, their art and their achievements occupy most of the first-floor rooms,
including daguerreotypes (early photographs). Rooms 30–33 cover the period
from World War I to 1990 and include a collection of portraits of the royal family.
The Balcony Gallery, also on the first floor, covers 1960–90 with photographs,
busts and figurines, and back on the ground floor, Britain since 1990 is
represented in a constantly changing exhibition of contemporary portraits, with
new acquisitions also displayed here.

WHAT TO SEE

SECOND FLOOR

The Tudor Galleries

A magnificent series of royal, aristocratic and family portraits makes this whole,
compact section of the gallery a must-see. Among the most stunning works is
the dazzling Ditchley Portrait of Elizabeth I by Marcus Gheeraerts the Younger
(1592), a tour de force of political propaganda. Gheeraerts shows the Queen

Above *The Statesmen's Gallery contains
portraits and busts of eminent Victorians*

triumphantly standing on a map of Britain with storm clouds behind her to the right, intended to represent the defeated Spanish Armada, and bright skies to the left, signalling a glorious future under the Virgin Queen's reign. Look out too for the huge ink-and-watercolour cartoon of Henry VIII by Hans Holbein—a preparatory work for the mural showing Henry, his parents and his third wife, Jane Seymour, which hung in Whitehall Palace until its destruction by fire in 1698; Rowland Lockey's group portrait of Sir Thomas More and his household and five generations of descendants; the full-length portrait of Catherine Parr by Master John; and a fiery-cheeked Sir Francis Drake, by an unknown artist.

George Villiers, Duke of Buckingham (Jacobean Court)
William Larkin's sumptuous full-length portrait of James I's handsome favourite was painted in 1616, when its subject was 24 years old. Villiers is almost upstaged by the lush red velvet of his cape and the bronze folds of silk drapery above him. These curtains were, in fact, green until 1985, when experts found traces of the original paint and removed the top layer to reveal the artist's rich shades, now displayed as he had intended.

FIRST FLOOR
The Brontë Sisters (Victorian Rooms)
Branwell Brontë (1817–48) painted this portrait of his sisters Anne (1820–49), Emily (1818–48) and Charlotte (1816–55) in about 1834. Growing up in a remote North Yorkshire parsonage, the siblings shared a vivid imaginary world, and the three young women went on to produce passionate and dark novels including *The Tenant of Wildfell Hall* (Anne), *Wuthering Heights* (Emily) and *Jane Eyre* (Charlotte). Branwell failed in his attempts to make his name as a writer and as an artist, and succumbed to drink and opium. A poignant outline, clearly seen between Emily and Charlotte, shows where he has painted out the self-portrait that originally completed the group. Technically the painting may not be too impressive but the image of three remarkable 19th-century novelists is fascinating.

Zandra Rhodes (Balcony Gallery)
Andrew Logan's sculpture of the larger-than-life fashion designer is one of several late 20th- and early 21st-century pieces in the National Portrait Gallery using unconventional materials and forms to bring out the personalities of their subjects. Logan has opted for resin and bright, theatrical colours to express Rhodes' extrovert character and flamboyant style. It makes a striking contrast to the gallery's earlier sculptures, mainly in marble or bronze, as well as to contemporary works such as the cool ceramic figure of Coco Chanel.

TIP
» Find out more about portraits and artists at the Portrait Explorer, on the ground floor mezzanine—touch screens give access to 30,000 sitters and 65,000 portraits.

GALLERY GUIDE
GROUND FLOOR
Rooms 34–41: Contemporary portraits; new acquisitions; temporary exhibitions

FIRST FLOOR
Rooms 21–29: The Victorians. Introduction: Queen Victoria, Statesmen's Gallery, Expansion and Empire, Early Victorian Arts, Portraits and Politics, Portraits by G. F. Watts, Science and Technology, Late Victorian Arts, Turn of the Century

Room 30: We Are Making A New World: Britain 1914–18
Room 31: A National Portrait: Britain 1919–1959 and Britain and the World 1939–59.
Room 32 (Balcony Gallery): Artists and Sitters Britain 1960–1990

SECOND FLOOR
Rooms 1–3: Tudor Galleries. The Early Tudors, Elizabethan England, Miniatures Gallery
Rooms 4–8: 17th century. The Jacobean Court, Charles I and the Civil War, Charles II: the Restoration of the Monarchy, The Later Stuarts
Rooms 9–14: 18th century. The Kit-Cat Club, The Arts in the Early 18th Century, Britain in the Early 18th Century, The Arts in the Later 18th Century, Science and Industry in the 18th Century, Britain becomes a World Power, Jacobean Court to Revolution
Rooms 17–20: The Regency Weldon Galleries. Royal Celebrity and Scandal; Art, Invention and Thought: The Romantics; Art, Invention and Thought: Making the Modern World; The Road to Reform

Left *Historian and politician Thomas Macaulay (1800–59) is commemorated on the facade of the building*

ST. JAMES'S PARK

www.royalparks.gov.uk

St. James's Park is the most attractive of all London's green spaces. From the footbridge that crosses the lake at its heart there are uninterrupted views westwards to the facade of Buckingham Palace, while to the east is the rear of Sir George Gilbert Scott's classical government offices, and the turrets and onion domes of the National Liberal Club.

Three palaces surround the park: The oldest, Westminster, is now the Houses of Parliament (▷ 179–180); St. James's Palace, across the Mall, remains the official court; and since 1837 the monarch has lived at the third, Buckingham Palace (▷ 176–177), at the southern end. Clarence House, on the park's northwestern edge, was the home of Queen Elizabeth, the Queen Mother, and is now the home of Prince Charles (Aug–end Sep daily 10–5.30 by timed tour, must be pre-booked, tel 020 7766 7303). Admiralty Arch, at the northern tip of the park, marks the other end of the Mall.

The park's central feature is the pleasant lake, created by John Nash from the canal originally excavated from the marshy land for Charles II. Charles was responsible for introducing the geese and waterfowl whose descendants still live here. Duck Island is their sanctuary, maintained as a wildlife reserve. On the west side of the island are the park's resident pelicans, a gift to Charles II from a Russian ambassador. It's since become something of a tradition for ambassadors to offer a pelican to the park. You can watch the five pelicans being fed every day at 2.30pm near Duck Island Cottage.

Inn The Park is a highly regarded restaurant with landscaped turf roof and timbered promenade. Early evening band concerts take place from May to August.

✚ 173 H6 ✉ Park Office, The Store Yard, Horse Guards Road SW1A 2BJ ☎ 020 7930 1793 ◷ Daily 5am–midnight ◷ Free Ⓜ St. James's Park, Green Park 🚌 11, 12, 53, 88, 211

ST. MARTIN-IN-THE-FIELDS

www2.stmartin-in-the-fields.org

Steps lead up to the Corinthian portico of the church of St. Martin-in-the-Fields, at the northeastern corner of Trafalgar Square. Many consider this lovely church to be the square's finest building. Scottish architect James Gibbs (1682–1754) designed it in the 1720s, and the lavish interior is decorated with ornate Italian plasterwork. Officially the parish church of Buckingham Palace, St. Martin's has strong royal connections—George I was a warden here, and there's a royal box to the left of the high altar. For some 40 years there has been a Chinese congregation at the church with regular Sunday services. The church is also famous for its support for homeless people.

Inside the church, the recent £36 million restoration is magnificent, the perfect setting for a lunchtime or evening concert by top ensembles and choirs. The Café in the Crypt offers escape from the hustle of London's streets.

✚ 173 J5 ✉ Trafalgar Square WC2N 4JJ ☎ 020 7766 1100 ◷ Mon–Sat 8–6.30, Sun 8–7.30; brass-rubbing Mon–Wed 10–6, Thu–Sat 10–8, Sun 11.30–5 ◷ Free; brass-rubbing from £4.50 Ⓜ Charing Cross, Leicester Square 🚌 9, 11, 13, 15, 24, 453 ▯ ▦

SPENCER HOUSE

www.spencerhouse.co.uk

Built in the mid-18th century for Earl Spencer (an ancestor of the late Diana, Princess of Wales), Spencer House is London's finest surviving Palladian mansion.

To see the interior you must take a guided tour, which leads into eight state rooms restored to their original style by the current owners, the Rothschilds. Company executives occupy the rest of the building.

Interior decor is lavish, to say the least, from the ornate green and gold ceiling in the Great Room to the classical murals in the Painted Room. A highlight is the Palm Room, where gilded columns and painted fronds stretch out like palm trees.

During spring and summer the magnificent 18th-century gardens are also open occasionally.

✚ 172 H5 ✉ 27 St. James's Place SW1A 1NR ☎ 020 7514 1958 ◷ By guided tour only: Sun 10.30–5.45 (last tour 4.45); closed Jan, Aug. Times vary, so phone ahead ◷ Adult £9, child (10–16) £7. No admission to under 10s Ⓜ Green Park 🚌 9, 14, 19, 22, 38

TATE BRITAIN

▷ 192–193.

TRAFALGAR SQUARE

www.london.gov.uk/trafalgarsquare

One of the world's most famous squares sits at the northern end of Whitehall (▷ 191), where it was laid out to John Nash's design between 1829 and 1841, as a commemoration of Admiral Lord Nelson's victory against the French at the 1805 Battle of Trafalgar.

Feeding the pigeons in Trafalgar Square, once a must for any visitor to London, is now forbidden (▷ 24).

Nelson towers on his 56m (185ft) column at the centre of the square. The statue itself, though 5m (17ft) high, can be seen only from strategic viewpoints such as the National Portrait Gallery's top-floor restaurant (▷ 201), but the four huge bronze lions that guard him, sculpted in the 1860s by Sir Edwin Landseer, are clearly on view, as well as the reliefs around the base of the column, showing Nelson's naval victories. A 17th-century equestrian monument commemorating Charles I, by Hubert Le Sueur (1633), stands on a traffic island.

At the square's corners are four great plinths. Three support more statuary: George IV, again on horseback, by Chantrey and T. Earle (1834), originally meant for Marble Arch; Sir Henry Havelock, by William Behnes (1861); and Sir Charles Napier, by G. G. Adams (1855)—both celebrating military heroes of their time. The fourth plinth is currently devoted to hosting contemporary, sometimes controversial, sculpture, which will periodically change. Marc Quinn's striking white marble sculpture of disabled artist Alison Lapper—naked and pregnant—was the first.

The famous fountains, decorated with sculptings of mermaids and men, sharks and dolphins, were installed in the 19th century and embellished by Sir Edwin Lutyens in 1939.

Leaping into the water during New Year celebrations is another tradition that has now been ruled out on grounds of safety. However, the water still plays in the fountains from 10am daily.

✚ 173 J5 ⏰ Open access ✋ Free
🚇 Charing Cross, Leicester Square
🚌 3, 9, 11, 12, 24, 88, 176, 453

WELLINGTON ARCH
www.english-heritage.org.uk
England's answer to the Arc de Triomphe in Paris is a neoclassical arch erected in 1826 to celebrate the Duke of Wellington's victories in the Napoleonic Wars. A huge equestrian statue of the Duke was added 20 years later.

At one time the rooms inside the arch housed a police station; now there's a permanent exhibition on the statues and memorials of London, and you can enjoy the views from the platform beneath the sculpture.

✚ 172 G6 ✉ Hyde Park Corner W1J 7JZ
☎ 020 7930 2726 ⏰ Apr–Sep Wed–Sun

10–5; Nov–Mar Wed–Sun 10–4 ✋ Adult £3.70, child (5–16) £1.90, under 5s free, family £18.50 🚇 Hyde Park Corner 🚌 2, 8, 9, 10, 14, 16, 19

WESTMINSTER ABBEY
▷ 194–195.

WESTMINSTER CATHEDRAL
www.westminstercathedral.org.uk
Britain's premier Roman Catholic church is a striking Westminster landmark with its 83m (273ft) bell tower and striped patterning of red brick and white stone. Designed in Byzantine style by Victorian architect John Francis Bentley (1839–1902), it echoes the Basilica of St. Mark in Venice. Bentley's brief was that the church should have an extra wide nave to accommodate large congregations, and that it should bear no resemblance to the nearby Protestant Westminster Abbey. You can take a lift up to the top of the bell tower for great views of Big Ben, Buckingham Palace and Nelson's Column.

✚ 172 H7 ✉ 42 Francis Street SW1P 1QW ☎ 020 7798 9055 ⏰ Mon–Fri 9.30–5, Sat–Sun 9.30–6 ✋ Free. Treasures exhibition: adult £5, child (5–18) £2.50, family £11; joint ticket with campanile: adult £8, child £4, family £17.50 🚇 Victoria 🚌 11, 24, 148, 211, 507 🚆

WHITEHALL
Whitehall is the broad avenue connecting Trafalgar Square (▷ 190) with Parliament Square—and the heart of the British government—to the south. Heading south, the first building on the right is the Admiralty.

Next is Horse Guards, where two members of the Household Cavalry mount guard on horseback between 10 and 4—a tradition that persists although all that remains of the former royal palace is the Banqueting House (▷ 175), opposite. The soldiers keep to their stations without moving or making eye contact with passers-by.

Beyond Horse Guards is the gated entrance to Downing Street. This has been the official residence of the Prime Minister (No. 10) since 1731. No. 11 is the official home of the Chancellor of the Exchequer.

Farther along Whitehall is the poignant Portland-stone Cenotaph, designed by Sir Edwin Lutyens and unveiled in 1920 to commemorate the victims of World War I. This provides the focus of the Remembrance Day celebrations held annually since 1918 on the Sunday nearest 11 November.

✚ 173 J5 ⏰ Open access ✋ Free
🚇 Charing Cross, Westminster 🚌 11, 12, 24, 53, 88, 159, 453

Left *Detail of a fountain in Trafalgar Square, with St. Martin-in-the-Fields in the background*
Below *The neoclassical, triumphal Wellington Arch, illuminated at night*

INFORMATION

www.westminster-abbey.org
♦ 173 J6 ✉ Parliament Square SW1P
3PA ☎ 020 7222 5152 ⏰ Mon–Tue,
Thu–Fri 9.30–4.30, Wed 9.30–7, Sat
9.30–2.30. Sun worship only. Chapter
House, Pyx Chamber, accessible only on a
viewing platform. Abbey museum, Mon–
Sat 10.30–4. Cloisters daily 8–6 subject to
availability, closed during special events.
College garden Apr–Sep Tue–Thu 10–6;
Oct–Mar Tue–Thu 10–4. Free lunchtime
band concerts Jul–Aug Wed 12.30–2pm
✋ Adult £15, child (11–16) £6, under 11s
(max of 2 children per paying adult) free,
family £30–£42. Services free. Museum £1
(free with abbey church ticket). Cloisters,
college garden free, donations welcome
for upkeep of garden 🚇 St. James's
Park, Westminster 🚌 11, 12, 24, 159,
211 🎧 90-min tours, £3 per person. For
bookings and further details ☎ 020 7654
4834. Audioguides in 8 languages free
with entry ticket at North Door 📖 £5, in
English, French, German, Spanish, Italian,
Russian, Japanese, Chinese 🛍 Stall
in north cloister and outside west
towers; hot and cold drinks, light snacks,
sandwiches 🍴 Outside west door exit;
souvenirs, postcards, gifts, books

Above *The main entrance is through the
great triple doors on the north front*

INTRODUCTION

Benedictine monks occupied this marshy site on the bank of the Thames from
the middle of the 10th century, but it was Edward the Confessor who began the
present building—the Collegiate Church of St. Peter in Westminster—as a new
church for the abbey in 1050. Having died a week after its consecration, on
6 January 1066, he was the first monarch to be buried here. Almost a year later,
William the Conqueror was crowned here, confirming the royal status of the
church, which has seen the coronation of every subsequent English monarch
with the exception of Edward V and Edward VIII.

Edward the Confessor was later canonized, and Henry III embarked on
large-scale rebuilding in 1245 to make a shrine for the veneration of the
sainted king. Today's church, greatly influenced by the French Gothic cathedrals
of Amiens and Reims, was the result. In 1503 the Lady Chapel at the east end
was rebuilt by Henry VII, who added his name to the chapel, making it into the
architectural high point of the church. The west front was not completed until
1745, when the two towers were built to Nicholas Hawksmoor's design.

The abbey forms the south side of Parliament Square. You enter by the north
transept, through one of three great doorways beneath the large rose window,
whose pattern is repeated in the floor tiles of the chapter house. Inside, turn
left to take a one-way, clockwise tour of the church and cloisters, passing a
succession of chapels with a bewildering throng of tombs and monuments,
before leaving by the west door.

WHAT TO SEE

STATESMEN'S AISLE

The north transept by which you enter the abbey became known as Statesmen's
Aisle after the burial of prime minister William Pitt the Elder in 1778. He is
actually one of the few famous personages commemorated here whose mortal
remains actually lie within their tombs. Other major political figures whose
graves or memorials are to be found here include William Gladstone, Lord
Palmerston, Benjamin Disraeli and Sir Robert Peel, founder of the police force.
Some of the best funerary artwork is actually on display within the three side
chapels off Statesmen's Aisle. Most striking of all is the monument in

St. Michael's Chapel, sculpted by Rubiliac in honour of Lady Elizabeth Nightingale, who died in childbirth. It shows her husband trying to ward off the skeletal figure of Death, who is rising from below to claim her.

HENRY VII'S LADY CHAPEL
North of the sanctuary is the Lady Chapel, where you can view the white-marble effigy of Elizabeth I (died 1603), who shares a tomb with her half-sister, Mary I (died 1558). From the aisle you enter the main part of the chapel, with its exquisite fan-vaulted ceiling. It makes an impressive setting for the royal tombs arranged around the altar and aisles. Among the finest of these is the tomb of Henry VII, in front of the altar, and of his mother, Lady Margaret Beaufort, near the south aisle altar. They died in the same year (1509), and their tombs are the work of the Florentine sculptor Pietro Torrigiano (1472–1522), who, as a boy, often fought with Michelangelo. Note the carvings on the stall misericords (1512): Subjects include mermaids, monsters and a wife beating her husband.

POETS' CORNER
The south transept, also known as Poets' Corner, is where, since the 16th century, great poets, authors, artists and actors have been honoured with memorials. Here are the remains of poet Geoffrey Chaucer (c. 1345–1400), who lived in the abbey precincts while a royal clerk of the works (or buildings inspector). William Shakespeare's monument is here too, though his statue and assumed likeness date from 1740, over a century after his death.

Among the best monuments are the busts of 17th-century poets John Dryden, Ben Jonson and John Milton, and poet and artist William Blake (1757–1827) — the last sculpted in bronze by Sir Jacob Epstein in 1957.

THE QUIRE AND SANCTUARY
This is the ceremonial heart of the church, where services and royal coronations take place, and where Prince William married Catherine Middleton in April 2011. The high altar is a relatively late addition, designed by Sir Gilbert Scott in 1867. The nearby mosaic of the Last Supper was created by Antonio Salviati. Standing to the sides of the altar are four large statues of Moses, King David, St. Peter and St. Paul, while in front of the high altar is the Cosmati Pavement, a mosaic made of glass and precious stones such as onyx, porphyry and serpentine. It was laid by Italian craftsmen in 1268.

CHAPTER HOUSE, PYX CHAMBER AND ABBEY MUSEUM
A door in the south quire aisle leads to the cloister, with its flowing tracery and superb views of the flying buttresses supporting the nave. The chapter house is an octagonal building of 1253, whose floor is still covered in its original tiles. The Norman undercroft (crypt) houses the abbey museum, where you can see macabre wax effigies, including those of Queen Elizabeth I, Charles II and Lord Nelson, made using their death masks and real clothes. The Westminster Retable, recently restored, is England's oldest altarpiece.

The Pyx Chamber, also part of the original abbey, contains the building's oldest altar, dated at around 1240. It's now home to original pyxes (money chests) and the abbey's church plate.

THE NAVE
Here you can enjoy the majestic nave roof, 32m (105ft) high. The complex patterning carries the eye eastwards; only by looking up can you appreciate the enormous length of the building, since at ground level the view is blocked by the 19th-century choir screen, where Sir Isaac Newton and other scientists are remembered. The Tomb of the Unknown Soldier (▷ 38) and St. George's Chapel are near the west door. Just outside the chapel is a portrait of Richard II (reigned 1377–99), the oldest known true portrait of an English monarch.

TIPS
» Attend a service and hear the choirboys, accompanied by the abbey organ on which composer Henry Purcell (1659–95) once played.
» Note that the cloisters are free, entered through Dean's Yard.

Below *Remembrance Day poppies around the Tomb of the Unknown Soldier*

A ROYAL TOUR

A walk through the original bastion of royal power in England, taking in three royal residences. You'll pass the former house of three prime ministers, skirt Whitehall and walk along Constitution Hill to see its poignant war memorial.

THE WALK

Distance: 2 miles (3km)
Time: 2 hours minimum
Start at: St. James's Park Underground station
End at: Hyde Park Corner Underground station

HOW TO GET THERE

🚇 District or Circle line to St. James's Park 🚌 11, 24, 148, 211

★ The huge art deco building above St. James's Park station is the London Underground headquarters.

Start from St. James's Park station by turning immediately left after the ticket barriers and emerging into Petty France. Cross the road and continue ahead down Queen Anne's Gate. Pass through the black gates at the end of the road and cross Birdcage Walk to the entrance to St. James's Park (▷ 190).

❶ In the park, look for noticeboards with a map, history and guide to bird life. James I is said to have housed an 'ellefant' here, plus crocodiles and other beasts, all gifts from foreign princes. The 'ellefant' was given a gallon of wine every day.

Continue straight ahead to reach the lake. Cross the bridge and turn immediately right. At the fork go left and look over to your right to see Big Ben (▷ 37). Walk on to the far northeast corner of the park and exit on to the Mall.

❷ To the right of the Mall, beyond Admiralty Arch, are Trafalgar Square (▷ 190–191) and Whitehall (▷ 191). To the left is Buckingham Palace (▷ 176–177). Royal and parliamentary Britain come together at least once a year when the Queen leaves the palace and passes down the Mall on her way to open Parliament (▷ 295).

Cross the Mall to the Institute of Contemporary Arts (▷ 178). With a day pass you can return later for a drink. Go around to the left of the ICA and up the steps to Waterloo Place.

❸ Statues here commemorate the Duke of York (1763–1827), second son of George III; Florence Nightingale (▷ 71); Edward VII; and Robert Falcon Scott, the British Antarctic explorer who died in 1912 on an expedition to the South Pole. Scott's wife, Lady Kathleen, was the sculptor.

Leave Waterloo Place by the northern side and turn left down Pall Mall and right on to St. James's Square.

❹ As you walk counterclockwise round the square, look for the former home of Nancy Astor (1879–1964), the second woman to be elected to Parliament and the first to take her seat. It's now the In-and-Out Club, one of St. James's private societies. Part of Chatham House was home to three former British prime ministers: William Pitt (1708–78), the Earl of Derby (1799–1869) and William Gladstone (1809–98). The gardens in the square are open Monday to Friday 10 to 4.30.

Continue past the East India Club and turn right into King Street. Here you'll find Christie's auction house (▷ 233). At the end of the street, cross St. James's Street and go down towards St. James's Palace in front of you.

❺ St. James's Palace, former home of Prince Charles, is closed to the public. It was built for Henry VIII in 1532 on the site of a former lepers' hospital, and remained the principal royal residence until Queen Victoria moved to Buckingham Palace.

Take the first right into Little St. James's Street and follow the road round to Bridgewater House. In front of you across the little square is the entrance to Clarence House, home of Prince Charles (▷ 190).
   Continue round along the side of St. James's Palace into Marlborough Street, past the guard, to the Queen's Chapel.

❻ The Queen's Chapel was designed by Inigo Jones in 1627 for Charles I's French wife, Henrietta Maria.

Walk past the statue of Queen Alexandra on the left and rejoin the Mall at the bottom of the street. Turn right and continue to Buckingham Palace (▷ 176–177). If the Queen is in residence, the Royal Standard will be flying.

Above *Spring is a lovely time of year to stroll in St. James's Park*
Opposite *The Wellington Arch*

A detour around the far side of the palace takes you to the Guards Museum (▷ 178) and the Queen's Gallery (▷ 181).
   Otherwise, bear right and head up Constitution Hill.

❼ At the top of Constitution Hill are the 2002 Memorial Gates, a testament to the 5 million volunteers from the Indian subcontinent, Africa and the Caribbean who died in the two world wars.

Cross over to the Wellington Arch (▷ 191). The walk ends here, by Hyde Park Corner Underground station.

WHERE TO EAT
Stop by the bandstand in St. James's Park. Deckchairs cost £1.50 for 1 hour or £4 for 3 hours Apr–Oct. For further information tel 020 7930 1793. There are refreshment stalls in the parks, and the Institute of Contemporary Arts has a good café.

PLACE TO VISIT
QUEEN'S CHAPEL
✉ Marlborough Road SW1A 1BG ☎ 020 7930 4832 ⊘ Visitors are welcome to attend regular services of worship every Sunday, 8.30 and 11.15am Easter Day–Jul (Queen's Chapel); early Oct–Good Friday (Chapel Royal)

SHOPPING

ANDERSON & SHEPPARD
www.anderson-sheppard.co.uk
Established in 1906, Anderson's
is a traditional tailor, with wooden
counters and tape measures. Classic
English gentlemen's suits are hand-
crafted here by expert tailors at a cost
of nearly £2,000 per suit. They also
sell blazers and overcoats.
✚ 168 G4 ✉ 32 Old Burlington Street
W1S 3AT ☎ 020 7734 1420 🕐 Mon–Fri
8.30–5 🚇 Piccadilly Circus, Oxford Circus
🚌 12, 13, 15, 23, 139

FLORIS
www.florislondon.com
Established in 1730, Floris is known
for its perfumes, toilet waters,
bath salts, scented soaps, shaving
accessories and aftershave.
✚ 204 H5 ✉ 89 Jermyn Street SW1Y 6JH
☎ 0845 702 3239 🕐 Mon–Fri 9.30–6,
Sat 10–6 🚇 Green Park, Piccadilly Circus
🚌 9, 14, 19, 22, 38

FORTNUM AND MASON
www.fortnumandmason.com
Founded in 1707, this famous store
is lit with chandeliers. The food hall,
spread over two floors, is excellent.
Treat yourself to an ice cream in the
retro Parlour, or classic British food
in the St. James restaurant. Outside,
the clock chimes the hour and Mr.
Fortnum and Mr. Mason emerge
and bow.
✚ 204 H5 ✉ 181 Piccadilly W1A 1ER
☎ 020 7734 8040 🕐 Mon–Sat 10–8, Sun
12–6 🚇 Green Park, Piccadilly Circus 🚌 9,
14, 19, 22, 38

GIEVES AND HAWKES
www.gievesandhawkes.com
Enjoy understated luxury and the
epitome of elegance in this tailors,
set in a fine Georgian building.
Purveyors of the finest-quality suits
and military uniforms, they have three
royal warrants to prove it.
✚ 168 G4 ✉ 1 Savile Row W1S
3RJ ☎ 020 7432 6403 🕐 Mon–Fri
10–6.30 (Thu until 7), Sat 10–6, Sun 11–5
🚇 Piccadilly Circus, Bond Street

JOHN LEWIS
www.johnlewis.co.uk
Largest by far of the popular and
respected chain of department
stores, this is the place to shop for
very good quality household goods,
beauty products, conservatively
priced clothing and accessories, and
stationery. The store is clearly and
logically set out and claims to be
'never knowingly undersold'.
✚ 168 G4 ✉ 300 Oxford Street W1A 1EX
☎ 020 7629 7711 🕐 Mon–Wed, Fri–Sat
9.30–8, Thu 9.30–9, Sun 12–6 🚇 Oxford
Circus, Bond Street 🚌 8, 10, 12, 23, 73
🚇 🍴

LILLYWHITE'S
www.sportsdirect.com
A department store dedicated entirely
to sports, Lillywhite's can outfit you
for virtually any pastime, from golf
to skiing. It is particularly strong
on footwear.
✚ 168 H5 ✉ 24–36 Lower Regent Street
SW1Y 4QF ☎ 0844 332 5602 🕐 Mon–Fri
10–10, Sat 9.30–10, Sun 11.45–6
🚇 Piccadilly Circus 🚌 9, 14, 19, 22

MULBERRY COMPANY
www.mulberry.com
Ready-to-wear fashions for men
and women, plus accessories, bags,
luggage and items such as camera
cases, all in top-quality leather.
Founder Roger Saul originally started
out as a belt designer. This flagship
store has three floors and is fitted out
in oak, amber glass, bronze and, of
course, leather.
✚ 168 G4 ✉ 50 New Bond Street W1S
1BJ ☎ 020 7491 3900 🕐 Mon–Sat 10–6,
Thu 10–7, Sun 11–5 🚇 Bond Street 🚌 8,
10, 14, 19

POILÂNE
www.poilane.com
An English outpost of a truly Parisian
boulangerie patisserie. Poilâne uses
an enormous wood-fired oven to
bake 80 loaves of its delicious and
expensive sourdough bread every
two hours. Have a look at the bread
chandelier, the original of which was
made by artist Salvador Dalí.
✚ 204 G7 ✉ 46 Elizabeth Street SW1W
9PA ☎ 020 7808 4910 🕐 Mon–Fri 7.30–7,
Sat 7.30–6 🚇 Sloane Square, Victoria
🚌 11, 19, 22, 211, C1

ST. JAMES'S CHURCH PICCADILLY
www.st-james-piccadilly.org
There is an antiques market on
Tuesdays in the church courtyard
(▷ 199), and a general market with
crafts Wednesday to Saturday.
✚ 204 H5 ✉ 197 Piccadilly W1J 9LL
☎ 020 7734 4511 🕐 Tue–Sat 10–6
🚇 Piccadilly Circus 🚌 9, 14, 19, 22

Left *The Halkin Hotel is a model of gracious Georgian styling—all Portland stone and arched windows, with a garden at the back*

pleasant stroll away from Hyde Park. The bedrooms combine comfort with practicality and many include marble bathrooms, and Superior rooms overlook the gardens. There's also a gym, with personal trainers and yoga instructors on hand if required. You'd expect impressive food from this chic hotel, and it certainly delivers. The restaurant, Nahm, is run by chef David Thompson, whose way with Thai cuisine has even earned him a role as an advisor to one of Thailand's leading cooking institutes.

⊞ 204 G6 ✉ Halkin Street, Belgravia SW1X 7DJ ☎ 020 7333 1000 🖐 £288–£540 🛈 41 🔄 📺 🔲 Hyde Park Corner 🚌 9, 10, 14, 19, 22, 52, 74, 137

MELBOURNE HOUSE HOTEL
www.melbournehousehotel.co.uk
This family-run bed-and-breakfast is an easy walk from Victoria mainline train station. Rooms are modern, with flat-screen digital TVs, and some are suitable for families. Breakfast is served in the basement dining room. No visitors allowed in rooms.

⊞ 205 H8 ✉ 79 Belgrave Road SW1V 2BG ☎ 020 7828 3516 🖐 £90–£110 🛈 17 🔲 Pimlico 🚌 24

PREMIER INN LONDON VICTORIA
www.premierinn.com
This hotel is one of the most central of the Premier's 20 London branches and typifies the group's reputation for providing quality accommodation at very fair prices. The modern rooms may not have many frills but they are comfortable. There is also a bar and restaurant on site.

⊞ 204 G7 ✉ 82–83 Eccleston Square SW1V 1PS ☎ 0871 527 8680 🖐 £90–£180 🛈 107 🔲 Victoria 🚌 2, 24, 36, 185, 436

THE RITZ
www.theritzlondon.com
Synonymous with sophistication and attention to detail, the Ritz remains one of London's premier luxury hotels, favoured by the glitterati. All

bedrooms are furnished in Louis XVI-style, with marble bathrooms and every imaginable comfort and facility. A choice of elegant reception rooms includes the Palm Court, with its legendary afternoon tea, the beautifully refurbished Rivoli Bar and the sumptuous Ritz Restaurant, complete with delicate gold chandeliers and extraordinary trompe-l'oeil decoration.

⊞ 204 G5 ✉ 150 Piccadilly W1J 9BR ☎ 020 7493 8181 🖐 £360–£1,000 🛈 137 (44 family) 📺 🔲 Green Park 🚌 8, 9, 14, 19, 22, 38a

ROYAL HORSEGUARDS
www.guoman.com
This majestic hotel in the heart of Whitehall and on the River Thames won the AA's prestigious Hotel of the Year award for 2010–11. The Victorian setting belies an interior of modern comfort and style. Suites and bedrooms are luxuriously restrained and elegant. Dine on the terrace, or in the splendid One Twenty One Two Restaurant, complete with piano bar.

⊞ 205 J5 ✉ 2 Whitehall Court SW1A 2EJ ☎ 0871 376 9033 🛈 281 🔄 📺 🔲 Charing Cross, Embankment

THE RUBENS AT THE PALACE
www.rubenshotel.com
If you want to stay near Buckingham Palace, this is the hotel for you. Right opposite the Royal Mews, it has air-conditioned bedrooms with state-of-the-art entertainment systems and internet access. There is a choice of rooms and lavish suites, including the eight opulent royal rooms, which are named after different monarchs. Two dining rooms and a plush bar complete the facilities. Families and pets are welcome.

⊞ 204 G6 ✉ 39 Buckingham Palace Road SW1W 0PS ☎ 020 7834 6600 🖐 From £174 🛈 161 🔄 🔲 Victoria

SIDNEY
www.sidneyhotel.com
A pleasant budget hotel conveniently located close to Victoria train station. Several bedrooms are suitable for family use. The public areas include a bar lounge and an airy breakfast

room. Breakfast is included, but no evening meals are served.

⊞ 204 H8 ✉ 68–76 Belgrave Road SW1V 2BP ☎ 020 7834 2738 🖐 £89–£105 🛈 82 🔲 Victoria, Pimlico 🚌 24

THE STAFFORD LONDON BY KEMPINSKI
www.kempinski.com
From the pristine, tastefully decorated and air-conditioned bedrooms, to the highly professional yet friendly service, this classically styled boutique hotel maintains the highest standards and retains an air of understated luxury. The American Bar is a fabulous venue in its own right, festooned with an eccentric array of celebrity photos, caps and ties. Afternoon tea is a long-established tradition here. The stylish Stafford Mews has been added, offering 26 stunning mews suites across the courtyard. Tucked away behind Green Park in a quiet corner of St. James's, the Stafford is in an ideal position for excellent shopping and visiting the main sights.

⊞ 204 H5 ✉ 16–18 St. James's Place SW1A 1NJ ☎ 020 7493 0111 🖐 From £345 🛈 105 🔄 📺 🔲 Green Park 🚌 8, 14, 19, 22, 38

THE WESTBURY
www.westburymayfair.com
The Westbury is right in the heart of London's finest shopping area and counts many celebrities among its clientele. Standards of accommodation are high throughout. The public spaces offer a variety of eating and drinking options, including the Polo Bar for cocktails.

⊞ 168 G4 ✉ Bond Street W1S 2YF ☎ 020 7629 7755 🖐 £155–£510 🛈 246 📺 🔲 Bond Street 🚌 8

WINDERMERE
www.windermere-hotel.co.uk
A relaxed and informal family-run hotel within easy reach of Victoria mainline train station. The Pimlico Restaurant serves renowned evening meals and good breakfasts.

⊞ 204 G8 ✉ 142–144 Warwick Way SW1V 4JE ☎ 020 7834 5163 🖐 £119–£145 🛈 22 🔲 Victoria 🚌 24

AROUND HYDE PARK

This large swathe of the city, which is split between the three boroughs of Westminster, Chelsea and Kensington, and Camden, paints a canvas of this cosmopolitan capital at its most diverse. It also offers two of central London's largest green spaces, Hyde Park itself and Regent's Park; the former segues seamlessly into Kensington Gardens, famed for the palace inhabited by Princess Diana, while the latter is home to the zoo and London's largest mosque. Cultural, ethnic and social diversity abound in the various neighbourhoods, from the quiet, classy bastions of old money in Belgravia and Chelsea, through the Afro-Caribbean community that still holds its annual carnival in Notting Hill and the high percentage of Middle Eastern immigrants and wealthy visitors in parts of Kensington, Bayswater and Edgware Road, to the young punks and eccentrics who frequent Camden Lock and its fantastic market, where you can find quirky souvenirs and quality clothing and handicrafts from all over the world.

Eager shoppers have plenty more to choose from: the twin meccas of Harrods and Harvey Nichols are both in Knightsbridge, while the environs of nearby King's Road and Sloane Square are still packed with trendy boutiques. Kensington High Street offers more mainstream goods, like a mini Oxford Street, while lovers of art can cruise the Bayswater Road, on the north side of Hyde Park, every Sunday for works direct from the artist. As if all that wasn't enough, South Kensington is home to a trio of London's greatest museums—the Natural History Museum, the Science Museum and the Victoria & Albert Museum. The whole area also contains a profusion of lesser sights and even one of the world's great performance spaces in the rotund Albert Hall, opposite the memorial of Queen Victoria to her beloved consort.

2

3

4

5

6

7

8

9

KENSAL TOWN

WESTBOURNE GREEN

Paddington Community Hospital

NORTH KENSINGTON

CAMBRIDGE GARDENS

HARROW ROAD FLYOVER

PADDINGTON

MCC Museum

Alexander Fleming Laboratory Museum

St Mary's Hospital

PADDINGTON STATION

NOTTING HILL

BAYSWATER

Whiteleys Shopping Centre

New West End Synagogue

BAYSWATER

Spoke's Monument

Peter Pan Station

Kensington Gardens

Physical Energy Statue

Round Pond

Serpentine Gallery

Kensington Palace

Princess of Wales Diana, Memorial Fountain

Albert Memorial

HOLLAND PARK AVENUE

Holland Park

Holland House

Camden Hill Queen Elizabeth College

Duchess of Bedford's Walk

Kensington & Chelsea Town Hall

Kensington Market Court

KENSINGTON ROAD

HYDE PARK GATE

Royal College of Art

Royal Albert Hall

Polish Institute & Sikorski Museum

Royal Geographical Society

Imperial College

Imperial College of Science

Royal College of Music

Imperial College

Hyde Park Chapel

Imperial College

18 Stafford Terrace

Commonwealth Institute

Leighton House Museum

High Street Kensington

KENSINGTON HIGH STREET

KENSINGTON

St Alban's Grove

Cornwall

Science Museum

Earth Galleries

V&A Museum

Brompton Oratory

Natural History Museum

KENSINGTON (OLYMPIA) STATION

Olympia

Blythe Road

PEMBROKE ROAD

CROMWELL ROAD

Superstore

Chelsea & Westminster Hospital

SOUTH KENSINGTON

WEST KENSINGTON

West London County Court

West Kensington

HAMMERSMITH ROAD

TALGARTH ROAD

EARL'S COURT

EARL'S COURT STATION

Earl's Court

Earls Court Exhibition Centre

Hammersmith Cemetery

Baron's Court

WEST BROMPTON STATION

Brompton Cemetery

WEST BROMPTON

Normand Park

LILLIE ROAD

Turtle Key Arts Centre

Chelsea FC (Stamford Bridge)

Royal Marsden Hospital

Brompton & Harefield

A   B   C   D

London Central Mosque
Museum
Regent's Park
Sherlock Holmes' Museum
Madame Tussauds
MARYLEBONE
Wallace Collection
Selfridges
BLOOMSBURY
ST GILES
SOHO
CHINATOWN
STRAND
Marble Arch
MAYFAIR
PICCADILLY CIRCUS
Hyde Park
Apsley House
Green Park
St James's Park
ST JAMES'S
KNIGHTSBRIDGE
Harrods
Buckingham Palace
BELGRAVIA
Holy Trinity Church
WESTMINSTER
VICTORIA STATION
PIMLICO
Saatchi Gallery (Duke of York's Headquarters)
Royal Hospital
National Army Museum
Carlyle's House (NT)
Chelsea Physic Garden
Thames
Battersea Park

0   400 m
0   400 yds

F   G   H   J

18 STAFFORD TERRACE

www.rbkc.gov.uk

A mass of paintings, cartoons and photographs covers the walls in the Victorian house occupied by political cartoonist and illustrator Edward Linley Sambourne (1844–1910) from 1874 until his death.

The family continued to use the house as a family home until 1980, when it was opened as a museum. It remained almost totally unaltered during the intervening years, preserving its over-furnished, late 19th-century appearance, complete with the original William Morris wallpapers, Asian rugs, stained-glass windows and solid, heavy, Gothic-inspired furniture.

✚ 208 B6 ✉ 18 Stafford Terrace W8 7BH ☎ 020 7602 3316 🅖 Guided tours Wed 11.15, 2.15, Sat–Sun 11.15, 1, 3.30. Reservations advised 🖑 Adult £6, under 16s £1 🅠 High Street Kensington 🚌 9, 10, 27, 28, 49, 52, 70, 328

ALEXANDER FLEMING LABORATORY MUSEUM

www.imperial.uhs.uk

In 1928 Scottish bacteriologist Alexander Fleming (1881–1955) discovered penicillin while working in St. Mary's Hospital, next to Paddington Station. In the hospital's small museum, you can see the cramped laboratory where he cultivated the naturally antibiotic mould that revolutionized medicine. Museum volunteers are on hand to relate their personal experiences of the impact of antibiotics, and displays and a video tell Fleming's story and trace the role of penicillin in the fight against disease.

✚ 208 D4 ✉ St. Mary's Hospital, Praed Street W2 1NY ☎ 020 3312 6528 🅖 Mon–Thu 10–1, other times by prior appointment 🖑 Adult £2, child £1 🅠 Paddington 🚌 7, 15, 27, 36

APSLEY HOUSE

www.english-heritage.org.uk

Designed by Robert Adam in 1771, this aristocratic town house at the western end of Piccadilly on Hyde Park Corner became the London home of war hero and future prime

Above *Broad, tree-lined carriage drive in Battersea Park*
Opposite *Colonnaded Apsley House*

minister Arthur Wellesley, 1st Duke of Wellington, in 1817.

Known as 'No. 1 London', because it was the first house within the city toll gates on the western approach, it houses the Duke's outstanding collection of paintings, porcelain, silver, sculpture, furniture, medals and memorabilia — including his own death mask, and the Sèvres 'Egyptian' dessert service that Emperor Napoleon gave as a divorce present to Josephine, who rejected it. The Waterloo Gallery, 27m (90ft) long, contains the Duke's magnificent art collection, with works by Goya, Rubens and Murillo. Between 1992 and 1995 the interior of the house was restored to its early 19th-century appearance.

Although the 7th Duke gave the house and its contents to the nation in 1947, several apartments were retained for use as the family home.

✚ 209 F6 ✉ 149 Piccadilly W1J 7NT ☎ 020 7499 5676 🅖 Apr–Oct Wed–Sun 11–5; Nov–Mar Wed–Sun 10–4 🖑 Adult £6.30, child (under 18) £3.80 🅠 Hyde Park Corner 🚌 8, 9, 10, 14, 74

BATTERSEA PARK

www.wandsworth.gov.uk

Officially opened in 1858 by Queen Victoria, this riverside park was

created on marshy common land known as Battersea Fields, partly to rid it of a reputation for illegal racing, drinking and gambling.

It has since become one of London's most popular parks, with three million visitors a year. Attractions include the original Victorian carriage drives, sports facilities, an art gallery, two playgrounds, a boating lake, sculptures by Henry Moore and Barbara Hepworth and a Japanese Peace Pagoda, given to London in 1985 by the Buddhist Order as a symbol of peace. Cycling has been a popular pastime here since 1896. Extensive restoration work carried out in recent years has revitalized the park. The Vista Fountains (Mar–Nov) are the magnificent centrepiece of the formal gardens originally designed as part of the Festival of Britain in 1951, and a 19th-century Promenade Walk has been re-created by the river.

✚ 209 F9 ✉ Battersea Park SW11 4NJ ☎ 020 8871 7530 🅖 Daily 8am–dusk 🖑 Free 🅠 Sloane Square, then bus 🚌 East of park (Queenstown Road) 137; west of park (Battersea Bridge Road) 19, 49; south of park (Battersea Park Road) 45, 344, 345 🚉 Battersea Park, Queenstown Road ⛴ Cadogan Pier 🅿

INFORMATION

www.hrp.org.uk

✚ 208 C5 ✉ Kensington Palace State Apartments, Kensington Gardens W8 4PX ☎ 0870 751 5170 🕐 Mar–Oct daily 10–6; Nov–Feb 10–5 💷 Adult £12.50, child (5–15) £6.30, under 5s free, family £34 🚇 High Street Kensington, Queensway 🚌 9, 10, 49, 52, 70, 148 🎧 Sound guide included in entry; guidebook £3.95, in English and German 🍽 The Orangery (▷ 239) 🛍 Kensington Palace Shop, the Yellow Drawing Room Shop

Above *Sir Christopher Wren re-orientated the palace to face west*

INTRODUCTION

In 1689 the asthmatic William III set up home in Kensington Palace to escape from the damp and smoke of riverside Whitehall Palace. He bought the existing 1605 Jacobean mansion named Nottingham House and had it enlarged by Sir Christopher Wren (1632–1723); the renowned architect saved time by simply adding new blocks to the four corners so the king's entourage could be accommodated. William's wife Mary subsequently had the Queen's Gallery added to her apartments, while the South Front was added during William's reign. His successor Queen Anne bequeathed the nation the Orangery, while George I had further extensions added to the palace in the 1720s.

The palace has been home to many members of the royal family, but is most famously where Diana, Princess of Wales, lived until her death in 1997; it was her marital home before her marriage to Prince Charles ended. She and six other princesses who lived in Kensington Palace are celebrated in the innovative exhibition, Enchanted Palace, which incorporates installation art and performance by actors set against the backdrop of the State Apartments.

The Royal Ceremonial Dress Collection, a superb array of finery from the 18th to the 20th centuries, is closed pending restoration in 2012.

WHAT TO SEE

STATE APARTMENTS

First of the State Apartments, upstairs, are the Queen's Apartments, the largest of which is the 26m (85ft) Queen Mary's Gallery, a panelled room hung with royal portraits. Several smaller rooms are decorated with 17th-century furnishings and pictures, including the State Bed, in Queen Mary's Bedchamber, complete with its original hangings.

By contrast, the King's Apartments are very opulent. Italianate in style, the rooms have magnificent ceiling paintings by William Kent (c.1685–1748). Most impressive is the Cupola Room, with its pillars, figures of Greek and Roman deities, and busts of Roman emperors and ancient philosophers. Queen Victoria was baptized here. It is currently home to modern fashion installations.

Courtiers and visitors would have used the King's Grand Staircase, designed by Wren, with its scrolled wrought-ironwork by Jean Tijou and walls and ceiling coated in Venetian-style paintings by Kent. The trompe-l'oeil wall painting of a gallery crowded with figures includes many contemporary portraits of George I's courtiers and servants.

THE GARDEN

Don't miss the pretty sunken garden, made in 1909 in an area previously occupied by potting sheds. It was modelled on a similar garden at Hampton Court, with lime trees trained to form a hedge on three sides and flower beds framing the central lily pond (to which there is no public access).

TIPS

» Look for access to the palace from the Broad Walk in Kensington Gardens.
» Kensington Palace will close from January to March 2012 for the installation of major new displays.
» Remodelled gardens, a terrace café and a new entrance from the Broad Walk will be highlights in 2012.

Left *The garden is at its best between April and October, when the beds are planted with vibrant flower displays*
Below *Leaf and flower detail from the wrought-iron gates*

Above Victorian masterpieces on display in Leighton House Museum

been restored in period style; the most remarkable is the Arab Room, complete with pool and marble pillars and based on a Moorish banqueting hall in Palermo, Sicily. Islamic tiles collected by Leighton on his travels through Damascus, Cairo and Rhodes cover the walls and floor.

Other rooms, less exotically finished with red walls and ebonized wood, are hung with paintings by Leighton and many of his Pre-Raphaelite contemporaries, including John Everett Millais, Edward Burne-Jones and George Frederick Watts. Visitors are permitted to picnic in the walled garden.

Leighton's first-floor studio is still sometimes used by contemporary artists, with an 'artist in residence' scheme in operation.

✚ 208 B6 ✉ 12 Holland Park Road W14 8LZ ☎ 020 7602 3316 🕐 Wed–Mon 10–5.30 🖐 Adult £5, child (under 16) £1 🚇 High Street Kensington 🚌 9, 10, 27, 28, 49

JEWISH MUSEUM
www.jewishmuseum.org

This important museum celebrates Jewish life in Britain since 1066, with a permanent collection of art and artefacts displayed in four galleries, plus exhibitions relating to the Holocaust. The museum reopened in 2010 in an extensive new space.

✚ Off map 209 G2 ✉ Raymond Burton House, 129–131 Albert Street NW1 7NB ☎ 020 7284 7384 🕐 Sun–Thu 10–5, Fri 10–2 🖐 Adult £7, child (5–16) £3, family £17 🚇 Camden Town, Mornington Crescent 🍴 🏛

LEIGHTON HOUSE MUSEUM
www.rbkc.gov.uk

Victorian artist Frederic, Lord Leighton (1830–96) had this red-brick studio-house built to his own design on the edge of Holland Park. The result was a private palace devoted to art, equipped with only one bedroom as he didn't want to be bothered with house guests. Every room has

LONDON CENTRAL MOSQUE
www.iccuk.org

The showpiece Islamic Culture Centre and mosque, opened in 1978 on the eastern side of Regent's Park, provides a focus for London's many Muslim communities, with lecture and conference facilities, a bookshop and a library. About 4,500 worshippers can be accommodated in the mosque, which has marble floors and intricate mosaics. Sir Frederick Gibberd (1908–84) designed the building with its splendid golden dome, 25m (82ft) high, and white minaret.

✚ Off map 209 E2 ✉ 146 Park Road NW8 7RG ☎ 020 7725 2213 🕐 Daily 9.30–6.30 🖐 Free 🚇 Baker Street, Marylebone 🚌 13, 82, 113, 274 🏛

LORD'S TOUR AND MCC MUSEUM
www.lords.org

Cricket divides the British nation between devoted fans on the one hand and those who find it baffling and boring on the other. Lord's historic cricket ground has a wider appeal, however, and tours of the

Marylebone Cricket Club (MCC) give an intriguing behind-the-scenes glimpse of a venue that has been in use since the 18th century.

In the Long Room, the cricket-watching room at the heart of the Pavilion, an art gallery contains portraits of the game's celebrities. You can also take a look in the players' dressing rooms and visit the MCC Museum, where pictures and mementoes trace 400 years of cricketing history, and you can see the tiny, delicate Ashes urn.

The Brian Johnston Memorial Theatre shows footage of matches.

✚ Off map 208 D2 ✉ Lord's Cricket Ground, St. John's Wood NW8 8QN ☎ 020 7616 8500/8595 🕐 Tours daily 10, 12, 2, Apr–Oct; 12, 2, Nov–Mar. No tours during major matches or on preparation days. On other match days, only the 10am tour enters the Pavilion. MCC Museum included in tours 🖐 Adult £15, child (5–16) £9, under 5s free, family £40 🚇 Marylebone, St. John's Wood 🚌 139, 189 🍴 🏛

MADAME TUSSAUDS
▷ 217.

MARBLE ARCH

John Nash designed this elegant monument of white Carrara marble in 1828 as the main entrance to Buckingham Palace (▷ 176–177), but it was moved to its current site next to Speakers Corner in Hyde Park (▷ 212) when the palace was extended in 1851. At the time it was intended to form the park's principal entrance, but it now stands isolated on a grassy traffic island and the central gates remain closed most of the time. To this day, only members of the royal family are allowed to drive through.

The triple-arched design was inspired by the Constantine Arch in Rome and is carved with intricate reliefs of winged, wreathed Victories, a Roman warrior and Justice, Peace and Plenty, plus representations of England, Scotland and Ireland.

✚ 209 F4 🕐 Open access 🖐 Free 🚇 Hyde Park Corner, Marble Arch, Bond Street, Green Park 🚌 10, 36, 74, 137, 148, 436

MADAME TUSSAUDS

Madame Tussauds waxworks collection, a quirky eccentricity just beyond the southeast corner of Regent's Park, is one of London's most popular attractions. More than 2 million visitors come here every year to spot the likenesses of famous figures and pose beside heroes of sports and entertainment. The collection changes all the time: Celebrities know they've made it when their waxwork appears here, and they know they've had their day when their likeness is melted down to be turned into another rising star. Unlike fame, however, the techniques used to make the models are timeless and have barely changed since Madame Tussaud started her business 200 years ago. The hair used is real and the wax is similar to candlewax, which would melt in the heat of sunlight—thus explaining why the displays have to be kept in darkened rooms.

The oldest figure on display is Sleeping Beauty, made in 1765 and based on Louis XV's mistress, Madame du Barry, but the highlight of a visit for many is the ghoulish Scream, in the Chamber of Horrors, complete with live actors to terrify visitors even more (not recommended for children under 12). Elsewhere, you can mix with stars such as Brad Pitt and Kate Moss at the A-List Party. Spot Marilyn Monroe at Premier Night, and rub shoulders with Lady Gaga and Amy Winehouse among the Music Megastars.

Tours end with a Spirit of London time-travel trip in a taxicab (complete with sounds and smells) from Elizabethan times through the Plague and Great Fire to the Blitz and on to the Swinging Sixties.

Latest attractions feature an audience with the Queen and other members of the royal family. In 2010, Cheryl Cole made her debut here—at a cost of £150,000. The interactive Sports Zone enables you to test your sporting skills or team up with the greats, including Formula 1 champion Lewis Hamilton.

As you go round, keep an eye out for the anonymous-looking 'tourists', sitting on benches or standing around chatting. You'll find yourself caught out more than once.

MARVEL SUPER HEROES 4D

Marvel Comics created some of the world's most famous super-heroes, including Spiderman and the Incredible Hulk. This new exhibition brings them to life using a '4-D' animated movie—where the special effects hit the audience with wind, smoke, water spray and trembling seats. You can even join Spiderman on the ceiling of his upside-down office.

INFORMATION

www.madametussauds.com
➕ 209 F3 ✉ Marylebone Road NW1 5LR ☎ General enquiries 0871 894 3000; 0870 400 3000 (booking only; fee applies) 🕐 Daily 9.30–5.30 (until 7 in school summer holidays) ✋ Prices vary according to time of visit or if booked online. Adult from £25.20, child (5–16) from £21.60; discount available when booked with tickets for London Eye (▷ 75) and London Dungeon (▷ 73) 🚇 Baker Street 🚌 13, 27, 74, 82, 139 📖 £4, in English, French, German, Italian, Spanish 🍴 ♿

Above *The Beatles, forever young at Madame Tussauds*

NATIONAL ARMY MUSEUM

www.national-army-museum.ac.uk
The British army's story is traced
from the Middle Ages and the
1415 Battle of Agincourt to modern
conflicts including the Falklands
War, the Gulf War, Kosovo and Iraq.
Although wartime experience is
naturally to the fore, space is also
given to peacetime military life.

In addition to describing
campaigns and battles, the
museum focuses on the lives
of ordinary soldiers, using
paintings, photographs, uniforms
and equipment along with
reconstructions and life-size models.

Themed galleries bring military
history up to date. They include
Conflicts of Interest, which shows the
British army's role as a peace-keeping
force throughout the world.

Weekend special events follow a
different theme every month, with
uniformed interpreters, specialist
lectures and children's workshops all
making for an entertaining day out.
✚ 209 F8 ✉ Royal Hospital Road, Chelsea
SW3 4HT ☎ 020 7881 2455 🕐 Daily
10–5.30 ✋ Free 🚇 Sloane Square
🚌 11, 19, 22, 137, 170 ⛴ Cadogan Pier
💻 🏧

NATURAL HISTORY MUSEUM
▷ 220–221.

REGENT'S PARK

www.royalparks.gov.uk
Originally part of Henry VIII's royal
hunting grounds, Regent's Park
came into its own during the reign
of the Prince Regent, later George
IV, who gave the park its name. The
original, grandiose plans, devised by
John Nash, were to include a palace
to the south in St. James's and a
triumphal route up to the pleasure
gardens. The park itself was to be
girded by grand, stuccoed houses.
Money ran out before the plans could
be fully realized, but the park, some
of the terracing and the first part
of the triumphal route—Regent's
Street—were completed before work
came to a halt.

The York Gate entrance, near the
Baker Street Underground station,
lies just beyond the world-famous
Madame Tussauds (▷ 217). As you
walk up to the park you'll notice,
on the right, the Royal Academy
of Music, founded in 1822, where
some of the world's finest musicians,
singers and composers have trained.

On York Bridge, look back to see
St. Mary's Church, on Marylebone
High Street. When Nash laid out
Regent's Park he deliberately aligned
the York Gate axis to take in a view
of the church, with its majestic
Corinthian portico and circular tower.
York Bridge continues past Regent's
College, on the left, now a centre for
European studies. Beyond lie Queen
Mary's Gardens. Here, Nash had
intended a temple dedicated to the
memory of all who had contributed
to British history and culture. Instead,
the 6.8ha (17-acre) circle contains
London's finest rose garden, planted
to honour George V's wife, Queen
Mary, and the Open-Air Theatre
(▷ 235), founded in 1932. Near by
a new garden has been planted to
encourage wildlife.

To the west is the Y-shaped
boating lake, and a walk around the
upper part of the lake brings you
to Hanover Gate, where the park's
newer buildings are found. The
London Central Mosque (▷ 216)
is to the north, easily spotted with
its golden dome, and to the south,
fronting the Outer Circle, are Quinlan
Terry's neo-Nash villas of 1992.
✚ 209 F2 ☎ 020 7486 7905 🕐 Daily
5am–dusk ✋ Free 🚇 Baker Street,
Marylebone, Regent's Park, Great Portland
Street, Camden Town 🚌 27, 82, 113, 274,
C2 💻

ROYAL HOSPITAL

www.chelsea-pensioners.co.uk
Chelsea's Royal Hospital was built
by Sir Christopher Wren at the
behest of Charles II in the late 17th
century as almshouses for veteran
soldiers. It still serves that purpose
today, and the Chelsea Pensioners,
as the residents are known, are
a familiar sight in the area. Their
dress uniform is the scarlet tunic
of the Duke of Marlborough, worn
with blue trousers and a tricorn
hat; at other times you may see
them in blue tunics. To catch them
in their ceremonial garb, look out
on Oak Apple Day (29 May), when
they commemorate the Battle of
Worcester—from which Charles II
escaped by hiding in an oak tree in
1651—by festooning his statue in
the central courtyard with oak leaves.
The first women pensioners were
admitted in 2009.

In the small museum you can see
the pensioners' uniforms and medals,
the barrel-vaulted chapel and the
panelled Great Hall. Outside, you can

Below *Queen Mary's Gardens in Regent's Park; as well as the famous rose garden, there's an ornamental lake and the national delphinium collection*

Above *One of the residents of the Meet the Monkeys walkthrough enclosure at ZSL London Zoo*

ZSL LONDON ZOO
www.zsl.org

Occupying 15ha (37 acres) of the northeast corner of Regent's Park (▷ 218) and straddling the Regent's Canal, the London Zoological Gardens opened in 1828. It was the world's first institution dedicated to the scientific study of animals, and in its heyday in the 1950s attracted over 3 million visitors per year. Today conservation and study take preference over public display. Nonetheless, it is still a very popular and important visitor attraction offering the chance to see around 5,000 animals drawn from 650 species, many of which are endangered in the wild.

Highlights in the zoo include the famous Snowdon Aviary, designed by Lord Snowdon in 1964. There are plenty of new attractions too, such as the Clore Rainforest Lookout and Nightzone where small nocturnal animals scurry about in a simulated moonlight world; and the wonderful Gorilla Kingdom, a £35 million enclosure for a colony of western lowland gorillas.

Near the zoo entrance, you'll find the noisy primates and, by complete contrast, the silent world of the aquarium and the reptile house. The mountain-like Mappin Terrace (with wallabies and emus) was designed by Sir Peter Chalmers Mitchell (1864–1945), then secretary of the London Zoological Society, and J. J. Joass (1868–1952) in 1913; Joass also designed a new aquarium for the zoo in 1924. The modernist Penguin Pool, always crowded at feeding time, was designed by Berthold Lubetkin (1901–90) in 1931. The brilliant white building's intertwined ramps were an innovative design feature of their day.
➕ Off map 209 E2 ✉ Outer Circle, Regent's Park NW1 4RY ☎ 020 7722 3333 🕐 Early Mar–late Oct daily 10–5.30; late Oct–early Mar daily 10–4 🖐 Prices vary according to season, from adult £16.20, child (3–15) £13.20, under 3s free 🚇 Camden Town 🚌 274, C2 🚤 London Waterbus Company (020 7482 2550) runs scheduled services from Camden Lock and Little Venice: Apr–Sep daily 10–5 🛒 🎁

wander in the south grounds, site of the annual Chelsea Flower Show (▷ 294) since 1913.
➕ 209 F8 ✉ Royal Hospital Road SW3 4SR ☎ 020 7881 5200 🕐 Mon–Sat 10–12, 2–4; May–Sep Sun 2–4 🖐 Free 🚇 Sloane Square 🚌 11, 137, 170, 239

SAATCHI GALLERY
www.saatchi-gallery.co.uk
The gallery moved in October 2008 to its smart new Chelsea premises, which provide a state-of-the-art showcase for the work of young unknown artists, and for artists of international repute who are not normally exhibited in the UK.
➕ 209 F7 ✉ Duke of York's Headquarters, King's Road SW3 4SQ ☎ 020 7823 2363 🕐 Daily 10–6 🖐 Free 🚇 Sloane Square 🚌 11, 19, 22, 49, 211, 319 🛒

SCIENCE MUSEUM
▷ 222–223.

SHERLOCK HOLMES MUSEUM
www.sherlock-holmes.co.uk
Fictional detective Sherlock Holmes, created by Sir Arthur Conan Doyle (1859–1930), 'lived' at 221b Baker Street together with his friend and colleague Dr. Watson between 1881 and 1904. This 1815 house is actually No. 239 Baker Street, but 221b is now the number on the door. Dedicated to the life and times of Holmes, the house has been carefully furnished to reflect descriptions in Conan Doyle's stories, with Holmes's study overlooking Baker Street on the first floor.

'Personal' belongings include the detective's deerstalker hat, magnifying glass, violin and chemistry equipment, and papers include a variety of exhibits from Holmes's cases, and the 'diary' of Dr. Watson. The third-floor exhibition rooms house wax models of some of the characters and scenes from the stories.
➕ 209 F3 ✉ 221b (239 postal address) Baker Street NW1 6XE ☎ 020 7224 3688 🕐 Daily 9.30–6 🖐 Adult £6, under 16s £4 🚇 Baker Street, Marylebone 🚌 13, 82, 274, 453 🎁

VICTORIA & ALBERT MUSEUM
▷ 224–228.

WALLACE COLLECTION
▷ 229.

INFORMATION

www.nhm.ac.uk

➕ 208 D7 ✉ Cromwell Road SW7 5BD
☎ 020 7942 5000 ⏱ Daily 10–5.50.
Wildlife Garden Apr–Oct 10–5
💷 Free. Charge for some temporary
exhibitions 🚇 South Kensington 🚌 14,
49, 70, 74, 345, 414, C1 📖 £5, in
English only. Free floorplans and map
🍴 Restaurant: self-service meals and
snacks ☕ Cafés, snack bar 🏛 Museum
shop, Dino Store, Earth Shop

Above The Natural History Museum's
main entrance, with its twin towers, on
Cromwell Road

INTRODUCTION

Built on land purchased by Prince Albert from money raised at the Great
Exhibition of 1851 (▷ 36), the huge French Romanesque Natural History
Museum was designed by Alfred Waterhouse (1830–1905) to house the British
Museum's natural history collection, and opened to the public in 1881. Relief
panels in terracotta showing animals, fossils, plants and insects run the whole
length of the facade; living species of the time are shown to the left of the
entrance, extinct ones to the right.

Thousands of animal, plant and mineral specimens were bequeathed by
Sir Hans Sloane (▷ 139), including more than 10,000 animal specimens and
338 volumes of pressed plants. Sir Joseph Banks, who accompanied Captain
Cook on his first voyage around the world in the 1760s, was another important
benefactor. Today the museum owns more than 65 million specimens and more
than a million books and manuscripts.

The main entrance, approached via a grand flight of stone steps from
Cromwell Road, leads straight into the huge and richly decorated Central Hall,
which has been likened to the nave of a cathedral. The hall leads off to the left to
the Blue Zone, which has exhibitions on dinosaurs, mammals, creepy crawlies
(including a robotic scorpion), fish and other marine life, plants and minerals,

meteorites and the story of evolution. To the right and up the main stairs is the Green Zone, concentrating on ecology and evolution.

The museum's side entrance leads into the Red Zone, opened in 1996 and housed in rooms on the ground, mezzanine, first and second floors, linked by a central escalator which travels through a huge globe. State-of-the-art displays tell the story of the Earth's formation, with sections on volcanoes and earthquakes, hands-on stations demonstrating the forces of wind, water and heat, and galleries focusing on the Earth's natural geological treasury of gemstones and discussing ways of protecting our world for the future.

Outside the museum, the Wildlife Garden, in the Orange Zone, planted in 1993 on the west lawn, provides both peace and quiet and the chance to study some of Britain's habitats, from oak woodland to reedbeds. The futuristic and interactive Darwin Centre is also in this zone.

WHAT TO SEE
BLUE ZONE
Dinosaurs
This is one of the most popular galleries, with a high-level walkway bringing you eye to eye with some of the ancient monsters. The lighting is low and atmospheric, and there is an animatronic re-creation of the creatures in action, including one of the world's most advanced models of its kind, a terrifying 4m-high (13ft) *Tyrannosaurus rex*, now the subject of debate as to whether it was a hunter or a scavenger. Soaring staircases provide views of the hall's detailed decoration (note the monkeys scrambling up and down the arches) and look down on the plaster-cast skeleton of *Diplodocus carnegii* (which comes from Wyoming), 150 million years old, 26m (86ft) long, and one of the largest animals ever to have roamed the Earth.

The Blue Whale
Suspended from the ceiling in the Mammals section is another giant—a life-size model of a blue whale almost 28m (93ft) in length and dwarfing the African elephant, the largest land mammal.

GREEN ZONE
Ant Colony
The museum has its very own labour force of leafcutter ants, and you can watch as members of the thousands-strong colony grow and tend the fungus that provides its food, cut up the leaves collected from their feeding area and are guarded as they work by the soldier ants with vicious-looking jaws.

Giant Sequoia
One of the most intriguing exhibits is a passage cut through this enormous tree (*Sequoiadendron giganteum*) displayed on the stairs to the first floor. This particular specimen was cut down in 1892, by which time it was 84m (276ft) tall and measured 15m (49ft) around the girth. A tree ring count indicates that it was 1,335 years old when felled, having started its life in California in AD557.

RED ZONE
The Power Within/Earthquake
This unnerving series of displays has become one of the museum's top attractions. The exhibition explores the powerful forces of heat and pressure that are constantly on the move between the ground that we inhabit and the centre of the Earth. A simulator gives you some idea of how it feels to be in an earthquake; film footage of the Kobe earthquake in Japan in 1995 shows the terrors of the real thing, as a supermarket is shaken to its foundations. Volcano eruptions are re-created, and you can see an up-to-date record of the most recent earthquake occurrences around the world.

TIPS
» If the queues at the main entrance are very long, make for the side entrance on Exhibition Road.

» From early November to early January an ice rink on the east lawn and a traditional carousel create a winter wonderland.

GALLERY GUIDE
BLUE ZONE
GROUND FLOOR
Dinosaurs, Fishes, Amphibians, Reptiles
Marine Invertebrates
Human Biology
Mammals
Images of Nature

GREEN ZONE
Central Hall
Fossil Marine Reptiles
Fossils from Britain
Ecology
Creepy Crawlies
Bird Gallery
Primates
Minerals

FIRST FLOOR
Our Place in Evolution
Minerals
Primates
(stairs): Giant Sequoia
Tree
(Treasures: new gallery opens 2012)

RED ZONE
GROUND FLOOR
Today and Tomorrow
Lasting Impressions

MEZZANINE FLOOR
Earth Lab

FIRST FLOOR
From the Beginning
Earth's Treasury

SECOND FLOOR
The Power Within/Earthquake
Restless Surface

ORANGE ZONE
Wildlife Garden
Darwin Centre: Life-science laboratories and collections

INFORMATION

www.vam.ac.uk

208 E7 ✉ Cromwell Road SW7 2RL
☎ 020 7942 2000 🕐 Sat–Thu 10–5.45,
Fri 10–10 (selected galleries) 💷 Free,
except for some exhibitions and events
📣 Free introductory tours daily (1 hour)
10.30–3.30; also free gallery talks on Thu
at 1; meet in the Grand Entrance 📖 V&A
guidebook £5; The British Galleries at
the V&A £4.95, in English only 🚇 South
Kensington, Knightsbridge 🚌 14, 74,
414, C1 🍴 Morris, Gamble & Poynter
Rooms café on Level 1; open daily 10–5.15
(Fri until 9.30); Garden Café summer
only, for drinks and snacks 🎁 Gift shop
on Level 1 selling items inspired by the
permanent collections. Bookshop selling
gifts and exhibitions merchandise ❓ The
Fashion Collection galleries are scheduled
to reopen in spring 2012

Above *Room 23 is dedicated to garden
sculpture, which became very popular in
Britain in the 18th century*

INTRODUCTION

The V&A was founded in 1852 with profits from the Great Exhibition of 1851.
Its aim was to give the working classes access to great art and to inspire British
manufacturers and designers. Originally housed in Marlborough House, near
Buckingham Palace, it was moved to the present site in 1857 as the South
Kensington Museum. It was given its current name in 1899, when Queen Victoria
laid the foundation stone of a new building that later opened in 1909.

Contemporary glass sculptor Dale Chihuly's chandelier in twisted, colourful
blown glass dominates the entrance hall. The permanent collection comprises
thousands of items, including fashion and textiles, furniture and paintings,
jewellery, ceramics, glass, silver and ironwork. It is enhanced by temporary
exhibitions such as, in 2010, the Raphael Cartoons for Sistine Chapel tapestries.

The main entrance on Cromwell Road is on Level 1, but the galleries start
(numerically) one level down (Level 0) with the European collection. On Level
1 are sculpture, plaster casts and photography; Islamic and Asian and more
European collections; the Raphael Gallery, and the fashion collection.

The museum's 15 British Galleries begin on Level 2 and continue on Level
4. Level 3 features the Materials and Techniques galleries, including ironwork,
jewellery, musical instruments, paintings, tapestries and silver; glass objects are
on show on Level 4 and ceramics on the museum's top floor, Level 6.

WHAT TO SEE

EUROPEAN COLLECTION

The Becket Casket (Room 8)

Part of the medieval treasury, this gilt copper and blue enamel reliquary was
made in about 1180. It is the oldest and largest of about 50 items associated
with Thomas à Becket's martyrdom that survive from the workshops of the
Limoges enamellers—experts at making beautiful goods with hard-wearing
and cheap materials. The murder of Becket, the Archbishop of Canterbury who
incurred Henry II's wrath and was assassinated at the cathedral altar, is pictured
on the front; one of the knights can be seen hacking off the martyr's head. The
lid of the casket shows Becket's funeral.

The Burghley Nef (Room 62)
This dazzling salt-holder is one of the boat-shaped objects (known as nefs) that were all the rage in 16th-century France. It was made in Paris in about 1527, with a rare nautilus shell serving as the salt bowl and set into the 'hold' of an elaborate silver sailing ship, resting on a golden-haired mermaid. The intricately worked details on the ship include two tiny figures playing chess — representing Tristan and Iseult, the legendary ill-fated lovers associated with the tales of King Arthur and Camelot.

Raphael Cartoons (Room 48A)
Although their name conjures up images of *Peanuts*, these cartoons are actually works of extreme skill, painted in glue distemper as prototypes to be hung in the Sistine Chapel at the Vatican. The seven pieces were most likely completed in 1516 and then sent to Brussels for the weaving process. The cartoons portray various scenes from the Gospels and Acts.

ASIAN AND ISLAMIC COLLECTION
Chinese Pagoda (Room 47)
The centrepiece of the Gerard Godfrey Gallery of Chinese Export Art is a brightly coloured 2.7m (9ft) porcelain model of a 17-tier Chinese pagoda, one of only 10 of its kind believed to have survived. Each of the progressively smaller tiers is decorated with exquisitely delicate blues and golds and shows a tiny figure looking through an open window, shaded by green and silver canopies. At the time of its creation — between 1800 and 1815 — trade was booming between Europe and China, and mass production of souvenirs for European buyers was at a peak. This pagoda was specially made to an individual order, rather than put together on an assembly line, and is based on the 15th-century pagoda of Nanking (destroyed in 1853).

TIPS
» Colour-coded signs and banners, corresponding to key areas of the museum, help you find your way around.
» Take advantage of the late-night opening until 10pm every Friday.
» Sections of the museum are undergoing major refurbishment and may close for months at a time. If there is something you especially hope to see, check ahead.

Below *The main facade was created by Austin Webb, who won a competition in 1891 to design the museum expansion*

PHOTOGRAPHY AT THE V&A

Only four years after the opening of the V&A, when photography was still in its infancy and regarded as strictly inferior to other art media, the museum began a collection of photographic work. One of its first exhibitions was a display of life studies by Clementina, Lady Hawarden (1822–65), who took many photographs of her daughters in their home at South Kensington in London. Her experiments with light, shade and reflection give added interest to these early examples of photography as an art form.

The V&A has now amassed more than 500,000 works in its photographic collection.

Tipu's Tiger (Room 41)

One of the V&A's best-known objects is kept in the Nehru Gallery of Indian Art. The 18th-century model of a tiger savaging a man, complete with mechanically produced growls and screams, was made for Tipu Sultan, son of Haidar Ali Khan, ruler of the state of Mysore. Known as the Tiger of Mysore, Tipu had the tiger emblem worked into many of his surroundings and possessions, but this example, with its sound-effects organ built into the brightly coloured tiger's side, is unique. It may represent the actual fate of the son of General Sir Hector Munro in Bengal. Tipu suffered defeat at the hands of the British at Seringapatam in 1799, and his tiger was brought back as booty to be put on show in the East India Company Museum, later to be transferred to the Victoria & Albert.

BRITISH GALLERIES
Writing Box (Room 58)

Henry VIII owned this portable stationery set, made in 1525 and elaborately decorated. It's a rare survivor of the Tudor court. Inside the lid of the box, the gilded leather lining shows the coat of arms of the king and Catherine of Aragon, cherubs and copies of a German woodcut of Venus and Mars; other parts of the box are illustrated with miniature profiles and intricate motifs and designs. Drawers and compartments are built into the design, which incorporates a Latin inscription wishing Henry triumph over his adversaries.

The Great Bed of Ware (Room 57)

Celebrated in literature and lore, the Great Bed of Ware was made between 1590 and 1600 for an inn in Ware, Hertfordshire, as a kind of marketing ploy, enticing travellers with its unusually large dimensions and ornamental carving—which would originally have been picked out in vivid colours. To modern eyes, the

Below *The V&A café occupies the museum's three original refreshment rooms; the centre one was designed by James Gamble in Renaissance style*

bed itself may not seem remarkably large, but the frame is certainly massive. It includes panels made by German immigrant craftsmen and Dutch-influenced marquetry. The bed had fulfilled its promotional function by 1601, when it warranted a mention in Shakespeare's play *Twelfth Night*.

Strawberry Thief by William Morris (1834–96) (Room 125)

Reacting against the dehumanizing processes of 19th-century mass industry, William Morris and his contemporaries in the Arts and Crafts movement sought to revive the craftsmanship of the Middle Ages. *Strawberry Thief*, a repeated design of thrushes stealing fruit among leaves and flowers used on fabric and wallpaper, is an example of Morris's attempt to bring individualism and beauty into middle-class homes. He produced it using an ancient indigo-discharge printing technique; for the first time, with this pattern, he used red and yellow along with blue and white, a long and difficult process that made this one of his firm's costliest cottons. Morris's designs are shown alongside those of his contemporaries Charles Rennie Mackintosh and Christopher Dresser.

THE FASHION COLLECTION

Sack-Back Gown (Room 40)

A finely worked satin gown made in France in the 1770s illustrates the way fashion developed in high society, incorporating casual dress (which sack-back gowns originally were) and combining old and new. The bodice, with its front fastening, is the height of contemporary style, while the square, wide 'saddle-bag' hoops and elbow-length, ruffled sleeves harked back 20 years or so. Delicate blue padded satin and chenille lace are used to decorate the ivory-coloured gown and petticoat, along with embroidered floral sprigs and gathered ribbon.

Bar Suit, Christian Dior (1905–57) (Room 40)

Dior's New Look designs hit the fashion shows in 1947 and created an immediate sensation among women accustomed to the pared-down, austere styles of wartime Europe. The bar suit has a cream silk jacket nipped in to show off a 46cm (18in) waist; a full black wool crêpe skirt flares out beneath it, with a hem measuring 7.3m (24ft) in circumference. Topping the ensemble is a low-brimmed hat, adding the finishing touch to an overall image of elegant chic.

GALLERY GUIDE
MAIN FLOORS
LEVEL 6
Rooms 137–145: Ceramics

LEVEL 4
Rooms 118–125: British galleries
Rooms 127–128a: Architecture
Rooms 129–131: Glass gallery

LEVEL 3
Rooms 65–69 and 70a: Silver galleries
Rooms 70–73: Gold, silver and mosaics
Rooms 74 and 76: 20th-century
Rooms 81, 82, 87–88a: Paintings
Rooms 83–84: Sacred silver and stained glass
Room 90: Prints and drawings
Room 90a: Portrait miniatures
Rooms 91–93: Jewellery gallery
Room 94: Tapestries
Rooms 95–100: Textiles
Room 101: Furniture
Rooms 107 and 109: Frescoes by Victorian artist Frederic, Lord Leighton
Room 111: Sculpture
Rooms 113–114e: Ironwork
Room 116: Metalware

LEVEL 2
Rooms 52–58: British galleries, tracing the history of British design from the Tudor era to 1900
All other rooms are for exhibitions

LEVELS 0 AND 1
Rooms 1–9, 16a and 21–28: European displays (Rooms 21–24 Sculpture)
Rooms 17–20: Asian sculpture
Room 38a: Photography
Room 40: Fashion
Rooms 41–42, 44–45 and 47a–g: Asian and Islamic works
Room 46: Medieval
Rooms 46a and 46b: Cast courts
Room 48: Raphael gallery

HENRY COLE WING
LEVELS 4 AND 5
Study rooms
Lecture rooms

KEY
Main Floors
- Level 6
- Level 4
- Level 3
- Level 2
- Level 1
- Level 0

WALLACE COLLECTION

Four generations of the Hertford family amassed this world-class collection of art, on show in Hertford House, a beautiful 18th-century mansion. It was started when the 4th Marquess of Hertford, living as a recluse in Paris with his illegitimate son, Richard Wallace, during the French Revolution, bought French 18th-century paintings, porcelain and furniture to add to his inheritance of Sèvres porcelain and paintings by Canaletto and Gainsborough. Richard inherited the collection in 1870 and brought it to England, escaping the unstable political situation in France. He in turn added many fine examples of Renaissance ceramics, bronzes, armour and jewellery, and his widow left the collection to the nation in 1897, on condition that it remained intact and was never removed from central London.

FROM ARTWORKS TO ARMOUR

The rooms are packed with all sorts of beautiful objects, from paintings, furnishings and fittings originally made for the palaces of Fontainebleau and Versailles to 18th-century saucepans.

About 70 paintings from the 17th and 18th centuries hang in the Great Gallery. Most famously, these include *The Laughing Cavalier* by Frans Hals (1624), a portrait of an unknown young man (although he is neither a cavalier nor laughing) seated in sumptuous surroundings with a rural backdrop, and a marvellous portrait of King George IV by Sir Thomas Lawrence (1769–1830).

There's also a superb display of European arms and armour, much of it made by specialist metalworkers and embellished with fine inlay decoration. Seek out the late 15th-century set of armour for a man and his horse, made in Germany.

INFORMATION

www.wallacecollection.org

✚ 209 F4 ✉ Hertford House, Manchester Square W1U 3BN ☎ 020 7563 9500 🕐 Daily 10–5 💷 Free 🚇 Bond Street, Baker Street 🚌 2, 10, 13, 30, 74, 82, 94 🎧 Free guided tours weekdays 1pm, also Sat 11.30am, Sun 1pm, 3pm £5.99, in English only 🍽 The Wallace Restaurant (Sun–Thu 10–5, Fri–Sat 10am–11pm) 🎁 Gifts and books, many exclusive to the collection

Below *The Wallace Collection is housed in a Georgian mansion*

THE WALLACE COLLECTION OPEN DAILY | FREE ADMISSION

WALLACE COLLECTION
FREE & Open Daily 10am – 5pm

THE SEVEN WONDERS OF KENSINGTON

South Kensington became London's museum district in the 19th century. This simple route highlights the architectural masterpieces that were built here, drawing freely on Renaissance and Romanesque style.

THE WALK
Distance: 4km (2.5 miles)
Time: 1hr
Start/end at: South Kensington Underground station

HOW TO GET THERE
🚇 District, Circle or Piccadilly line to South Kensington 🚌 14, 74, 414, C1

★ This walk captures the spirit of the Great Exhibition of 1851, which was organized by Prince Albert, the Queen's Consort. The exhibition was so successful that it inspired him to establish a permanent centre for the study of the applied arts and sciences. He proposed that some of the profits from the exhibition should be used to buy land in South Kensington. The result was the concentration of world-class museums in South Kensington, and Imperial College.

From South Kensington Tube, cross Thurloe Street and turn left into Exhibition Road. Cross the road at the traffic lights.

On the right-hand corner is the Victoria & Albert Museum.

❶ The Victoria & Albert Museum (▷ 224–228) is regarded as one of the world's greatest museums. As it has more than 11.5km (7 miles) of galleries, it's hard to know where to begin. Take your time and wander around slowly. Your patience will be rewarded by the extraordinary visual input of the thousands of items on display, mostly decorative items and period clothing.

Cross the road to the splendid Natural History Museum.

❷ The neo-Gothic architecture of the Natural History Museum

(▷ 220–221) is extraordinary. Designed by Alfred Waterhouse, it uses the decorative terracotta that was so fashionable in the Victorian era (see also the Royal Albert Hall, ▷ 231 and above) to full effect. A series of lion sculptures also feature in the design.

The walk continues along Exhibition Road past the Science Museum, on the left, followed by Imperial College (for science, technology and medicine).

❸ The Science Museum (▷ 222–223) is less impressive from the outside—even some of its staff say that it resembles a small Selfridges. In the early stages it was a humdrum assortment of wooden buildings. The chief architect, Sir Richard Allison, had been asked to maintain strict economy in the new building, which

Left *The design of the Royal Albert Hall was inspired by Roman amphitheatres; the continuous terracotta frieze that runs around the outside of the dome shows allegorical figures engaged in various cultural activities*

was on a grand scale, as was the rambling hulk that is Imperial College.

Turn left into Prince Consort Road, which is home to the 600 students of the Royal College of Music.

❹ If you see some oddly shaped rucksacks and bags, they probably belong to a musician or student at the Royal College of Music, which provides courses for performers and composers. In the concert hall is an organ donated by composer Hubert Parry, who taught here, as did Charles Villiers Stanford and Ralph Vaughan Williams.

Halfway along Prince Consort Road, on the right, there are some steps that lead up to the round Royal Albert Hall, with its familiar glass-domed roof.

❺ Completed in 1871, 10 years after the death from typhoid of Queen Victoria's Prince Consort, the imposing auditorium of the Royal Albert Hall (▷ 235) had actually been planned during his lifetime. The project was funded by selling seats on 999-year leases, which theoretically still exist today. The venue hosts all sorts of musical styles, most famously the summer series of classical Proms concerts (▷ 295).

At the top of the steps bear right to reach the main road, Kensington Road (in this short stretch known as Kensington Gore). Cross this road at the traffic lights for a closer look at the Albert Memorial.

❻ The grandiose Albert Memorial was finished in 1876 in honour of Victoria's late husband. The pediment hosts a crowd of 187 life-size figures of famous men, while elsewhere bronzes and mosaics represent the

different sciences and arts. Four surrounding marble groupings stand for the continents. Amid all of this sits a gilt statue of Albert himself, as if embarrassed by all the fuss.

Spend some time beyond the memorial and wander through the lovely Kensington Gardens.

❼ In effect the eastern half of Hyde Park, Kensington Gardens (▷ 213) are generally more serene. They were first opened to the public during the reign of George II but only on Sunday, and formal garb was de rigueur. The prettiest section of the Serpentine, here known as Long Water, the statue of Peter Pan and, of course, the grandeur of Kensington Palace (▷ 214–215) are among the attractions here.

Retrace your steps to the Royal Albert Hall. With the building on your left, continue along Kensington Gore, past the rather dull exterior of the Royal College of Art, until you reach Queen's Gate. Turn left, pass the Gore Hotel and cross Prince Consort Road. On the left is the other end of

Imperial College and soon you'll see the wildlife garden of the Natural History Museum, behind the railings where Queen's Gate meets Cromwell Road.

Turn left along Cromwell Road and then take the right turn to take you back to South Kensington Underground station.

WHERE TO EAT AND DRINK
All the museums along this walk have either a café or a restaurant. The café at the V&A serves wine and beer, the food is particularly fresh and the surroundings opulent. Alternatively, you could wait until the end of the walk and take your pick of the pubs on Earl's Court Road, such as the Blackbird at No. 209.

WHEN TO GO
As this walk features such popular museums, it is best done on a weekday morning, when the crowds should be smaller, especially out of season. If you only concentrate on the outdoor section, however, then a sunny afternoon enhances the beauty of the tree-lined streets and the park.

SHOPPING

ALFIE'S ANTIQUE MARKET
www.alfiesantiques.com
London's largest indoor antiques market, Alfie's is home to 100 dealers specializing in art deco, silver, furniture, paintings and prints, jewellery, ceramics, vintage clothing and lots more. You'll be competing against dealers and may well spot some celebrity faces too.
➕ 246 E3 ✉ 13–25 Church Street, Marylebone NW8 8DT ☎ 020 7723 6066 🕐 Tue–Sat 10–6 🚇 Marylebone, Edgware Road 🚌 6, 13, 16, 82, 98, 139, 189, 274 ▣

BONHAM'S
www.bonhams.com
Operating since 1793, this international auction house deals in a wide variety of interesting lots—including football and cricket memorabilia. Fine art, furniture, carpets, and silver and plate are among their auction themes.
➕ 247 E6 ✉ Montpelier Street SW7 1HH ☎ 020 7393 3900 🕐 Mon–Fri 9–5.30 🚇 Knightsbridge 🚌 9, 10, 14, 74, C1

BOUTIQUE GIORGIO ARMANI
www.armanistores.com
Comparatively understated fashion. This shop is one of a number of showcases of big Italian names along this street, including Alberta Ferretti at No. 205 and Prada at No. 43.
➕ 247 F6 ✉ 37–42 Sloane Street SW1X 9LP ☎ 020 7235 6232 🕐 Mon–Tue, Thu–Sat 10–6, Wed 10–7 🚇 Knightsbridge 🚌 19, 22, 137, C1

BRORA
www.brora.co.uk
Cashmere heaven. Beautiful, soft classics for all the family in sometimes startling hues, plus blankets, tweedy bags and slippers. Not cheap, but great quality.
➕ 246 E8 ✉ 344 King's Road SW3 5UR ☎ 020 7352 3697 🕐 Mon–Sat 10–6, Sun 12–5 🚇 South Kensington, Sloane Square 🚌 11, 19, 22, 211, 328

BROWNS
www.brownsfashion.com
The latest and funkiest labels for women makes this smart boutique look intimidating, and it isn't cheap, but the people here know what's in vogue. See Browns Focus (No. 38) across the road for younger lines and Browns Labels for Less (No. 50) along the street for sale items. Small men's selection.
➕ 247 G4 ✉ 24–27 South Molton Street W1K 5RD ☎ 020 7514 0016 🕐 Mon–Wed, Fri–Sat 10–6.30, Thu 10–7 🚇 Bond Street 🚌 8, 10, 12, 73, 139

CAMDEN LOCK MARKET
www.camdenlockmarket.com
This vibrant, arty market, in a lovely setting around Camden Lock, has expanded and sprawled to fill every patch of space from the canal back to Camden Lock Place. You'll find everything from trendy designer clothes to art, food and furniture.
➕ Off map 247 G1 ✉ Camden Lock Place/Chalk Farm Road NW1 ☎ 020 7485 7963 🕐 Daily 10–6 🚇 Camden Town, Chalk Farm 🚌 24, 27, 29, 31, 74, 134 🚢 London Waterbus route links to Little Venice

CATH KIDSTON
www.cathkidston.co.uk
Cath Kidston's pretty and now famous floral designs, inspired by 1950s' patterns, are available on fabrics, wallpapers, bed linen, table linen, vintage jewellery and ornaments in this charming Sloane Square shop. The original store is at Clarendon Cross, Holland Park, and there are others around town.
➕ 247 F7 ✉ 27 King's Road SW3 4RP ☎ 020 3463 4840 🕐 Mon–Sat 10–7, Sun 12–6 🚇 Sloane Square 🚌 11, 19, 22, 211, 319

CHELSEA TOYS
www.chelseatoys.co.uk
Chelsea Toys is the place to come for beautiful traditional wooden toys, as well as soft toys, dressing-up costumes for children, fairy-tale dolls and puppets.
✚ 247 E8 ✉ 53 Godfrey Street SW3 3SX ☎ 020 7352 1718 🕐 Mon–Sat 10–6, Sun 12–6 🚇 South Kensington, Sloane Square 🚌 11, 19, 22, 211

CHRISTIE'S
www.christies.com
James Christie conducted his first sale in 1766 and went on to hold the greatest auctions of his time. Christie's salerooms are world famous, auctioning major works such as Monet's *Le Bassin aux Nymphées*, sold in 2008 for more than £40 million. Most auctions are free and public.
✚ 246 D7 ✉ 85 Old Brompton Road SW7 3LD ☎ 020 7930 6074 🕐 Mon 9–7.30, Tue–Fri 9–5, Sat–Sun 11–5 🚇 South Kensington 🚌 14, 22, 70, 74, 345, 414, C1

THE CONRAN SHOP
www.conranshop.co.uk
Housed in the magnificent Michelin Building, The Conran Shop was the pioneer of bringing late 20th-century design to the everyday household. Beautiful displays include furniture, kitchenware, books, gadgets, ceramics, fabrics and just about everything for the home.
✚ 246 E7 ✉ Michelin House, 81 Fulham Road SW3 6RD ☎ 020 7589 7401 🕐 Mon–Tue, Fri 10–6, Wed–Thu 10–7, Sat 10–6.30, Sun 12–6 🚇 South Kensington 🚌 14, 49, 360

GENERAL TRADING COMPANY
www.generaltradingcompany.co.uk
A stylish emporium, General Trading Company stocks furniture, tableware and ornaments. Since 1920 it's provided stylish wedding gifts and holds all current royal warrants. You might spot a celebrity or two in the organic foods café.

✚ 247 F7 ✉ 91 Pelham Street SW7 2NJ ☎ 020 7225 6470 🕐 Mon–Sat 10–7, Sun 12–6 🚇 South Kensington 🚌 14, 70, 360, C1

GRAYS ANTIQUE MARKET
www.graysantiques.com
A labyrinth of alleys concealed within an attractive 19th-century building. More than 200 dealers specialize in diverse items dating from 40BC to the 20th century. Keep your eyes open for a bargain.
✚ 247 G4 ✉ 58 Davies Street W1K 5AB ☎ 020 7629 7034 🕐 Mon–Fri 10–6, Sat 11–5 🚇 Bond Street 🚌 6, 7, 10, 13, 15, 27, 73, 88, 94, 98, 134, 137, 159, 189, 390

GUINEVERE
www.guinevere.co.uk
The original antiques emporium on this now famous strip of the King's Road, and probably the best. The 10 rooms give a vastly eclectic selection of fine antiques, ranging as much in price as in age and origin.
✚ Off map 246 D9 ✉ 574–580 King's Road SW6 2DY ☎ 020 7736 2917 🕐 Mon–Fri 9.30–6, Sat 10–5.30 🚇 Fulham Broadway 🚌 11, 14, 22

HARRODS
www.harrods.com
More than just a department store, Harrod's is a miniature kingdom. The vast, terracotta building occupies 1.8ha (4.5 acres)—a far cry from its origins as a small grocer's shop in 1849. Its Latin motto is *omnia, omnibus, ubique*—'everything for everyone, everywhere'. Pick up the Store Guide at the entrance for details of exhibitions and demonstrations. For many, the ground-floor food halls are the highlight, partly for the range of good foods on display, but also for W. J. Neatley's tiled ceilings (1902). Equally lavish art deco ceramics decorate both the men's hairdressing rooms and the women's toilets. Recent innovations include a dog spa, with facials and massage for pets.
✚ 247 E6 ✉ 87–135 Brompton Road SW1X 7XL ☎ 020 7730 1234 🕐 Mon–Sat 10–8, Sun 11.30–6 🚇 Knightsbridge 🚌 9, 10, 14, 19, 22, 52, 74, 137, 414, C1 🛍 🍴

HARVEY NICHOLS
www.harveynichols.com
Chic department store with marvellous window displays and an ultra-trendy beauty bar that can even sell you 10 minutes of fresh air! Six floors of clothing, housewares and a food market on the fifth floor. Stylish café, restaurant and sushi bar.
✚ 247 F6 ✉ 109–125 Knightsbridge SW1X 7RJ ☎ 020 7235 5000 🕐 Mon–Sat 10–8, Sun 11.30–6 🚇 Knightsbridge 🚌 9, 10, 14, 74, C1

HEAL'S
www.heals.co.uk
A top destination for contemporary interior design and furnishings for the past two centuries, with striking, high-quality furniture, rugs, beds, fabrics, bed linen and home accessories. The main store, on Tottenham Court Road, is immense.
✚ 247 E8 ✉ 234 King's Road SW3 5UA ☎ 020 7349 8411 🕐 Mon–Tue, Fri 10–6, Wed–Thu 10–7, Sat 9.30–6.30, Sun 12–6 🚇 Sloane Square, South Kensington 🚌 11, 19, 22, 211, C1

JACK WILLS
www.jackwills.com
Chic casual wear is the order at this flagship store of the 'university outfitters', but its appeal goes beyond students. You'll find everything from designer denim to colourful flannel pyjamas and branded accessories. A coffee shop is on the upper floor.
✚ 247 F7 ✉ 72 King's Road SW3 4UG ☎ 020 7581 0347 🕐 Mon–Wed 9am–10pm, Thu 8am–10pm, Fri 8–4, Sun 10.30–5 (closed Sat) 🚇 Sloane Square 🚌 11, 19, 22, 211, 319

JIMMY CHOO
www.jimmychoo.com
The best place in the West to find sexy high-heeled shoes, this store is in Knightsbridge, the playground of the beautiful rich. Your wallet could be stretched by these fabulous items, but trying them on costs nothing and they make you feel like a superstar.
✚ 247 F5 ✉ 32 Sloane Street SW1X 9NR ☎ 020 7823 1051 🕐 Mon–Sat 10–6, Wed 10–7, Sun 12–5 🚇 Knightsbridge 🚌 19, 22, 137, C1

247 F7 ✉ Sloane Square SW1W 8AS
☎ 020 7565 5000 🖐 £18–£25 🚇 Sloane
Square 🚌 11, 19, 22, 211, C1

WIGMORE HALL
www.wigmore-hall.org.uk
London's favourite intimate concert
and recital venue, with acoustics
of legendary perfection. Opened
in 1901 as the Bechstein Hall. The
architectural elegance matches the
peerless quality of the great classical
performances.
✚ 247 G4 ✉ 36 Wigmore Street
W1U 2BP ☎ 020 7935 2141 🖐 £12–£26
🚇 Bond Street, Oxford Circus 🚌 8, 10,
73, C2

SPORTS AND ACTIVITIES
CHELSEA FOOTBALL CLUB
www.chelseafc.co.uk
This club has been reinvigorated
since 2003 by the money of Russian
oil tycoon Roman Abramovich.
They have been Premier League
champions and FA Cup winners.
✚ 246 C9 ✉ Stamford Bridge,
Fulham Road SW6 1HS ☎ 0871 984
1955 🚇 Fulham Broadway 🚌 11, 414
⛴ Riverboat to Chelsea Harbour,
Mon–Fri

CHELSEA SPORTS CENTRE
www.courtneys.co.uk/chelsea
Refurbished in 2007 to provide
modern facilities in a building that
retains its early 1900s' charm, the
centre has a sports hall, swimming
pool, gym, fitness centre and
dance studio.
✚ 247 E8 ✉ 2 Chelsea Manor Street,
SW3 5PL ☎ 020 7352 6985 🕐 Mon–Fri
6.30am–10pm, Sat 8–8, Sun 8am–10pm
🖐 £3.50–£8 (depending on activity)
🚇 Sloane Square, South Kensington
🚌 11, 19, 22, 49, 319

FULHAM FOOTBALL CLUB
www.fulhamfc.co.uk
A snug little ground by Premier
League standards, where the team
owned by Mohamed Al Fayed, play
entertaining football.
✚ Off map 246 C8 ✉ Craven Cottage,
Stevenage Road SW6 6HH ☎ 0843 208
1222 🚇 Putney Bridge 🚌 74, 85, 190, 211,
220, 295, 424, C4

HYDE PARK
www.royalparks.gov.uk
The Serpentine (▷ 212), an 11ha
(27-acre) lake, offers rowing,
canoeing and hiring paddle boats,
plus a lido in summer. There are also
tennis courts and a bowling green.
✚ 247 E5 ✉ Hyde Park W2 2UH ☎ 020
7263 3473 🚇 Hyde Park Corner, Marble
Arch, Knightsbridge 🚌 9, 10, 12, 14, 73

REGENT'S PARK
www.royalparks.org.uk
In addition to boating facilities on the
lake, multisports are accommodated
at the Hub. There's also tennis.
✚ 247 F2 ✉ The Hub, Outer Circle,
Regent's Park NW1 4RU ☎ 020 7935 2458
🚇 Baker Street 🚌 274

HEALTH AND BEAUTY
BALANCE
www.balancetheclinic.com
This retreat offers health treatments—
including nutrition advice, colonics
and lymph drainage, and reflexology.
✚ 247 E8 ✉ The Courtyard, 250
King's Road SW3 5UE ☎ 020 7565 0333
🕐 Mon–Thu 9–8, Fri 9–7, Sat 9–6, Sun
9–5.30. Booking advisable 🖐 Treatments
from £45 🚇 South Kensington, Sloane
Square 🚌 11, 19, 22, 49, 211, 319

BHARTI VYAS
www.bharti-vyas.com
Holistic beauty centre offering
treatments such as aromatherapy,
acupressure and massage, tailored
for individual customers.
✚ 247 F3 ✉ 5 and 24 Chiltern Street W1U
7QE ☎ 020 7935 5312 🕐 Mon–Sat 9–6
(Wed, Fri till 7). Booking essential 🖐 Facial
from £80 🚇 Baker Street 🚌 2, 13, 30, 74,
82, 113, 139, 189, 274

BLISS LONDON
www.blissworld.co.uk
Originally opened in New York,
this salon promises highly trained
experts. The glass of wine and rich
chocolate brownies you're given
before a treatment is surely bliss!
✚ 247 E7 ✉ 60 Sloane Avenue SW3 3DD
☎ 020 7590 6146 🕐 Mon–Fri 9.30–8,
Sat 9.30–6.30, Sun 12–6. Booking essential
🖐 Facial from £110 🚇 Sloane Square,
South Kensington 🚌 14, 49, 345

PORCHESTER SPA
www.courtneys.co.uk
West London's best-value spa
includes three Turkish hot rooms, two
Russian steam rooms, a cold plunge
pool, a Finnish sauna and an art deco
swimming pool.
✚ 246 C4 ✉ Porchester Centre,
Queensway W2 5HS ☎ 020 7792 3980
🕐 Daily 10–10. Women only Tue, Thu,
Fri, Sun (10–4). Men only Mon, Wed, Sat.
Mixed couples Sun 4–10 🖐 From £22.50.
Mixed couples ticket £29.35 (Sun only)
🚇 Bayswater, Queensway 🚌 7, 15, 27, 36

VIDAL SASSOON
www.sassoon.com
The famous salon from the Swinging
Sixties is now a slick, modern
operation with a unique three-
year training school and six salons
throughout London.
✚ 247 G4 ✉ 60 South Molton Street W1K
5SW ☎ 020 7491 8848 🕐 Mon–Wed, Fri
9–6, Thu 9–6.45, Sat 9–4.30, alternate Sun
12–4.30. Booking advisable 🖐 Cut and
blow dry from £68 🚇 Bond Street 🚌 8,
10, 15, 73, 139

FOR CHILDREN
DIANA, PRINCESS OF WALES
MEMORIAL PLAYGROUND
www.royalparks.gov.uk
Creative fun for children up to the
age of 12. The playground has a Peter
Pan theme and includes a pirate ship,
crocodile, fountains and wigwams.
✚ 246 E5 ✉ Kensington Gardens W2 2UH
☎ 020 7298 2141 🕐 Daily 10am–dusk
🖐 Free 🚇 Lancaster Gate, High Street
Kensington, Queensway 🚌 9, 10 🚇

NATURAL HISTORY MUSEUM
▷ 220–221.

QUEENS ICE AND BOWL
www.queensiceandbowl.co.uk
A supermodern ice rink, plus 12
lanes of tenpin bowling, hi-tech
amusements and a karaoke bar.
✚ 246 C5 ✉ 17 Queensway W2 4QP
☎ 020 7229 0172 🕐 Daily 10am–11pm
🖐 Prices vary 🚇 Bayswater, Queensway
🚌 7, 23, 27, 70 🚇

SCIENCE MUSEUM
▷ 222–223.

PRICES AND SYMBOLS

The prices given are the average for a two-course set lunch (L) and a three-course à la carte dinner (D) for one person, without drinks. The wine price is for the least expensive bottle.

For a key to the symbols, ▷ 2.

AMAYA

www.amaya.biz

Brainchild of the team behind Chutney Mary, this Indian grill scooped nearly every award in 2005 by taking regional Indian food and bringing it up to date. Most of the food, designed for sharing, is prepared in full view of customers, ensuring freshness. The seafood platter is a particular highlight, or try the Caesar salad with chicken tikka and an ever-changing small selection of in-season curries, soups and biryanis. Booking is essential.
➕ 247 F6 ✉ Halkin Arcade, Motcomb Street SW1X 8JT ☎ 020 7823 1166 🕐 Mon–Sat 12.30–2.15, 6.30–11.30, Sun 12.45–2.45, 6.30–10.30 ✋ L £19.95, D £60, Wine £20 🚇 Knightsbridge

ASSAGGI

A relaxed and traditional Italian restaurant with bare floorboards, wooden tables and plenty of yellow and terracotta, set above the Chepstow pub. Starters may include buffalo mozzarella, *gamberoni con carciofi* (prawns cooked with artichokes) and *calamari ripieni* (stuffed squid). Main courses include *quaglia ripiena* (stuffed roasted quail) and *filetto di vitello al rosmarino* (pan-roasted fillet of white veal, rosemary and glazed baby onions). Perfectly accompanied by a selection of Italian and Sardinian wines.
➕ 246 C4 ✉ 39 Chepstow Place W2 4TS ☎ 020 7792 5501 🕐 Mon–Sat 12.30–2.30, 7.30–11. Closed public hols ✋ L £33, D £45, Wine £23 🚇 Notting Hill Gate, Bayswater (W of Lancaster Gate)

BABYLON

www.roofgardens.virgin.com

At this superb roof-garden restaurant, proceed through the cavernous foyer, hop into the lift and then walk past the fishtanks that form a wall of the small bar area. The generous and varied menu may offer delights such as tender baby squid bursting with king prawns and Cornish bourride perfumed with ginger and spring onions. Desserts might include chestnut crème brûlée with chestnut noodles and almond ice cream.

Above *Babylon restaurant is known for its sumptuous seafood*

➕ 246 C6 ✉ The Roof Gardens, 99 Kensington High Street W8 5SA ☎ 020 7368 3993 🕐 Mon–Sat 12–2.30, 7–10.30, Sun 12–2.30. Closed 25 Dec ✋ L £19, D £40, Wine £21 🚇 High Street Kensington (SW of Lancaster Gate)

BIBENDUM

www.bibendum.co.uk

Housed in the large remarkable art deco Michelin building, this restaurant is light and airy with fabulous stained-glass windows depicting Bibendum, the Michelin Man, riding his bicycle, kick-boxing and drinking champagne. The Bibendum motif is also picked up on the glasses, decanters, vases, tables and even the chair legs. The set menus are good value. Great emphasis is placed on wine service, with guidance from the sommeliers through the list of some 600 wines. The less formal Oyster Bar is open all day (from noon) serving all manner of crustacea, plus salads and daily specials.
➕ 247 E7 ✉ Michelin House, 81 Fulham Road SW3 6RD ☎ 020 7581 5817 🕐 Mon–Fri 12–2.30, 7–11, Sat 12.30–3,

7–11, Sun 12.30–3, 7–10.30. Closed 25–26 Dec, 1 Jan 🖐 L £26.50, D £50, Wine £17.95 🚇 South Kensington

CAMBIO DE TERCIO
www.cambiodetercio.co.uk
Voted the best Spanish restaurant outside Iberia in 2003, this attractive, friendly venue serves up exquisite modern Spanish cooking, including tapas. Dishes range from the innovative—Cuba libre of foie (duck liver mousse, coca-cola and rum gelée) lemon snow—to the classic such as beef solomillo, oxtail or grilled tuna, albeit with a modern twist. The desserts are superb: leave room for the creamy thyme-lemon ice cream. The wines are all Spanish, and are expensive.
🕂 246 D8 ✉ 163 Old Brompton Road SW5 0LJ ☎ 020 7244 8970 🕘 Mon–Fri 12–2.30, 7–11.30, Sat 12–3, 7–11.30, Sun 12–3, 7–11 🖐 L £30, D £37, Wine £24 🚇 Gloucester Road (W of South Kensington)

CARAFFINI
www.caraffini.co.uk
Friendly service greets you at this popular neighbourhood Italian restaurant. The pale yellow painted walls are hung with mirrors and prints and the pale wood floors contrast with Venetian blinds, blue chairs, banquettes and plants. The lengthy menu includes a risotto with fresh baby artichokes and prawns, and an excellent tiramisu among the desserts. There's a good selection of vegetarian dishes and a range of Italian wines.
🕂 247 F8 ✉ 61–63 Lower Sloane Street SW1W 8DH ☎ 020 7259 0235 🕘 Mon–Sat 12.15–2.30, 6.30–11.30. Closed 25–26 Dec, public hols 🖐 L £26, D £32, Wine £15.70 🚇 Sloane Square

CHEZ BRUCE
www.chezbruce.co.uk
This small, unassuming place—that looks more like a bistro from the outside rather than Wandsworth's culinary star—is set in a parade of shops overlooking the common, and is heaving most of the time. First-timers should look for the

large planters bursting with flowers outside, or just follow the savvy crowd who are full of admiration for Bruce Poole's memorable classic regional French cuisine with a twist. Noteworthy flavours, perfect balance and impeccable skill make for a memorable time.
🕂 Off map 246 D9 ✉ 2 Bellevue Road SW17 7EG ☎ 020 8672 0114 🕘 Mon–Sat 12–2, 6.30–10.30, Sun 12–3, 7–9.30. Closed 24–26 Dec, 1 Jan 🖐 L £25, D £45, Wine £18 🚇 Balham 🚆 Wandsworth Common

CHUTNEY MARY
www.chutneymary.com
This popular King's Road Indian restaurant has a romantic look and a changing menu that combines established dishes with exciting new specialities, such as buttered crab (popular in Mumbai) and the restaurant's own foie gras dish cooked with seared mango and mild chilli marsala jelly. Don't miss one of the interesting and unusual desserts, such as the crème brûlée with strawberries and marsala spice.
🕂 Off map 246 D9 ✉ 535 King's Road SW10 0SZ ☎ 020 7351 3113 🕘 Mon–Fri 6.30–11, Sat 12.30–3, 6.30–11.30, Sun 12.30–3, 6.30–10.30. Closed 25 Dec 🖐 L £22, D £45, Wine £20 🚇 Fulham Broadway

CIBO
www.ciborestaurant.net
Cibo is at once exciting and relaxing. The cooking is straightforward and concentrates mainly on seafood; there is a fine selection of grilled fish and shellfish and modern Italian specialities such as baked monkfish tails with courgette flowers or baked rack of lamb on a potato crust with baby artichokes. The wine list is interesting, with some hidden classics from overlooked regions. Set lunches are reasonably priced and the atmosphere is quieter than in the evening. The staff are friendly at all times.
🕂 246 A6 ✉ 3 Russell Gardens W14 8EZ ☎ 020 7371 2085 🕘 Mon–Sat 12–3, 6.30–11, Sun 12–3. Closed 25–26 Dec 🖐 L £17.50, D £33, Wine £21 🚇 Kensington Olympia, Shepherd's Bush

LE GAVROCHE RESTAURANT
www.le-gavroche.co.uk
No other restaurant in Britain is as faithful to classic French tradition as the long-established Le Gavroche, the name now synonymous with the French Roux brothers and carried on by Michel Roux Jr. Tables are set with crystal and silver and the staff are professional and well informed. Dishes might include scallops baked in their shells and perfumed with truffles; lobster salad with mango, avocado, basil and lime; Scotch fillet of beef and foie gras, port sauce and truffled macaroni cheese; whole baked sea bass stuffed with fennel and wild rice. Desserts include a choice of soufflées, ice creams and sorbets. For a suitable accompaniment to your meal, choose from one of the most comprehensive wine lists in London. Male diners will need to wear a jacket.
🕂 247 F5 ✉ 43 Upper Brook Street W1K 7QR ☎ 020 7408 0881 🕘 Mon–Fri 12–2, 6.30–11, Sat 6.30–11. Closed 25 Dec–1 Jan, public hols 🖐 L £50 (set 3 courses), D £90, Wine £30 🚇 Marble Arch

KAI MAYFAIR
www.kaimayfair.co.uk
Located on a quite street parallel to Park Lane, this acclaimed gem of Chinese cooking could easily be bypassed. Inside it is chic and sleek, the menu a mix of authentic Chinese classics with some Westernized specialities. Try scallop and tiger prawns with glass noodles, perhaps, followed by sea bass with chopped snow leaf and a topping of shrimp crumble. Don't miss the special dessert of pumpkin cream with purple rice and coconut ice cream.
🕂 247 F5 ✉ 65 South Audley Street W1K 2QU ☎ 020 7493 8988 🕘 Mon–Fri 10–2, 6.30–10.30, Sat–Sun 12.30–2.30, 6.30–10 🖐 L £27 (3 courses), D £55, Wine £39 🚇 Marble Arch

LANGTRY'S
www.langtrysrestaurant.com
Named after the famous actress Lillie Langtry, who lived in this house, now the Cadogan Hotel. This new restaurant, with its modern British

menu from chef Oliver Lesnik, is a welcome addition to the London hotel dining scene. The food served in the historic dining room offers fine cooking using the best seasonal ingredients. Start with delights such as sun-dried tomato and fennel soup, move on to main dishes including chargrilled rib of Scottish beef and finish off with yummy sherry trifle.

✚ 247 F7 ✉ 21 Pont Street SW1X 9SG ☎ 020 7201 6619 🕐 Mon–Fri 7–10.30, 12–2.30, 6–10.30, Sat 8–11, 12–2.30, 6–10.30, Sun 8–11, 12–2.30. Closed 25 Dec ✋ L £32, D £49, Wine £22 🚇 Knightsbridge, Sloane Square

LEVANT

www.levant.co.uk

The perfume of roses drifts up the stairs to greet you at this Lebanese restaurant. Downstairs it is modern with polished stone floors and subtle lighting. Meze selections include spicy Armenian sausages, fried aubergine (eggplant) with pomegranate dressing, and of course hummus and falafel. Made to share, they're eaten with warm pitta bread. Staff are happy to guide newcomers, and be prepared for the belly dancer.

✚ 247 G4 ✉ Jason Court, 76 Wigmore Street W1H 9DQ ☎ 020 7224 1111 🕐 Mon–Wed 5–12, Thu–Fri 5–1, Sat 12–2.30, Sun 12–11. Closed 25–26 Dec, 1 Jan ✋ L £23, D £29, Wine £18 🚇 Bond Street

MADSEN

www.madsenrestaurant.com

Located very close to South Kensington Underground station, this stylish, clean-cut restaurant is dedicated to Scandinavian cuisine. Eco-ethics are big here, so materials used in the light, healthy meals are sustainably sourced and low on food miles. A classic starter of sweet-cured herring with dill-marinated potatoes and mustard cream sets the tone, followed perhaps by pork meatballs and red cabbage. Smushi—small Danish open sandwiches topped with thinly sliced meat or fish and vegetables—are a lunchtime treat.

✚ 246 D7 ✉ 20 Old Brompton Road SW7 3DL ☎ 020 7225 2772 🕐 Mon 12–10.30, Tue–Thu 12–11, Fri–Sat 12–11.45, Sun 12–5 ✋ L £9.50, D £35, Wine £17.25 🚇 South Kensington

MARCO

www.marcorestaurant.org

A Premier League venue for a top-notch modern British brasserie, thanks to a collaboration between flamboyant chef Marco Pierre White and club owner Roman Abramovich. The setting is elegant and glamorous, the cooking skilful and clean, with classics such as wild halibut with brown shrimps, roast venison, and desserts including caramelized apple pie and Eton mess.

✚ 246 C9 ✉ Chelsea Football Club, Stamford Bridge, Fulham Road SW6 1HS ☎ 020 7915 2929 🕐 Tue–Sat 6–10.30 (may be affected by match fixtures) ✋ D £47, Wine £15 🚇 Fulham Broadway

MAZE

www.gordonramsay.com

Yet another member of the Gordon Ramsay stable, under the rising star of chef Alex Marks. He delivers a modern French approach with Asian influences, producing highly accomplished dishes such as Suffolk pork cheek and belly, with mostada of pear and swede, quince purée and choucroute. There's a wide range of wines by the bottle and half bottle, and more than 25 choices available by the glass.

✚ 247 F4 ✉ 10–13 Grosvenor Square W1K 6JP ☎ 020 7107 0000 🕐 Daily 12–2.30, 6–10.30. Closed public hols ✋ L £30 (set 3 courses), D £37, Wine £32 🚇 Bond Street

THE ORANGERY

www.hrp.org.uk/KensingtonPalace

The quintessential English tea venue. Take tea or a light lunch in the beautiful Orangery designed for Queen Anne in 1704. You eat on the terrace or in the dining room in elegant surroundings overlooking the formal palace gardens. You can start with breakfast—from Continental to full English or even one with champagne. Lunch offers British

delights such as steak or salmon followed by strawberry tart with lavender cream. For many, afternoon tea is the speciality—cucumber sandwiches or scones with cream and jam.

✚ 246 C6 ✉ Kensington Palace, Kensington Gardens W8 4PX ☎ 020 7376 0239 🕐 Mar–Sep daily 10–6; Oct–Feb 10–5. Closed 24–26 Dec ✋ L £15, full tea from £14.85, Wine £15 🚇 High Street Kensington, Queensway

ORIGINAL TAGINES

www.original-tagines.com

As you would expect from the name, this Moroccan restaurant in Marylebone serves many versions of the eponymous dish among its main courses. Other specialities include a range of couscous dishes. Friendly staff and a warm, welcoming atmosphere. The charcoal grill is visible through a glass wall.

✚ 247 F3 ✉ 7a Dorset Street W1U 6QN ☎ 020 7935 1545 🕐 Daily 11am–12am ✋ L £18, D £24, Wine £11 🚇 Baker Street

LA POISSONERIE DE L'AVENUE

www.poissoneriedelavenue.com

This elegant family-run Chelsea restaurant and oyster bar boasts its own shop next door selling the freshest of fish and shellfish. The menu is seasonally driven, but might include a starter of yellowfin tuna carpaccio with spring onions, followed by poached fillet of turbot in a champagne and mushroom sauce. Other menu options include roasted quail, and beef fillet in a Béarnaise sauce.

✚ 247 E7 ✉ 82 Sloane Avenue SW3 3DZ ☎ 020 7589 2457 🕐 Mon–Sat 12–3, 7–11.30, Sun 12–4, 7–11 ✋ L £24, D £36, Wine £26 🚇 South Kensington

RACINE

www.racine-restaurant.com

It doesn't get much more Gallic this side of the English Channel than in this popular Knightsbridge brasserie just opposite the South Kensington museums. There's an authentic bustle and a rather masculine look of dark wood and deep brown leather. Expect hearty bourgeois

STAYING

PRICES AND SYMBOLS

The prices given are the lowest and highest for a double room for one night, unless otherwise stated. Breakfast is not usually included. All the hotels listed accept credit cards unless otherwise stated. Note that rates vary widely throughout the year.

For a key to the symbols, ▷ 2.

22 YORK STREET

www.22yorkstreet.co.uk
This elegant five-storey, Georgian terraced town house is a charmer, set in a quiet corner in the heart of central London, near Baker Street Tube station. Rooms are individually furnished in a comfortable and elegant, yet simple, style, with wooden floors, rugs, French antique furniture and quilts. The Continental breakfast (included), taken around a large antique dining table, is one of the tastiest and healthiest in town. Tea or coffee and biscuits are always available for guests in the welcoming lounges.
✚ 247 F3 ✉ 22 York Street W1U 6PX ☎ 020 7224 2990 🖐 £109–£129 ❶ 18 (no children under 5) 🚇 Baker Street

BARRY HOUSE

www.barryhouse.co.uk
A smart, friendly, family-run property that offers bed-and-breakfast near Hyde Park, Marble Arch and many of London's main sights. There are budget rooms on the upper floor.
✚ 246 D4 ✉ 12 Sussex Place, Hyde Park W2 2TP ☎ 020 7723 7340 🖐 £79–£120 ❶ 17 🚇 Paddington, Lancaster Gate 🚌 7, 15, 23, 27, 36

THE BEAUFORT

www.thebeaufort.co.uk
A chic boutique hotel, the Beaufort is in a tree-lined cul-de-sac just a few minutes' walk from Knightsbridge. Air-conditioned bedrooms are well furnished and equipped with chocolates, CD players and free internet and satellite TV, including Sky movies. Complimentary drinks and afternoon tea are served in the attractive drawing room. A good Continental breakfast is served in guests' rooms.
✚ 247 E7 ✉ 33 Beaufort Gardens SW3 1PP ☎ 020 7584 5252 🖐 £156–£276 ❶ 29 🚇 South Kensington, Knightsbridge 🚌 14, 74, C1

BERJAYA EDEN PARK HOTEL

www.berjayahotel.com
An elegant 1860 Bayswater town house, on a tree-lined terrace a few minutes' Tube ride from Oxford Street and the West End. Rooms are simply furnished. Suites have a private entrance and adjoining family living room or private patio and sitting room area, including sofa bed. There's a convenient restaurant, too.
✚ 246 C4 ✉ 35–39 Inverness Terrace W2 3JS ☎ 020 7221 2220 🖐 From £69 ❶ 114 🚇 Bayswater, Queensway 🚌 12, 70, 94

THE BERKELEY

www.the-berkeley.co.uk
The Knightsbridge Berkeley never fails to impress. Bedrooms are coolly elegant and modern, each one furnished with perfect attention to detail. The public spaces are decorated with magnificent flower arrangements and the Blue Bar is strikingly furnished, its blue tones and white ceiling, complete with opulent chandelier, setting the scene for a relaxed pre-dinner drink. The health spa offers a range of

treatments and there's an open-air rooftop pool. Two restaurants provide a contrast of styles: choose from the upmarket brasserie at Koffman's and the Michelin-starred haute cuisine of Marcus Wareing at the Berkeley.

🕂 247 F6 ✉ Wilton Place SW1X 7RL ☎ 020 7235 6000 🖐 £360–£710 🛈 214 🌀 🏊 📺 🍴 🚇 Hyde Park Corner, Knightsbridge 🚌 9, 10, 14, 19, 22, 52, 74, 137

BLAKEMORE
www.starcrown.com

This basic hotel enjoys a quiet yet central position just a few minutes' walk from Hyde Park (▷ 212). The bedrooms are neatly decorated and the executive rooms have been tastefully refurbished. Spacious public areas include the Rossetti bar lounge, smart lobby and the attractive Wellington and Terrace restaurants.

🕂 246 C4 ✉ 30 Leinster Gardens W2 3AN ☎ 020 7262 4591 🖐 From £168 🛈 163 🚇 Bayswater, Queensway 🚌 12, 70, 94

BYRON
www.capricornhotels.co.uk

This hotel in a row of Georgian houses has been restored to provide comfortable accommodation and to retain a number of original features. Bedrooms vary in size, but all are tastefully furnished and equipped with modern facilities. There's a dining room where you can have breakfast, an attractive guest lounge and licensed bar.

🕂 246 C4 ✉ 36–38 Queensborough Terrace W2 3SH ☎ 020 7243 0987 🖐 £109–£185 🛈 45 🚇 Bayswater

THE CADOGAN HOTEL
www.cadogan.com

This Victorian hotel in Chelsea overlooks the lovely gardens in Cadogan Place. Bedrooms are air-conditioned and stylishly furnished. The elegant drawing room is popular for afternoon tea, and the grand purple and silver Langtry's restaurant (▷ 238–239) serves traditional classic British dishes.

🕂 247 F7 ✉ 75 Sloane Street SW1X 9SG ☎ 020 7235 7141 🖐 £200–£390 🛈 65 🌀 📺 🚇 Sloane Square 🚌 19, 22, 137, C1

CAPITAL
www.capitalhotel.co.uk

This small, family-owned hotel near Harrods (▷ 233) has individually designed, fresh and light bedrooms with antique furniture and marble bathrooms. A highlight of any visit to this outstanding hotel is dinner in the two-Michelin-star Capital restaurant, where head chef Jérlome Poncelle serves innovative French-inspired dishes.

🕂 247 F6 ✉ 22 Basil Street SW3 1AT ☎ 020 7589 5171 🖐 £240–£456 🛈 50 🌀 🚇 Knightsbridge 🚌 19, 22, 137, C1

CLARIDGE'S
www.claridges.co.uk

Impressive standards of luxury, style and service are upheld at this iconic bastion of British hospitality. The sumptuously decorated, air-conditioned rooms have Victorian or art deco themes to reflect the architecture of the building. Gordon Ramsay at Claridge's, the hotel restaurant, is run by the renowned British chef; the food and service are superb. The sleek cocktail bar is a popular meeting place, and the lobby is a stylish place to have afternoon tea.

🕂 247 G4 ✉ Brook Street W1K 4HR ☎ 020 7629 8860 🖐 £390–£800 🛈 203 🌀 📺 🚇 Bond Street 🚌 8

THE DORCHESTER
www.thedorchester.com

One of London's finest hotels, The Dorchester is sumptuous. The bedrooms all have individual design schemes, are beautifully furnished and have huge, luxurious bathrooms. Leading off from the lobby, The Promenade is perfect for afternoon tea or drinks. In the evening you can catch live music in the bar, and enjoy a cocktail or an Italian meal. The main restaurant is the traditional Grill Room, which looks almost exactly as it did in 1931 when the hotel first opened. A new restaurant was added

in 2007 with Alain Ducasse at the helm, and China Tang offers some of the best Cantonese food in London.

🕂 247 F5 ✉ Park Lane W1K 1QA ☎ 020 7629 8888 🖐 £510–£795 🛈 250 📺 🚇 Hyde Park Corner, Marble Arch 🚌 2, 10, 16, 36, 73, 74, 82, 137, 148

FOUR SEASONS HOTEL
www.4seasonshotel.co.uk

Not to be confused with the Four Seasons London Hotel on Park Lane, this small family-run hotel is on the edge of Regent's Park (▷ 218) and within easy walking distance of London Zoo (▷ 219) and Madame Tussauds (▷ 217). Breakfast (included) is served in the pretty conservatory, which gives the impression of being away from the bustling city.

🕂 247 F3 ✉ 173 Gloucester Place, Regent's Park NW1 6DX ☎ 020 7724 3461 🖐 £71–£198 🛈 16 🚇 Baker Street, Marylebone 🚌 2, 13, 30, 74, 82, 113, 139, 189, 274

THE GAINSBOROUGH
www.eeh.co.uk

This Georgian town house is in a quiet street in South Kensington, near the Natural History Museum (▷ 220–221). The bedrooms have been individually designed and are decorated with fine fabrics and quality furnishings. There is a small public lounge. Some refurbishment was undertaken in 2011.

🕂 246 D7 ✉ 7–11 Queensberry Place SW7 2DL ☎ 020 7957 0000 🖐 £99–£182 🛈 48 🚇 South Kensington 🚌 14, 49, 70, 74, 345, 360, 414

THE GALLERY
www.eeh.co.uk

This stylish property, close to Kensington and Knightsbridge, offers friendly hospitality, attentive service and sumptuously furnished bedrooms, some with a private terrace. Public areas include several lounges (one with internet access) and an elegant bar. Room service is available 24 hours a day. There are no evening meals.

🕂 246 D7 ✉ 8–10 Queensberry Place SW7 2EA ☎ 020 7915 0000 🖐 £99–£188

WESTBOURNE
GREEN

KENSAL TOWN

NORTH
KENSINGTON

PADDINGTON

PADDINGTON
STATION

Norfolk
Plaza

Barry
House

NOTTING
HILL

Assaggi

New Linden

Berjaya Eden
Park Hotel

BAYSWATER

Blakemore

Byron

Mornington
Hotel

Lancaster
Gate Hotel

Lancaster
London

The Ladbroke
Arms

Kensington
Gardens

Peter Pan
Statue

The Churchill
Arms

Vicarage
Hotel

Kensington
Palace

The Orangery

Kensington
House

Holland
Park

Babylon

High Street
Kensington

KENSINGTON

Cibo

KENSINGTON
OLYMPIA
STATION

Olympia

London
Kensington Forum

The
Gallery

The
Gainsborough

HAMMERSMITH

WEST
KENSINGTON

Rushmore
Hotel

Maranton
House Hotel

SOUTH
KENSINGTON

Madsen

EARL'S
COURT

K&K Hotel
George

EARL'S
COURT
STATION

Cambio de
Tercio

WEST
BROMPTON
STATION

WEST
BROMPTON

The Atlas

The Cross
Keys

The River Café &
Hotel Orlando

Marco

Chez Bruce,
Chutney Mary,
The Chelsea Ram

A   B   C   D

Four Seasons

The Landmark London
22 York Street
Hart House
Lincoln House
Original Tagines
The Mandeville
Levant
Marble Arch Inn
Texture
Maze
Claridge's
Le Gavroche Restaurant
Kai Mayfair
The Dorchester

The Berkeley
Salloos
Zuma
The Levin
Capital
The Beaufort
Racine
Langtry's
La Poissonerie de l'Avenue
The Admiral Codrington
Nag's Head
Zafferano
Amaya
Jumeirah Carlton Tower Hotel
The Grenadier
The Lanesborough
The Cadogan Hotel
Caraffini
Restaurant Gordon Ramsay

Hyde Park

Green Park

Serpentine

Thames

MARYLEBONE
LISSON GROVE
BLOOMSBURY
ST GILES
SOHO
CHINATOWN
STRAND
MAYFAIR
ST JAMES'S
KNIGHTSBRIDGE
BELGRAVIA
WESTMINSTER
PIMLICO

Buckingham Palace

400 m
400 yds

E   F   G   H   J

EXCURSIONS

Although central London has enough to keep you occupied for months, it is worth getting a feel for the city a little way farther out. There are many lesser-known attractions that can be visited in a couple of hours, such as Dulwich Picture Gallery or Horniman Museum, which double up nicely. These are still within city postcodes, as is Greenwich, which easily merits a full day's exploration on its own. The site of the Meridian boasts a beautiful riverside setting, as well as a bustling market, the vast maritime museum, the Royal Observatory and the Millennium Dome, now the O2 Arena, a huge entertainment complex. About the same distance on the north side of the centre, Hampstead offers a couple of minor sights and untrammelled beauty on its sprawling heath.

In the outlying suburban boroughs you can choose between famous royal residences of the past and present at Hampton Court and Windsor Castle, the latter sitting squatly across the river from Eton, a quaint place renowned for its exclusive public (that is, private) school. The River Thames itself offers a rich vein for exploration on tours both east and west of the centre. In the southwestern suburbs, an unmissable sight for any horticulturalist is the Botanical Gardens at Kew, only a couple of miles from the huge expanse of Richmond Park, still home to wild deer.

For a real getaway from the London area, perhaps best done as an overnight stay although both can be reached easily within a couple of hours, two standout options are Oxford and Bath. Oxford is dominated by the leisurely academic atmosphere emanating from the medieval spires and courtyards of its university colleges, while Bath has its roots in Roman times but impresses most for its exquisite Georgian architecture.

A10
B156
ey
Goff's
Oak
Cheshunt
Waltham
Cross
M25
Enfield
thgate
A105 A10
A1010
A1055
Wood
Green
Tottenham
Dalston
A105 A503
A10
A104
A107
A1
olborn
City
A501
A11
A13
A100
LONDON
Thames
Peckham
xton
Dulwich
Picture
Gallery
Dulwich
A205
eatham
Crystal
Palace
A212
A214
A215
A222
Croydon
A212
Purley
Sanderstead
ulsdon
A22
Caterham
A22
Godstone
A25
M23

Epping
Green
Cambridge
M11
North Weald
Bassett
A414
Chipping Ongar
Ingatestone
A10
B194
Waltham
Abbey
M25
A121
Theydon
Bois
M25
A13
B181
Epping
B1393
A113
A128
Brentwood
A12
A1168
A104
A121
A112
Loughton
Abridge
A12
Chingford
A113
A12
Woodford
Chigwell
A1112
Harold
Hill A12
A127
28
A127
William
Morris
Gallery
A406
A1400
A118
A127
Romford
A124
Walthamstow
Hornchurch
B187
Upminster
B186
29
Leytonstone
A406
Ilford
A1112
Leyton
M25
Stratford
A17
Barking
Dagenham
South
Ockendon
Hackney
A12
A124
East Ham
A13
A13
A1306
Rainham
Aveley
A13
30
A13
Thames
Barrier
A1020
London
City
Thamesmead
A13
West
Thurrock
A1306
Thames
Woolwich
A2016
Greenwich
A206
Erith
Purfleet
New
Cross
A2
A207
Bexleyheath
Dartford
Crossing
A226
Lewisham
A20
A205
A2
Crayford
Greenhithe
Horniman
Museum
Eltham
Eltham
Palace
Bexley
Dartford
A2
Gravesend
Catford
A208
Sidcup
A223
A205
A21
A208
A20
A222
A222
Swanley
B260
Beckenham
A225
B260
Meopham
Bromley
A208
St Mary
Cray
A20
A232
West
Wickham
Crockenhill
A232
A2022
A232
Orpington
Eynsford
West
Kingsdown
M20
A227
A224
A225
A20
A21
A33
M25
A224
Otford
Kemsing
Wrotham
Biggin Hill
M26
Warlingham
B269
A233
Borough
Green
Limpsfield
A25
Riverhead
A25
A227
M25
Brasted
Sevenoaks
A225
A26
Westerham
B2042
A25
Oxted
B269
B8026
Crockham
Hill
A21
Four Elms
B245
Hildenborough

0   8 km
0   5 miles

251

HOW TO GET THERE
Cambridge is 96km (60 miles) north of London

🚆 From King's Cross or Liverpool Street (55 min)

🚌 National Express service from Victoria Coach Station (2 hours 30 min)

🚗 M11 northeast to junction 14, then A414 northwest (1 hour 30 min)

✈ Stanstead Airport (25 min)

TIPS
» Avoid visiting on a Monday, when most museums are closed.

» If you're driving, use the park-and-ride scheme to avoid the congestion and high parking prices of the city centre.

» Many college chapels offer free lunchtime organ recitals during the Cambridge Festival (mid-Jul to early Aug).

CAMBRIDGE

Its beautiful, compact heart makes historic Cambridge a great destination for a day or weekend away from the capital. Its venerable university buildings surround quadrangles and gardens. There are a clutch of superb museums, good places to eat out, and shopping too, in the new Grand Arcade centre.

A guided walking tour is a great way to find your bearings—a selection of excellent themed tours leave the tourist office (daily), just off the Market Place, and take in the most picturesque colleges. Alternatively, pick up the *Cambridge and beyond* leaflet (free), which includes a map, suggested routes and other useful information. One of the best ways to see the city is from the diminutive River Cam. Hire a flat-bottomed punt (poled boat) for an hour and explore for yourself (instruction given), or take a chauffeured option. The stretch of the river within Cambridge is known as the Backs—it takes you along the dreamy lawns and backs of the colleges, including King's College and the Bridge of Sighs. For a longer adventure, take a picnic and punt up-river to the village of Grantchester, 4km (2.5 miles) away.

WHAT TO SEE
Students first arrived here in 1209, and the first college, Peterhouse, was founded in 1284. The university now comprises 31 colleges, and the most attractive lie along Trumpington Street/King's Parade/Trinity Street, and Sidney Street. Most are private, though you may often walk through their open courtyards to visit chapels and other historic highlights (all close mid-Apr to Jun during examinations). King's College was founded in 1441 by Henry VI, and its chapel (daily) is the most famous, with its soaring gothic stone fan-vaulting and medieval stained glass. Catch a choral service if you can (daily in term-time).

The Fitzwilliam Museum (Tue–Sun, free) contains an outstanding collection of art and artefacts, including ceramics, paintings by Monet, Renoir and Van Gogh, and exquisite relics of ancient Greece. Twentieth-century art and craft is celebrated at the fascinating Kettle's Yard House and Gallery (Tue–Sun). Other museums linked to the university include relics of Captain Scott and others at the Scott Polar Research Institute (Tue–Sat), and fabulous fossils at the Sedgwick Museum of Earth Science (Mon–Sat).

There are plenty of green spaces where you can get away from the crowds, including Midsummer Common and Jesus Green by the river. The Botanic Garden is a welcome retreat, just 1.6km (1 mile) south of the city centre (daily). Just outside the city, historic aircraft are displayed (and frequently flown) at the Duxford Imperial War Museum (daily), the leading aviation museum in Europe; and the American Military Cemetery (daily) at Madingley is a moving tribute to around 9,000 US servicemen killed in World War II.

Above *Punting on the River Cam is an enjoyable way to see the colleges*

CHISWICK HOUSE

www.chgt.org.uk

This superb example of Palladian architecture is the work of Richard Boyle, 3rd Earl of Burlington (1694–1753), who made it his mission to promote the style in Britain. The perfectly symmetrical exterior, with its octagonal central dome and classical portico with six Corinthian columns, gives no clue to the sumptuously decorated rooms inside. Don't miss the gilding in the Blue Velvet Room or the domed saloon, lit from the drum windows, which were derived from the Roman Baths of Diocletian. The classical Italianate gardens were restored to splendour in 2010.

10km (6 miles) W of Tralfagar Square ✉ 50 Burlington Lane W4 2RR ☎ 020 8995 0508 🕓 May–Oct Sun–Wed 10–5 🖐 Adult £5, child (5–15) £2.50, under 5s free, family £12.50 🚇 Turnham Green 🚌 27, 190, 391 🚉 Turnham Green, Chiswick ☕ 🏛

DULWICH PICTURE GALLERY

www.dulwichpicturegallery.org.uk

More than 300 masterpieces make up this exceptional art collection, most painted in the 17th and 18th centuries and including works such as Van Dyck's *Madonna and Child*, Poussin's *Return of the Holy Family from Egypt* and Rembrandt's portrait of *Jacob III de Gheyn*, stolen several times from the gallery but recovered on each occasion. The neoclassical building, designed by Sir John Soane in 1811, was England's first purpose-built art gallery. A striking addition by Rick Mather, opened in 2000, provides more exhibition space, an education centre for children and adults, and a café overlooking the large garden.

The gallery also serves as a mausoleum: At the rear of the building are the tombs of Noel Desenfans, who was responsible for putting the collection together in the 1790s, and Sir Francis Bourgeois, who bequeathed it to Dulwich College in 1811.

8km (5 miles) SE of Trafalgar Square ✉ Gallery Road, Dulwich Village SE21

7AD ☎ 020 8693 5254 🕓 Tue–Fri 10–5, Sat–Sun 11–5. Free tours Sat–Sun 3pm (normal admission charge) 🖐 Adult £5, under 18s free. Exhibitions adult £9, child (under 18) free 🚌 P4 from opposite Brixton Tube or Lewisham bus station; 3 to West Dulwich station; 37 to North Dulwich station 🚉 West Dulwich, North Dulwich ☕ 🏛

ELTHAM PALACE

www.english-heritage.org.uk

Moated parkland surrounds the remains of one of England's largest but least-known royal medieval palaces and the flamboyant house built next door by film director Stephen Courtauld in the 1930s and furnished in art deco style.

Inside it's fitted out with the modern conveniences of the day, including an electrically operated central vacuum cleaner, some loudspeakers relaying jazz to the ground floor, and an internal phone system. Check out the distinctive dining room with its pink leather upholstered chairs and black-and-white doors, and also Virginia Courtauld's exotic bathroom lined with onyx and gold mosaic and featuring a bust of Psyche. Other curious features include the centrally heated cage once occupied by the Courtaulds' pet lemur. The grounds include a rose garden and a moat stocked with carp.

19km (12 miles) SE of Trafalgar Square ✉ Court Yard, Eltham SE9 5QE ☎ 020 8294 2548 🕓 Apr–Oct Sun–Wed 10–5; Nov–23 Dec, Feb–Mar Sun–Wed 11–4. Palace and grounds closed 23 Dec–31 Jan 🖐 Adult £9.30, child (5–16) £5.60, family £24.20 🚌 132, 161 🚉 Eltham, Mottingham ☕ 🏛

FENTON HOUSE

www.nationaltrust.org.uk

This red-brick house built in 1695 is one of the best of its kind surviving in London. Period furnishings are complemented by a fine collection of ceramics, Georgian furniture and 17th-century needlework. The Benton Fletcher Collection of keyboard instruments from the 17th and 18th centuries is regularly put to use for concerts given in the house. Outside, roses grow in the charming walled garden, and there's an orchard and vegetable garden as well.

8km (5 miles) NW of Trafalgar Square ✉ Hampstead Grove, Hampstead NW3 6SP ☎ 020 7435 3471, general information 01494 755563 🕓 Mar Sat–Sun 2–5; Easter–Oct Sat–Sun 11–5, Wed–Fri 2–5 🖐 Adult £5.70, child (5–16) £2.80, under 5s free, family £14.20 🚇 Hampstead 🚌 46, 268 🚉 Hampstead Heath

FREUD MUSEUM

www.freud.org.uk

Sigmund Freud (1856–1939), Austrian neurologist and founder of psychoanalysis, lived at 20 Maresfield Gardens in south Hampstead from 1938 (when he escaped from Nazi-occupied Vienna). His youngest daughter, Anna, herself a psychoanalyst, continued to live there up until her death in 1982. The house is now a museum devoted to Freud's life and work, and contains his famous couch, along with his collection of antiquities, books, letters, diaries and other personal mementoes.

8km (5 miles) NW of Trafalgar Square ✉ 20 Maresfield Gardens NW3 5SX ☎ 020 7435 2002 🕓 Wed–Sun 12–5 🖐 Adult £6, child (12–16) £3, under 12s free 🚇 Finchley Road 🚌 13, 82, 113 🚉 Finchley Road and Frognal, Hampstead Heath 🏛

Below *Red-brick Fenton House in Hampstead has lovely gardens and an orchard*

INFORMATION

www.cuttysark.org.uk
www.oldroyalnavalcollege.org
www.nmm.ac.uk
www.english-heritage.org.uk
(for Ranger's House)

11km (7 miles) SE of Trafalgar Square on the south bank

✉ Cutty Sark: Cutty Sark Gardens SE10 9HT. Old Royal Naval College SE10 9LW. National Maritime Museum: Greenwich Park, SE10 9NF. Ranger's House: Chesterfield Walk, Blackheath, SE10 8QX

☎ Old Royal Naval College: 020 8269 4747. National Maritime Museum: 020 8858 4422, recorded information 020 8312 6565. Ranger's House: 020 8853 0035

🕐 Old Royal Naval College: daily 10–5, grounds 8–6. National Maritime Museum: daily 10–5. Ranger's House Apr–Sep

✋ Old Royal Naval College: free; guided tours £5. National Maritime Museum: free, charge for special exhibitions. Ranger's House: adult £6.30, child (5–15) £3.80, under 5s free 🚆 DLR via Canary Wharf 🚌 188 ⛴ River boat from Westminster Pier (1hr 10 min) 🚉 DLR to Island Gardens, then walk through the tunnel 🍴 The Gallery café, ground floor, and Paul Coffee Bar, Level 2 of National Maritime Museum; also Astronomy Café in Royal Observatory 🏛

INTRODUCTION

This lively riverside town is home to some of London's finest historic buildings, set against a backdrop of beautiful parkland, and the largest maritime museum in the world. In the town are plenty of places to eat, shops and street markets. In North Greenwich the space-age Millennium Dome has been transformed into the huge O2 entertainment complex, containing performance spaces, clubs, shops, restaurants and the British Music Experience (▷ 257).

The best way to reach Greenwich is by river, as the view from the riverside is one of the finest in London. Most people come here to admire the assembly of historic buildings—the former Royal Naval College, the National Maritime Museum in the Queen's House and the Old Royal Observatory, in Greenwich Park. It's also worth browsing the craft stalls at the covered weekend market and sampling some of the many good pubs and restaurants.

An off-beat place worth visiting is the Fan Museum at 12 Croom's Hill (Tue–Sat 11–5, Sun 12–5), dedicated to the ancient art of fan-making. There are over 3,500 fans in the collection, dating from the 11th century onwards, on show in changing, themed exhibitions and in permanent displays.

WHAT TO SEE

CUTTY SARK

This sleek tea clipper anchored by Greenwich Pier was built in 1869 to carry cargoes between Britain and the Orient. In 1871 she broke the world record for sailing between London and China, completing the trip in only 107 days. Following a devastating fire in May 2007, the ship is closed for restoration until 2012, when a new museum will open on the site.

OLD ROYAL NAVAL COLLEGE

This monumental group of buildings was laid out by Sir Christopher Wren in 1664 as a hospital for infirm and aged seamen. After the hospital closed in 1869, the complex was taken over by the Royal Naval College, training officers from all over the world, and it's now used by the University of Greenwich and the Trinity College of Music.

Two areas are open to the public: the Painted Hall and the chapel. The Painted Hall, created by Sir James Thornhill in 1707–17, features the largest painting in Great Britain, *Triumph of Peace and Liberty*, showing joint monarchs William (1650–1702) and Mary (1662–94) surrounded by allegorical figures. It measures 32 x 15m (106 x 51ft), and Thornhill and his assistants worked on it for some 20 years and received a fee of £6,685—then a princely sum—for their labours. The chapel (1718–25), restored by James Stuart after a fire in 1779, is in neo-Grecian style. The vast altar painting, *St. Paul Shaking Off the Viper,* is by American artist Benjamin West (1738–1820).

NATIONAL MARITIME MUSEUM

A suite of stunning galleries centred on the glass-roofed Neptune Court, and opened for the Millennium, gives the museum more space to tell the story of Britain's maritime history from the failed 16th-century invasion of the Spanish Armada to the 19th century. It focuses on exploration, trade and empire and explores themes such as luxury liners and naval heroes. Among the huge collection of ships (including hundreds of models), paintings, navigational instruments and the relics of sailors and explorers, seek out the luxurious state barge made for Frederick, Prince of Wales, in 1732, and the jacket Nelson was wearing when he was fatally wounded at the Battle of Trafalgar in 1805.

The museum's central building, the Queen's House, was England's first example of the neoclassical Palladian style, brought from Italy by Inigo Jones (1573–1652). Begun in 1616 as a palace for James I's wife, Anne of Denmark, it was not completed until 1635 in the reign of Charles I for his queen, Henrietta Maria. Inside, the best feature is the Tulip Stair, named after the decorative pattern on its balustrade.

Also in the care of the National Maritime Museum is the Old Royal Observatory, founded by Charles II in 1675 to tackle the problem of finding longitude at sea. The original building, Flamsteed House, was designed by Sir Christopher Wren for John Flamsteed, the first Astronomer Royal. The large Gate Clock (adult £10, child £5) measures Greenwich Mean Time, the standard by which time is set all round the world. In the courtyard you can straddle the eastern and western hemispheres by standing astride the simple brass strip that marks the Greenwich Meridian. The Royal Observatory has undergone a £15 million redevelopment with new galleries, an education centre and the Peter Harrison Planetarium, with its excellent range of shows (tel 020 8312 6608; adult £6.50, child £4.50).

RANGER'S HOUSE

At the southern end of Greenwich Park is the 18th-century Ranger's House, which became the official residence of the 'Ranger of Greenwich Park'. It's now a showcase for the Wernher Collection, formerly at Luton Hoo in Bedfordshire, which belonged to diamond and gold merchant Sir Julius Wernher. There are more than 700 works of art including paintings, tapestries, furniture, ceramics, ivories and jewels from the 16th and 17th centuries.

BRITISH MUSIC EXPERIENCE

London's newest museum is a highly entertaining history of pop culture and music tracing developments from the 1940s to the present day. It concentrates mainly on UK artists and bands, while showing their US influences and counterparts when appropriate. There are seven chronological sections, featuring plenty of paraphernalia like original stars' instruments and some amazing stage costumes. Other highlights are the Gibson Interactive Studio and Dance the Decades display.

Your visit starts and ends with lively (and loud) video presentations. One excellent feature is that you can bookmark any information that especially interests you by touching your smart ticket on to the electronic pads, to be retrieved at your leisure on the museum's website.

✉ 02 complex, North Greenwich SE10 0DX ☎ 020 8463 2000 🕐 Daily 10–7.30 (last entry 6.30) 🎫 Adult £12, child (5–16) £6, under 5s free 🚇 North Greenwich 🚌 108, 129, 132, 161, 188, 422, 472

Above *Compass on the dome of the Old Royal Naval College*
Opposite *Greenwich Park and the Royal Observatory*
Below *The* Cutty Sark *is being restored to its former glory*

HAMPSTEAD HEATH

www.cityoflondon.gov.uk

Hampstead Heath is a wonderfully diverse public open space of 320ha (790 acres), with areas of ancient woodlands, bogs, hedgerows and natural grassland. Londoners come to walk, jog, ride horses, enjoy picnics, fly kites, play petanque and swim in the three ponds and the lido. The Men's Pond and Ladies' Pond are life-guarded. Just east of the ponds is Parliament Hill, offering views over London. Local legend claims that Queen Boadicea (Boudicca), who led her Iceni people against the Roman occupiers (▷ 27), lies buried here.

At the northern end of the heath is Kenwood House (Apr–Oct daily 11–5; Nov–Mar 11.30–4), built in 1616 and remodelled by Robert Adam in 1764–79 for the Earl of Mansfield. It was left to the nation in 1927 by the 1st Earl of Iveagh, along with its outstanding collection of paintings. Here you will find Rembrandt's *Portrait of the Artist* (c.1665), Vermeer's *The Guitar Player* (c.1676) and Gainsborough's fine portrait of *Mary, Countess Howe* (c.1764), among other important works by English and Dutch masters.

Open-air lakeside concerts are held in the grounds in June, July and August, with fireworks as a spectacular finale to some performances.

8km (5 miles) NW of Trafalgar Square
Hampstead Heath Information ☎ 020 7332 3322 🕒 Open access 🖐 Free 🚇 Hampstead 🚌 46, 210, C11 🚉 Hampstead Heath

HAMPTON COURT PALACE

▷ 260–261.

HIGHGATE CEMETERY

www.highgate-cemetery.org

During the 19th century everyone who was anyone in London was laid to rest in Highgate Cemetery. When it fell out of use, the main buildings became dilapidated and the landscape choked with brambles and sycamores. In the 1980s volunteers rescued and restored the grounds, clearing the tombs and

graves but leaving enough greenery to create a romantic air.

The cemetery is divided in two by Swain's Lane: the original West Cemetery, Victorian Gothic in style, and the newer East Cemetery, peaceful, leafy and less visited. You can visit the West Cemetery by guided tour only; don't miss the Egyptian Avenue and Terrace Catacombs here. The exceptional collection of Victorian funerary architecture here includes the graves of about 850 famous figures, including German political theorist Karl Marx (1818–83), novelist George Eliot (1819–80) and chemist Michael Faraday (1791–1867, ▷ 181), plus 18 Royal Academicians, six Lord Mayors of London and 48 Fellows of the Royal Society. The surroundings are laid out as a mixed woodland of hornbeam, exotic lime, oak, hazel, sweet chestnut, tulip and field maple.

8km (5 miles) N of Trafalgar Square
✉ Friends of Highgate Cemetery, Swain's Lane N6 6PJ ☎ 020 8340 1834 🕒 Eastern Cemetery: Mar–Oct Mon–Fri 10–5, Sat–Sun 11–5; Nov–Feb Mon–Fri 10–4, Sat–Sun 11–4. Closed during funerals. Western Cemetery: Admission by tour only, advance booking essential, Mar–Nov Mon–Fri 2pm, Sat–Sun 11, 12, 1, 2, 3. No weekday tours Nov–Feb. No children under 8 🖐 All tickets cash only. Eastern Cemetery £3 (no video cameras). Western Cemetery adult £7, child (8–16) £3

(no video cameras or tripods) 🚇 Archway 🚌 143, 210, 271 to Lauderdale House 🚉 Upper Holloway 🏛

HOGARTH'S HOUSE

www.hounslow.info

Today, Hogarth's House stands close to a busy roundabout, but when the 'little country box by the Thames' was used as a summer home by artist and satirical engraver William Hogarth (1697–1764), it was set in open fields. The simple rooms are hung with copies of his work, including the moral tales *Marriage à la Mode* (1745) and *The Rake's Progress* (1735).

10km (6 miles) W of Trafalgar Square
✉ Hogarth Lane, Great West Road, Chiswick W4 2QN ☎ 020 8994 6757 🕒 Reopens summer 2011—phone for times and costs 🚇 Turnham Green 🚌 27, 190, 391

HORNIMAN MUSEUM

www.horniman.ac.uk

A real gem, whose elegant clock tower stands proudly on the hilltop as you approach Forest Hill from Dulwich, this museum is named after Victorian tea merchant Frederick John Horniman, who originally displayed the many items he had collected during his travels in his house before founding the museum in 1901. The main collections, which

Below *The epitome of Georgian elegance, Marble Hill House is surrounded by public parkland*

EXCURSIONS SIGHTS

have grown tenfold in the ensuing century, cover Horniman's favourite subjects of natural history and anthropology. The former still largely consists of old-fashioned cases crammed full of stuffed and mounted creatures, with the noble exception of the small but delightful aquarium, but the displays on human culture and ethnology are first rate and up to date. There is also a massive collection of musical instruments with some interactive features. The magnificent gardens underwent a £2.3 million redevelopment in 2011.

10km (6 miles) S of Trafalgar Square ✉ 100 London Road, Forest Hill SE23 3PQ ☎ 020 8699 1872 🕐 Daily 10.30–5.30 🎟 Free 🚉 Forest Hill 🚌 176, 185, 197 ☕ 🏛

KEATS HOUSE
www.keatshouse.cityoflondon.gov.uk
Poet John Keats (1795–1821) came to live here in 1818, fell in love with the girl next door, Fanny Brawne, and became engaged to her in 1819. In 1820 he left for Italy for health reasons; it was there that he died in 1821. During his brief time in this house he wrote some of his best-loved poems, including *Ode to a Nightingale*; the plum tree under which he wrote it has gone, but a replacement in the garden marks the spot.

The newly refurbished house displays letters, manuscripts and furnishings, synonymous with the period style.

8km (5 miles) NW of Trafalgar Square ✉ Keats Grove, Hampstead NW3 2RR ☎ 020 7435 2062 🕐 May–Oct Tue–Sun 1–5; Nov–Apr Fri–Sun 1–5. Regular guided tours 🎟 Adult £5, under 16s free; entry to garden free 🚇 Belsize Park, Hampstead 🚌 46, C11 🚉 Hampstead Heath

LONDON WETLAND CENTRE
www.wwt.org.uk
The world's first wetland habitat created within a capital city sprawls over 42ha (105 acres) on the site of the former Barnes Elms reservoirs. The area has been landscaped to form different wetland environments, including ponds, reedbeds,

sandbanks and grazing marshes. These support a surprising diversity of wildlife, from frogs and newts, bats, damselflies and dragonflies to ducks, sand martins, kingfishers and even the rare bittern—180 species in all. There's a visitor centre to explore, and an adventure playground for children. Guided tours are free, at 11 and 2.

10km (6 miles) SW of Trafalgar Square ✉ Queen Elizabeth's Walk, Barnes SW13 9WT ☎ 020 8409 4400 🕐 Apr–Oct daily 9.30–6, Nov–Mar 9.30–5 🎟 Adult £10.55, child (4–16) £5.85, under 4s free, family £29.40 🚇 Hammersmith 🚌 283 from Hammersmith Underground to Wetland Centre; 33, 72, 209 to Red Lion pub 🚉 Barnes ☕ 🏛

MARBLE HILL HOUSE
www.english-heritage.org.uk
Built to make the most of the views over the river towards Richmond Hill, Marble Hill House is an exemplary Palladian villa. It was designed as a rural retreat for Henrietta Howard, mistress of the Prince of Wales, the future George II, in 1724; later it was given to another royal consort, Mrs Fitzherbert, who was secretly married to the future George IV in 1785 but had to give way to Caroline of Brunswick.

As with all Palladian villas, the main rooms are on the second floor. The Great Room is a perfect cube, in keeping with the Palladian love of geometry. It is furnished as it would have been in Henrietta Howard's time, when regular visitors included the writers John Gay, Horace Walpole and Alexander Pope, who advised on the layout of the garden, with its groves of statuesque trees and manicured lawns. Today the grounds provide an atmospheric riverside backdrop for a series of outdoor concerts.

16km (10 miles) SW of Trafalgar Square ✉ Richmond Road, Twickenham TW1 2NL ☎ 020 8892 5115 🕐 Apr–Oct Sat 10–2, Sun 10–5. Entry by guided tour only. Tours Sat 10.30, 12; Sun 10.30, 12, 2.15, 3.30 🎟 Adult £5.30, child (5–16) £3.20, under 5s free, family £13.80 🚇 Richmond 🚌 65, 371 🚉 St. Margarets ☕ 🏛

NATIONAL ARCHIVES
www.nationalarchives.gov.uk
All central national government records, from the Norman Conquest in 1066 to the present day, are stored here, as well as all law court records, stacked away on 167km (104 miles) of shelving.

You can order up particular documents, and there is a small, changing display of some of the most significant pieces of the collection, most significantly the Domesday Book, the great land survey of 1086, plus curiosities such as Shakespeare's will, and the last telegram sent from the *Titanic* before it sank.

15km (9 miles) W of Trafalgar Square ✉ Ruskin Avenue, Kew TW9 4DU ☎ 020 8876 3444 🕐 Archive Tue, Thu 9–7, Wed, Fri–Sat 9–5; museum Tue–Sat 9–5 🎟 Free 🚉 Kew Gardens 🚌 65, 237, 267, 391, R68 🚉 Kew Bridge ⛴ Kew Pier 🍴 🏛

OSTERLEY PARK
www.nationaltrust.org.uk
One of London's largest surviving estate parks, with an elegant neoclassical villa at its heart, Osterley feels a thousand miles from the bustle of central London. The original Elizabethan villa was built by Thomas Gresham in 1576 and remodelled by Robert Adam in the late 18th century for Sir Francis Child, head of Child's Bank. Don't miss the Eating Room, with its elaborately decorated plaster ceiling, statues and paintings, or the Gobelin tapestries in the Tapestry Room. There is a fascinating glimpse into life below stairs in the servants' quarters. Audiovisual handsets help to bring it all to life.

The house is surrounded by pleasure gardens, ornamental lakes and parkland.

19km (12 miles) W of Trafalgar Square ✉ Jersey Road, Isleworth TW7 4RB ☎ 020 8232 5050 🕐 House and gardens: Apr–Oct Wed–Sun 12–4.30; Nov–Mar Sat–Sun 12–3.30. Park daily 8–7.30 🎟 House and gardens: adult £8.80, child (5–16) £4.40, under 5s free, family £22. Garden only: adult £5, child £1.95 🚇 Osterley 🚌 H28, H91 🚉 Isleworth ☕ 🏛

INFORMATION

www.hrp.org.uk

21km (13 miles) SW of Trafalgar Square

✉ East Molesey, Surrey KT8 9AU

☎ 0844 482 7777; bookings: 0844 482 7799 ⊙ Palace, maze Apr–Oct daily 10–6; Nov–Apr daily 10–4.30. Gardens close 1–2 hours earlier 🎟 Adult £15.95, child (5–15) £8, under 5s free, family £38. Maze only: adult £3.85, child £2.75, family £10 🚌 111, 216, 411, 461, 513, R68 🚇 Hampton Court 🚢 Summer services from Westminster Pier 🎧 Tours, audioguides, exhibitions 📖 £4.95 in English, French, Italian, Japanese, Spanish ☕ Privy Kitchen Coffee Shop; Tiltyard café, palace gardens 🛍 Barrack Block Shop in former palace barracks; Garden Shop; Henry Shop, between Base Court and Clock Court; Tudor Kitchens Shop, next to Tudor Wine Cellar

INTRODUCTION

Hampton Court is one of the oldest and most interesting of London's royal palaces, with beautiful riverside gardens.

Cardinal Thomas Wolsey, Archbishop of York and chancellor to Henry VIII, built Hampton Court in 1514 as a country residence, almost completely obliterating all traces of the previous country manor belonging to the Knights Hospitallers of St. John of Jerusalem, which dated from the 13th century. In 1528 he made an unsuccessful bid to retain the king's favour by handing over his new home. Henry spent around £62,000 extending it, turning it into a royal palace with features such as a huge communal dining room, a chapel, bowling alleys, tennis courts and a hunting park. Apart from a few minor alterations by Elizabeth I and later the Stuarts, the layout remained unchanged until the 1690s, when William and Mary employed Sir Christopher Wren to make further modifications and additions. The main alterations were completely new apartments for both the king and the queen, costing a startling £113,000. The result was the striking mix of Tudor and baroque styles still in evidence today.

WHAT TO SEE
AROUND THE PALACE

You approach the palace through the Trophy Gates, surrounded by all manner of turrets and castellations, with the Tudor Great Gatehouse ahead in Base Court, now only half the size it was during Cardinal Wolsey's day. Terracotta roundels, originally painted and gilded, depict Roman emperors in the two side turrets.

Carved on the opposite gateway are the intertwined initials 'H' and 'A'—Henry and Anne. Having declared his marriage to Catherine of Aragon invalid, Henry married Anne Boleyn in 1533, but the marriage lasted only four years, and Anne was beheaded at the Tower (▷ 112–117). Ahead, to the right, an exhibition tells the story of Henry as a young man.

Clock Court comes next, named after the huge astronomical clock on the gateway's inner side. This was made in 1540 for Henry VIII and was used to calculate the high tide at London Bridge, essential for working out when to move the king's entourage downstream.

INSIDE THE PALACE

On the left of Clock Court is Henry VIII's Great Hall, with its hammerbeam roof, oriel window, minstrels' gallery and splendid tapestries depicting the story of Abraham. It was constructed during 1534 in great haste at the king's bidding, the workers toiling away by candlelight. Nearby, in the Tudor kitchens, more than 200 staff cooked for 600 people at a time. Opposite, through Wren's elegant colonnade, you enter Henry VIII's State Apartments (1689–94), decorated with paintings, furnishings and tapestries. Jean Tijou (fl. 1689–c. 1711), a French blacksmith, made the ironwork balustrades of the staircases, Grinling Gibbons (1648–1721) carved the woodwork and Antonio Verrio (c. 1639–1707) painted many of the ceilings. Two of the most interesting rooms in this section of the palace are the Great Watching Chamber, with its fine ceiling of gilded oak, and the Haunted Gallery, so named as it is supposedly the home of the spirit of Henry's fifth wife, executed Catherine Howard. From here it is a few steps to the beautiful Chapel Royal, where services, open to the public, are still held regularly.

Accessed by the grand King's Staircase, are William III's apartments, which include the Guard Chamber, complete with 3,000 pieces of armoury, the Privy Chamber with its imposing throne, and the Great Bedchamber, boasting a throne of a different sort—the king's velvet toilet. The smaller Queen's Apartments look over Wren's Fountain Court, and the public rooms look out on to avenues, canals and fountains. Inside, the opulent Queen's Drawing Room contains an impressive array of paintings, including a rather self-aggrandizing ceiling portrait of Queen Anne as Justice. The Georgian Rooms include the Cumberland Suite, inhabited by George II before he acceded to the throne, the Cartoon Gallery, designed by Wren to accommodate the Raphael Cartoons, now in the Victoria & Albert Museum (▷ 224–228), and the Queen's Private Chapel. Finally, the four early Tudor Wolsey Rooms serve as reminders of the cardinal's original palace, although they now display works from the monarchy's huge Royal Collection.

THE GARDENS

Today's formal landscaping of avenues and lakes originated in William and Mary's time. To the south, the Privy Garden was for the use of the royal family and was separated from the river by Tijou's wrought-iron screen. Nearby are Henry VIII's Pond Garden and an Elizabethan knot garden of aromatic herbs. The Great Vine, planted in 1768 by Capability Brown, still produces black Hamburg grapes.

North of the palace are the Rose Gardens, formerly the tiltyards, where jousting took place, and the Wilderness, 4ha (10 acres) of natural woodland. The Maze, laid out in the 1690s, is in the top corner and covers 60sq m (645sq ft). The most famous labyrinth in the world is for many people the best-known feature of Hampton Court and the principal reason for coming here. Its original hornbeam hedges were replaced by yew as visitor numbers grew exponentially in the 1960s, as yew withstands wear and tear better. Although not the most elaborate maze in the world, it is still deceptively tricky and many visitors find themselves spending more time inside than they had planned. In July the grounds and gardens are taken over by the world's largest annual flower show. The spectacle lasts for one weekend only, so check ahead for dates.

TIPS
» Take a free introductory tour from one of the guides.
» Buy a combined train and palace entry ticket—it gives 10 per cent off admission.
» Tudor cookery demonstrations take place in the Royal Court kitchens at weekends—check the website for dates and details.

Opposite *The mellow red brick of Hampton Court seems to glow in the sun*
Below *The unicorn statue outside faces his lion counterpart*

Above *Classical Roman statues decorate the rooms of 16th-century Syon House*
Opposite *The Thames Barrier was built to protect London against flooding*

OXFORD
▷ 264–265.

RICHMOND PARK
www.royalparks.gov.uk
Originally enclosed as a hunting
ground by Charles I in 1637,
Richmond Park is, at 1,011ha (2,500
acres), London's largest open
space. Its diverse landscape takes in
grassland, areas of bog and bracken,
wetland, woodland and ancient
parkland trees, and herds of fallow
(350) and red (300) deer still graze
here—but in safety, nowadays. In
spring, when camellias, magnolias,
azaleas and rhododendrons come
into flower, the Isabella Plantation is a
treat to visit.
15km (9 miles) W of Trafalgar Square
✉ Park Office, Holly Lodge, Richmond Park,
Richmond, Surrey TW10 5HS ☎ 020 8948
3209 ⓘ Open access during daylight hours
✋ Free 🚆 Richmond, then bus 371 or 65
to Lass of Richmond Hill stop 🚌 72 85, 371,
K3 🚇 Richmond, then bus 371 or 65 to Lass
of Richmond Hill stop 🚻 🍴

THE RIVER THAMES
▷ 266–267.

ROYAL BOTANIC
GARDENS, KEW
▷ 268–269.

STRAWBERRY HILL
www.strawberryhillhouse.org.uk
Historian and politician Horace
Walpole (1717–97) built a charming
fantasy of a villa which would inspire
the first ever gothic novel: *The Castle
of Otranto*. A tourist attraction when
it was first built, it is now nearing the
end of its £9-million refurbishment,
and has opened its doors once more
to visitors, who can admire the frothy
confection of plaster, papier mâché
and woodwork, and glow in the
reflected colours of the magnificent
stained glass. Restoration of the
gardens includes the re-creation of a
remarkable shell-backed bench.
19km (12 miles) W of Trafalgar Square
✉ 268 Waldegrave Road, Twickenham,
TW1 4ST ☎ 020 8744 3124 ⓘ Apr–Nov
Mon–Wed 2–4.20, Sat–Sun 12–4.20
✋ Adult £8, child (5–15) £5, family £20.
Entry by timed ticket, advance booking
recommended 🚆 Richmond, then 33 bus
🚌 33, R68 🚇 Strawberry Hill 🚻 🏧

SYON HOUSE AND PARK
www.syonpark.co.uk
Outside, this historic seat of the
Dukes of Northumberland looks
forbidding, but the battlemented
mid-16th-century building contains
some of the most elegantly
decorated rooms in England. Robert

Adam (1728–92) remodelled the
interior between 1761 and 1768
using marble, gilded statues and
plasterwork.
   Among the duke's private
rooms, now on view, are the Green
Drawing Room with its splendid
Adam fireplace, rescued from
Northumberland House in the
Strand when it was demolished in
1874. Upstairs is the suite of rooms
furnished for the young Princess
Victoria, to whom the 3rd Duchess of
Northumberland was governess.
   Capability Brown landscaped the
grounds of Syon House between
1767 and 1773 by creating an idyllic
version of the countryside, with lakes,
lawns and fine specimen trees. The
centrepiece, linking lake and garden,
is the Great Conservatory, built
between 1820 and 1827 by Charles
Fowler, the architect of Covent
Garden market (▷ 142–143). Several
different planting environments are
housed in the Conservatory, ranging
from damp fernery to the hot, dry
cactus beds.
   The rose garden was replanted in
1995 with more than 8,000 roses.
Farther off, a stroll around the lakes
takes in many moisture-loving plants,
flowering shrubs and unusual trees.
   In the London Tropical Forest
(separate admission charge, open
daily 10–5.30, www.tropicalforest.
co.uk, tel 020 8847 4730), rescued
exotic animals, including monkeys,
lemurs, snakes, lizards, baby
crocodiles and more, are kept in near-
natural habitats. Within the grounds
there is also a giant indoor adventure
playground, a garden centre and a
trout fishery.
15km (9 miles) W of Trafalgar Square
✉ Syon Park, Brentford, Middlesex TW8
8JF ☎ 020 8560 0881 ⓘ House: Mid-Mar
to Oct Wed–Thu, Sun 11–5; gardens mid-
Mar to Oct daily 10.30–5; Nov to mid-Mar
Sat–Sun 10–4; miniature steam railway open
late Jun–late Aug Sun, and Apr–Aug bank
hol weekends ✋ House, gardens and Great
Conservatory: adult £10, under 16s £4, family
£22; gardens and Great Conservatory: adult
£5, child £2.50, family £11 🚇 Gunnersbury,
then bus 🚌 237, 267, E2, E8 🚇 Kew
Bridge or Gunnersbury, then bus 🚻 🏧

THAMES BARRIER

www.environment-agency.gov.uk

In 1953, 300 people died when the Thames broke its banks and flooded London. Since then the river has risen by another 50cm (20in)—and it will continue to rise by about 1m (3ft) every hundred years. The Thames Barrier was opened in 1984 to prevent further flooding, and its spectacular stainless steel gates, 61m (200ft) wide, are now a familiar landmark. Electrically powered hydraulic power packs, housed immediately below the stainless steel roofs, rotate the gates, which are regularly closed and reopened for experiments and inspection. Exhibits explain river tides, anti-pollution strategies and the return of river wildlife. In the information office there's a working model of the barrier and a re-creation of the great Victorian stench.

16km (10 miles) E of Trafalgar Square ✉ 1 Unity Way SE18 5NJ ☎ 020 8305 4188 🕐 Thu–Sun 10.30–5 💷 Adult £3.50, under 16s £2 🚊 Greenwich 🚌 177, 180 🚆 Charlton Barrier Pier 🅿 📷

WILLIAM MORRIS GALLERY

www.walthamforest.gov.uk

This is the only public museum devoted to the designer, craftsman, writer and socialist William Morris (1834–96). Along with his contemporaries in the Arts and Crafts movement, he reintroduced craftsmanship into everyday domestic objects as a reaction against industrialization. Their work

and Morris's life and influence are illustrated with displays of their fabrics, rugs, carpets, wallpapers, furniture, stained glass and painted tiles. There are also examples of Arts and Crafts furniture, textiles, ceramics and glass from the 1880s to the 1920s. The gallery is closed for major refurbishment until 2012.

15km (9 miles) NE of Trafalgar Square ✉ Lloyd Park, Forest Road, E17 4PP ☎ 020 8496 4390 🕐 Check ahead for current times 💷 Free 🚊 Walthamstow Central 🚌 34, 97, 123, 215, 275, 357 🚆 Walthamstow Central 📷

WIMBLEDON COMMON

www.wpcc.org.uk

Together with Putney Lower Common, this slice of greenery covers about 461ha (1,140 acres). Among the areas of woodland, scrubland, heathland and recreation parks are a nature trail, an 18-hole golf course, cricket pitches, 26km (16 miles) of bridle paths, several football and rugby pitches and athletics facilities.

A restored 1817 windmill now houses a museum (Apr–Oct Sat 2–5, Sun 11–5) with models, flour-grinding machinery and a collection of woodworking tools.

East of the common, on Church Road, is the All England Lawn Tennis Club, venue for the annual world championships (▷ 294–295). The excellent Tennis Museum, opened in 2006, provides a chronicle of the game of tennis from its origins in the 1860s to the present day (daily 10–5).

In the cinema you can see footage of championship matches.

13km (8 miles) SW of Trafalgar Square ✉ The Ranger's Office, Windmill Road, Wimbledon Common SW19 5NR ☎ 020 8788 7655 🕐 Open access 💷 Free 🚆 Tours (charge) tel 020 8946 6131; book in advance 🚊 Putney Bridge, Southfields, Wimbledon 🚌 93 🚆 Wimbledon 📷

WINDSOR AND ETON

▷ 270–271.

WORLD RUGBY MUSEUM

www.rfu.com

Rugby Union fans will love this collection of memorabilia dating back to the 1800s. You can see the Calcutta Cup, the oldest rugby jersey in existence and use the interactive touch-screen computers to learn about the history of the game. Or test your strength on the scrum machine, relive the greatest-ever tries, and witness the highs and lows of the world's most prestigious competitions in the audiovisual theatre. The museum may be closed during events.

18km (11 miles) SW of Trafalgar Square ✉ Twickenham and Twickenham Stadium Tours, Rugby Road, Twickenham TW1 1DZ ☎ 0871 222 2120 🕐 Tue–Sat 10–5, Sun 11–5. Tours Tue–Sat 10.30, 12, 1.30, 3, Sun 1, 3 💷 Museum and stadium tour: adult £14, child (5–16) £8, family £40; museum only (match day ticket-holders only): £6 🚊 Richmond, then R68 or 33 to Twickenham centre; Hounslow East, then 281 🚌 33, 110, 267, 281, 290, 490, H22, R68, R70 🚆 Twickenham

INFORMATION

Tourist information office

www.visitoxfordandoxfordshire.org

✉ 15–16 Broad Street, Oxford OX1 3AS

☎ 01865 252200

HOW TO GET THERE

Oxford is 92km (57 miles) northwest of London

🚉 From Paddington (1 hour)

🚌 Victoria Coach Station: National Express service OXX90 (1 hour 40 min)

🚗 M4 west, then M40 to junction 7 (1 hour 15 min)

Above *The Radcliffe Camera, part of the Bodleian Library, with Brasenose College on the left and All Souls on the right*

INTRODUCTION

Home of one of the world's oldest universities, Oxford is a vibrant city of ancient buildings and riverside walks, with excellent shopping.

Everywhere in this city of spires and greenery there's a sense of the long tradition of learning. There's been a university here since the arrival in 1167 of a number of English scholars expelled from the Sorbonne in Paris after a dispute between the English and French kings.

Every student is attached to one of the 39 individual colleges. They are all different in character but most have their buildings, including a chapel and a high-ceilinged dining hall, set around quadrangles (quads). Most of the central colleges have medieval origins and display an interesting mixture of architectural styles from Renaissance to Victorian.

Oxford is not huge, but its layout can be confusing. High Street, which students call the High, runs from Carfax Tower east to Magdalen Bridge over the River Cherwell, dividing the city into north and south. To get your bearings, climb the towers of St. Michael's Church, in Cornmarket Street, the city's oldest building; the University Church of St. Mary the Virgin, High Street, dating from 1280 and serving the university; or the Carfax Tower, a remnant of the 14th-century St. Martin's Church, at the busy crossroads known as Carfax.

WHAT TO SEE

COLLEGES

Christ Church, St. Aldate's, founded in 1525, is the largest and most visited college and has the biggest quadrangle. Its chapel is Christ Church Cathedral, which predates the college and is England's smallest cathedral. Christ Church Picture Gallery includes works by Dürer and Michelangelo.

To the south and east spreads the bucolic Christ Church Meadow (entrances at St. Aldate's, Rose Lane and Merton Street), still grazed by cattle—a pocket of green countryside in the heart of the city. You can walk from the meadow or the High into the Oxford Botanic Garden (daily), the oldest botanic gardens in Britain, founded in 1621 and filled with plants from around the world.

Magdalen College (pronounced 'maudlin') is one of the richest and most spacious colleges, founded in 1458 and with its own deer park. Also worth a visit are Merton College, its peaceful gardens partly enclosed by the old city wall; New College, famous for its handsome hall, cloister and gardens; the Queen's College, with buildings by Sir Christopher Wren (1632–1723) and Nicholas Hawksmoor (1661–1736); and, farther out in Parks Road, Keble College, a relative newcomer whose red-brick buildings are a Victorian tour de force.

UNIVERSITY BUILDINGS

Between Broad Street and High Street is a trio of eye-catching university edifices. The Sheldonian Theatre (built between 1664 and 1669), the first major architectural work by Sir Christopher Wren, assumes the shape of a Roman theatre and hosts university functions and concerts. Nearby are several buildings housing the Bodleian Library, the world's oldest library, opened in the 14th century and now housing over 6 million books (tours Mon–Sat). The circular, domed Radcliffe Camera, completed in 1749, serves as one of the library's reading rooms.

MUSEUMS

The pick of the museums is the Ashmolean in Beaumont Street (Tue–Sun), Britain's oldest public museum, opened in 1683, and undergoing refurbishment. It contains Oxford University's priceless collections from the time of early man to 20th-century paintings. The cavernous and old-fashioned Pitt Rivers Museum in Parks Road (daily) has a celebrated anthropology collection of more than 250,000 objects, among them masks and shrunken heads. Next door is the University Museum of Natural History (daily), in a splendid neo-Gothic building.

For a succinct survey of the city from prehistoric times to the present, from mammoths to Morris Minor motor cars, visit the Museum of Oxford, St. Aldate's (Tue–Thu, Sat).

TIPS

» To get the real atmosphere, visit in term time.

» Use the park-and-ride on the outer ring road and take a bus into the heart of the city. The centre is pedestrianized and parking is expensive.

» Feel free to wander into many of the university and college buildings. Some charge for admission, and most have a notice indicating which areas are open and at what times.

» For an overview, join a guided walking tour of the city and colleges at the tourist information centre.

» Hire a punt or rowing boat from the Cherwell Boathouse in Bardwell Road for a classic boating trip.

WHERE TO EAT
BRASSERIE BLANC

www.brasserieblanc.com
Authentic provincial French cuisine from monkfish, scallop and shellfish ragout to confit of rabbit leg.

✉ 71–72 Walton Street, Oxford OX2 6AG
☎ 01865 510700 ⊙ Mon–Fri 12–2.45, 5.30–10, Sat 12–10.30, Sun 12–9
✋ L £12.95, D £32, Wine £14.95

QUOD BRASSERIE AND BAR

www.quod.co.uk
A place that's buzzing all day long. Its Italian brasserie menu includes pizzas and pastas as well as locally sourced meat, and heavenly desserts.

✉ Old Bank Hotel, 92–94 High Street, Oxford OX1 4BN ☎ 01865 202505
⊙ Mon–Sat 7am–11pm, Sun 7am– 10.30pm ✋ L £11.95, D £31, Wine £12

OXFORD

HOW TO GET THERE
Embankment Pier
🚇 Circle, District, Bakerloo or Northern line to Embankment 🚌 9, 11, 12, 24
Westminster Pier
🚇 Circle, District or Jubilee line to Westminster 🚌 11, 12, 24, 453

INTRODUCTION

A cruise along the Thames is a leisurely way to see the city. It gives a new perspective to London's development and history, which is inextricably linked with this long and majestic river.

As the Thames flows west to east into Greater London, on the last stages of its 346km (215-mile) journey to the sea, it loops around Hampton Court Park and the 16th-century palace of Hampton Court itself (▷ 260–261), a reminder of the Tudor era. It's a fitting introduction to the river's course through the capital and recalls a period when the Thames was a place of regal processions, magnificent mansions and palaces, and thriving trade.

However, the river's significance in the commercial and royal life of the nation goes back much further—probably to the Bronze Age and earlier—and, having turned northwards, the river flows past Kingston upon Thames, the site of many Saxon coronations.

WHAT TO SEE
TEDDINGTON TO KEW

Navigating the river and its ebb and flow was a problem for centuries, alleviated with the building of locks and weirs such as those at Teddington, a little farther north at the point between the non-tidal and tidal sections of the river.

During the 17th and 18th centuries the lush banks of this stretch of the river became a fashionable setting for aristocratic homes and gardens. You pass Ham House, Marble Hill House (▷ 259) and Syon House (▷ 262) as the river makes its way past the affluent town of Richmond and up past Kew Gardens (▷ 268–269) to the Hanoverian Kew Palace.

RIVERBOATS

Sailing times vary according to seasons, tides and conditions.

Thames Clippers

www.thamesclippers.com

High-speed catamarans offer a frequent daily hop-on, hop-off service between Woolwich (east) and Millbank (west), stopping at QEII (for the O2 Arena), Greenwich, Masthouse, Greenland, Canary Wharf, Tower, London Bridge, Bankside, Blackfriars, Embankment and Waterloo. Also the Tate-to-Tate service, every 40 min, and the O2 Express service (evenings only).

☎ 0870 781 5049

Crown River Circular Cruise

www.crownriver.com

Hop-on, hop-off circular service between Westminster and St. Katharine's Pier, calling in at Festival, Bankside and London Bridge City piers every hour, with commentary.

☎ 020 7936 2033

Thames River Services

www.thamesriverservices.co.uk

Sightseeing boats operate between Westminster and Greenwich, with some extensions to the Thames Barrier. Tours run approximately every 40 min, year-round.

☎ 020 7930 4097

Thames River Boats

www.wpsa.co.uk

Boats run up-river from Westminster to Kew, Richmond and Hampton Court, Apr–Oct. Tides affect travel times, so allow plenty of time. The route includes two locks.

☎ 020 7930 2062

KEW TO BATTERSEA

From here the Thames winds through Chiswick, with its lovely Georgian riverside houses, and past Barnes, now home of the London Wetland Centre (▷ 259), passing under the elaborate Victorian suspension bridge at Hammersmith. Fulham Palace (Museum/Gallery Sat–Wed 1–4; gardens daily dawn–dusk), formerly the private residence of the Bishops of London, is on the approach to the last southern dip of the river—where the Oxford and Cambridge Boat Race (▷ 294) starts at Putney—before it flows under Battersea Bridge and between the Chelsea Embankment and Battersea Park (▷ 211).

BATTERSEA TO BANKSIDE

This marks the point where the river enters central London and becomes a working highway, until recently lined with shipping, docks and warehouses. Today this is tourist London proper: The Thames flows between Lambeth Palace (▷ 82) and the Houses of Parliament (▷ 179–180) and past the London Eye (▷ 75) and the Southbank complex of concert, theatre and film venues (▷ 77), making a northern loop past the Victoria Embankment (▷ 147) and towards the Millennium Bridge (▷ 77), linking St. Paul's Cathedral (▷ 104–109) and Tate Modern (▷ 80–81).

BANKSIDE TO THE THAMES BARRIER

Beyond Shakespeare's Globe (▷ 78) and Southwark Cathedral (▷ 79) the river reaches London Bridge, the modern crossing that replaced the 1831 version, itself replacing its arched medieval predecessor, which was crammed with houses and shops. The next crossing is Tower Bridge (▷ 111), designed to allow tall ships passage between the city and the sea. Guarding the north bank is the Tower of London (▷ 112–117), William the Conqueror's fort placed strategically to protect access to the Port of London.

From this point the river passes through an area once dominated by shipping docks and warehouses, and now extensively redeveloped as smart office and residential blocks.

Seafaring is the theme from Docklands onwards, as the Thames reaches Greenwich (▷ 256–257) before continuing its course to the Thames Barrier (▷ 263) at Woolwich Reach and beyond the Greater London boundaries towards Gravesend and the sea.

Opposite *Cruise boat at Westminster Pier*
Above *Cruise boat passing under the Millennium Bridge*

INFORMATION

www.kew.org

13km (8 miles) W of Trafalgar Square

✉ Kew, Richmond, Surrey TW9 3AB

☎ 020 8332 5655 🕓 Apr–Aug Mon–Fri 9.30–6.30, Sat–Sun 9.30–7.30; Sep–Oct daily 9.30–6; Nov–Feb daily 9.30–4.15; Mar daily 9.30–5.30 💷 Adult £13.90, under 17s free 🚇 Kew Gardens 🚌 65, 391 🚉 Kew Bridge 📖 £4.95, in English only 📷 Victorian Terrace Café, White Peaks café 🍴 The Orangery; The Pavilion (mid-Feb to Oct only) 🎁 At Victoria Gate and White Peaks

INTRODUCTION

Kew has a royal palace, magnificent glasshouses, mature trees and—above all—120ha (300 acres) of spectacular gardens.

The gardens were created by combining two royal estates in 1772. Under the patronage of George III they developed into one of the world's foremost centres of horticultural research, largely thanks to botanist Sir Joseph Banks (▷ 220), who became the King's adviser in 1773 after his voyage around the world with Captain Cook. The early botanic garden occupied just a small area; the rest was landscaped by Capability Brown (his lake and Rhododendron Dell remain) and dotted with fanciful buildings to amuse courtly visitors.

WHAT TO SEE

The oldest building is the 10-storey pagoda, built in 1761–62 to the designs of William Chambers. Kew began to change after 1841, when the gardens were handed over to the State, and several greenhouses were added. The Palm House, designed by Decimus Burton, opened in 1848. It was thoroughly refurbished in 1985. Apart from a bewildering variety of palms and other tropical species, its basement hides the fascinating Marine Display, which includes examples of coral reefs, mangrove swamps, rocky shores and salty marshes.

Next was the Temperate House, also by Decimus Burton, begun in 1859. On completion, 40 years later, it was the world's largest greenhouse. From its

Above *The Temperate House*

elevated gallery you get a good view of the plants, including the Chilean wine palm, planted in 1846 and now claimed to be the largest greenhouse plant in existence.

The Princess of Wales Conservatory opened in 1987. Much of it is below ground level (for insulation) and is lit by a series of low, tentlike glass roofs. You pass through different climate zones, from arid desert at one end to orchid-filled tropics at the other.

British native wild flowers are the theme at Queen Charlotte's Cottage and Gardens on the southwestern fringes of the site, named after George III's queen. This is now a woodland nature reserve, as requested by Queen Victoria. Also tucked in a secluded corner of the gardens is the Rhododendron Dell, one of the few features left pretty much as it was in Capability Brown's original design; the other being the lake. The dell contains an amazing 700 varieties of the colourful shrub and is at its best in May, though flowering spans most of the year from November to August.

Apart from these famous attractions, there are plenty more horticultural delights that can easily stretch your visit into a full day. The Bamboo Garden has 120 specimens from all over the world, some up to 3m (10ft) high, and is a good year-round exhibit. The Aquatic Garden, opened in 1909, comprises a set of tanks filled with water lilies, rushes and sedges; it is at its best when the plants bloom in summer. The beautifully landscaped Rock Garden dates from 1882 and was redesigned in modern times to incorporate a bog garden and cascade. It is arranged into six geographical areas, showcasing mainly Alpine, Mediterranean and woodland plants, so there will always be something in flower. Finally, especially constructed around the 18th-century Ice House for grey days, the Winter Garden contains a collage of hardy specimens such as wintersweet, viburnum, witch hazel, cornelian cherry and aconite, whose various hues stand out against the evergreen backdrop.

For children (age 3–9) there's the excellent indoor Climbers and Creepers play area, with various giant plants to explore, and a glass-walled apiary. Treehouse Towers is an adventure playground just outside.

TIPS
» Take the Kew Explorer, a hop-on-hop-off mini land train that tours all the key sites in 40 minutes. Tickets are £4, child (under 17) £2, available on board. The Royal Botanical Gardens were given UNESCO World Heritage Site status in July 2003. Their magnificent glasshouses have been renovated and updated to make them more accessible to today's visitors.
» Picnic concerts of swing music take place in July, with headline acts such as Jools Holland and Brian Ferry.

Left *Giant lily pads up to 2m (6.5ft) across are grown annually from seed*
Below *The Palm House*

EXCURSIONS | SIGHTS

INFORMATION

Tourist information office

www.windsor.gov.uk

✉ The Old Booking Hall, Windsor Royal Shopping, Thames Street, Windsor SL4 1PJ ☎ 01753 743900

HOW TO GET THERE

Windsor is 40km (25 miles) west of central London

🚇 District Line to Richmond (30 minutes from Embankment), then South West Trains to Windsor and Eton Riverside station

🚆 55 min from Waterloo to Windsor and Eton Riverside station or 25 min from Paddington to Slough, then 10 min from Slough to Windsor (▷ 62)

🚌 Daily Green Line services from Victoria Coach Station, London: 1 hour 10 min

🚗 M4 to junction 6 or M3 to junction 3, then A322/A332 (30 min)

Above Windsor Castle's Henry VIII Gate
Opposite An imposing statue of Queen Victoria stands in front of the castle

INTRODUCTION

Less than an hour from London are two neighbouring towns that offer a full day out: Windsor, with the largest castle in Europe, and Eton, with one of Britain's most famous public schools.

WHAT TO SEE
WINDSOR CASTLE

Windsor Castle is an unforgettable sight, towering above the town on a chalk cliff. It's the largest inhabited castle in the world and one of the principal residences of the sovereigns of England since the 12th century. Much of its present appearance dates from the 19th century, but the stone castle was built for Henry II in 1165, replacing William the Conqueror's original 11th-century fort.

There are several buildings to visit within the castle complex. St. George's Chapel is a masterpiece of Perpendicular Gothic architecture, begun in 1475 by Edward IV and completed in 1511. Queen Elizabeth the Queen Mother is buried here beside her husband, King George VI, and her daughter Princess Margaret. The monument in the northwest chapel to Princess Charlotte, who died in childbirth in 1817, shows her ascending to heaven with an angel carrying her stillborn child. The chapel's fan-vaulted ceiling is particularly beautiful, as are the elaborate 15th-century choir stalls covered in vignettes of animals, jesters, the Dance of Death and biblical stories, and surmounted by banners of the 26 Knights of the Garter, the highest order of knighthood, whose investiture has taken place here since 1348. It was here that the Queen's youngest child, Edward, married Sophie Rhys-Jones in 1999, and the service of blessing for Prince Charles and Camilla Parker-Bowles was held in April 2005 after their wedding in the town's Guildhall.

The baroque State Apartments, restored after a devastating fire in 1992, are hung with works from the Royal Collection, one of the world's finest private art collections. Also on display is Queen Mary's Dolls' House, designed by Sir

Edwin Lutyens in 1924. The furnishings are designed at one-twelfth life-size, the plumbing and lighting really work, and eminent writers and artists contributed handwritten books and miniature paintings to the library.

Don't miss the Changing of the Guard at Windsor Castle: Apr–Jul Mon–Sat 11am weather permitting; Aug–end Mar alternate days 11am (not Sun).

WINDSOR TOWN

After visiting the castle, it's worth exploring Windsor's many shops and public buildings. The Guildhall on the High Street was completed in 1689 by Sir Christopher Wren. Its Tuscan columns, on the ground floor, don't quite touch the ceiling; apparently the town council insisted on having them, but Wren left the gap at the top to make the point that they were structurally superfluous. Farther up the High Street pass the 19th-century parish church of St. John the Baptist and continue up Park Street to the Long Walk, a 5km-long (3-mile) avenue of trees in Windsor Great Park. Savill Garden (daily), 14ha (35 acres) of woodland within the park, is lovely in spring when the azaleas and camellias are in bloom.

ETON

Across the river from Windsor is Eton, its appealing main street fronted by Britain's best-known public school. Eton College was founded by Henry VI in 1440 for 70 King's Scholars, also known as Collegers, who lived in the college and were educated free, and a small number of 'Oppidans', who lived in the town of Eton and paid for their education.

Today Eton takes about 1,280 boys between the ages of 13 and 18, all of whom are boarders. You can see the school yard, the college chapel, the cloisters and the Museum of Eton Life (tel 01753 671177 for opening times) throughout the summer season. Princes William and Harry both went to Eton.

TIPS
» Ask your hotel about group tours to Windsor; many companies offer them daily and will pick you up at your hotel.
» You can take a horse-drawn carriage tour around Windsor, or a sightseeing bus, or a variety of walking tours are available — contact the tourist office for details.
» Call ahead before leaving London. Windsor Castle's State Apartments and Chapel sometimes close at short notice. St. George's Chapel is open only to worshippers on Sundays.

WHERE TO EAT
BROWNS
www.browns-restaurants.co.uk
Part of a small popular chain of brasseries, Browns offers tasty treats such as tempura-battered cod and chips, and steak, mushroom and Guinness pie.
✉ The Promenade, Barry Avenue, Windsor SL4 1QX ☎ 01753 831976
🕐 Mon–Sat 12–11, Sun 12–10.30
🖐 L £11.95, D £32, Wine £13.95

STROK'S AT SIR CHRISTOPHER WREN'S HOUSE
www.sirchristopherwren.co.uk
Former home of the great architect, this art deco restaurant has views of the Thames. Old favourites with a modern twist include baked cod on feta cheese and chive mashed potatoes.
✉ Thames Street, Windsor SL4 1PX
☎ 01753 442422 🕐 Daily 12.30–2.30, 6.30–10 🖐 L £22.50, D £44, Wine £22.50

PLACE TO VISIT
WINDSOR CASTLE
✉ Windsor SL4 1NJ ☎ 020 7766 7304
🕐 Mar–Oct daily 9.45–5.15, Nov–Feb 9.45–4.15 🖐 Adult £16.50, child (under 17) £9.90, under 5s free, family £43.50

There are many organized tours in and around London and beyond. Choices range from escorted walking tours around the streets of the city to tailor-made tours in luxury chauffeur-driven limousines. River cruises, evening tours and specialist interest tours can all be found. Most tours are available in different languages and car or coach tours will pick you up from and take you back to your hotel.

For more organized tour options, see the Around Town section of the magazine *Time Out* or contact any tourist information office.

BICYCLE TOURS

See Cycling in London, ▷ 60.

BUS TOURS

BIG BUS COMPANY

www.bigbustours.com

Tours (lasting about two hours) of the main central London sights are in open-top buses with a live commentary. Board on any signed stop on three routes: Green Park–St. James's Palace; Victoria Station–London Hilton; Marble Arch–Kensington Palace.

✉ 48 Buckingham Palace Road SW1W 0RN ☎ 020 7233 9533 ✋ Adult £26, child (5–15) £10, under 5s free, family £62. Tickets valid for 48 hours and interchangeable from route to route

THE ORIGINAL TOUR

www.theoriginaltour.com

Open-top buses are run by a company founded during the Festival of Britain in 1951. The commentary is in several languages. Board at any signed stop (there are more than 90 of them to choose from).

✉ 17–19 Cockspur Street, Trafalgar Square SW1Y 5BL ☎ 020 8877 2120 ✋ Adult £25, child (5–15) £12, under 5s free, family £80

CANAL TRIPS

JASON'S TRIP

www.jasons.co.uk

Ninety-minute trips are operated in beautifully painted canal boats with a live commentary. They start from Little Venice, past Regent's Park (▷ 218) and London Zoo (▷ 219), to Camden Lock.

✉ Jason's Wharf, Blomfield Road W9 2PD ☎ 020 7286 3428 🕙 Apr–Nov daily 12.30, 2.30 ✋ Adult from £7.50, child (4–14) £6.50, under 4s free 🚇 Warwick Avenue 🚌 6, 46, 187

LONDON WATERBUS COMPANY

www.londonwaterbus.com

These boats travel the same route as Jason's Trip (see below), but without the live commentary. They also go to London Zoo.

✉ West Yard, Camden Lock NW1 8AF ☎ 020 7482 2660 🕙 Apr–Sep daily, every hour 10–5; Nov–Mar 11–4 ✋ Adult £9.70–£19.50, child (3–15) £7.70–£16.50, under 3s free 🚇 Camden Town/Chalk Farm, Warwick Avenue 🚌 6, 46, 187

COACH TOURS

EVAN EVANS TOURS

www.evanevanstours.co.uk

A wide range of half-day and full-day tours are offered.

✉ 258 Vauxhall Bridge Road SW1V 1BS ☎ 020 7950 1777

RIVER TRIPS

See The River Thames, ▷ 266–267.

TAILOR-MADE TOURS

TOUR GUIDES LTD

www.tourguides.co.uk

Blue Badge guides take you on a tour tailor-made to your specification, either within London or beyond. Walking, car and coach tours are available. Themed tours include antiques, literature and pubs.

✉ 72 Temple Chambers, Temple Avenue EC4Y 0HP ☎ 020 7936 2568 ✋ Half day in English £122, most other languages £142. Full day in English £193, other languages £219

TAXI TOUR

www.blacktaxitours.co.uk

Personalized tours in a black cab (maximum five people) come complete with commentary from the cabbie. Tours, usually lasting two hours, operate by day or by night.

You can be picked up from and returned to your hotel.

✉ Black Taxi Tours of London ☎ 020 7935 9363 ✋ A two-hour guided tour around London by day between 8 and 6 costs £100 per taxi cab; by night the cost is £110 per taxi cab. Out-of-town trips are priced on request

WALKING TOURS

Walking tours take place throughout London daily. Typically, they start and finish at Underground stations—meet the guide outside the station designated. Normally, there's no need to book unless you are in a large group.

BLOOD AND TEARS WALK

www.shockinglondon.com

London's grim past is described by actor Declan McHugh. Tours depart from Barbican station. Call for times.

✉ 31 Dibdin House, Maida Vale, London W9 1QE ☎ 07905 746733 ✋ Adult £9, child (12–14) £7. Not suitable for children under 12

ORIGINAL LONDON WALKS

www.walks.com

Probably the best walking tour operators in London offer lots of interesting themed walks, with different options every day.

✉ PO Box 1708 NW6 4LW ☎ 020 7624 3978 ✋ Adult £8, child (under 15) free

BLUE BADGE GUIDES

The Blue Badge is the British national standard guiding qualification. Each Blue Badge guide is selected, trained and examined by the official British tourist boards. Companies with Blue Badge guides offer a wide range of languages (up to 40) and specialist knowledge. They are known for their punctuality and reliability.

PRACTICALITIES

Practicalities gives you all the important practical information you will need during your visit, from money matters to emergency phone numbers.

LONDON

TEMPERATURE

RAINFALL

BEFORE YOU GO

CLIMATE AND WHEN TO GO

» London's sprawl of heated buildings has created its own microclimate, so frost and lingering snow are very rare. The temperature seldom falls below freezing, although northerly winds can make it feel very chilly in the winter. On average, January remains the coldest month. The temperature in London is generally two degrees above that of the rest of Britain.

» Be prepared for rain at any time of year. Officially, the wettest weeks are from late September to the end of November, but it can be just as wet in the middle of summer.

» The period between June and August is the warmest and busiest (school holidays run from late July to early September). Spring and September are appreciably quieter, but the weather is less reliable. May and June have the bonus of long daylight hours (see table below).

» The winter months can be a good time for visiting London, as sights are far less crowded and accommodation is often cheaper.

WEATHER REPORTS

» Daily forecasts are given at the end of television and radio news shows. They are also available by phone, fax, text or on the internet. Telephone 09068 500401 for Greater London weather (calls cost 60p per minute from a BT landline), or fax 09065 300128 for South East (including London weather).

» For forecasts texted to a mobile (cell) phone type wthr5 followed by a UK town or city. Send this message to 82222 (available on all networks except Virgin).

WHAT TO TAKE

You may find the following checklist useful, but if you forget or need to replace any items, there's every chance that you'll be able to find its equivalent in London.

DAYLIGHT HOURS

January	8
February	9
March	11
April	13
May	15
June	17
July	16
August	15
September	13
October	11
November	10
December	8

» A selection of clothing for a wide range of weather conditions. Rainwear is essential all year. Umbrellas can be more trouble than they're worth, especially on windy days; a lightweight waterproof jacket is a better option.

» Addresses and phone numbers of emergency contacts.

» Driver's licence (if you hold a licence or permit from Australia, Canada, Ireland, New Zealand or the USA, this will suffice) or International Driver's Licence (if your licence is not in English).

» Photocopies of passport and travel insurance (or send scanned versions

TIME ZONES

Britain is on GMT (Greenwich Mean Time—also known as Universal Time or UTC) during winter. In summer (late March to late October) clocks go forward one hour to British Summer Time (BST). The world is divided into 24 time zones. The chart shows time differences from GMT.

City	Time difference	Time at 12 noon GMT
Amsterdam	+1	1pm
Auckland	+10	10pm
Berlin	+1	1pm
Brussels	+1	1pm
Chicago	-6	6am
Dublin	0	noon
Johannesburg	+2	2pm
Madrid	+1	1pm
Montréal	-6	6am
New York	-5	7am
Paris	+1	1pm
Perth, Australia	+8	8pm
Rome	+1	1pm
San Francisco	-8	4am
Sydney	+10	10pm
Tokyo	+9	9pm

WEATHER WEBSITES

ORGANIZATION	NOTES	WEBSITE
BBC	London, UK and world weather reports and forecasts, plus many related topics. Includes satellite imagery	www.bbc.co.uk/weather/
The Met Office (UK)	Clear government site with good specialist links	www.metoffice.gov.uk

of these to an email account that you can access while you are away).

>> Credit cards (preferably more than one credit card), and/or travellers' cheques, and a small amount of cash in sterling.

>> Numbers of credit/debit cards, registration numbers of mobile (cell) phones, cameras and other expensive equipment (in case you need to report loss to the police). Keep these separately from the items.

>> Spare passport photos for Travelcards (▷ 48).

DOCUMENTS
PASSPORTS

>> Visitors from outside the UK must have a passport valid for at least six months from the date of entry into the country.

>> The United Kingdom (England, Wales, Scotland and Northern Ireland), the Channel Islands and the Isle of Man form a common travel area. Once you have entered any part of it through immigration control, you do not need further customs clearance to travel within it.

>> You must show photographic ID, such as a passport or driver's licence with a photo, for all internal flights.

VISAS

>> Before travelling you should double-check visa requirements: see www.ukvisas.gov.uk.

>> Citizens of countries in the European Economic Area (EEA)—the European Union (EU), Switzerland, Norway and Iceland—can enter the UK for purposes of holiday or work for any length of stay, without requiring a visa.

>> If you are a citizen of the United States, Australia, Canada or New

Zealand, you do not require a visa for stays of up to six months. However, you must have enough money to support yourself without needing to work or receiving any money from public funds.

>> Those wishing to stay longer, and nationals of certain countries, require a visa—check with the embassy or consulate in your own country.

>> You are usually allowed to enter and leave the UK as many times as you like while your visa is valid. On arrival in the UK, you must be able to produce documentation establishing your identity and nationality.

TRAVEL INSURANCE

>> Make sure you have adequate travel insurance. Some visitors (including citizens of EU countries, Australia and New Zealand) receive free or reduced-cost medical

treatment under the National Health Service (▷ 278) with the relevant documentation, but travel insurance including medical expenses is still recommended. However, visitors from countries not included in this arrangement, such as the United States and Canada, must make provision for their own medical insurance.

>> An annual travel insurance policy may be the best value for those who make several trips away from home in any 12-month period. Be aware, however, that long trips abroad—typically stays longer than 30 or 45 days—may not be covered.

OTHER HEALTH DOCUMENTS

>> European Health Insurance Card for EU citizens (formerly the E111 form; ▷ 278).

CUSTOMS

Goods you buy in EU countries

If you bring into the UK large quantities of alcohol or tobacco, a Customs Officer is likely to ask about the purposes for which you hold the goods. This particularly applies if you have with you more than the amounts listed below:

• 3,200 cigarettes	• 10 litres of spirits
• 400 cigarillos	• 90 litres of wine (of which only 60 litres can be sparkling wine)
• 200 cigars	
• 3kg of smoking tobacco	• 20 litres of fortified wine (such as port or sherry)
• 110 litres of beer	

Bringing goods to the UK from outside the EU

You are entitled to the allowances shown below only if you travel with the goods and do not plan to sell them. For further information see the HM Customs and Excise website: www.hmce.gov.uk.

• 200 cigarettes; or	• 2 litres of fortified wine, sparkling wine or other liqueurs
• 100 cigarillos; or	
• 50 cigars; or	• 16 litres of beer
• 250g of tobacco	• £390 worth of all other goods including gifts and souvenirs
• 4 litres of still table wine	
• 1 litre of spirits or strong liqueurs over 22% by volume; or	

BRITISH EMBASSIES AND CONSULATES ABROAD

COUNTRY	ADDRESS	WEBSITE
Australia	High Commission, Commonwealth Avenue, Yarralumla, Canberra ACT 2600, tel 02 62706666	http://ukinaustralia.fco.gov.uk
Canada	High Commission, 80 Elgin Street, Ottowa, ON K1P 5K7, tel 613 237-1530	http://ukincanada.fco.gov.uk
Ireland	29 Merrion Road, Ballsbridge, Dublin 4, tel 01 2053700	http:/britishembassyinireland.fco.gov.uk/en
New Zealand	High Commission, 44 Hill Street, Wellington 6011, tel 04 924 2888	http://ukinnewzealand.fco.gov.uk
South Africa	High Commission, 255 Hill Street, Arcadia 0002, Pretoria, tel 12 421 7500	http://ukinsouthafrica.fco.gov.uk/en
US	3100 Massachusetts Avenue NW, Washington DC 20008, tel 202 588-6500	http://ukinusa.fco.gov.uk

MONEY

>> Britain is an expensive country to travel in, so it's a good idea to explore your options for carrying and changing money.

>> Expect to spend a minimum of about £45 per day excluding accommodation, if you're touring independently.

>> The best idea is to carry money in a range of forms—cash, at least one credit card, bank card/charge card/Maestro card and travellers' cheques. This gives you the maximum degree of flexibility.

CASH

>> Britain's currency is the pound sterling (£), which is divided into 100 pence (p).

>> Scotland has its own notes, which are legal tender throughout the UK, although some smaller shops may be reluctant to accept them.

>> There is no limit to the amount of cash you may import or export.

>> It is worth keeping a few 10p, 20p, 50p and £1 coins handy for pay-and-display parking machines and parking meters.

CREDIT CARDS

>> Credit cards are widely accepted throughout London and Britain; Visa and MasterCard are the most popular, followed by American Express, Diners Club and JCB.

>> Credit cards can also be used for withdrawing currency at cashpoints (ATMs) at any bank displaying the appropriate sign.

>> If your credit cards or travellers' cheques are stolen or lost, call the issuer immediately, then report the loss to the police; you'll need a reference number for the insurance.

CASHPOINTS (ATMs)

>> Most bank branches have ATMs. Check with your bank if you are not sure whether you will be charged for using another bank's ATM.

>> LINK is the UK's only branded network of self-service cash machines. Use of LINK machines is free, except for credit, charge and store cards, for which you pay a cash advance fee.

>> You will be charged for using the convenience machines at certain private locations (such as fuel garages); fees are displayed, and are usually £1.25–£1.50.

TRAVELLERS' CHEQUES

>> These are the safest way to carry money, as you will be refunded in the

MAJOR BANKS

There are four main banks in the UK and they have branches all over London. All have foreign exchange facilities.

NAME	HEAD OFFICE ADDRESS	TELEPHONE
Barclays	1 Churchill Place E14 5HP	020 7116 1000
Lloyds TSB	25 Gresham Street EC2V 7HN	020 7626 1500
NatWest/RBS	135 Bishopsgate EC2M 3UR	0800 200 400
HSBC	8 Canada Square E14 5HQ	020 7991 8888

EVERYDAY ITEMS AND HOW MUCH THEY COST

Take-away sandwich	£4
Bottle of water	£1.20
Cup of tea or coffee	£1.20–£2
Pint of beer	£2.50–£3.80
Glass of house wine	£3–£5
British national daily newspaper	50p–£2
20 cigarettes	£6.65
Ice cream	£1–£1.50
Litre of unleaded petrol	£1.33

event of loss usually within 24 hours (keep the counterfoil separate from the cheques themselves).

BANKS
>> Most banks open Monday to Friday 9.30 to 4.30. Some branches also open on Saturday morning.
>> It pays to shop around for the best exchange and commission rates on currency. You do not pay commission on sterling travellers' cheques, provided you cash them at a bank affiliated with the issuing bank.
>> You will need to present ID (usually a passport) when cashing travellers' cheques.

POST OFFICES
>> Most post offices are open Monday–Friday 9–5.30 and Saturday 9–12.
>> Apart from the main post offices offering full postal services, there are sub-post offices, often forming part of a newsagent.
>> Many post offices offer commission-free bureaux de change services through an online ordering service available through www.postoffice.co.uk. Payment can be made in cash, or by cheque, banker's draft, Visa, MasterCard, Delta, Solo or Maestro.

BUREAUX DE CHANGE
>> These money-changing operations can be found at most major rail and Underground stations in central London, as well as at airports and at on-street locations, and are mostly open 8am to 10pm. Rates of exchange may be higher than at banks; it pays to shop around.

LOST OR STOLEN CREDIT CARDS
American Express
01273 696933
Diners Club
0870 1900 011
MasterCard/Eurocard
0800 964767
Maestro/Solo
www.maestro.com
Visa/Connect
0800 895 1725

24-HOUR EXCHANGE SERVICES IN LONDON

Chequepoint
550 Oxford Street W1C 1LY
Tel 020 7723 1005
Marble Arch Underground
71 Gloucester Road SW7 5BW
Tel 020 7373 9682
Gloucester Road Underground
2 Queensway W2 3RX
Tel 0800 699799
Bayswater Underground

Commission rates for currency and travellers' cheques should be clearly displayed.
>> Beware of commission-free bureaux as they often offer very poor rates of exchange, and should generally be used only for changing small amounts.

DISCOUNTS
>> Reduced, or free fares, on buses, Underground services and trains are available for children under 16.
>> Over 60s and 16- to 25-year-olds can purchase railcards for £26, giving a one-third reduction on off-peak national rail services (▷ 45).

THE EURO
>> Britain has not yet committed itself to the euro currency, but it is possible to spend euros in Britain.
>> One euro is made up of 100 cents. Euro notes come in denominations of 5, 10, 20, 50, 100, 200 and 500 euros. Coins come in denominations of 1 and 2 euros, and 1, 2, 5, 10, 20 and 50 cents.
>> It is not always clear where you might be able to spend euros, but many major high-street chain stores accept them in some or all of their branches: for example the Body Shop, Boots, Habitat, HMV, Marks and Spencer, Selfridges, WH Smith and the bookstore Waterstone's.
>> Some pubs owned by JD Wetherspoon, Scottish and Newcastle and Shepherd Neame take euros, as do some BP fuel stations.
>> Train tickets for travel on the Stansted Express, the Gatwick

TIPPING	
Restaurants (where service is not included)	10%
Tour guides	£1–£2
Hairdressers	10%
Taxis	10%
Chambermaids	50p–£1 per day
Porters	50p–£1 per bag

Express and Virgin trains can be paid for in euros.
>> Outside London, in general the bigger the city, the more places will accept euros.

WIRING MONEY
>> Having money wired from your home country can be expensive (agents charge fees for the service) and time-consuming.
>> Money can be wired from bank to bank, which takes up to two working days, or to agents such as Travelex (tel 0845 872 7627, www.travelex.co.uk) and Western Union (tel 0800 833 833, www.westernunion.com).

VAT REFUNDS
▷ 290.

Barbados
British Virgin Islands
Bulgaria
Channel Islands
Falkland Islands
Montserrat
New Zealand
Romania
Russia
St. Helena
Turks and Caicos Islands
Republics of the former USSR except Latvia, Lithuania and Estonia
Yugoslavia (that is, Serbia and Montenegro) and successor states (Croatia, Bosnia-Herzegovina and Macedonia)

HEALTH

>> Britain's National Health Service (the NHS) was set up in 1948 to provide health care for the country's citizens based on need rather than the ability to pay. It is funded by the taxpayer and managed by a government department.

>> While NHS care for British citizens is free, private health care can also be bought from organizations such as BUPA.

>> Visitors from the EU are entitled to free or reduced-cost NHS treatment (see below), although health insurance is still advised for non-British citizens.

BEFORE YOU DEPART

>> Consult your doctor at least six to eight weeks before leaving.

>> Free or reduced-cost medical treatment is available through the NHS for visitors from EU countries, but you'll need to have a valid European Health Insurance Card (EHIC).

>> Several non-EU countries have reciprocal health care agreements with the United Kingdom (see below), although health insurance is still advised. In most cases a passport is sufficient identification for hospital treatment. Most countries, however, including the United States and Canada, do not have agreements with the UK, and for citizens of these countries a comprehensive travel insurance policy is required.

>> No inoculations are required to enter Britain. However, it is advisable

to have an anti-tetanus booster. Check with your doctor whether you need immunization or health advice for: meningococcal meningitis; hepatitis B; diphtheria booster; or measles/MMR.

COUNTRIES WITH RECIPROCAL HEALTH AGREEMENTS WITH THE UNITED KINGDOM

Anguilla
Australia

WHAT TO TAKE WITH YOU

>> Visitors from the European Union should bring a valid EHIC card and a photocopy of it, which should be kept separately from the card and in a safe place.

>> Visitors from outside the European Union should bring their travel insurance policy and a photocopy.

HEALTHY FLYING

• Visitors to the UK from as far as the US, Australia or New Zealand may be concerned about the effect of long-haul flights on their health. The most widely publicized concern is deep vein thrombosis, or DVT. Misleadingly called 'economy class syndrome', DVT is the forming of a blood clot in the body's deep veins, particularly in the legs. The clot can move around the bloodstream and could be fatal.

• Those most at risk include the elderly, pregnant women and those using the contraceptive pill, smokers and the overweight. If you are at increased risk of DVT see your doctor before departing. Flying increases the likelihood of DVT because passengers are often seated in a cramped position for long periods of time and may become dehydrated.

To minimize risk:
Drink water (not alcohol)
Don't stay immobile for hours at a time
Stretch and exercise your legs periodically
Do wear elastic flight socks, which support veins and reduce the chances of a clot forming

Exercises

Ankle rotations	**Calf stretches**	**Knee lifts**
Lift feet off the floor. Draw a circle with the toes, moving one foot clockwise and the other counterclockwise	Start with heel on the floor and point foot upward as high as you can. Then lift heel high, keeping ball of foot on the floor	Lift leg with knee bent while contracting your thigh muscle. Then straighten leg pressing foot flat to the floor

Other health hazards for flyers are airborne diseases and bugs spread by the plane's air-conditioning system. These are largely unavoidable but if you have a serious medical condition seek advice from a doctor before flying.

PRACTICALITIES | ESSENTIAL INFORMATION

>> Visitors with existing medical conditions and allergies, for example to commonly used drugs, should wear a warning bracelet or tag.

IF YOU NEED TREATMENT

>> If you are injured or in an accident, go immediately to a hospital casualty department (emergency room).

>> Dial 999 for an ambulance if it is an emergency.

>> If you are staying at a hotel or bed-and-breakfast, members of staff should be able to help you if you need to contact a doctor. Emergency telephone numbers are often on a noticeboard in a central area or in your room.

>> Another option is to contact NHS Direct (tel 0845 4647 or www. nhsdirect.nhs.uk) and explain the problem. Free medical advice from a qualified nurse is available to everyone through this government-funded service. You do not have to give personal details.

>> Non-urgent medical appointments can be made with any doctor or surgery listed in the Yellow Pages. There are also 10 NHS walk-in centres in London; these are open seven days a week and give fast access to treatment. Initial advice, such as if you need to go to hospital, will be given, but those visitors without a reciprocal arrangement with the UK, such as the United States and Canada, will be charged to speak to a nurse (approximately £25) or doctor (approximately £55) and for any prescription drugs required. You will be issued with a receipt to give to your insurance company.

>> To find the nearest doctor, dentist or pharmacy, ask at your hotel, or search the website www.nhs.uk/servicedirectories.

>> Major pharmacies and large supermarkets have a wide range of medicines that you can buy over the counter, although items such as antibiotics will require a prescription from a doctor.

>> Pharmacists operate a roster system of out-of-hours opening times

in many areas, with times of the duty pharmacist displayed in the shop window and in the local newspaper.

WATER

>> Tap water is safe to drink everywhere, but bottled water is readily available, though quite expensive in tourist hotspots.

SUMMER HAZARDS

>> Between May and September the sun can be strong and a high-factor sunscreen of SPF 15 or above is recommended.

>> Insect bites are irritating rather than dangerous, but it is advisable

to take insect repellents in hot weather, especially if you are going near water.

DENTAL TREATMENT

>> Non-British residents will have to pay for dental treatment as private patients.

>> Dentists are listed in telephone directories or you can use the British Dental Association's online service at www.bda-findadentist.org.uk to find one.

OPTICIANS

>> Bring your own prescription or a spare pair of spectacles in case of loss or breakage.

MAJOR PHARMACIES

NAME	TELEPHONE	WEBSITE
Boots the Chemist	0845 609 0055	www.boots.com
Lloyds Pharmacy	0845 600 3565	www.lloydspharmacy.com
Numark	0800 783 5709	www.numarkpharmacists.com
Superdrug	0800 096 1055	www.superdrug.com

HOSPITALS WITH EMERGENCY DEPARTMENTS

NAME	ADDRESS	TELEPHONE
Charing Cross Hospital	Fulham Palace Road W6 8RF	020 3311 1234
Chelsea and Westminster Hospital	369 Fulham Road SW10 9NH	020 8746 8000
Royal Free Hospital	Pond Street, Hampstead NW3 2QG	020 7794 0500
St. Mary's Hospital	Praed Street W2 1NY	020 3312 3333
St. Thomas's Hospital	Westminster Bridge Road SE1 7EH	020 7188 7188
University College Hospital	235 Euston Road NW1 2BU	020 3456 7890
	Call 999 for an ambulance	

OPTICIANS

NAME	TELEPHONE	WEBSITE
Boots Opticians	0845 609 0055	www.boots.com
David Clulow (London)	020 8515 6700	www.davidclulow.com
Dollond & Aitchison	0845 602 9539	www.danda.co.uk
Specsavers (Marble Arch branch)	020 7706 0404	www.specsavers.co.uk
Vision Express	08444 771 177	www.visionexpress.com

ALTERNATIVE MEDICAL TREATMENTS

A wide range of alternative treatments is available in the UK. These treatments are chargeable for visitors. The listings below are a starting point; local telephone directories will have more details.

NAME	TELEPHONE	WEBSITE
British Chiropractic Association	0118 950 5950	www.chiropractic-uk.co.uk
British Osteopathic Association	01582 488455	www.osteopathy.org
The Society of Homeopaths	0845 450 6611	www.homeopathy-soh.org

>> Additionally, some payphones allow you to send text messages and email—look for the sign that indicates this.

>> Thousands of libraries have free internet access; for details go to www.peoplesnetwork.gov.uk.

>> In addition to internet cafés and web phones, BT has introduced hundreds of wireless hotspots in locations such as airports, hotels, service stations and bars. These hubs allow laptop- and pocket PC-users broadband access to the internet, using wireless technology known as WiFi. You need a laptop or pocket PC PDA running Microsoft Windows XP, 2000 or Microsoft Pocket PC Vista 2002, and a wireless LAN card. You need to be within a radius of 100m (330ft) of the hub.

>> Any WiFi approved card should work with BT Openzone, but this service is an expensive, if convenient, way of surfing the net.

USING A LAPTOP

>> If you are bringing your laptop from another country, remember to bring a plug adaptor for your charger (see Electricity, ▷ 280). A surge protector is also useful.

>> Wireless technology, such as Bluetooth, allows you to connect to the internet using a mobile phone; check beforehand what the charges will be. Dial tone frequencies vary from country to country, so set your modem to ignore dial tones.

POST

>> For all post office information, call Customer Services (tel 0845 722 3344).

>> Post boxes are painted bright red (except some in post offices) and are either set into walls or are stand-alone pillar boxes. Collection times are shown on each post box.

>> Stamps are available from newsagents, supermarkets and some other shops in addition to post offices. Look for the sign.

>> Generally, airmail is preferable for mail sent outside Europe; for bulky items surface mail is substantially cheaper, but typically takes around

eight weeks outside Europe. Airmail to Europe takes around three days, and to the rest of the world from five days.

>> Large post offices have poste restante (mail holding) services. Mail addressed to the recipient and inscribed with the words Poste Restante will be kept at the specified post office until collected by the addressee, who will need to bring along a form of identification to collect it.

>> To send items within the UK for guaranteed next-day delivery, use special delivery. This service also enables you to insure the items in case of loss, and to trace the item on its journey and confirm that it has been delivered.

TELEPHONE PRICES FROM PUBLIC TELEPHONES	
Minimum charge	60p
All UK calls	60p for first 30 min, then 10p each 5 min thereafter
Calls to mobile phones	From 45p Mon–Fri 7–7, 38p per minute Mon–Fri after 7pm and before 7am, and 15p per minute all other times
US and Canada	£2 per minute at all times
Belgium, France, Germany, Italy, Netherlands and Sweden	£1 per minute at all times
Australia and New Zealand	20p per minute at all times
Call charges	These are lower after 6pm on weekdays and all day Saturday and Sunday. Local calls are cheaper than long-distance calls within Britain, and calls to mobile phones are generally more expensive than other calls

POSTAGE RATES		
First class within UK	Up to 100g (3.5oz) (usually arrives next day, but not guaranteed)	41p
Second class within UK	Up to 100g (3.5oz) (usually two days)	32p
Airmail Rates		
Europe	Postcard and letter up to 20g (0.6oz)	60p
	Letter up to 40g (1.3oz)	88p
	Letter up to 100g (3.5oz)	£1.65
Rest of world	Postcard and letter up to 10g (0.3oz)	67p
	Letter up to 40g (1.3oz)	£1.46
	Letter up to 100g (3.5oz)	£3.04

OPENING TIMES AND TICKETS

ENTRANCE FEES

Most attractions in London charge reduced admission fees for children under 16, holders of student cards, those on unemployment benefit and those aged 60 and over (proof may be required). Family tickets, generally for two adults and two children, are also widely available.

HERITAGE ORGANIZATIONS

>> National Trust (NT) membership is excellent value if you wish to visit more than two properties owned by the National Trust (there are 13 in London and many more within easy reach of the city).

>> You can join at any NT property. Membership gives free admission to all properties. The NT Touring Pass (available to overseas visitors in advance only) gives free entry to all NT properties for 7 or 14 days for one or two persons or a family. See www.nationaltrust.org.uk.

>> For further information contact the National Trust, PO Box 39, Warrington WA5 7WD, tel 0844 800 1895, www.nationaltrust.org.uk.

>> English Heritage (EH), CADW in Wales and Historic Scotland (HS) in Scotland manage hundreds of historic properties, statues and monuments in Britain. EH membership gives free entry to all EH properties plus half-price admission to CADW and HS properties for one year, and free entry thereafter.

>> You can join at any EH, CADW or HS staffed property: English Heritage, Kemble Drive, Swindon SN2 2YP, tel 0870 333 1181, www.english-heritage.org.uk.

DISCOUNT PASSES

>> If you are planning extensive sightseeing, buy a discount card. The following are all available from the Britain and London Visitor Centre in Lower Regent Street (▷ 286), major tourist offices and airports.

London Pass

This gives free admission to more than 55 attractions in and around London, free travel options and a pocket guide. Passes are for one, two, three or six days and cost £41 for a one-day adult pass (£51 inc. transport, zones 1–6) to £94 for six days (£144 inc. transport); www.londonpass.com.

Great British Heritage Pass

Aimed at North American visitors, this pass allows free entry to more than 400 historic properties and gardens. Passes for 3, 7, 15 days or 30 days. Passes range from £39 for a 3-day adult pass to £119 for 30 days. See www.british heritagepass.com.

NATIONAL HOLIDAYS

Although banks and businesses close on public (bank) holidays, the trend in London is for tourist attractions and shops to remain open, except on 25 and 26 December and 1 January, when almost everything closes. If any of these days falls on a Saturday or Sunday, the next weekday is a holiday.

New Year's Day (1 January)
Good Friday
Easter Monday
First Monday in May
Last Monday in May
Last Monday in August
Christmas Day (25 December)
Boxing Day (26 December)

OPENING TIMES

Opening hours can vary so check in advance with individual sights.

Banks	Monday–Friday 9.30–4.30	Some large branches also open Saturday morning.
Doctors and Pharmacies	Most pharmacies open Monday–Saturday 9–5 or 5.30 Doctors' surgeries only Monday–Friday, typically 8.30–6.30 and on Saturday morning	Notices in the window and in local newspapers indicate extended-hour rosters of local pharmacies (usually for a few extra hours in the evening and for short periods on Sunday). Doctors and dentists are usually closed on Sunday.
Museums, Houses and Galleries	Many open Monday–Saturday 10–5, Sunday 12–5, but hours vary	Some do not admit visitors who arrive less than 30 minutes before closing time.
Post Offices	Monday–Friday 9–5.30, Saturday 9–12	
Pubs	Changes in licensing laws mean that pubs now negotiate their own individual opening hours	Most pubs, however, still maintain the traditional hours, which are from about 11–11. Some close between 3 and 6pm. In England and Wales pubs open on Sunday 12–10.30pm. Many stay open all afternoon, although food may not be available from 2/2.30pm until around 6.30–8.30pm.
Restaurants	No hard-and-fast opening hours, but typically around 12–2.30pm and 6–9pm	Take-away restaurants stay open until around 11pm or later. Many places in the City are closed on Saturday and Sunday. or 6–11pm (slightly earlier on Sundays).
Shops	Usually open Monday–Saturday 9–5 or 5.30 but London shop hours vary (▷ 290)	Newsagents open on Sunday morning as well. Some corner shops and convenience stores open longer hours— 8am–10pm or 11pm, seven days a week.
Supermarkets	Usually 8am–9pm or later and for six hours (usually 10–4) on Sunday	Some are open 24 hours.

TOURIST OFFICES

TOURIST INFORMATION CENTRES (TIC)

>> TICs are a useful source of brochures and information on places to stay, where to eat out, entertainment venues and local events in London. Many will also supply free street maps and sell guidebooks and souvenirs.

>> Most tourist information centres will book accommodation for you free of charge (the hotelier pays a commission); for bookings outside London, you may be charged a small fee (about £2.50) for this service.

>> After office hours, some tourist information centres display lists of available accommodation in their office windows.

TOURIST INFORMATION CENTRES

LONDON AND AROUND

Britain and London Visitor Centre
1 Lower Regent Street SW1Y 4XT
www.visitlondon.com
Apr–Sep Mon 9.30–6.30, Tue–Fri 9–6, Sat–Sun 10–4; Oct–Mar Mon 9.30–6, Tue–Fri 9–6, Sat–Sun 10–4.
Visit London information line 08701 566 366 open Mon–Fri 9–9, Sat–Sun 9–5.
This is the official London tourist office and website.

City Information Centre
St. Paul's Churchyard (opposite St. Paul's Cathedral) EC4M 8BX
Tel 020 7332 1456
Mon–Sat 9.30–5.30, Sun 10–4

Greenwich (Town) TIC
Pepys House
2 Cutty Sark Gardens
Greenwich SE10 9LW
Tel 0870 608 2000
Daily 10–5

King's Cross St. Pancras TIC
LUL Western Ticket Hall
Euston Road N1 9AL
Mon–Sat 7.15am–9.15pm, Sun 8.15–8.15

LGBT Tourist Office
(lesbian, gay, bisexual, transgender)
25 Frith Street
Soho W1D 5LB
www.gaytouristoffice.co.uk

Liverpool Street TIC
Liverpool Street Underground station EC2M 7PP
Mon–Sat 7.15am–9.15pm, Sun 8.15–8.15

Piccadilly Circus TIC
Piccadilly Underground station
Daily 9.15–7

Twickenham TIC
The Atrium, Civic Centre
York Street
Twickenham, Middlesex TW1 3BZ
Tel 020 8891 7272
Mon–Thu 9–5.15, Fri 9–5

Victoria station TIC
Opposite Platform 8
Victoria Railway Station SW1V 1JU
Mon–Sat 7.15am–9.15pm, Sun 8.15–8.15

OUTSIDE LONDON

Visit Britain
Thames Tower
Black's Road W6 9EL
Tel 020 7578 1000
www.visitbritain.com
The website has a search facility for tourist information centres across Britain, giving addresses, telephone numbers and opening hours.

Tourism South East England
40 Chamberlayne Road
Eastleigh, Hampshire SO50 5JH
Tel 02380 625400
www.visitsoutheastengland.com

South West England
Woodwater Park, Exeter, Devon EX2 5WT
www.visitsouthwest.co.uk

VISIT BRITAIN OFFICES OVERSEAS

Australia
Level 3, Suite 2
32 Walker Street
N. Sydney
NSW 2060
Tel 02 9021 4401

Canada
160 Bloor Street East
Ontario M4W 1B9
Tel 1 416 646 6674

New Zealand
151 Queen Street
Level 17, IAG House
Auckland 105-652
Tel 09 357 6620

South Africa
Regus Bryanston
The Campus, Twickenham Building
Bryanston
Johannesburg 2021
Tel 011 575 6817

US
551 Fifth Avenue, Suite 701
New York
NY 10176
Tel 1 800 462 2748

Website for visitors to Britain:
www.visitbritain.com

MEDIA

Britain has a vibrant media culture, with some of the world's oldest newspapers, publicly funded TV channels, and the global media presence of the BBC (British Broadcasting Corporation).

TELEVISION

There are five main national terrestrial channels in Britain. There is no advertising on the BBC channels, which are funded by a licence fee from all owners of a TV.

>> **BBC1** focuses on soaps, lifestyle shows, children's TV, documentaries and drama.

>> **BBC2** specializes in cultural programmes, comedy and history.

>> **ITV 1** is the home of popular broadcasting, including soaps, quiz shows, children's programmes, reality TV, drama and films.

>> **Channel 4** broadcasts quality films, documentaries, comedy and quiz shows, science and natural history programmes.

>> **Channel 5** shows children's programmes, game shows, popular films, top US shows like *CSI* and reruns of soaps.

Cable and Digital

>> Although the number of homes with cable in Britain is rapidly increasing, there are few cable-specific channels. However, it is possible to get a greater variety of free channels via cable.

>> Digital satellite receivers allow viewers to receive an increasing number of free digital channels.

>> You have to pay a subscription to view sports and film channels.

>> Digital terrestrial television receivers can be purchased with one payment of around £40, allowing viewers to watch more channels than on normal terrestrial services.

>> Digital television offers many interactive services, such as shopping, email and games.

>> Beginning in 2009, over a period of three years, terrestrial channels will be phased out throughout Britain, making digital the only option.

RADIO

>> Analogue FM and AM stations are now also available digitally.

>> Digital technology allows for more stations and choice while offering better sound quality with no interference.

>> Digital radio is free, but the radios themselves are quite expensive. It is also possible to listen to digital radio through digital television.

>> Information about current digital radio stations can be found at www.radiostations.co.uk.

Radio Stations

The television licence funds the BBC's national and regional radio stations. There are also plenty of independent, commercial stations.

>> **Radio 1** A diverse selection of the latest music from mainstream dance, rock and pop to indie and R&B. There are regular national, international and entertainment news bulletins and every Sunday from 4 to 7pm the UK singles chart.
97–99 FM; www.bbc.co.uk/radio1

>> **Radio 2** New and old classic rock, pop, country, folk, reggae and soul interspersed with chat, regular news and travel bulletins and music documentaries.
88–91 FM; www.bbc.co.uk/radio2

>> **Radio 3** Classical and jazz to new and world music along with culture and drama. The BBC Proms, a classical music festival held every summer in the Royal Albert Hall, is broadcast live every summer.
90–93 FM; www.bbc.co.uk/radio3

>> **Radio 4** Topical and political news, comedy, art, drama and quiz shows, along with radio plays, interviews and documentaries. There are also in-depth news bulletins.
92–95 FM; www.bbc.co.uk/radio4

>> **Capital FM** bills itself as London's No. 1 hot music station and appeals to young, hip listeners.
95–106 FM; www.capitalfm.com

>> **Classic FM** is an independent station broadcasting classical music and music news.
100–102 FM; www.classicfm.co.uk

>> **Absolute Radio** is a commercial radio station transmitting rock and new music along with sports and music news.
105.8 FM; www.absoluteradio.co.uk

NEWSPAPERS

>> National newspapers in Britain are divided into quality papers known as broadsheets (although only two are still in the large broadsheet format) and tabloids. Broadsheets focus on relatively objective news reporting while most tabloids cover seemingly sensational human-interest stories and celebrity gossip.

>> The Sunday newspapers are more expensive and bigger than their daily counterparts. The broadsheets have special sections on travel, property, finance, the arts and media, and contain supplements with listings, reviews and articles.

>> The streets and transport network are inundated with the free morning *City A.M.* and *Metro* and afternoon *Evening Standard*.

International Newspapers

>> Newspapers from around the world, including foreign-language papers, can be purchased at airports and larger train stations.

>> The bookstore and newsagents WH Smith also stocks major international newspapers, including the *International Herald Tribune*.

MAGAZINES

>> *Time Out* is issued weekly and contains articles and features detailing what's on in London, from concerts and musicals to exhibitions and films, and with information and reviews on restaurants, pubs, shopping and accommodation.

BOOKS AND FILMS

London's vitality, variety, glamour and squalor have always provided rich pickings for writers and film-makers. Many have sung the city's praises; for some it's been a love-hate affair.

LITERATURE

Eminent historian Peter Ackroyd's biography of the great city, *London: The Biography* (Vintage, 2000), has been meticulously researched and presented and is essential reading for those wishing to understand the capital that defines the country. His third book in the series, *Thames: Sacred River* (Chatto & Windus 2007), explores the history of the river so central to London's existence.

The London Encyclopaedia, by Ben Weinreb and Christopher Hibbert (Macmillan, 1983), is a vast undertaking, and provides comprehensive information about London's buildings past and present.

Perhaps the most famous book about London is *The Diary of Samuel Pepys*, in which the observer, Pepys, recorded events in Britain from 1600 to 1669.

Jeremy Paxman's *The English: a Portrait of a People* (Penguin, 1999) makes delightful reading. A galloping overview of the English as a whole, the celebrated broadcaster's book covers topics such as their attitude to private property, and astutely perceives what elements define the English character.

Several of Charles Dickens's novels were set in London—*Oliver Twist* (1837), *Bleak House* (1853) and *Little Dorrit* (1857). *Oliver Twist* is the story of an orphan born into a workhouse who runs away to London, only to fall in with thieves. Dickens's social conscience is evident in this tale of hardship and reward.

William Blake (1757–1827), born in London, was another writer to express a keen awareness of cruelty

and injustice, notably in his poem 'London', in *Songs of Experience*.

In 1887, Sir Arthur Conan Doyle first introduced his creation, Sherlock Holmes, perhaps the most famous fictional detective of all, in the novel *A Study in Scarlet*. Holmes lived at 221b Baker Street (▷ 219).

The amusing *Bridget Jones's Diary*, by Helen Fielding (Picador, 1997), defined a generation of 30-something single women living in London in the late 1990s. It and its sequel, *The Edge of Reason*, were made into hugely successful films.

Zadie Smith's *White Teeth* (Penguin, 2001) is the story of three generations of families—one white, one Indian and one mixed-race—living in north London in the 1990s.

Monica Ali has written sharply on a similar subject—multinational, multidenominational London, in her 2003 novel *Brick Lane* (Doubleday); the film appeared in 2007.

Three of Nick Hornby's successful novels, *Fever Pitch* (Cassell, 1992), *High Fidelity* (Cassell, 1995) and *About a Boy* (Cassell, 1998), are set in London, in the varying worlds of football (Arsenal in particular), record shops and single mothers. All of them have been made into films.

Will Self's novel *The Book of Dave* (Viking, 2006) is a complex parody of modern religion, where in a new post-global-warming world society bases its beliefs on the fragments of an unhappy London cabbie.

Edward Rutherford's *London* (Arrow, 2010) is a hefty romp through 2,000 years of London life, weaving fact and fiction to bring episodes of history alive. At 1,328 pages, it's not for the faint-hearted.

FILMS

In the opening sequences of *The World Is Not Enough* (1999), James Bond hurtled from the MI6 building

by Vauxhall Bridge, pursued by a beautiful assassin, and provided a fantastic high-speed river chase all the way to the Greenwich Dome.

Lock, Stock and Two Smoking Barrels (1998), directed by Guy Ritchie, is a pastiche of the old gangster movies.

Classic Ealing comedies such as *Passport to Pimlico* (1948), starring Stanley Holloway, were all made at Ealing Studios, founded in 1929 and the first British sound-film studios.

My Beautiful Launderette caused something of a stir in 1985 when Daniel Day-Lewis starred in this well-observed story of the relationship between two young gay men (one Asian) in intolerant times.

Other classic films that might transport you to your favourite part of London are *Alfie* (1966), which sees Michael Caine ducking and diving around town, *An American Werewolf in London* (1981), a comedy horror movie about a visiting American who gets bitten, and *A Fish Called Wanda* (1988), starring John Cleese, Jamie Lee Curtis and Michael Palin. More recent releases, with some great shots of London, are *Notes on Scandal* (2006), a sinister tale set around a London school starring Judi Dench and Cate Blanchett, and *Breaking and Entering* (2006), a London melodrama with Jude Law and Juliette Binoche.

GUIDEBOOKS

AA CityPack London
Pocket book and map.
London: A City Revealed
A visual tribute to London, with more than 350 large colour photographs.
Fodor's London
In-depth illustrated guide updated annually.
The AA Hotel Guide
The AA Restaurant Guide

MAPS

AA Street by Street Central London
Street by Street Z Maps

WEBSITES

A vast amount of information can be found online.

GENERAL TOURIST INFORMATION

www.visitbritain.com—the official website for the Britain and London Tourist Information Centre
www.southeastengland.com
www.fco.gov.uk—Foreign and Commonwealth Office
www.english-heritage.org.uk
www.nationaltrust.org.uk
www.hrp.org.uk—historic royal palaces
www.royal.gov.uk—royal residences
www.artsline.org.uk—information on arts and attractions for visitors with disabilities

ABOUT LONDON

www.visitlondon.com
www.londontown.com—a directory covering sights, events and accommodation
www.ukeverything.co.uk—a portal to London websites and the rest of the UK
www.londonforfun.com—information on attractions and sights
www.travellondon.com
www.londonnet.co.uk
www.virtual-london.com
www.visiting-london.com
www.thelondonvisitor.com—a monthly guide to London
www.tripadvisor.com
www.gingerbeer.co.uk—the London lesbian and bisexual scene
www.royalparks.gov.uk

NEWS AND REVIEWS

www.bbc.co.uk/london
www.guardian.co.uk
www.timesonline.co.uk

THEATRE/MUSIC

www.londontheatre.co.uk
www.ticketmaster.co.uk—tickets
www.ambassadortickets.com—information on what's on, what's coming up and where to get tickets
www.reallyuseful.com—the Really Useful Theatre group

www.southbankcentre.co.uk—the website for the South Bank Centre, including the Royal Festival Hall, Purcell Room and Queen Elizabeth Hall
www.royalalberthall.com
www.roh.org.uk—Royal Opera House

CINEMA

www.bfi.org.uk—British Film Institute
www.ugicinemas.co.uk
www.odeon.co.uk

TRAVEL

Airports

www.gatwickairport.com
www.heathrowairport.com
www.stanstedairport.com
www.london-luton.co.uk
www.londoncityairport.com

Bus/Coach

www.greenline.co.uk
www.nationalexpress.com
www.megabus.com

Rail

www.firstcapitalconnect.co.uk
www.heathrowexpress.com
www.gatwickexpress.com
www.stanstedexpress.com

www.eurostar.com
www.thetrainline.com—book tickets and find out fares and journey times
www.nationalrail.co.uk—general information and train times

London Transport

www.tfl.gov.uk—official Transport for London website
www.thamesriverservice.co.uk

Car Rental

www.alamo.co.uk
www.avis.co.uk
www.europcar.co.uk
www.hertz.co.uk

Car Breakdown

www.theaa.com
www.rac.co.uk

WEATHER REPORTS

www.bbc.co.uk/weather
www.metoffice.com
www.weathercall.co.uk

HEALTH

www.nhsdirect.nhs.uk
www.medicentre.co.uk—walk-in private doctor and health service

MAJOR SIGHTS

SIGHT	WEBSITE	PAGE
British Museum	www.britishmuseum.org	134
Buckingham Palace	www.royal.gov.uk	176
HMS *Belfast*	www.hmsbelfast.iwm.org.uk	72
Houses of Parliament	www.parliament.uk	179
Imperial War Museum	www.iwm.org.uk	74
Kensington Palace	www.hrp.org.uk	214
London Eye	www.londoneye.com	75
Madame Tussauds	www.madametussauds.com	217
Museum of London	www.museumoflondon.org.uk	103
National Gallery	www.nationalgallery.org.uk	182
National Portrait Gallery	www.npg.org.uk	188
Natural History Museum	www.nhm.ac.uk	220
St. Paul's Cathedral	www.stpauls.co.uk	104
Science Museum	www.sciencemuseum.org.uk	222
Shakespeare's Globe	www.shakespeares-globe.org	78
Sir John Soane's Museum	www.soane.org	148
Somerset House	www.somerset-house.org.uk	150
Tate Britain/Modern	www.tate.org.uk	192/80
Tower Bridge	www.towerbridge.org.uk	111
Tower of London	www.hrp.org.uk	112
Victoria & Albert Museum	www.vam.ac.uk	224
Wallace Collection	www.wallacecollection.org	229
Westminster Abbey	www.westminster-abbey.org	194

SHOPPING

London offers shoppers a vast range, from smart department stores and speciality shops to market stalls and bargain basements. Many people come to London just to shop. Oxford Street and Regent Street can be crammed to bursting point in summer and during the Christmas shopping season—which starts in November. Particularly long queues can be expected at the most popular stores such as Hamleys, the world-famous toy shop, but there are quieter areas too.

Shops have adopted increasingly flexible opening hours and it is difficult to generalize. Late opening, until 9 or 10, is common in the busiest areas and many shops also open on Sundays at varying times.

SALE TIME

Twice a year, stores traditionally slash their prices in order to sell off the previous season's remaining stock. The best bargains are at the January sales, starting immediately after Christmas—sometimes before—and continuing well into February. Determined bargain-hunters camp out in the streets in advance to be first in line when the sales open at Harrods (▷ 233) or Selfridges (▷ 234–235). Summer sales begin in June or July and last to the end of August. Nowadays mid-season reductions are also common.

Strict rules govern the way that sales operate in Britain, and the fact that you buy an item in a sale does not affect your statutory rights as a consumer. You are, for example, entitled to a full refund if the goods prove faulty—but you must retain your receipt as proof of purchase.

TAX-FREE SHOPPING

If you are visiting from a non-European Union country, you are exempt from Value Added Tax on certain goods that you take out of the country if you spend a minimum amount (VAT is a 20 per cent sales tax). This can amount to a hefty saving. Most leading stores have details of the tax-free shopping policy and can help with your claims.

PAYING

Most shops accept the major credit cards, but there are exceptions. Travellers' cheques may be accepted, but you will need to show your passport. Personal cheques must be drawn from a UK bank account. Street markets may not accept credit cards or cheques.

STREET SELLERS

With the exception of market traders, who pay to maintain regular spots at established markets, it's smart to beware of street sellers anywhere in London. The products they sell may not be what they're claimed to be.

MARKETS

Markets come in all shapes and sizes in London, from the stylish to the basic. For wonderful atmosphere, cheeky traders' patter and piled-high goods ranging from leather jackets to second-hand records, visit Petticoat Lane (▷ 120) near Liverpool Street or Brick Lane (▷ 120), both in the East End and reached from Liverpool Street or Aldgate East Underground station. At Camden Lock, reached from Camden Town Underground station, students and antique-hunters flock to the stalls of bric-a-brac and trendy clothes (daily 10–6). Berwick Street market (▷ 154) sells produce and an assortment of household goods.

SHOPPING AREAS

If you want department stores and brand-name shopping and can stand the crowds, head to the West End around Oxford Street, Regent Street and Bond Street. Covent Garden is full of quirky specialist shops and street entertainment, the King's Road in Chelsea has more avant-garde labels among the mainstream stores, while Knightsbridge has the most exclusive and expensive shopping.

Below *London's most famous shopping street is 2km (1.5 miles) of major brands' flagship outlets, imposing department stores—and tacky souvenir shops*

ENTERTAINMENT AND NIGHTLIFE

The range and variety of performing arts and entertainment in London is enough to make you dizzy. Just wandering through the West End gives an idea of what's on offer, but it's also worth looking beyond central London and scanning the pages of *Time Out*, the city's most comprehensive guide to what's on in and around the city. And if you've got the energy and the inclination you can party 24 hours a day in London. After a period when superclubs for the young and affluent ruled the scene, there's now a variety of venues and styles to cater for every taste, budget and age range. Note that almost all performance venues, other than clubs, do not permit smoking in the auditorium.

CINEMA
The choice of films in London is huge. In addition to the multiscreen chain complexes that show new release blockbusters (many on and around Leicester Square), there are independent repertory cinemas that screen a range of special-interest films and international fare with English subtitles. These include the Institute of Contemporary Arts (ICA), (▷ 178) at Carlton House Terrace and the National Film Theatre (▷ 77 and 87) on the South Bank, which has themed festivals and guest speakers.

CLASSICAL MUSIC, DANCE AND OPERA
A useful place to start is the Southbank Centre (▷ 77), which has a full schedule of dance (staged by the English National Ballet) and concerts, either in the Royal Festival Hall or the more intimate Queen Elizabeth Hall or Purcell Room (▷ 88). For conventional classical music and big names, check the Barbican (▷ 120–121), where the

London Symphony Orchestra has its base. The Royal Opera House (▷ 158, 160), Covent Garden, still has a reputation for high prices and stuffiness, despite its flashy new setting. Productions by the Royal Ballet Company, based here, cost less than opera performances. For opera sung in English, head for the London Coliseum (▷ 158), home of the English National Opera.

Between July and September the Proms season (BBC Henry Wood Promenade Concerts, ▷ 295) gets underway at the Royal Albert Hall (▷ 235), with lunchtime chamber concerts as well as evening performances. If you don't mind standing, it doesn't cost that much to get in.

Churches also host excellent recitals and concerts, particularly St. James's Piccadilly (▷ 199) and St. Martin-in-the-Fields (▷ 199).

CONTEMPORARY LIVE MUSIC
At one end of the spectrum, the live-music scene features massive stadium gigs. At the other, rock

bands frequently perform in local pubs, and there's much in between—for example jazz at Ronnie Scott's (▷ 158) in Soho, among other venues. Free live music is available in the Royal Festival Hall and sometimes in the National Theatre foyer at lunchtime.

For folk, world music, blues, rock 'n' roll, salsa and what-ever else, stray into outlying areas such as Camden, Kentish Town or Islington for lively pub-and-club scenes.

THEATRE
Much of the West End's long-established Theatreland now seems obsessed with long-running musicals, and to get tickets to these you must book several months in advance. The National Theatre stages classic and experimental work on the South Bank—cross Waterloo Bridge to see the current schedule digitally displayed on the facade.

Above *Leicester Square is ringed by luxurious cinemas showing the latest movies*

Fringe theatre finds its place in pub rooms and other cramped or quirky venues, as well as in more conventional spaces such as The Gate in Notting Hill (▷ 235), dedicated to staging work by new writers.

To book major theatrical and musical performances it's often easiest to use the internet. Visit www.ticketmaster.co.uk or www.keithprowse.com.

CLUBBING

London has a diverse choice of nightclubs so you need to do a bit of homework to find the club that's right for you. Look in listings magazines (such as *Time Out*), pick up flyers, talk to other clubbers in the trendy pre-club bars near your chosen nightspot. Once you've decided on where to go you must also check out what is happening on that particular night, as many clubs have different theme nights throughout the week. The good news is you can go clubbing most nights—even on Mondays and Tuesdays, you'll find places that are buzzing.

Queues usually start to form outside popular venues from around 11pm. Some clubs offer free admission early in the evening, relying on the price of drinks to make up the cost (and that often doesn't take long). Others also ratchet up their charges later at night. Theme nights, special events, guest bands and DJs are generally advertised at the club or online. Clubs with restaurants and/or shows sometimes offer special menu deals to keep you going.

Always check your chosen venue's dress code. Some are relaxed, some insist on 'smart' dress (definitions vary wildly), and some object to specific items of clothing such as jeans or trainers. Once there you will often have to pass muster with tough-looking doormen (bouncers). If they refuse to admit you, just accept it and walk away. They don't need to give a reason and there's no point arguing—they won't listen, you won't win, and it may lead to trouble. Just try your luck elsewhere. A sure way of invoking the bouncers' displeasure is to turn up drunk.

Once past the door, you may be frisked by security staff.

OTHER CLUB OPTIONS

For moderate sound volume, more space and a wider age range, head for clubs hosting salsa or other Latin sessions or a classic cabaret-and-dinner club—not all of these charge exorbitant prices, but many require smart dress (again, definitions vary). One of the best things about some of these places is that they offer dance lessons (often free) before the night starts properly. All you have to do is swallow a little pride and turn up early!

OLDER CLUBBERS

If techno, hip-hop, electro and drum 'n' bass gives you a headache and you'd like to dance to some music that you might recognize, then look for nightspots offering mainstream, disco or 1970s' and 80s' music.

The official website www.visitlondon.com is a good source of ideas, but double-check with venues for events and times.

'ADULT'

You don't have to look far in Soho to find a fairly dubious assortment of peep shows and sex shows, where sharks await tourists. It's easy to wander into Soho by accident, but it is best to stay well away from these places.

COMEDY

Comedy clubs boomed in the 1980s, and there's still an impressive choice of revues, improvised shows and stand-up comedy to choose from, from open-mike novice spots to crowd-pulling big names such as Jack Dee and Lee Evans.

GETTING HOME

Before setting out, plan how you're going to get back. Night buses and some regular routes run all night (▷ 53), but if the venue is out on a limb or too far from the bus stop it's best to ask about taxis (there's often a rank outside). Remember that Underground trains stop running at around midnight.

SPORTS AND ACTIVITIES

Sport is a passion for the British, despite their tendency to caricature themselves as good-humoured losers.

London is the setting for several iconic sporting venues, including historic Lord's Cricket Ground (▷ 216), Wimbledon's All England Lawn Tennis Club (▷ 263), where the world-famous championships are held every June–July (▷ 294–295), and Wembley Stadium. The old Wembley Stadium, loved for its historical associations rather than its antiquated facilities, has now been replaced by a state-of-the-art arena. The new stadium (▷ 17) was finally opened in March 2007. The iconic Twin Towers have been replaced by a massive arch 133m (440ft) high which can be seen from 21km (13 miles) away. There are no quibbles with the quality of the new facility but the location, in one of London's least pleasant suburbs and awkward to get to by all forms of transport, still riles many people, particularly in the provinces. Rugby's main London stadium, which hosts international contests, is at Twickenham (▷ 263), in west London. There are countless other, small-scale venues, but the easiest way to catch a game of cricket, football or rugby is simply to turn up at a surburban municipal park or playing field and stand on the sidelines as local teams battle it out.

There's nothing more quintessentially English than watching a local game of cricket on a sunny Sunday afternoon. Kew Green is the perfect venue but there are lots of others around town which are free and open to everyone. By contrast, tickets for football matches in the Premiership (England's top flight) are particularly difficult to get hold of and very expensive (from £35 to £60), though they do attract the cream of world talent.

The football and rugby seasons run from late August to the middle of May; cricket is played between April and September.

Two of Britain's most famous horse-racing events take place close to London: the Epsom Derby in early to mid-June, and Ascot Week (▷ 294), in mid-June. The latter is attended by royalty, the rich and famous and anyone wanting to see and be seen, as well as crowds of punters there for the thrill of placing

a bet—and is known as much for the women's outrageous hats as for the races themselves.

To book tickets for most major sporting events contact Ticketmaster (tel 0844 844 0444, www.ticketmaster.co.uk) or Keith Prowse (tel 0844 209 0381, www.keithprowse.com).

Innumerable sports centres have sprung up around the capital over the past 20 years. These range from expensive clubs, where you may be able to buy short-term membership to use gyms, saunas, swimming pools and squash courts, to municipal operations providing no-frills versions of the same kind of facilities at much lower prices.

If you want to be part of a real London institution, consider applying (well in advance) to join the thousands of participants in April's

annual London Marathon, when everyone from top athletes to TV celebrities and charity collectors in chicken outfits pounds the course between Blackheath and the Mall (▷ 17 and 294). Contact Virgin London Marathon (tel 020 7902 0200, www.virginlondonmarathon. com) or Sportstours International (tel 0161 703 8161, www.sportstours international.co.uk) for details, though unless you are a serious club runner your chances are restricted.

London's greatest offerings for the active of all ages are its parks, greens and commons. Nothing beats walking, jogging, flying a kite or sailing a model boat at Hampstead Heath, Hyde Park, Battersea Park, Wimbledon Common or Clapham Common—each of which provides a little slice of countryside and breathing space in the city.

HEALTH AND BEAUTY

The health and beauty industry is one of London's most rapidly growing sectors. There are scores of clinics and clubs throughout the capital offering every kind of treatment, from acupressure to zero balancing, cosseting you quite literally from head to toe. After a day's shopping or sightseeing amid the bustle, noise and traffic fumes of the metropolis, it's heaven to relax in a quiet space with a facial, a pedicure, a massage or some aromatherapy.

For most visitors these basic therapies and techniques will more than suffice, though if you seek more specialist treatment you will no doubt find it. The best source of information and advice on where to go is the *Time Out London's Health & Fitness Guide*. All reputable clinics abide by

local regulations, are fully insured and have qualified staff, so safety is never an issue.

Some venues are for members only, with monthly or annual charges which are prohibitive to most short-term visitors. Many more, however, take short-notice bookings and some

are just walk-in, though it's always best to call first. Most clubs are open to both sexes, though one of the more recent trends is for men to start discovering their 'inner-self' via health and beauty treatments and a small number of men-only salons have opened.

CHILDREN'S LONDON

London is particularly well equipped with a host of attractions and museums of all kinds that set out to capture and engage young imaginations. There are children's areas and playgrounds and, of course, there's no lack of costumed ceremonial display to appeal to all ages.

Most fee-charging attractions have children's prices and discounted family tickets, though definitions of 'child' and 'family' vary considerably. Many places have free entry for children under five or six. Inevitably, the most crowded times are during school holidays—two

weeks at Easter, from mid-July to the first week of September, two weeks at Christmas and week-long half-term breaks throughout the year. During those times, prices are often lower and opening hours longer.

One of the most useful sources of information on special events, shows

and regular attractions alike is *Time Out's* annual *London for Children* magazine (available in bookshops). It's also worth checking the children's section of *Time Out* each week, and the website www.visitlondon.com also has an entertaining children's section.

London has many festivals and traditions. Listed below, month by month, are the major events that take place annually. They are free unless stated otherwise.

DAILY CEREMONIES
CEREMONY OF THE KEYS
www.hrp.org.uk
Every evening at 9.53pm the ceremony of locking up the Tower begins. For free tickets, apply in writing to the Ceremony of the Keys Office, Tower of London (▷ 116) at least two months in advance.
✉ Tower of London EC3N 4AB ☎ 020 3166 6278 ⊕ Nightly ⊜ Tower Hill ⊟ 15, 42, 78, 100, RV1

CHANGING OF THE GUARD
www.royal.gov.uk
Footguards in full dress uniform can be seen changing shifts in a stirring display of pageantry at two locations in London. You should arrive early to get into position for a good view.
✉ Buckingham Palace SW1A 1AA, Horse Guards SW1A 2AX, Tower of London EC3N 4AB ⊕ Buckingham Palace forecourt: May–Jul (and alternate days rest of the year) daily 11.30am (no ceremony in very wet weather). Horse Guards Arch: Mon–Sat 11am, Sun 10am ⊜ Buckingham Palace: St. James's Park; Horse Guards: Charing Cross ⊟ Buckingham Palace: 11, 139, 211, C1; Horse Guards: 11, 12, 24, 159

JANUARY
NEW YEAR'S DAY PARADE
www.londonparade.co.uk
Around 10,000 dancers, musicians and floats gather along Piccadilly outside the Ritz just before noon, and parade around Trafalgar Square and along Whitehall, to finish in Parliament Square.
✉ Piccadilly to Parliament Square ☎ 020 8566 8586 ⊕ 1 Jan

JANUARY–FEBRUARY
CHINESE NEW YEAR
End January/early February
www.londonchinatown.org
Enormous Chinese dragons snake their way through and around Chinatown (▷ 140) collecting money and gifts.
✉ Around Trafalgar Square and Chinatown

MARCH–APRIL
OXFORD AND CAMBRIDGE BOAT RACE
www.theboatrace.org
Annual race held on the Thames, from Putney to Mortlake, between rowing eights from Oxford and Cambridge universities.
⊕ Mar or Apr ⊜ Putney Bridge, Hammersmith, Ravenscourt Park ⊟ Central London–Putney 14, 22; Central London–Hammersmith 9, 10, 27; Hammersmith–Mortlake 209; Chiswick Bridge 190

APRIL
VIRGIN LONDON MARATHON
www.virginlondonmarathon.com
More than 30,000 runners compete in one of the world's biggest road races (▷ 17).
☎ 020 7902 0200 ⊜ Start: North Greenwich. Finish: Green Park, St. James's Park ⊟ Start: 188. Finish: 11, 12, 24, 159, 453

MAY
CHELSEA FLOWER SHOW
www.rhs.org.uk
Fabulous flower show at the Chelsea Royal Hospital, attended by the Queen and huge crowds.
✉ Royal Hospital, Royal Hospital Road SW3 4SR ☎ 0844 338 7505 ⊌ £47 ⊜ Sloane Square ⊟ 11, 137, 170

JUNE
DERBY DAY
www.epsomderby.co.uk
The premier flat race (a type of horse race) of the year, with a lively fairground atmosphere.
✉ Epsom Downs Racecourse, Epsom KT18 5LQ ☎ 01372 726311 ⊕ First Sat in Jun ⊌ £25–£105 ⊟ Epsom Town Centre or Tattenham Corner, then take the shuttle bus

ROYAL ACADEMY SUMMER EXHIBITION
▷ 21.

TROOPING THE COLOUR
www.royal.gov.uk
On the Queen's official birthday the 'colour' (flag) of one of her seven Household regiments is carried for her inspection at a military ceremony on Horseguards Parade. Tickets are allocated by ballot in March—see the website for details.
✉ Horse Guards Parade, Whitehall SW1A 2AX ☎ 020 7414 2479 ⊕ Second Sat in Jun ⊜ Westminster, Charing Cross ⊟ 11, 12, 24, 159

ROYAL ASCOT
www.ascot.co.uk
One of the world's most famous race meetings, dating back to 1711, this is attended by the Queen. There is a strict dress code, and usually there is as much attention paid to the ladies' often startling outfits as to the racing.
✉ High Street, Ascot SL5 7JX ☎ 0870 727 1234 ⊕ Mid-Jun ⊌ £17–£69 ⊠ Ascot

JUNE–JULY
CITY OF LONDON FESTIVAL
www.colf.org
Dance, music, theatre, cinema and literary events take place, plus walks, across the City of London.
✉ Fitz Eylwin House, 25 Holborn Viaduct EC1A 2BP ☎ 0845 120 7502 ⊕ Late Jun to mid-Jul

WIMBLEDON LAWN TENNIS CHAMPIONSHIPS
lwww.wimbledon.com
This is the oldest major tennis championship in the world and the only such tournament played on grass. In the early rounds, you can queue for tickets on the day, but the

only way for members of the public to get tickets for the final four days is to enter a public ballot the previous autumn.

✉ All England Lawn Tennis and Croquet Club, Church Road, Wimbledon SW19 5AE ☎ 020 8971 2473 ⏱ Last week in Jun, first week in Jul 💷 £35–£110 Ⓜ Southfields 🚌 493 🚉 Wimbledon

JULY
HAMPTON COURT PALACE FLOWER SHOW
www.rhs.org.uk
This is the world's largest annual flower show, set amid the grounds of the historic royal palace.

✉ Hampton Court Palace, East Molesey KT8 9AU ☎ 0844 338 7505 ⏱ Second week in Jul 💷 £29 🚌 111, 216, 411, R68 🚉 Hampton Court 🚢 From Westminster, Richmond, Kingston

BBC HENRY WOOD PROMENADE CONCERTS
www.royalalberthall.com
The world-famous Proms feature an eclectic mix of music from startling modern music to classical standbys. The Last Night, also held in Hyde Park, draws huge crowds.

✉ Royal Albert Hall, Kensington Gore SW7 2AP ☎ 0845 401 5045 ⏱ Mid-Jul to mid-Sep 💷 £5 (standing; on the door only)–£40. Proms in the Park £20 Ⓜ South Kensington 🚌 9, 10, 52, 70, 360

LONDON PRIDE PARADE
www.pridelondon.org
Themed floats and exotic costumes celebrate London's gay and lesbian community, ending a two-week festival with a Pride in the Park event in Hyde Park.

✉ 27 Old Gloucester Street WC1N 3AX ☎ 0844 884 2439 ⏱ Early Jul Ⓜ Start: Embankment. End: Hyde Park 🚌 Start: 9, 11, 13. End: 12, 73, 74

AUGUST
NOTTING HILL CARNIVAL
www.nottinghill-carnival.co.uk
More than a million people get together for one of the biggest street parties in Europe. Expect fabulous costumes, steel drum, bands and mega sound systems.

✉ Notting Hill W10/W11 ☎ 020 7727 0072 ⏱ Aug bank holiday Sun and Mon Ⓜ Ladbroke Grove, Holland Park, Notting Hill Gate 🚌 23, 52, 94

SEPTEMBER
GREAT RIVER RACE
www.greatriverrace.co.uk
Around 300 Cornish gigs, Chinese dragonboats with drummers, cutters, longboats and other craft compete to win the UK Traditional Boat Championship.

✉ On the River Thames from Docklands to Ham House, Richmond ☎ 020 8398 9057 ⏱ Mid-Sep; dates vary Ⓜ Start: Docklands. Finish: Richmond

OCTOBER
PEARLY KINGS AND QUEENS HARVEST FESTIVAL
www.pearlysociety.co.uk
Victorian costermongers (market traders) elected their own 'royalty' to protect their trading interests. Today, the pearly kings and queens, who mostly devote their spare time to raising money for charity, gather in their elaborate outfits covered in mother-of-pearl buttons.

✉ St. Paul's Church, Bedford Street WC2E 9ED ☎ 020 8778 8670 ⏱ First Sun in Oct Ⓜ Covent Garden, Leicester Square 🚌 24, 29, 176

OCTOBER–NOVEMBER
LONDON FILM FESTIVAL
www.lff.org.uk
The UK's biggest film festival is centred on the National Film Theatre (▷ 87) and various West End cinemas.

✉ National Film Theatre, South Bank SE1 8XT ☎ 020 7928 3232 ⏱ Two weeks in late Oct/early Nov 💷 £7.50–£30

NOVEMBER
STATE OPENING OF PARLIAMENT
www.parliament.uk
The Queen arrives in a State coach attended by the Household Cavalry to reopen Parliament officially following its summer recess.

✉ House of Lords, Parliament Square, Westminster SW1A 0PW ☎ 020 7219 4496 Ⓜ Westminster 🚌 3, 11, 12, 24

LORD MAYOR'S SHOW
www.lordmayorsshow.org
The newly elected Lord Mayor of London processes with about 140 floats to the Royal Courts of Justice, where the oath of allegiance is taken before the return journey. There are spectacular fireworks in the evening from a barge moored between Waterloo Bridge and Blackfriars Bridge.

✉ Streets between Mansion House and Royal Courts of Justice in the Strand ☎ 01328 824420, box office 01908 300106 ⏱ Second Sat in Nov 💷 Free along route; grandstand tickets £29 Ⓜ Procession: Mansion House, Temple; fireworks: Blackfriars, Embankment 🚌 Procession: 11, 15, 23; fireworks: 1, 45, 100, 168, RV1

REMEMBRANCE SUNDAY PARADE
The Queen, the Prime Minister and other dignitaries lay wreaths to commemorate those who have died fighting in wars.

✉ Cenotaph, Whitehall SW1 ⏱ Sun nearest 11 Nov Ⓜ Charing Cross 🚌 11, 12, 24, 159

NOVEMBER–DECEMBER
CHRISTMAS LIGHTS
Celebrities are invited to switch on the Christmas lights decorating the most famous shopping streets, plus a huge Norwegian spruce in Trafalgar Square—an annual gift from Norway since 1947 to express the nation's gratitude for British support during World War II.

✉ Trafalgar Square, Oxford Street, Regent Street, Bond Street, Covent Garden ⏱ Late Nov–early Dec Ⓜ Charing Cross, Leicester Square 🚌 24, 29, 176

Britain's reputation for food has undergone a radical change in the last few years, and now ranks with the best in the world. The public has become more discerning, chefs have higher profiles and the country now creates its own culinary trends. Top restaurants celebrate traditional British food, adding glamorous touches to such staples as bangers and mash, fish and chips or steak and kidney pie.

These are also standard dishes on most pub menus, along with adventurous offerings served in the new breed of 'gastropubs', which provide first-class meals as well as good beer.

Britain's colonial past adds to its culinary mix: curry is said to be the nation's favourite dish. London has exciting modern restaurants serving traditional Indian, Pakistani or Bangladeshi dishes, fusions of Indian and European cooking or the latest innovations from Mumbai. Thai food is currently enjoying a boom, and Middle Eastern and North African restaurants are particularly popular in the City.

Another long-standing British favourite is Italian food. As well as the home-grown pasta and pizza chains there are innumerable Italian-run restaurants and cafés — often the best bet for a decent cup of coffee and a snack.

London is at the hub of all this gastronomic innovation and you can find pretty well anything in its streets, from cutting-edge modern cuisine through to the Bangladeshi delights of Brick Lane. In some parts of the City basic cafés still sell pie and mash and jellied eels, the latter being something of an acquired taste, but worth trying as part of London's culinary heritage.

RESERVATIONS

In many restaurants, especially on quieter days, it's possible to walk in off the street and get a table, but if you have your heart set on dining in a particular place, it's always best to book a table in advance. Less formal establishments, especially pubs,

A QUICK GUIDE TO TRADITIONAL BRITISH FOOD

BREAKFAST

Traditional British breakfasts are filling, fatty and enormously comforting. A 'fry-up' is based on fried egg and bacon, usually accompanied by fried bread or toast, sausages, mushrooms, grilled tomatoes, baked beans and sometimes black pudding (made from barley, oats and pigs' blood).

In hotels a cooked breakfast will usually be preceded by orange juice and cereals, and followed by toast.

PIE AND MASH SHOPS

London's East End's eel, pie and mash shops are still a popular café option. Steak or steak and kidney pies are cooked in the back of the shop then served up with mashed potatoes.

Pie and mash shops also sell eel, either cooked or jellied. Cooked eels are served with mash and a thin green parsley sauce; jellied eels are cooked in large, white basins, then left to cool, so that the liquor sets, and served cold.

FISH

Another traditional London catch is whitebait, and these days very small quantities are actually caught in the River Thames. These tiny fish — the mixed fry of fish such as herring and sprat — are deep fried and eaten whole, crunchy. Whitebait dinners were customarily eaten in the Houses of Parliament at the end of the parliamentary session.

One of Britain's perennial favourites is fish and chips: white fish — usually cod or haddock — coated in batter then deep fried and served with chips, and, optionally, mushy peas.

DRINKS

Traditional British wine is usually made from fruit or even flowers such as elderflower, but there is a growing number of vineyards in southern England and occasionally a wine list might offer a native white wine. Cider, made from cider apples, remains a popular British drink, and is available in most pubs.

Traditional British ale (beer) is more strongly flavoured and less fizzy than lagers and European beers. There are hundreds of independent brewers in Britain, each one producing a distinctive style of beer. Local London brewers include Fuller's and Young's, who both produce traditional award-winning beers. Try Fuller's ESB or Young's Double Chocolate Stout.

AFTERNOON TEA

This great British institution remains popular and is widely available in hotels and tea rooms from about 2 or 3pm. There are many variations, but it always includes a pot of tea and something to eat. In the top hotels it's an impressive spread, including cucumber and other sandwiches, and cakes; cream teas include a scone (small, doughy bun) with cream, butter and jam.

Tea arrived in Britain in the 17th century. By the 19th century it was a very fashionable drink, with tea merchants creating special blends.

may tell you that they do not accept bookings but work on a 'first come, first served' basis. At the other end of the spectrum, you may find that many of the UK's top restaurants are booked up for weeks or even months in advance.

It's fairly common for a table booking to last only a couple of hours, after which time guests will be expected to move on to make way for the next sitting. Many restaurants stop serving food relatively early, compared with other – particularly Mediterranean – European countries. Don't expect to turn up at 10.30pm and be fed unless you've checked in advance.

DRESS CODE
In the past the British loved to dress for dinner and the more formal restaurants tended to have strict dress codes, especially where jackets and ties were concerned. These days things are far more flexible, though it's unwise to turn up at a pricey restaurant wearing jeans and a T-shirt.

SMOKING
It is illegal to smoke in any enclosed public space, including pubs, bars and restaurants. Smokers have to smoke outside.

LICENSING LAWS
Since November 2005 '24-hour drinking' laws have been in operation. In practice, most premises only open for a couple of extra hours more than the standard 11pm, and only on Thursday, Friday and Saturday nights. Children aged 16 to 18 can drink alcohol only if it accompanies a meal. Some restaurants – especially those not licensed to sell alcohol – operate a 'bring your own' system, in which case it's usual for diners to pay a small corkage fee.

VEGETARIAN MEALS
Most British restaurants offer some meat-free dishes, and the choices are generally becoming greater and more imaginative. Some restaurants

SAVOURY DISHES
Bangers and mash
Sausages and mashed potato usually served with onion gravy
Bubble and squeak
Pre-cooked cabbage and potato fried up together
Cottage pie
Minced beef (and vegetables) topped with mashed potato
Kedgeree
Smoked haddock, eggs and rice with curry powder
Lancashire hotpot
Casserole of lamb and vegetables topped with sliced potato
Scotch egg
Hard-boiled egg covered with sausage meat; eaten cold, often as a snack
Shepherd's pie
Minced lamb and vegetables topped with mashed potato and baked
Toad in the hole
Sausages baked in batter
Welsh rarebit
Thick cheese sauce spread on toast, then grilled

Yorkshire pudding
Batter cooked in the juices of roast beef, its accompaniment

PUDDINGS
Bakewell tart
Almond-flavoured flan, with jam and a pastry base
Bread-and-butter pudding
Slices of bread and butter baked with dried fruit, milk and eggs
Fruit crumble
Stewed fruit with a topping of crumbled flour and butter, baked in the oven and served warm, with custard
Fruit fool
Cooked soft fruit blended with cream or custard (served cold)
Spotted dick
Hot pudding made with suet pastry and raisins
Summer pudding
Cooked soft fruit in a shell of white bread; served cold with cream
Trifle
Layers of sponge cake, fruit, jelly and custard, topped with whipped cream; served cold

do not include a vegetarian option on the menu but are happy to prepare one on request. Thai, Vietnamese and Indian restaurants are usually good options for vegetarians.

CAFÉS, BRASSERIES AND BISTROS
These days the word 'café' refers to the stylish, urban, Continental-style establishments that bridge the gap between pubs, restaurants and coffee bars by selling hot drinks, snacks, wine and meals. Like brasseries and bistros, they often stay open all day – in fact it can be difficult to distinguish between the three. The 'greasy spoon' is a cheap-and-cheerful version of the café, usually serving simple traditional, calorie-filled British meals such as sausage and mash, fish and chips and fry-up

breakfasts (served all day), as well as tea, coffee and other hot drinks.

PUBS
You'll find Irish bars, sports bars, traditional street corner pubs and slick futuristic bars. Bare stone walls, open fires and wooden beams typify older establishments, often imitated in modern chains, though many London pubs feature trendy modern styling or themed decor.

One of the newest trends is the gastropub – a fusion of pub and restaurant that promises not only a place to drink, but also good-quality food. Pub menus have traditionally included bar snacks – lighter, cheaper meals such as sandwiches, baked potatoes with fillings and savoury dishes – but these days most also serve substantial meals.

EATING

PRACTICALITIES

London has some of the best hotels in the world, but the cost of accommodation is generally high. You can expect to pay around £150 a night for a room of a reasonable standard, and the rates begin to soar if you stay at one of the grand old establishments such as Claridge's, the Dorchester or the Savoy. Good value hotels and guest houses do exist, but these rooms are very much in demand and you must book in advance.

Many hotels will ask you to confirm your reservation and will charge a fee if you cancel at short notice or fail to turn up. You may lose your deposit and some hotels will charge the cost of the room to your credit card.

CHEAPER ACCOMMODATION

Consider alternatives to hotels, such as renting apartments or staying with a London family. The London Tourist Board has leaflets on these and other options.

Youth hostels run by the Youth Hostel Association (YHA) are a good option for visitors on a tight budget. You need to be a member of the association; either join in advance or in person at any hostel or online at www.yha.org.uk. Annual membership for British residents

is £15.95, and family membership (£22.95) includes children or young people under 18 travelling with you; under 26s pay £9.95). More adventurous types may like to try getting a free stay via www.couchsurfing.org.

HOTEL FACILITIES

The biggest problem with London hotels (after price) is noise, as many are on busy streets. Some have double glazing, but that can make rooms unbearably stuffy, especially since air-conditioning is not standard. If you value peace and quiet, look for hotels on side streets in residential areas; or request a room at the rear or higher up in the building. Most hotels also have rooms of different sizes, so always ask whether there

is a choice. You will not necessarily automatically be allocated the best room available.

For facilities such as parking, 24-hour room service, gyms and swimming pools, expect to pay a high premium in central London.

TIPS

›› Many hotels offer cheaper rates on Saturday and Sunday. Sometimes big chains offer weekend discounts. Some hotels also offer lower rates for stays of a week or more.
›› Rates can be cheaper during February and March, and October and November.
›› The higher the rate, the more chance there is of getting a significant discount. Go online to check out any special offers.

ROMAN

London's growth as a city began when the invading Romans founded their base of Londinium, occupying roughly the same area as today's City. A well-preserved remnant of the thick stone wall built around the city after its sacking by Queen Boadicea in AD61 stands next to Tower Hill Underground station and Cooper's Row. The unearthed Temple of Mithras is now adjacent to the Bucklersbury House office block on Queen Victoria Street.

ANGLO-SAXON

Churches were built of stone and characterized by their simple arched windows with thick central supports. The first St. Paul's Cathedral was founded in AD604 and Edward the Confessor had Westminster Abbey (▷ 194–195) completed in 1066.

NORMAN

In the late 11th and 12th centuries the Norman conquerors brought new styles and craftsmen from Normandy. Massive fortified buildings and churches were thrown up in the wake of the Norman invasion, recognizable by their round arches, heavy masonry and decorated walls and doorways.

Examples: Westminster Hall, the oldest remaining part of the medieval Westminster Palace, erected in 1097 (but renovated in the 14th century).

The White Tower, at the heart of the Tower of London (▷ 112–117), built in 1078.

EARLY ENGLISH AND DECORATED

Architecture of the late 12th and 13th centuries became lighter, using pointed rather than rounded arches, especially in lancet windows. This period marked the move towards the long, vertical lines of the Gothic style and an increasing focus on window space. As windows became bigger, buttresses were added to transfer the outward thrust of the roof to the ground.

Examples: Southwark Cathedral's choir and retrochoir (▷ 79); Westminster Abbey.

PERPENDICULAR GOTHIC

Evolving from the Decorated style, simpler lines and more uniform tracery on windows and walls emerged during the late 14th and 15th centuries, with much use of fan-vaulting and four-centred arches. Designs used greater areas of glass.

Examples: Henry VII Chapel, Westminster Abbey.

TUDOR AND EARLY STUART

The late 15th and 16th centuries marked a shift from the Gothic to the Renaissance styles, with the emphasis on domestic architecture for the gentry. Brick and wood-panelling became popular.

Examples: Hampton Court Palace (above; ▷ 260–261); Shakespeare's Globe Theatre (▷ 78), Southwark – a painstaking reconstruction of the 16th-century original.

LATE STUART

The Palladian style, recalling the work of 16th-century Italian architect Andrea Palladio, reflected classical Roman influences in porticoes and restrained symmetrical facades. Classical styles merged in the 18th century with baroque ornamentation and rich detail.

Major Architects: Inigo Jones (1573–1652): designed the Queen's House (▷ 257), Greenwich, and Banqueting House (▷ 175). Brought the Palladian style into fashion, as well as the use of movable scenery and the proscenium arch.
Sir Christopher Wren (1632–1723): designed St. Paul's Cathedral

(▷ 104–109), Greenwich Hospital and many of the City churches following the Great Fire of 1666. Professor of Astronomy at London and Oxford.
Nicholas Hawksmoor (1661–1736): Wren's assistant, who favoured monumental classicism. Designed many churches, including St. George's Bloomsbury, St. Mary Woolnoth, Christchurch Spitalfields.
James Gibbs (1682–1754): Scottish architect who designed St. Martin-in-the-Fields (▷ 190) and St. Clement Danes (▷ 147).

GEORGIAN AND REGENCY
During the Georgian period architects turned back to the Palladian style, and in the late 18th and early 19th centuries Greek classical influences came to the fore, prompting an emphasis on simplicity and symmetry, especially in the new terraced town houses. The Regency period saw the introduction of floor-to-roof bow windows and wrought-ironwork in staircases and balconies.
Major Architects: Robert Adam (1728–92): designed Osterley House (▷ 259) and Syon House (▷ 262) and undertook decoration and furniture as well as exteriors.
William Kent (1684–1748): a Yorkshireman who advocated the return to Palladianism. Designed Chiswick House (▷ 255) and Kensington Palace (▷ 214–215).
John Nash (1752–1835): known for his Regency houses and responsible for Regent's Park (▷ 218) terraces.
Sir John Soane (1753–1837): favoured austere classical designs. Responsible for the Bank of England (▷ 101) and Dulwich Picture Gallery (▷ 255).
Sir William Chambers (1726–96): first treasurer of the Royal Academy; designed Somerset House (▷ 150–151).

VICTORIAN
Architecture of the period 1837–1901 called on a mish-mash of influences as new public buildings such as railway stations and municipal

offices sprang up. These were notable for their neo-Gothic designs, romanticized medieval motifs, rich details and extensive use of steel, iron and glass. Examples: Houses of Parliament; Natural History Museum; Albert Memorial; St. Pancras Station; Tower Bridge.
Major Architects: Sir Charles Barry (1795–1860): designed the Houses of Parliament (▷ 179–180) after their destruction by fire in 1834.
Sir George Gilbert Scott (1811–78): designed St. Pancras Station; compelled to tone down his neo-Gothic design for the Foreign Office.
Augustus Welby Northmore Pugin (1812–52): led the neo-Gothic movement and worked with Barry on the Houses of Parliament, as well as designing several churches.
Alfred Waterhouse (1830–1905): designed the Natural History Museum (▷ 220–221) and many churches.
William Butterfield (1814–1900): leading exponent of the Gothic Revival. Used red brick and a wooden spire in All Saints' Church (▷ 133).
Sir Aston Webb (1849–1930): a president of the Royal Academy, who designed Admiralty Arch, the facade of Buckingham Palace's east front (▷ 176–177), and the Victoria & Albert Museum (▷ 224–228).

LATE VICTORIAN AND EDWARDIAN
In the late 19th century the Arts and Crafts movement was promoted by William Morris as a reaction against mass production, with the aim of making hand-made objects and fine art an integral part of daily life. Its influence extended to architecture as suburban brick houses, with terracotta panelling, balconies and large gardens. The organic motifs of art nouveau were popular until about 1914.
Examples: Red House, Bexleyheath; Holy Trinity Church, Chelsea.
Major Architects: Philip Webb (1831–1915): an exponent of simple domestic architecture who worked with Morris on the Red House.
Sir Edwin Lutyens (1869–1944):

designed the Cenotaph in Whitehall (▷ 191), as well as many characterful country houses.
Sir Herbert Baker (1862–1946): worked with Lutyens. Best known in Britain for his controversial reconstruction of the Bank of England. Designed India House, on Aldwych, and South Africa House, overlooking Trafalgar Square, in Cape Dutch style.

INTER-WAR
Public and domestic buildings made full use of art deco's geometric lines, bold colours and exotic motifs, often using Egyptian themes, marking the huge public interest in archaeologist Howard Carter's discovery of the tomb of Tutankhamun. Traditional materials such as coloured tiles and stained glass were combined with modern chromium plating.
Examples: BBC Broadcasting House, Langham Place; Odeon Cinema, Islington; Hoover Building, Perivale; Daily Express Building, Fleet Street.
Major Architects: Berthold Lubetkin (1901–90): Russian architect who was prolific in the 1930s, designing the Gorilla House and Penguin Pool in London Zoo (▷ 219).

POST WORLD WAR II
After 1945 designs became increasingly stark and massive, using materials such as concrete, especially in the tower blocks of the 1960s and the rough, unfinished designs of Brutalism. In contrast, the hi-tech style of the 1970s and 1980s exposed the inner workings of public buildings. Stainless steel and glass were popular materials.
Examples: National Theatre and SouthBank Centre (▷ 77); Lloyd's Building (▷ 118); Millennium Bridge (▷ 77).
Major Architects: Sir Richard Rogers (1933–): designed the Lloyd's Building.
Sir Norman Foster (1935–): responsible for the Millennium Bridge (▷ 77) and the 30 St. Mary Axe (The Gherkin, ▷ 21).

anticlockwise .... counterclockwise
aubergine .... eggplant

bank holiday .... a public holiday,
when all banks
are closed ($\triangleright$ 285)
bill .... check (at restaurant)
biscuit ....cookie
bonnet .... hood (car)
boot ....trunk (car)
busker ....street musician

caravan .... house trailer or RV
car park .... parking lot
carriage .... car (on a train)
cashpoint .... ATM or cash machine
casualty ....emergency room
(hospital department)
chemist .... pharmacy
chips .... french fries
coach ....long-distance bus
concessions .... reduced entrance
fees or fares
coriander .... cilantro
courgette .... zucchini
crèche ....day care
crisps .... potato chips

directory enquiries .... directory
assistance
dual carriageway .two-lane highway

en suite .... a bedroom with its own
private bathroom; may
also just refer to the bathroom

football ....soccer
full board .... a hotel tariff
that includes all meals

garage ....gas station
garden ....yard (residential)
GP ....doctor

half board ....hotel tariff that
includes breakfast and
either lunch or dinner
high street .... main street
hire...rent

inland .... within the UK

jelly .... Jello™
jumper, jersey......................sweater
junction .... intersection

layby .... pull-off
level crossing .... grade crossing
lorry .... truck
licensed .... a café or restaurant
that has a licence to serve
alcohol (beer and wine only
unless it's 'fully' licensed)
lift..elevator
listed building...... protected building

mainline station .... a train station
as opposed to an underground or
subway station (although it may be
served by the underground/subway)

nappy...................................... diaper
newsagent ... newsstand, newspaper
shop
note............................. paper money

off-licence .... liquor store

pants.................. underpants (men's)
pavement .... sidewalk
petrol ....gas
phone box ....phone booth
plaster .... Band-Aid or bandage
post...mail
public school .... private school
pudding ....dessert
purse.......................... change purse
pushchair .... stroller

quay ....wharf/pier

return ticket.............. roundtrip ticket
rocket (salad leaves)........... arugula
roundabout ...... traffic circle or rotary

self-catering............ accommodation
including a kitchen
single ticket.............. one-way ticket
solicitor ....lawyer
stalls ....orchestra seats (in theatre)
subway ....underpass
surgery .... doctor's office
swede .... American turnip

tailback, traffic jam .... stalled line of
traffic
take away............................ takeout
taxi rank ....taxi stand
terrace ....row houses
tights ....pantyhose
T-junction ....an intersection where
one road meets another
at right angles (making a T shape)
toilets................................restrooms
torch ....flashlight
trolley .... cart
trousers .... pants

vest ....undershirt

waistcoat ....vest
way out ....exit

zebra crossing .... crosswalk

BRITISH FLOOR NUMBERING

In Britain the first floor of a building
is called the ground floor, and the
floor above it is the first floor. So
a British second floor is a US third
floor, and so on. This is something to
watch for in museums and galleries
in particular.

304-305   Regent's Park   REGENT'S PARK   306-307   SHOREDITCH   308-309

CLERKENWELL   ST LUKE'S   SPITALFIELDS

BLOOMSBURY

MARYLEBONE   British Museum   HOLBORN   Museum of London

PADDINGTON   Wallace Collection   Sir John Soane's Museum

BAYSWATER   SOHO   Covent Garden   CITY   St Paul's Cathedral   WHITECHAPEL

MAYFAIR   Somerset House   Shakespeare's Globe   Tower of London

Kensington Gardens   Hyde Park   National Gallery   National Portrait Gallery   Tate Modern   HMS Belfast   Tower Bridge   Thames

Kensington Palace   KNIGHTSBRIDGE   ST JAMES'S   London Eye   THE BOROUGH

KENSINGTON   Science Museum   Buckingham Palace   Houses of Parliament   LAMBETH

Natural History Museum   V&A Museum   BELGRAVIA   WESTMINSTER   Westminster Abbey

310-311   CHELSEA   Tate Britain   VAUXHALL   Imperial War Museum

312-313   314-315

304-315

| 0 | | | | | 500 m |
| 0 | | | | | 500 yds |

Main through road		Recommended sight
Secondary road		Building of interest
Other road	•	Monument
Dual carriageway	ℹ	Tourist information centre
Road in tunnel	✝	Church
Congestion Charging Zone	⊖	Underground station
Footpath	℗	Car parking
Railway station	🚌	Bus / Coach station
Park or garden		

MAPS

Map references for the sights refer to the individual locator maps within the regional chapters. For example, Buckingham Palace has the reference ✚ 172 G6, indicating the locator map page number (172) and the grid square in which Buckingham Palace sits (G6). These same grid references can also be used to locate the sights in this section. For example, Buckingham Palace appears again in square G6 within the atlas, on page 312.

5

monument

Peter Pan
Statue

Physical Energy
Statue

Hyde Park

Norwegian/British
Monument

Serpentine   Road

Serpentine   Road

Serpentine
Gallery

The Serpentine

Lido Café

Diana,
Princess of Wales
Memorial Fountain

Rotten   Row

Prince of Wales   New   Ride
Gate

Albert
Memorial

Alexandra
Gate

Albert
Gate

South   Carriage   Drive

Edinburgh
Gate

KNIGHTSBRIDGE

6

KENSINGTON   ROAD

A315   KENSINGTON   ROAD

KNIGHTSBRIDGE

A315

A4

KNIGHTSBRIDGE

Seville Street

Wilton
Place

William Mews

Wilton
Crescent

P

KENSINGTON

Royal
College
of Art

Royal
Albert
Hall

Royal
Geographical
Society

Polish Institute
& Sikorski Museum

Imperial
College

Westminster
Synagogue

Trevor
Square

Trevor
Place

Raphael St

Knightsbridge

ROAD

Basil Street

A3216

Pavilion
Road

Harriet
Street

Lowndes
Square

Kinnerton
Street

Motcomb
Street

West Halkin
Street

Wilton
Terrace

Imperial College
of Science

Ennismore

Ennismore
Gardens

Ennismore
Mews

Montpelier Square

Sterling St

Montpelier
Place

Lancelot Place

Walk

Hans

Hans

Road

Harrods

Basil Street

Hans Crescent

Cadogan

Lowndes Street

Prince Consort Road

Royal College
of Music

Ayrton Road

imperial
ollege

Unwin Road

Prince's

Gardens

Ennismore

Ennismore
Gardens

Gardens Mews

Cheval Place

Brompton
Place

Beaufort Gardens

Road

Brompton
Road

Hans
Road

Place

Sloane
Street

Cadogan

CHESHAM

Imperial College

Imperial College Road

P

Hyde Park
Chapel

Cottage Place

Brompton

BEAUCHAMP   PLACE

Pont St
Mews

Ovington
Gardens

Ovington
Gardens

PONT

B319

Hans St

Pavilion
Road

Cadogan
Square

Chesham
Street

Lyall

CHESHAM

Frankland
Road

Science
Museum

V&A
Museum

Brompton
Oratory

Egerton

Egerton
Gardens

Yeoman's Row

First Street

Sumner Place

312

Pie

BELGRAV

Natural History
Museum

Earth
Galleries

Ismaili
Centre

THURLOE   PLACE

North
Terrace

BROMPTON

BROMPTON

Walton

Bonne Place

Ives St.

Hasker Street

Garden Mews

Milner

Lennox
Gardens

Moore Street

Clabon

Cadogan
Square

Cadogan
Gate

Cadogan
Gardens

Cadogan
Place

Ellis Street

7

CROMWELL   ROAD

A4

THURLOE

Thurloe
Square

Alexander
Place

BROMPTON
ROAD

Mossop
Street

Denyer Street

Rawlings Street

Halsey Street

Draycott

Cadogan
Gardens

Pavilion

Holy Trinity
Church

A3217

Sloane

Queensberry
Place

Harrington Road

Onslow
Square

Thurloe
Street

South Terrace

Pelham   Street

South
Kensington

Pelham
Crescent

Draycott

Lucan
Place

Makins
Street

Sloane

Elystan
Street

Rosemoor
Street

Cadogan

Coulson
Street

SLOANE SQ

SYMONS ST

SIMONS ST

Sloane Ter

Sloane
Square

Holbein
Place

ROAD

B304

ONSLOW

Onslow
Square

Sydney
Mews

Cranley
Place

Foulis Terrace

FULHAM

Stewart's Grove

Ikworth
Place

Whitehead's Grove

Spmont
Place

Avenue

Draycott
Place

Bray Place

Blacklands
Terrace

Cadogan
Gardens

Culford
Gardens

Symons St

Coulson
Street

A3217

KING'S

LOWER SLOANE
STREET

Sloane
Gardens

CLIVEDEN PL

CHELSEA BRIDGE RD

Royal
Hospital

Queen's
Gate

Onslow
Gardens

Onslow
Gardens

Sydney

Neville
Street

Bury
Walk

SYDNEY

STREET

Cale   Street

Elystan Place

St. Luke's
Street

Astell Street

Markham Street

Bywater Street

Markham
Square

Royal
Avenue

Cheltenham
Terrace

W Walpole Street

ROAD

Saatchi Gallery
(Duke of York's
Headquarters)

Turk's Row

Holbein
Mews

B302

PIML

Royal
Hospita

Royal
Marsden
Hospital

Dudmaston
Mews

South
Parade

Royal
Brompton
Hospital

Britten

Chelsea
Manor
Street

Dovehouse Street

Godfrey Street

Jubilee
Place

Burnsall St

Chelsea Manor

KING'S

Smith

Radnor Walk

Shawfield
Street

Flood   Street

St Leonard's Terrace

Royal
Avenue

Franklin's
Terrace

St Woodfall
Street

Smith Terrace

Burton's
Court

Chelsea
Synagogue

Franklin's
Row

Royal
Hospital

The Infirmary
Royal Hospital

8

FULHAM

Elm Park
Gardens

Carlyle Square

Old Church Street

Manresa Road

Chelsea
Leisure Centre

Chelsea Manor Street

B304

Flood Street

Tedworth
Square

Redburn Street

Christchurch Street

ROYAL HOSPITAL ROAD

National Army
Museum

Royal
Hospital RD

St Stephen Walbrook Church
St Mary Abchurch
CANNON STREET STATION
Market
Lime
Street
FENCHURCH STREET STATION
Friars
Haydon Street
South Tenter Street
PRESCO'T STREET
P

GRACECHURCH
Fenchurch
Street
Clement's
Lane
Philpot Lane
St Clement's Lane
Rood Lane
Fenchurch
Plantation
Lane
Mincing
Lane
Hart Street
Cooper's Row
Crutched
Pepys Street
Trinity House
Crosswall
GOODMAN'S YARD
Portsoken Street
Chamber Street
B126
4

Monument
ARTHUR STREET
KING WILLIAM STREET
FISH STREET HILL
Eastcheap
Great Tower Street
Mark Lane
Seething Lane
St Mary At Hill
Idol
Monument Street
Byward Street
Trinity Square
Tower Hill
Tower Gateway
TOWER HILL
A1211 SHORTER ST
A1202 ROYAL MINT STREET
Cartwright Street
John Fisher Street
Ensign Street
Wilton's Music Ha

STREET
Laurence Pountney La
Suffolk Lane
Swan Lane
LOWER
THAMES
STREET
Monument
All Hallows-by-the-Tower
Lower Thames Street
A100
A1203 EAST
SMITHFIELD
Royal Mint Court
ST GEORGE IN THE EAS
Thomas More Street

London Bridge Sports Centre
Fishmonger's Hall
Custom House
Tower of London
TOWER BRIDGE APPROACH
A100
London Commodity Exchange
West Dock
St Katharine Docks
East Dock
Nesham St
Vaughan
More St
P
Anthony St
5

Swan Lane Pier
LONDON BRIDGE
Tower Stairs
Thames
Way
Mews Street
Wapping High Street

Golden Hinde
London Bridge Hospital
London and City Pier
Tower Millennium Pier
RNLI Lifeboat Station
TOWER BRIDGE
St Katharine Pier
St Katharine's Way

Montague Close
chester walk
Thames Path
HMS Belfast
Hay's Galleria
Tower Bridge
Butler's Wharf Pier
Wapping High Street

Southwark Cathedral
DUKE STREET HILL
Tooley Street
London Dungeon
Battle Bridge Lane
Southwark Crown Court
The Scoop
Shad Thames
Design Museum

borough Market
Railway Approach
London Bridge Street
TOOLEY
Winston Churchill's Britain at War Experience
Greater London Authority Headquarters (City Hall)
Potters Fields
Thames Path
Shad Street
Gainsford Street
Curlew Street
Maguire
Shad Thames
Bermondsey Wall
West Providence Square
Jacob Street
Chambers Stree

A200
ST
The Shard
LONDON BRIDGE STATION
STREET
Magdalen Street
Stand Street
Barnham Street
A200
Down Lane
Queen Elizabeth Street
Three Oak Lane
St Saviour's Dock
Mill Street
Wolseley Street
George Row

Kings College London
Guy's Hospital
THOMAS
STREET
A2205
Holyrood Street
CRUCIFIX LANE
London City Mission
DRUID
Fair Street
TOOLEY STREET
Dockhead
JAMAICA
John Felton Road
6

Newcomen Street
maid Court
Crosby Row
Mellor Street
Weston Street
Snowsfields
Snowsfields
Guy Street
Kirby Grove
BERMONDSEY
Fashion & Textile Museum
White's Grounds
Brunswick Court
Reverdy Lane
TOWER
BRIDGE
Tanner Street
TANNER STREET
A200
Druid
Millstream
Sweeney Crescent
Scott Lidgett Crescent

Empire Square
Tennis
Sterry Row
Porlock Street
Kipling
Weston Street
Morocco St
Tyers Gate
Leathermarket Gardens
Lamb Walk
Tanner Street
City Walk
Purbrook Street
Riley Road
Mill Street Road
Old Jamaica Road
ROAD
Enid Street
B202

LONG
Tabard Garden
Manciple
Staple Street
LANE
Wild's Rents
Decima Street
Leathermarket Street
Cluny Place
A200
ABBEY
STREET
Kendall Walk
The
Grange Walk
Neckinger
Frean Street
Marine Street
B202
Spa
Dunlop Place
Road
Lucey Road
Thurland Road

GREAT
Pardoner Street
Law Street
STREET
Grange
A2206
Grange Yard
Bacon Grove
Spa Road
Henley Drive
Cadbury Way
Yalding Road
Rouel Road
Dockley Road

DOVER
Spurgeon Street
Burbage Close
Priorfess Street
BRIDGE
GRANGE
Grange Walk
Ascot
Lingley Street
Macks Road

STREET
Deverell Street
Bartholomew Street
NEW KENT ROAD
Rothsay Street
Alice Street
TOWER
Webb Street
ROAD
Crimscott Street
Willow
Curtis
Street
Alscot Way
Setchell Road
Ascot Way
Fort
Grove
Balaclava Road
Alma Road
SOUTHWARK PARK ROAD
A2206
7

ROAD
John Maurice Close
Henshaw Street
Searles Road
Darwin St
Mason Street
A2
A100
Swan Mead
Aberdour Street
Leroy St
Page's Walk
Guinness Square
Page's Walk
Willow Walk
Mandela Way
Setchell Road
DUNTON
Lynton
Monnow
Reverdy Road
Simms Road
Esmer Road

Chatham Street
Hillery Close
Barlow
Catesby Street
Elsted Street
Flint Street
Tisdall Pl
Darwin Street
Townsend Street
Comus Place
Congreve Street
OLD KENT ROAD
Hendre Road
Marcia Road
B203
MANDELA WAY
Milton Close
Bushwood Dr
Chaucer Drive
P

N
315

MAPS | INDEX

MAPS INDEX

320

MAPS INDEX

MAPS | INDEX

322

INDEX LONDON

PICTURES

The Automobile Association would like to thank the following photographers, companies and picture libraries for their assistance in the preparation of this book.

Abbreviations for the picture credits are as follows:
(t) top;
(b) bottom;
(l) left;
(r) right;
(AA) AA World Travel Library.

2 AA/M Moody;
3t V&A Images;
3c AA/J Tims;
3b AA/J Tims;
4 AA/R Victor;
5 AA/J Tims;
6 AA/J Tims;
8 AA/R Mort;
9 AA/M Jourdan;
10 AA/J Tims;
11 Courtesy of the Landmark Hotel;
12l Britain on View/photolibrary.com;
12r AA/M Jourdan;
13 AA/S Montgomery;
14 AA/J Tims;
15t AA/M Jourdan;
15b Nathan King / Alamy;
16 Londonstills.com / Alamy;
17l AA/N Setchfield;
17r AA/J Tims;
18 Wireimage/Getty Images;
19l AP/PA Photos;
19r AA/R Strange;
20 Dan Kitwood/Getty Images);
21t Image Source/Corbis;
21b Pictorial Press Ltd / Alamy;
22 AA/J Tims;
23t AA/N Setchfield;
23b Rolf Richardson / Alamy;
24l Edward Parker / Alamy;
24r Rob Judges London / Alamy;
25 Private Collection/The Bridgeman Art Library, London;
26 AA/P Kenward;
27t AA/S&O Mathews;
27b AA/T Woodcock;
28 Roy 18 E 1 f.175 Death of Wat Tyler (*d.*1381) in front of Richard II, killed by Lord Mayor Walworth for wishing to abolish serfdom, from Vol II (covering the period 1377–89), by Jean Froissart, (*c.*1460–80),/British Library, London, UK/©British Library Board. All Rights Reserved/The Bridgeman Art Library;
29l The Lions of London, Jackson,

Peter (1922–2003) / Private Collection / © Look and Learn / The Bridgeman Art Library;
29r Bettmann/CORBIS;
30 AA/R Strange;
31t Mary Evans Picture Library;
31b AA/S&O Mathews;
32 AA/P Kenward;
33t AA;
33b Giffard Stock / Alamy;
34 Angelo Hornak / Alamy;
35t Mary Evans Picture Library;
35b Trinity Mirror / Mirrorpix / Alamy;
36 Mary Evans Picture Library;
37t AA/M Jourdan;
37b Mary Evans Picture Library;
38 Mary Evans Picture Library;
39l AA/J Tims;
39r Popperfoto/Getty Images;
40l AA/S Montgomery;
40r Jonathan Goldberg / Alamy;
41 AA/J Tims;
42 Digitalvision;
45 AA/J Tims;
48 AA/B Smith;
49 AA/J Tims;
50 AA/J Tims;
51 AA/J Tims;
52 AA/S Montgomery;
53t AA/J Tims;
53b AA/N Setchfield;
56 Britain on View/photolibrary.com
57 AA;
62 tony french / Alamy;
63 AA/J Tims;
65 AA/C Sawyer;
66 AA/M Jourdan;
70 derek webb / Alamy;
71 David R. Gee / Alamy;
72 AA/S McBride;
73 AA/S Montgomery;
74 AA/B Smith;
75 AA/M Moody;
76 AA/J Tims;
77 AA/J Tims;
78 AA/R Turpin;

79 AA/S Montgomery;
80 AA/S Montgomery;
81 AA/M Jourdan;
82 AA/M Jourdan;
84 AA/J Tims;
86 AA/M Jourdan;
87 AA/M Jourdan;
89 Splinter Images / Alamy;
90 Courtesy of the Oxo Tower;
92 London Bridge Hotel;
93 London Bridge Hotel;
96 AA/W Voysey;
100 Anthony Hatley / Alamy;
101 Geffrye Museum;
102 Holmes Garden Photos / Alamy;
103 Britain on View/photolibrary.com;
104 AA/J Tims;
105 AA/S Montgomery;
106 AA/R Strange;
107 AA/B Smith;
109l AA/R Strange;
109r AA/P Baker;
110 AA/J Tims;
111 AA/J Tims;
112 AA/S Montgomery;
114 AA/S Montgomery;
115 Britain on View/photolibrary.com;
116l AA/M Trelawny;
116r AA/S Montgomery;
118 AA/R Turpin;
119 AA/P Kenward;
120 AA/R Turpin;
122 Courtesy of Lanes Restaurant and Bar;
125 Courtesy of the Chamberlain Hotel;
128 AA/J Tims;
132 AA/J Tims;
133 AA/J Tims;
134 Helmet, from the Sutton Hoo Ship Burial, *c.*625–30AD (iron & gilt bronze), Anglo-Saxon, (7th century)/ British Museum, London, UK / The Bridgeman Art Library;

136 AA/G Wrona;
137l AA/J Tims;
137r AA/J Tims;
139 AA;
140 AA/R Victor;
141 AA/J Tims;
142 AA/M Jourdan;
143l AA/J Tims;
143r AA/J Tims;
144 AA/J Tims;
145 AA/M Jourdan;
146 AA/J Tims;
147 Adrian Chinery / Alamy;
148 Derry Moore;
149l Martin Charles;
149r Martin Charles;
150 AA/M Jourdan;
151 AA/M Jourdan;
152 AA/S Montgomery;
153 AA/J Tims;
154 AA/J Tims;
157 AA/J Tims;
159 AA/J Tims;
161 Courtesy of The Sanctuary;
162 Courtesy of L'Escargot;
164 Roberto Herrett/Alamy;
165 INTERFOTO / Alamy;
166 Courtesy of One Aldwych;
167 AA/J Tims;
170 AA/J Tims;
174 AA/J Tims;
175 AA/J Tims;
176 AA/J Tims;
177l AA/J Tims;
177r Derry Moore/The Royal Collection © 2010 Her Majesty Queen Elizabeth II;
178 AA/J McMillan;
179 AA/J Tims;
180l AA/J Tims;
180r AA/J Tims;
181 AA/S Montgomery;
182 AA/J Tims;
184 AA/R Strange;
185 Credit: *Sunflowers*, 1889 (oil on canvas), Gogh, Vincent van (1853–90) / Private Collection / Photo © Christie's Images / The Bridgeman Art Library;
186 *The Beach at Trouville*, 1870 by Claude Monet (1840–1926) National Gallery, London UK/Bridgeman Art Library;
187 AA/J Tims; **188** AA/J Tims; **189**

AA/R Turpin;
191l AA/J Tims;
191r nagelestock.com / Alamy;
192 AA/S Montgomery;
193 Britain on View/photolibrary.com;
194 AA/S Montgomery;
195 AA/J Tims;
196 AA/S McBride;
197 AA/B Smith;
198 AA/J Tims;
200 L'Oranger;
202 The Halkin Hotel;
206 AA/S Montgomery;
210 AA/S Montgomery;
211 AA/S Montgomery;
213 AA/J Tims;
214 AA/P Kenward;
215l AA/J Tims;
215r AA/P Kenward;
216 AA/R Mort;
217 AA/J Tims;
218 AA/J Tims;
219 AA/N Setchfield;
220 AA/S Montgomery;
222 AA/J Tims;
224 Richard Waite;
225 V&A Images;
226 V&A Images;
227l Edina van der Wyck;
227r V&A Images;
229 AA/S Montgomery;
230 AA/J Tims;
232 AA/J Tims;
237 Babylon;
241 Andrew Holt / Alamy;
242 AA/J Tims;
248 Roman Baths & Pump Room;
252 Travelshots.com/Alamy;
254 AA/L Noble;
255 AA/S Montgomery;
256 AA/N Setchfield;
257t AA/N Setchfield;
257b Cutty Sark Trust;
258 AA/R Strange;
260 AA/R Turpin;
261 AA/R Turpin;
262 AA/M Trelawny;
263 AA/T Woodcock;
264 AA/S&O Mathews;
266 AA/J Tims;
267 AA/N Setchfield;
268 AA/N Setchfield;
269l AA/R Mort;

269r Patricia Spinelli / Alamy;
270 AA/R Strange;
271 AA/J Tims;
273 AA/S Montgomery;
276 AA/R Strange;
277 AA/S Montgomery;
278 AA/J Tims;
282 AA/M Jourdan;
284 Photodisc;
290 AA/P Kenward;
291 AA/P Wilson;
298 Strand Palace Hotel;
299 AA/P Baker;
303 Kevin Allen/Alamy.

ACKNOWLEDGEMENTS LONDON

CREDITS

Series editor
Sheila Hawkins

Project editor
Lodestone Publishing Ltd

Design
Tracey Butler

Picture research
Michelle Aylott

Image retouching and repro
Neil Smith

Mapping
Maps produced by the Mapping Services
Department of AA Publishing

Main contributors
Judith Bamber, Richard Cavendish, Nick Edwards, Colin
Follett, Stephen Frost, Tim Locke, John Mabbett, Heather
Morley, Michael Nation, Nia Williams

Updater
Ann Stonehouse

Indexer
Marie Lorimer

Production
Lorraine Taylor

Published by AA Publishing, a trading name of AA Media Limited, whose registered office is
Fanum House, Basing View, Basingstoke, RG21 4EA. Registered number 06112600.
A CIP catalogue record for this book is available from the British Library.

ISBN 978-0-7495-6585-5

KeyGuide is a registered trademark in Australia and is used under licence.
Colour separation by AA Digital Department
Printed and bound by Leo Paper Products, China

Find out more about AA Publishing and the wide range of travel publications and services the AA provides by visiting our website at
theAA.com/shop